The Soul's Economy

The Soul's

Economy

Market Society and Selfhood in
American Thought, 1820–1920

JEFFREY SKLANSKY

The University of North Carolina Press

Chapel Hill and London

Now these things are so in Nature. All things ascend, and the royal rule of economy is that it should ascend also, or, whatever we do must always have a higher aim. Thus it is a maxim that money is another kind of blood. *Pecunia alter sanguis:* or, the estate of a man is only a larger kind of body. . . . The counting-room maxims liberally expounded are laws of the Universe. The merchant's economy is a coarse symbol of the soul's economy.
—Ralph Waldo Emerson,
The Conduct of Life, 1860

CONTENTS

ACKNOWLEDGMENTS

The great pleasure of writing this book has been the opportunity to learn from so many fine teachers, colleagues, and friends. My parents, to whom this work is gratefully dedicated, have taught me most of all, not least because of their own spacious love of learning. Their dogged interest and bottomless encouragement have blessed this book and its author far more than I can say.

This project began, too long ago, as a dissertation at Columbia University. There I learned much about how to write history from Barbara Fields, who advised my master's thesis, and much about how to teach it from James Shenton, with whom I was privileged to lead an undergraduate seminar. Richard Bushman and Kenneth Jackson helped me to find my way through the doctoral program, while Joshua Freeman, Susan Kemp, and Anders Stephanson steered me in the right direction at crucial junctures. Much of my understanding of American history comes from discussions and debates with fellow graduate students, particularly Michael Berkowitz, Aaron Brenner, Nancy Cohen, Barbara Cutter, John Gillooly, Sarah Henry, Anne Kornhauser, Rebecca McLennan, Alice Nash, Adele Oltman, Michael Sappol, Gary Stone, and Cyrus Veeser. Stuart Svonkin offered invaluable advice and assistance, not to mention moral support, throughout my research and writing. My graduate work was funded in part by fellowships from Columbia and from the Mrs. Giles Whiting Foundation.

For introducing me to the history of science and thoughtfully responding to much of the dissertation in various forms, I thank Nancy Leys Stepan. Alan Brinkley, Eric Foner, and Alice O'Connor gave the finished dissertation their careful attention and offered many constructive comments. So did James Livingston, who graciously helped me to sharpen my argument (even where he

Introduction

T his book traces a shift in American social thought that played a defining part in the development of industrial capitalism. The story begins in the early nineteenth century with rising dissent against conventional views of selfhood and society— among Romantic writers in industrializing New England, economic theorists in the metropolitan Middle Atlantic, and proslavery polemicists in the plantation South. It continues through the cultural crisis wrought by large-scale industrialization after the Civil War, seen in popular demands to reform the monetary system, elite attempts to reorganize the system of poor relief, and especially efforts across the political spectrum to reconceive the system of political economy born of the Revolutionary Era. It culminates at the century's end in the creation of the professional disciplines of psychology and sociology, along with a new social economics and a new view of the common law.

This project itself, however, began with a concern about the limits of public discussion of economic inequality in recent years. In the United States, as throughout much of the industrialized world, the last quarter of the twentieth century saw a draconian restructuring of business and government: defunding and privatizing of public services; consolidation of transnational control over industry, finance, and trade; downsizing and outsourcing of the paid workforce, and the wedding of new technology to old forms of casual and sweated labor. As the fall of Communism and the rise of multilateral trade agreements expanded the dominion of American-style private enterprise around the globe, inequalities of wealth and income, of rights as well as resources, widened precipitously worldwide.[1]

At the same time, the demise of social democracy in Europe along with New Deal liberalism in the United States marked the eclipse of equality as a cardinal principle for the traditional parties of the left, which embraced instead the neo-liberal gospel of the free market. Increasingly isolated in the academy, many left-leaning writers and scholars emphasized claims for recognition of racial, sexual, and ethnic difference over demands for redistribution of property. Others found in the fragmented, flexible regime of global capitalism the dawn of a postindustrial or postmodern age in which the old categories of class and state, of economic and political power, simply no longer applied. Even as the rule of the market (as well as organized resistance to its dictates) grew ever more universal, both the system of private accumulation and the working class it created became increasingly outmoded as subjects of political debate. Their very existence as coherent objects of inquiry was called into question by much contemporary scholarship.[2]

For all the talk of a "new economy" and a "new world order," much of this is oddly familiar to historians of the late nineteenth century, America's Gilded Age. The dismantling of the regulatory and welfare state has recreated some of the competitive conditions under which big business first rose to power. A little over a century ago, leading industrialists wrested control of the shop floor from organized labor, then reorganized the productive process to maximize speed and minimize skill. They seized command of the domestic market through a revolutionary upheaval of corporate combination and integration, then mobilized the burgeoning power of the national government to conquer new markets abroad. The distance between rich and poor, owners and workers, rapidly multiplied in the new industrial empire.[3]

But then, as now, the political and economic reconstruction underway was so profound as to appear to undermine the very concepts of property and power that had long informed egalitarian calls for redistribution.[4] The turn-of-the-century movement among European social democrats from revolutionary struggle to evolutionary reform mirrored a different but parallel shift on the American left. In the United States, a Populist tradition that viewed property as either the proper reward of productive labor or the ill-gotten gains of class privilege was decisively defeated. In its place arose a Progressive tradition that conceived both wealth and work as societal rather than individual resources, demanding a fair instead of full return for personal effort or enterprise. Among many labor leaders, as well as their middle-class allies, the nineteenth-century critique of the "money power" and "wage slavery" yielded to a growing acceptance of finance capital and wage labor as the new grounds of economic democracy, not its antithesis.[5]

Since the Revolutionary War, democratic thinkers had commonly identified republican rule with a broad distribution of the means of subsistence. Self-government depended upon the independence of the self-employed farmer or artisan, the master of his household and the sovereign of his state. But as the corporation finally replaced the household as the main owner of productive resources, a rising generation of Progressive social scientists declared the once revolutionary ideals of self-ownership and self-rule retrograde if not obsolete. Born of the new research university, the modern disciplines of psychology, sociology, anthropology, political science, and economics together reconceived market society as a fast-moving mainstream of culturally created desires, habits, and mores, instead of an unchanging arena of contract and competition among independent proprietors. Seen in this way, liberty as well as equality appeared to depend less on the distribution of property than on popular participation in the spiritual and material rewards of industrial progress. Even as the unprecedented depression of the 1870s through the 1890s deepened the divides between corporate goliaths and small business owners, employers and employees, and creditors and debtors, reformist academics happily hailed the death of "economic man" and the birth of a new "social self" in his place.[6] Their vision of an increasingly "interdependent" society, in which each shared in the rising prosperity of all while the means of production remained under corporate control, provided the point of departure for later generations of progressive thinkers from the New Deal to the Great Society.[7]

Historical hindsight is a dangerous thing. At the zenith of both capitalist growth and liberal reform in the 1960s, historians might be forgiven for cynically conflating the two, discerning the smiling face of big business behind the entire career of "corporate liberalism" originating in the Progressive Era.[8] The resurgence of laissez-faire politics since then has helped prompt renewed appreciation for the original radicalism and breadth of the Progressive tradition, which encompassed widely divergent views of social progress.[9] In recent years, leading scholars on the academic left have found in Progressivism and its philosophical twin, Pragmatism, an undogmatic alternative to free-market fundamentalism, one in tune with the embrace of cultural diversity and the disavowal of universalistic models of human nature and social order.[10] Yet in reopening the vital debates about selfhood and society raised by the epochal shift in political culture around 1900, we risk once again closing off discussion of the no less fundamental issues that Progressive social theorists left behind but never really resolved. Chief among these nineteenth-century concerns was the distribution not only of wealth but of the basic resources required to create it—the underlying issue, once posed by the displacement of the household by the corporation, that has resurfaced in new ways as the cover provided by the welfare state has been stripped away.

Throughout the nineteenth century, many Americans rejected the nascent association of freedom with the right to sell one's labor and of democracy with the equal right to purchase what others produced. Yet to a growing avant-garde of abolitionists, feminists, trade unionists, and social scientists—not to mention merchants, manufacturers, and bankers—attacks upon the commodification of labor as well as consumer goods seemed inextricably bound up with a doomed defense of patriarchal privilege against the socializing force of the free market. Some of the most incisive historians of market culture in recent years have upheld that verdict, relegating agrarian and artisanal protests to the realm of reaction, nostalgia, and myth. By eroding the basis of individual autonomy in men's mastery of their households, the argument goes, capitalist development led people to define themselves in less individualistic, paternalistic, and parochial terms, fostering more inclusive notions of personal identity and social solidarity.[11] Such an ironic reading of economic history underlines the tendency of commercial culture to outgrow the forms of private ownership and enterprise from which it arises. At the same time, such faith in the subversive power of corporate and consumer consciousness tends to overlook the reciprocal ways in which the irreverent, protean, footloose spirit celebrated by recent writers has sustained market relations in the very act of subverting them and, accordingly, to dismiss the need as well as the possibility of any systemic challenge to capitalist imperatives.[12]

A central premise of this book, however, is that nineteenth-century concerns about property and sovereignty amounted to something more than fear of progress, while twentieth-century notions of interdependence and social selfhood represented something less than an unambiguous advance upon outdated ideals. The dissolution of the self-employed household did not simply render irrelevant the concepts of productive labor and class privilege that framed the political battles of the nation's first hundred years any more than the breakdown of the New Deal order made moot the questions of participation and inclusion that shaped much of the second century. The cultural reformation of the Gilded Age reflected the promise and possibilities of the emerging industrial regime but also its enduring limits. New bases for social reform and social thought set new boundaries as well.[13]

With that in mind, this book charts a change in the generally accepted terrain and borders of public debate. It focuses in particular on shifting conceptions of human nature and the nature of society, conceptions rooted in the Enlightenment quest for the universal laws that govern human affairs. Such "social science" was hardly the only source of prevailing ideas about social relations, but it occupied a privileged place in American social thought, deeply influencing religious and philosophical discourse as well as commonplace assumptions from the eighteenth century onward.

The original science of American society derived largely from eighteenth-century British and French writings on philosophy, jurisprudence, political theory, and economics, echoed in such founding texts as the Declaration of Independence, the *Federalist Papers*, Benjamin Franklin's *Autobiography*, Thomas Paine's *Common Sense*, and scores of lesser-known works. It took its specifically American shape from the commercial republic of yeoman farmers and shopkeepers, where the household, which controlled both the family labor and the farm or shop itself, formed the basic unit of social life. Independence or autonomy was the unifying principle, linking the constitution of each individual to the constitution of the social order as a whole in a chain of self-government. Through the exercise of human reason, individuals mastered their own passions. By regulating their passions, they controlled their actions, turning their efforts to productive use. Productive labor, in turn, enabled people to claim possession of land and tools as well as the fruits of their handiwork. Such property then formed the foundation of contracts among individuals and ultimately of the social compact between citizens and their state. Leading social theorists accordingly identified citizenship with ownership, popular sovereignty with private property, the political with the economic. Thus did "political economy," broadly conceived, define the parameters of public debate in the early republic, informing notions of private conscience and public virtue as well as individual and class interest, of duties as well as rights.

In resting moral and social identity upon individual ownership of productive resources, political economy elevated private property and contractual relations into unalterable laws of nature, as C. B. Macpherson and others have well argued.[14] So too, by defining itself in contrast to the "domestic economy" that governed the household, the classical social science set aside familial and gender relations as apolitical, often along with other relations of dependence, such as slavery. Many writers likewise excluded from consideration those they deemed wanting in the faculties of reason or productive labor, such as women, black people, and Indians. Yet in so restricting the realm of public discussion, political economy set the stakes of social struggle as well. The common presumption that sovereignty went hand-in-hand with property fueled fundamental debates over the relationship between public policy and the distribution of wealth in the new nation. The identification of liberty and equality with ownership provided a rationale for the sanctity of property, but it inspired as well the demands of the dispossessed, from debt and tax relief to enfranchisement, emancipation, and equal rights.

Amid the expansion of northern wage labor and southern slavery in the antebellum era, the revolutionary ideal of independence proved increasingly divisive, even explosive. Burgeoning manufacturers and planters laid claim to the mantle of the autonomous individual as they consolidated control over land, labor, and capital, finding sanction in orthodox economics for the single-minded pursuit of profit. At the same time, early labor leaders demanded equal access to the means of self-support as an inalienable human right, invoking the tradition of Jefferson and Paine on behalf of the rising ranks of the property-less, railing against the incipient aristocracy of moneyed men. Across the Atlantic, the class analysis that had informed the earlier revolt against what Adam Smith called "mercantilism" provided the point of departure for a mounting socialist critique of capitalism. Political economy's central concern with the bonds between work and wealth, ownership and rulership, defined the conflicting claims of both sides in the widening class divide.

The growing stridency of the struggle prompted a handful of prominent antebellum writers to question the common understanding of selfhood and society inherited from the Revolutionary Era. Inspired by the Romantic Movement abroad, New England Transcendentalists recoiled from the pervasive preoccupation with political and economic power in contemporary culture. The philosopher Ralph Waldo Emerson, the theologian Horace Bushnell, and the cultural critic Margaret Fuller each exalted the passionate, intuitive side of human nature as opposed to the cold calculation of pecuniary interests. They celebrated the subliminal spiritual unity that bound every individual to society, to nature, and to the divine. Yet the target of their varied protests was not so much market society itself as it was the increasingly utilitarian science of political economy, which bolstered popular resistance to the emerging industrial order as well as conventional rationales for it.

The same could be said of the more thoroughgoing repudiation of the ideal of independence by two contemporary southern critics of "free society." George Fitzhugh and Henry Hughes based their eccentric defense of slavery upon the new science of "sociology," created by the French theorist Auguste Comte to counter the corrosive cultural legacy of the French Revolution. Like Comte, they envisioned an organic affinity between owners and workers or rulers and ruled, a relationship of reciprocity rather than equality, of fellow feeling rather than contract. The sentimental "socialism" they espoused presented an impassioned polemic against economic individualism and the competitive market along with an innovative apology for class inequality at its most absolute.

A similar blend of criticism and apologetic characterized the work of the most influential antebellum political economist, Henry C. Carey of Philadelphia. Carey sternly rejected the supposedly "iron laws" of British economic dogma that foresaw an increasingly fierce contest over diminishing returns from labor and capital. Drawing upon both Romantic psychology and Comtean sociology, he described market society as an irenic melting pot for rival economic interests, whether between employer and employee, master and slave, agriculture and industry, or North and South. The basis of true commerce for him was not competitive self-interest but cooperative "association," the watchword of utopian socialism, dissolving caste and class lines in a rising tide of shared abundance and brotherly love. For Carey, as for Emerson and Fitzhugh and Hughes, the aim of reform was less to transform property relations than to transcend them, to invest the existing economic structure with new social and spiritual value.

In much the same spirit, monetary reformers seized upon the national currency created during the Civil War as the potential instrument of Careyite association, reuniting honest labor and industrial capital as it had helped reunite the nation, liberating northern workers as it had southern slaves. Flying the frayed banner of the "producing classes," they called for free access to cash and credit instead of equal rights to factories and fields. Such claims entailed rethinking the basic principle of classical political economy that the distribution of income depended upon the distribution of the means of production, not the means of exchange. To middle-class reformers seeking to reconstruct the system of private charity and public relief, the rapid growth of poverty alongside industrial wealth warranted a related reconsideration of the laws of social science. The founders of the American Social Science Association in 1865 and the host of professional societies that grew out of it thought the tendency of the times favored a harmonious balance between the responsibilities of the rich and the needs of the poor instead of an increasing imbalance of power. Under the guidance of an enlightened elite, in their view, the postbellum era would herald the mutual dependence of all Americans rather than the dependence of the many upon the few.

The sudden collapse of the midcentury economic boom in the 1870s, inaugurating a quarter-century of cutthroat competition and class strife, threw the fields of social science and social reform into crisis as well. Political economy practically split in two, pulled in competing directions by the respective exponents of the rights of labor, such as Henry George, and of capital, such as William Graham Sumner. Perhaps the best-known American political economists of their day, George and Sumner both sought to repair the broken bond between labor and property, only in opposite ways. George called for confiscating and redistributing rent in order to free the landless from starvation or slavery. Sumner, by contrast, demanded an end to redistributive taxation in order to stop "paupers" as well as "plutocrats" from extorting the fruits of others' industry.

Yet even as they both strived to save the embattled ideal of propertied independence, each critically redefined it. George reconceived labor's right to land as a claim to a fair share in the societal abundance resulting from market relations, or to a decent standard of living. Likewise, Sumner shifted from his early defense of economic individualism to an embrace of corporate organization as a means of subordinating individual interests to the needs of the group and, ultimately, of society as a whole. Equally significant was his deliberate turn from political economy to sociology, or from the study of property and sovereignty to that of "mores" and "folkways," a departure subtly discernible in George's work as well. From opposite ends of the political spectrum, their parallel moves reflected a broader change in the terms of public debate, defined by a new kind of social science.

That new view of social relations arose in particular from the twin birth of modern psychology and sociology in the late nineteenth century. For the pioneers of the "new psychology," led by William James, John Dewey, and G. Stanley Hall, the practical challenge to individual autonomy amid the rise of industrial capitalism posed a philosophical problem as well. The disunity of property and production, experienced in different ways by absentee owners, wage earners, and professionals like themselves, disrupted the whole chain of self-command in classical moral philosophy and political economy. From the sovereignty of mind over body to that of individuals over their government, the eighteenth-century model of the masterful self seemed under siege.

Much like George and Sumner, the new psychologists sought to rescue the Enlightenment faith in human agency by radically reinterpreting it. In an age of titanic organizations and impersonal forces apparently beyond individuals' control, James, Dewey, and Hall championed free will. But they redirected willpower away from controlling labor and property, toward controlling belief and habit instead. Rather than retreating from the industrial turmoil around them, they insisted that psychic freedom only gained meaning from social "practice." But they conversely maintained that social practices like private property and market exchange essentially consisted of the psychological significance that people ascribed to them. They held that the true progress of society required the personal development of each of its members, and vice versa, entailing a far greater degree of inclusion and participation than the earlier concept of self-government. Yet such self-fulfillment did not appear to depend upon individuals' access to productive resources and the political rights that went with them, as the older ideal did. While the new psychology described a much more seamless relationship between self and society, in so doing it tended to set aside older questions about the structure of political and economic power.

It could be argued, of course, that the new industrial revolution was rendering those classical concerns increasingly anachronistic—that wealth was in fact no longer tied to work, nor income to ownership, nor sovereignty to property, as they once had been.[15] Such was the implicit premise of modern sociology and the allied field of "social economy," which jointly presented a new picture of market society at the turn of the century. As the market finally came to mediate every aspect of economic life, leading economists in Europe and the United States abandoned the presumption that market relations were anchored in something more solid: the "natural price" that commodities derived from the labor and tools and materials required to produce them. "Neoclassical economics" unmoored the subjective process of buying and selling from the objective cost of what was being bought and sold. The value of anything was simply what people were willing to pay for it. Yet in explaining what people would pay, neoclassical writers remained wedded to the old individualistic psychology of their forebears, assuming an innate human propensity to seek the greatest gain at the lowest price.

In the United States, where neoclassical largely meant laissez-faire, reform-minded economists took the logic of the market in a more social direction. To many of the founders of the American Economic Association in 1885, the market was not just a mechanism for the exchange of wealth among self-interested individuals, but rather the social source of economic values and interests to begin with. Such social economists maintained that modern Americans' desires as well as the means to satisfy them emerged from the process of exchange itself, not from the process of production that formed the foundation of market relations in classical political economy. For enthusiasts of the new "consumer culture," such as Simon N. Patten, as for its sharpest critics, such as Thorstein Veblen, the fundamental force governing economic affairs lay in the social norms, conventions, and customs that set the standard of living, not in individual rights to material resources. Like their German mentors, American social economists reconceived the market as a medium of common culture rather than social contract.

The founding theorists of modern American sociology, such as Lester F. Ward and Edward A. Ross, similarly regrounded political power in the psychosocial stream of "public opinion" instead of the contractual model of majority rule. They drew upon the French sociological tradition of Comte and his fin-de-siècle successor, Émile Durkheim, in redefining republican politics in terms of "organic solidarity" rather than the older understanding of popular sovereignty. The changed notion of sovereignty as an amalgam of shared traditions, values, and beliefs, not an aggregate of separate interests, likewise guided the new field of political science as well as the sociological reconception of the common law by constitutional scholars such as Thomas M. Cooley.

As political economy broke down into the technical disciplines of neoclassical economics and political science, modern psychology and sociology formed the central pillars of a new master science of market society. Those who straddled the two main fields, like Cooley's son, Charles H. Cooley, called their creation, "social psychology," by which they meant a general understanding of human nature and social relations rather than the narrower subdiscipline that goes by that name today. They and their colleagues found the new source of social power in mental as well as material commerce, or in what the younger Cooley called "communication" as well as "transportation," instead of in property and production. They envisioned a new world psychically knit together as never before along with a newly socialized psyche freed from the confines of class and individual self-interest. As an ideal model of market society, social psychology represented a progressive challenge to the reigning ethic of competition and accumulation, which had become closely identified with the old science of wealth.

As a description of actual political and economic development, however, social psychology elided the ways in which the bond between ownership and rulership, between private property and social power, was becoming increasingly absolute, not increasingly obsolete. The dominion of property in productive resources grew only more autocratic as capital was centralized and concentrated under corporate auspices. Conversely, neither the mechanization of production nor the separation of ownership from management nor the rise of mass consumption signaled the beginning of the end of the working class, premature postmortems then and since to the contrary. As a prescription for reform, social psychology revealed the democratic potential of the new corporate order while concealing its limits. By shifting the grounds of legitimate opposition away from the traditional terrain of political economy, the transformation of social science raised crucial new questions about social identity and participation, cultural assimilation and pluralism. But it left equally pressing questions about property and class unanswered, and more importantly, unasked.

To be sure, what Progressive social theorists and subsequent historians have called the "labor question" hardly disappeared with the frontier.[16] The issues of property and sovereignty at the core of classical political economy have risen repeatedly to the surface of public debate in times of crisis, and they appear poised to do so again. By the same token, the notions of spiritual solidarity and material interdependence that modern social psychology brought to the fore were far from unknown to social theorists a century earlier. Indeed, social scientists in the Gilded Age frequently recalled important elements of eighteenth-century moral philosophy, seeking to revive what they saw as the lost heart of the original science of society. The movement from political economy to social psychology is best understood as a slow, subtle shift in the center of gravity of American social science and social thought, not a sharp, clean break with the past.

Nor is that rough trajectory meant to encapsulate American thought and culture as a whole. From the dense web of intellectual and cultural history between the Revolutionary Era and the Progressive Era, only a single thread is traced here, and that one only at a few points along the way represented by the small group of historical figures selected for discussion. They were chosen because they seemed especially important in articulating the change in "social science," loosely defined, that accompanied the market and industrial revolutions of the nineteenth century. Many others would need to be included in a comprehensive survey, which this is not. Much else, as well, would need to be said in order to do full justice to those who are considered here. Though they played leading roles in the fall of political economy and the rise of social psychology, that movement scarcely encompassed the range of their intellectual ambitions and achievements.

Nonetheless, the seismic shift in the conventional understanding of market society, reflected in the work of these influential authors, altered the landscape of American political culture in deep and lasting ways. They and like-minded colleagues did not merely register the rise of industrial capitalism, translating old ideals into terms appropriate for the new age. They creatively reinterpreted the meaning of capitalist development when it was still open for vigorous debate. The story they together told, of a passage from the realm of individual needs and interests to that of social desires and norms, was partial in more ways than one. The rise of social psychology animated sweeping efforts to temper political and economic individualism by humanizing the industrial order and "socializing" human nature. At the same time, the fall of political economy discredited demands for a democracy of means rather than wants or for the socialization of property rather than the psyche. A century later, the fading promise of progressive reform calls for a reconsideration not only of what modern social science once made conceivable, but of what it made unimaginable as well.

CHAPTER ONE

Political Economy in Revolutionary America

T here is no Science, the Study of which is more useful and commendable than the Knowledge of the true Interest of one's Country," Benjamin Franklin wrote in 1729, opening one of his earliest essays on political economy.[1] Franklin shared with many in colonial British America an essentially scientific understanding of social power and social order, of duty and right, authority and allegiance, status and privilege. Such a social-scientific worldview was premised upon the idea that the behavior of individuals as well as societies followed certain fundamental laws that could be discovered and explored in the manner of the natural sciences.

Social science and the American colonies were both born of the crisis of religious, political, and economic authority in seventeenth-century Europe. The social as well as intellectual turmoil accompanying the decay of feudalism and the related conflicts over church, state, and land, which sparked European colonization of the New World, also gave rise to scientifically inspired movements in mental and moral philosophy, political theory, jurisprudence, and economics.[2] Emerging especially from English and French efforts to find in human nature and the nature of society a new basis for social order, Enlightenment social science reached its apotheosis in mid-eighteenth-century Scotland. It received its most famous expression in Adam Smith's *Wealth of Nations*, published in 1776.[3] But it was above all in Revolutionary America, which provided both the political backdrop and the most avid audience for Smith's work, that the new science of society took practical form.[4]

The name commonly given that synthetic science by Smith and his contemporaries was "political economy," by which they meant the study not solely of the production and distribution of wealth, the main focus of Smith's masterpiece. Political economy concerned as well the basis of social order broadly conceived to comprise psychology and ethics, law and politics, the subjects of Smith's earlier lectures and writings. In this inclusive sense as the science of human nature and society, political economy provided the foundation for late eighteenth-century Anglo-American political thought.[5]

Drawing together divergent social-scientific traditions—the egoistic psychology of Thomas Hobbes, the "political arithmetic" of William Petty, the "philosophical history" of James Harrington, the natural-rights theory of John Locke—political economy presupposed a few core concepts. The basic unit of social life was the individual, endowed with the natural capacities of rational willpower and productive labor, variously motivated by the dictates of passion, self-interest, and conscience. Social relations were constituted through control of land, labor, and the wealth they together produced. In order to secure their property, individuals vested authority in government. Political power was therefore founded upon property rights, which were themselves rooted in land and labor.

From these widely accepted premises, the American colonists derived the revolutionary ideals of independence and self-determination, for individuals as well as society as a whole. After the Revolution, the precepts of political economy informed the class-conscious struggles over public policy in the new nation. By the early nineteenth century, political economy had become closely identified with the increasingly contested character of American society itself. "As our country has had the high honour of laying the true foundations of civil government," wrote the author of one of the first American textbooks in the subject in 1823, "it must also have the honour of laying the true foundations of political economy."[6]

While political economy defined the terms of political debate in Revolutionary America, however, crucial areas of contemporary social thought remained beyond the bounds of social science. Reformed Christianity shared much with scientific conceptions of the social as well as natural worlds: Jonathan Edwards drew deeply upon Locke, just as Locke grounded his theories of labor and private property in Puritan theology.[7] Yet Christian belief also animated commonplace visions of the good life dedicated to the service of God rather than the pursuit of individual or collective interest, along with images of the good society predicated upon spiritual communion instead of private property and social compact. Many if not most Americans looked to Scripture as the ultimate authority on their place in the cosmos, even as they relied implicitly or explicitly upon social science for their understanding of political and economic institutions.[8]

At the same time, political economy by definition largely excluded the central social institution in most people's lives: the family.[9] The classical distinction between household and polity informed the Enlightenment assumption that family relations were essentially apolitical, governed by different laws than those of free will and voluntary association.[10] Relations between husbands and wives, like those between parents and children, masters and servants, guardians and wards, remained legally as well as culturally within the feudal fold of patriarchy, outside the framework of political economy.[11] While householders' property in the labor and earnings of their families provided the basis of men's political-economic identity, married women, along with children, servants, and slaves, were largely subsumed within the family, denied the mental as well as material attributes of political-economic "man."[12] Nevertheless, the social-scientific model of universal human nature and the revolutionary ideology of universal human rights incited feminist as well as antislavery thought in the early republic, along with a "revolution against patriarchal authority" within the family itself.[13] Though political economy generally did not question the relations of dependence that governed the household, neither did it simply afford a new rationale for familial hierarchy.

Most Americans, of course, never read Hobbes or Harrington or Smith, and in this sense political economy was largely the domain of an educated, cosmopolitan elite. Yet the Revolutionary Era witnessed a dramatic widening of the circle of political discussion as well as political action, so that backcountry farmers, urban mechanics, and even common laborers took part in the "American Enlightenment," claiming the rights of liberty and property for themselves. If in eighteenth-century England the laboring poor scorned political economy in favor of a "moral economy" indebted to pre-Enlightenment patriarchal principles, Americans of little means tended by contrast to articulate a plebeian political economy as the basis for an expansive understanding of equal rights. Indeed, it was the way in which political economy supported the often opposing claims of wealthy creditors and cash-strapped debtors, land speculators along with tenants and squatters, merchants as well as yeomen, that made the original science of society so central to the political battles of the early republic.[14] In the antebellum era to follow, the explanatory force of political economy for both sides in the widening class divide would spark growing opposition to the Smithian science itself.

Human Nature

At the base of classical political economy was a new science of human nature that highlighted the uniquely human capacities of rational will and productive labor. "[A]s there is but one species of man," wrote Thomas Paine in *Rights of Man* (1791), "there can be but one element of human power; and that element is man himself."[15] The Western concept of a universal human nature was originally rooted in the Book of Genesis, in which the unity of humankind mirrors that of God. The Calvinist rejection of church dominion over the soul in favor of a radically individual relationship between Christians and their Creator further bolstered notions of human nature as innate and independent of society.[16]

Christian conceptions of the solitary soul provided the point of departure for the Enlightenment psychology of "Reason," the spiritual source of independence for Revolutionary Americans. Seventeenth-century psychological theorists such as Hobbes and Benedict de Spinoza followed the example of the natural sciences in analyzing human nature by abstracting the individual from social relations, much as Galileo imagined how falling bodies would behave in a vacuum by abstracting from their friction with other bodies. The profoundly egalitarian implications of individualistic psychology underlay nearly all eighteenth-century republican or revolutionary thought, which largely defined itself against a deeply conservative cultural relativism and environmental determinism that denied the existence of universal natural law or concomitant natural rights.[17]

It was not that the social science of the Age of Revolution assigned little significance to nurture as opposed to human nature. Rather, psychological writers beginning with Locke identified the capacity for learning and self-improvement as among the distinctive traits of human nature itself and as the basis of the utopian promise of revolutionary experiments in social engineering. "The dimensions of the human mind are apt to be regulated by the extent and objects of the government under which it is formed," wrote Benjamin Rush, a prominent signer of the Declaration of Independence and founder of American psychiatry, on behalf of the new national Constitution in 1792. "Think then, my friend, of the expansion and dignity the American mind will acquire, by having its powers transferred from the contracted objects of a state, to the more unbounded objects of a national government?"[18]

Rush and other Revolutionary writers drew much of their understanding of human nature from the "faculty psychology" most fully developed by Scottish moral philosophers such as Dugald Stewart, Lord Kames, and Thomas Reid.[19] For the American apostles of the Scottish Enlightenment, "Reason"—comprising both "prudence" and "conscience," both self-interest and virtue—reigned supreme. "How great are our obligations to Christianity," Rush wrote, "which, by enlightening—directing—and regulating our judgments—wills—and passions, in the knowledge—choice—and pursuit of *duty*—*truth* and *interest*, restores us to what the apostle very emphatically calls 'a sound mind.'"[20] In this much, even orthodox American Calvinists with little faith in human nature agreed with their more liberal contemporaries. "God has given us rational minds. Let us then act a rational part," the Connecticut minister Nathaniel Niles urged his anxious parishioners on the eve of the Revolution.[21]

Reason represented for Revolutionary thinkers the power of psychological self-government, the ability to master one's irrational passions. "Self-command is not only itself a great virtue," Adam Smith wrote in *The Theory of Moral Sentiments* (1759), "but from it all the other virtues seem to derive their principal lustre."[22] Few American writers appeared to share David Hume's dour conviction that humans were wholly incapable of rational self-rule, though virtually all believed that the ideal required masterful effort, upon which free government no less than free will depended. "But it is the reason of the public alone that ought to controul and regulate the government," James Madison wrote in *The Federalist*, sounding a pervasive refrain. "The passions ought to be controuled and regulated by the government."[23]

The highest human "faculty" was generally considered the "conscience," which Locke and other religious dissenters in Restoration England had cherished as the chief protection of a free people. Rush and others in the Scottish tradition similarly valorized what they called the "moral faculty," or the "capacity in the human mind of distinguishing and choosing good and evil, or, in other words, virtue and vice."[24] The strongest force in human nature, however, as many American writers emphasized, was the instinct of self-preservation that Hobbes had argued humans shared with all living things. Properly enlightened and directed, self-preservation became the rational pursuit of self-interest basic to the economic writings of William Petty and Pierre Boisguilbert, and later Adam Smith and the French Physiocrats.[25] "Now it ought not to be wonder'd at, if People from the Knowledge of a Man's Interest do sometimes make a true Guess at his Design," Franklin observed, "for, *Interest*, they say, *will not lie*."[26] "Though we allow benevolence and generous affections to exist in the human breast, yet every moral theorist will admit the selfish passions in the generality of men to be the strongest," John Adams wrote in his *Defence of the Constitutions of the Government of the United States of America* (1786–1787). " . . . We are not, indeed, commanded to love our neighbor better than ourselves."[27] "Man is a being made up of self-love, seeking his own happiness to the misery of all around him," agreed William Manning, the Massachusetts farmer known for his advocacy of a national labor alliance in *The Key of Liberty* (1799).[28]

Yet "interest," a central concern of Revolutionary social thought, meant more than the calculated pursuit of purely economic ends. It encompassed as well the quest for social esteem in which Smith found the source of the universal desire for wealth, power, and eminence.[29] Self-interest did not necessarily imply selfishness, inherently opposed to morality or virtue. Carefully channeled, "prudence" could be enlisted on the side of "conscience" rather than against it, so that doing well meant doing good, and vice versa. Arguably the guiding question for moral philosophers from Smith to Franklin was how to align the dictates of self-interest with those of the moral faculty.[30] As historians such as Joyce Appleby and Gordon Wood have shown, one of the signal features of eighteenth-century Anglo-American political thought was the belief that enlightened self-interest promoted the prosperity of society as a whole, epitomized in Smith's valorization of the "frugal man" as a "public benefactor" in the *Theory of Moral Sentiments* as well as the *Wealth of Nations*.[31] Equally importantly, by anchoring self-interest in human nature, writers on social science tended to identify the "pursuit of happiness" with freedom from unnatural restraint. Madison's famous argument in *The Federalist* concerning the danger of political factions was based upon the presumption that individuals naturally followed their separate interests, so that the causes of factionalism could not be removed without denying human nature itself. "The latent causes of faction are thus sown in the nature of man," he wrote, and "relief is only to be sought in the means of controling its *effects.*"[32] Interests could be regulated and harnessed, but they could no more be denied than the instinct of self-preservation from which they stemmed. Political economy, often considered the science of wealth, might better be seen as the science of interest.

The increasing identification of free will with enlightened self-interest, rather than with "disinterestedness," was closely related to the Enlightenment idea that labor instead of leisure was the natural human condition.[33] The Calvinist exaltation of work as a sacred calling helped inspire the social-scientific model of *homo faber*, endowing humans with the natural capacity of creative labor as well as rational will. Classical political economy was founded upon this vision of "man the maker," of work as the source of wealth, which distinguished Petty and his successors from their mercantilist contemporaries who conceived of national wealth in terms of gold and silver bullion instead of human labor.[34] "The annual labour of every nation is the fund which originally supplies it with all the necessaries and conveniences of life which it annually consumes," Smith wrote. The division of labor, itself the product of the natural human "propensity to truck, barter, and exchange" in the pursuit of self-interest, was the wellspring of "that universal opulence which extends itself to the lowest ranks of the people" in a naturally growing economy.[35]

From the fundamental premise that labor created wealth, political economists derived two main concepts that directly or indirectly informed much of Revolutionary American social thought. First, classical writers from the late seventeenth to the early nineteenth century characteristically conceived of labor as the ultimate measure of economic value in one form or another. "Trade in general being nothing else but the Exchange of Labour for Labour," as Franklin explained, "the Value of all things is . . . most justly measured by Labour."[36] In other words, the classical economists defined "value" as an absolute magnitude or measure of the cost of producing goods, meaning on the most basic level the required expenditure of social effort. This notion of a "natural price," toward which the market price of goods naturally gravitated, led political economists to their main concern with the social "surplus" of revenues over costs. They located the source of that critical surplus not in trade but in the social relations that emerged in the production of wealth, or class relations.[37] More broadly, the cost theory of value underlay the pervasive eighteenth-century preoccupation with the relation between individuals' income and their place in the productive process, which Americans increasingly understood in class terms. "The great question will forever remain, *who shall work?*" Adams wrote in his *Discourses on Davila* (1791), and the "labor question" was indeed central to political thought in the Revolutionary Era.[38] Smith's disquieting distinction between "productive" occupations that created value and "unproductive" occupations supported by others' labor helped crystallize the revolutionary critique of aristocracy upon which the new nation was in many ways founded.[39]

The popular ideology of the "producing classes" had its roots as well in the second major principle that writers on political economy drew from the elevation of productive labor, alongside Reason, to a primary place in human nature. As labor became the main measure of value, it was also deemed the basis of property. Ownership of one's labor and its products became widely regarded as the most basic human right, the material manifestation of "self-command." "[E]very man has a *property* in his own *person*," Locke famously wrote in his *Second Treatise of Government*. "This no body has a right to but himself. The *labour* of his body, and the *work* of his hands, we may say, are properly his."[40] The natural right to the "fruits of labor" became a ubiquitous theme in Revolutionary writings, often drawing explicitly upon Locke or Smith.[41] Patriots commonly portrayed parliamentary taxation of colonial commerce as an ominous appropriation of the products of American labor. "How sweet are the labors that Freemen endure, / That *they* shall enjoy all the Profit, secure—," ran a popular song of the 1760s, "No more such sweet Labor AMERICANS know / If Briton shall *reap* what Americans sow."[42] Americans' prosperity, like the wealth of nations in general, was the rightful reward of their own efforts rather than a gift from abroad. As Paine wrote in 1782, "Ask the man who with his axe hath cleared a way in the wilderness and now possesses an estate, what made him rich, and he will tell you the labour of his hands, the sweat of his brow and the blessing of heaven. Let Britain but leave America to herself and she asks no more."[43]

In the 1790s, the labor theory of property became especially prominent in the democratic opposition to the Hamiltonian program of taxing middling Americans in order to fund the public debt held by wealthy creditors. "[T]o prohibit a great people from making all that they can of every part of their own produce . . . is a manifest violation of the most sacred rights of mankind," wrote the Philadelphia physician and wealthy landowner George Logan in 1792, citing Smith for support.[44] "Therefore no person can possess property without laboring," William Manning pointedly concluded in 1799, "unless he gets it by force or craft, fraud or fortune, out of the earnings of others."[45]

Rational will and productive labor formed the mental and material sides of human nature in early American political economy. Together they made up what Daniel Walker Howe has termed the "autonomous self," the child of the union of Reformation and Enlightenment in the New World.[46] "[F]ree agency is the gift of God to man," wrote the Congregationalist pastor Moses Mather in 1775, encapsulating the Revolutionary understanding of individual identity, and he concluded, "hence man has an absolute property in, and right of dominion over himself, his powers and faculties; with self-love to stimulate, and reason to guide him, in the free use and exercise of them, independent of, and uncontrolable by any but him, who created and gave them."[47]

Of course, the vision of human nature enshrined in the phrase, "all men are created equal," was rather less than universal. Enlightenment writers bestowed the sanction of science upon emerging conceptions of innate human difference that served to naturalize racial and sexual inequality, effectively restricting the natural equality of political economy to men like themselves. Political economy was founded not solely upon the universalistic models of seventeenth-century psychology and economics, but also upon contemporary works in historical jurisprudence as well as ethnographic studies of non-European peoples by commercial explorers and Jesuit missionaries, which bolstered belief in the distinctiveness and superiority of European civilization.[48] "In the beginning all the World was *America*," Locke wrote, anticipating the theory of progress articulated by Smith and other Scottish philosophers through which political economy defined its subject as the most advanced stage of society, by contrast to native American "savagery."[49] In the eighteenth century, earlier views of aboriginal peoples rooted in perceived differences of culture or civilization yielded to a developing scientific belief in biological differences between races, helping to justify the expansion of Anglo-American slavery and the continuing conquest of native land.[50]

While Thomas Jefferson's infamous ability to reconcile his espousal of human equality with his ownership of slaves highlights the limits of Enlightenment universalism, his seminal observations on race in the *Notes on the State of Virginia* (1787) betray a representative ambivalence. Refuting the brutal depiction of American Indians by Georges Louis Le Clerc, Comte de Buffon, the leading theorist of racial science, Jefferson contended that further study would likely "find that they are formed in mind as well as in body, on the same module with the 'Homo sapiens Europæus'" identified by the Swedish botanist Carolus Linnaeus. But he suspected science would demonstrate that "the blacks, whether originally a distinct race, or made distinct by time and circumstances, are inferior to the whites in the endowments both of body and mind," and therefore unsuitable for the assimilation to white civilization that he urged upon Indians.[51]

Social science inscribed sexual as well as racial difference upon human nature, in contrast to the "ungendered soul" of earlier Christian teaching.[52] Prior to the demise of the household economy in the nineteenth century, the capacity for productive labor was commonly ascribed to women and men alike, but women were rarely credited with an equal capacity for rational willpower and the equal rights associated with it.[53] Faculty psychology incorporated the gendered ideal of masculine reason mastering feminine desire, which was common to the traditions of classical republicanism, Lockean liberalism, and Protestantism. Revolutionary writers identified liberty, virtue, and individual identity itself with manly self-command.[54] Yet the universalist, egalitarian dimension of Enlightenment psychology inspired founding works of feminist social theory on both sides of the Atlantic in the 1790s—by Anne-Marie-Nicolas Caritat de Condorcet in France, Catherine Macaulay and Mary Wollstonecraft in Britain, and the Federalist essayist Judith Sargent Murray in New England.[55]

In her influential "Gleaner" essays, published in the *Massachusetts Magazine* from 1792 to 1794 and as a three-volume set in 1798, Murray endorsed women's subservience within the household as a model of natural inequality within society as a whole. But elsewhere in the same collected work, she heralded "a new era in female history" in which women would cultivate the mental as well as material independence formerly reserved for men. Insisting that "the minds of women are *naturally* as susceptible of every improvement, as those of men," Murray declared: "*The idea of the incapability* of women is, we conceive, in this *enlightened age*, totally *inadmissible*; and we have concluded, that establishing the *expediency* of admitting them to share the blessings of equality, will remove every obstacle to their advancement."[56] Here, at least, the new science of human nature seemed to support a vision of sexual as well as social equality in tension with more traditional conceptions of home and family.

Society

The science of human nature arose in tandem with a new science of society in which property and contract formed the central subjects. Underlying the racial and sexual exclusiveness of political economy was the widely shared understanding that political and economic relations depended upon private property. What chiefly distinguished modern European "commercial society" in Enlightenment thought from what Smith called "that early and rude state of society which precedes both the accumulation of stock and the appropriation of land" was the dual development of productive labor and the property rights that flowed from it.[57] While the apparent absence of private property in American Indian societies exemplified the pre-political "state of nature" for social theorists beginning with Hobbes, black slaves in eighteenth-century America were denied property in their persons and possessions by law.[58] Single women legally enjoyed the same property rights as men, but few could support themselves without marrying.[59] Once married, women forfeited the rights to own, manage, convey, or devise property in their own name under the common law of coverture, by which husbands assumed full title to their wives' labor and personal property along with management of their real estate.[60]

To be propertyless in Revolutionary America was to be essentially without political-economic identity, ineligible to vote or hold public office, to engage in contracts or commerce on one's own behalf.[61] For as virtually all political writers affirmed, property was the atom of society, the basis of social relations. "Property is surely a right of mankind as really as liberty," wrote Adams, and even those on the opposite end of the political spectrum generally agreed. " . . . The moment the idea is admitted into society that property is not as sacred as the laws of God, and that there is not a force of law and public justice to protect it, anarchy and tyranny commence."[62] For servants and slaves, wives and children, apprentices and tenants, who together made up the bulk of the working population of every region at any given time in eighteenth-century America, the identification of proprietorship with selfhood as well as society meant in important respects unfreedom, dependence, subordination. But for white men, the great majority of whom could expect to own their own farms or shops by their early 30s, and in a vital sense for the families they headed, property represented self-rule.

Unlike in England, where ownership of real property was the privilege of a dwindling minority, in the American colonies ownership of the land as well as the family labor needed to support a household was the norm rather than the exception.[63] The freehold farm, unburdened by feudal bonds, had been the primary economic and political unit since the first English settlements in the seventeenth century. The American Revolution was in many ways dedicated to the defense of the freehold against monarchical and aristocratic encroachment.[64]

From the English Whig tradition of which Harrington and Locke were the founding theorists, Americans learned to equate ownership of the means of subsistence with the freedom, virtue, and independence of the autonomous individual, the master of his household. Such proprietary independence did not imply individual self-sufficiency, for it rested upon the labor of household dependents as well as the cooperation and assistance of neighbors and friends.[65] Neither did autonomy necessarily mean the endless pursuit of riches through industry, frugality, and accumulation that Franklin called "the Way to Wealth," reminding aspiring tradesmen that "TIME is Money."[66] For the broad mass of yeoman farmers and self-employed artisans, the meaning of independence was closer to the ideal of "competency," described by Daniel Vickers and other historians as the ability to support a family at a basic level of comfort without working for others. Property in productive resources, as many American writers viewed it, was less a means of getting rich than a means of remaining self-employed and bequeathing a comparable competency to one's children.[67] "My farm is small; my servants are few, and good; I have a little money at interest; I wish for no more," wrote John Dickinson of Pennsylvania, a leading polemicist of the Revolution and later author of the Articles of Confederation. "My employment in my own affairs is easy; and with a contented grateful mind (undisturbed by worldly hopes or fears, relating to myself,) I am completing the number of days allotted to me by divine goodness."[68] For gentry as well as commoners, property commonly represented the material means of self-governance as much as self-interest, and the basis of the individual's responsibilities to his household and his state as much as his rights to labor and land.[69]

The bedrock belief in individual autonomy provided the foundation for dominant American conceptions of society and government in the Revolutionary Era. "[T]he rights of the whole," as Jefferson wrote to Madison in 1789, "can be no more than the sum of the rights of individuals."[70] Central to seventeenth-century and eighteenth-century political theory was the notion that society originated, theoretically if not literally, in a voluntary contract between independent proprietors, from which the state derived its sovereignty.[71] "Every man is a proprietor in society, and draws on the capital as a matter of right," Paine wrote in his *Rights of Man.* " . . . *[I]ndividuals themselves*, each in his own personal and sovereign right, *entered into a compact with each other* to produce a government: and this is the only mode in which governments have a right to arise, and the only principle on which they have a right to exist."[72]

Individuals entered into political society, as contemporary writers generally presumed, in order to secure their persons and property against transgression by others. Such security remained the sole legitimate purpose of government. In so exchanging the "natural right" to full freedom of action for the "civil right" to lawful protection of property, individuals nevertheless retained those "inalienable rights" of self-rule that government was meant to insure. "The intention for which a man resigns any portion of his natural sovereignty over his own actions is, that he may be protected from the abuse of the same dominion in other men. No greater sacrifice is therefore necessary than is prescribed by this object," as George Logan explained in 1792.[73] Further, as the Massachusetts jurist Theophilus Parsons noted in 1778, "Each individual also surrenders the power of controuling his natural alienable rights, ONLY WHEN THE GOOD OF THE WHOLE REQUIRES it."[74]

The American version of popular sovereignty, rooted in Puritan covenant theology as well as the relative autonomy of the provincial assemblies, rose to the forefront of political discourse in response to perceived Parliamentary violations of colonists' property rights. Colonial opposition to the Sugar and Stamp Acts drew upon the strong identification of the sovereignty of the British state with that of propertied individuals, underlined by Harrington and Locke as well as later Commonwealth writers such as John Trenchard and Thomas Gordon. Anglo-Americans commonly understood taxation as a special gift granted by the ratepayers to the king via their representatives in the House of Commons. In directly taxing American commerce without the colonists' consent, Parliament appeared to threaten the sanctity of property upon which legitimate government depended, inciting fears of dispossession and despotism.[75]

"The *common people* of *Great-Britain* very liberally give and grant away the property of the *Americans* without their consent, which if yielded to by us must fix us in the lowest bottom of slavery," wrote the revolutionary lawyer Silas Downer of Rhode Island in 1768. "For if they can take away one penny from us against our wills, they can take all. If they have such power over our properties they must have a proportionable power over our persons; and from hence it will follow, that they can demand and take away our lives, whensoever it shall be agreeable to their sovereign wills and pleasure."[76] The need to guard individuals' property against the government designed to protect it gave rise to the idea that "the People" must collectively rule themselves, the guiding principle behind American independence. As the democratic theorist John Taylor of Virginia explained in his 1814 treatise on American political economy, "The sovereignty of the people arises, and representation flows, out of each man's right to govern himself."[77]

While property rights were conventionally held by individuals, Revolutionary Americans identified the various interests to which such rights gave rise with different classes, as did Smith and other classical economists. The ideal of popular sovereignty therefore entailed a vision of representative government as an arena of competing class interests, which were defined by ownership of different productive resources. Since the essential purpose of government was the protection of property, the early national struggles over the meaning of popular sovereignty focused upon how to represent and reconcile different forms of property within a single state, as Charles A. Beard argued nearly a century ago.[78]

The aristocratic Adams and the self-styled "laborer" Manning alike recognized an inevitable conflict of interests between rich and poor, "the Few" and "the Many," which republican government must mediate.[79] "[T]hose classes which have not their centinels in government, in proportion to what they have to gain or lose, must infallibly be ruined," warned the "Federal Farmer," a leading opponent of the proposed national Constitution in 1787. Different propertied interests fostered different political virtues, he argued in classically republican fashion, deeming the yeomanry "nervous and firm," mechanics "honest and credulous," merchants "frugal" and "industrious," and calling upon government to "unite and balance" these rival tendencies.[80] The most renowned discussion of class interests and representative government came from the other side in the debate over the Constitution. "Those who hold, and those who are without property, have ever formed distinct interests in society," Madison wrote in *Federalist* No. 10, echoing the opposition. "Those who are creditors, and those who are debtors, fall under a like discrimination. A landed interest, a manufacturing interest, a mercantile interest, a monied interest, with many lesser interests, grow up of necessity in civilized nations, and divide them into different classes, actuated by different sentiments and views. The regulation of these various and interfering interests forms the principal task of modern legislation."[81] Federalist and Anti-Federalist, patrician and plebeian generally concurred that property formed the basis of politics and set the stakes of political struggle.

At the same time, however, Revolutionary writers often envisioned a common good that transcended individual or class interest, and some denied the legitimacy of private interests altogether. The most thoroughgoing American dissent from the individualistic model of the social contract came from orthodox Calvinism, which recalled the Puritan vision of a commonwealth of souls.[82] In his representative *Two Discourses on Liberty* (1774), the Rev. Nathaniel Niles proclaimed God "the original owner of all things," whose creation remained a "common property . . . committed to mankind to be managed for the whole." Society delegated responsibility for particular "parts of the common inheritance" to individuals, who were obliged "to use the public interests deposited in [their] hands" on behalf of "the good of the community." Yet, in compensation for their public service, individuals were assured a reasonable income from their separate labors and forbidden "to take from another that part of the public property which is committed to him; or to impede him in making the best use of it," according to Niles. Not unlike Adam Smith, the Connecticut pastor found that by protecting individual claims upon the common stock, society provided the proper incentive for each to maximize the good of all. "When we enjoy liberty, and are sure of its continuance, we feel that our persons and properties are safely guarded by her watchful eye. . . . This excites to industry, which tends to a competency of wealth," he wrote. While insisting that society originated in a common commission from God rather than a compact between individuals, Niles nevertheless agreed that "contracts are sacred things," which it was the state's duty to enforce as well as to obey. "And when those in the seat of government become regardless of their contracts, and break through them, in so doing, they throw the state, directly, into the depths of anarchy," he pointedly concluded. " . . . When Kings, therefore, infringe on chartered rights they dissolve all manner of union between themselves and their subjects."[83]

A different rapprochement between communitarian Calvinism and contractarian radicalism appeared in the writings of Joel Barlow, perhaps the best-known member of the "Connecticut Wits" literary circle in the Revolutionary Era.[84] After serving the cause of American independence as both epic poet and army chaplain, Barlow left religious and political conservatism behind in his native New England to become an ardent Jacobin in revolutionary France. In his acclaimed *Advice to the Privileged Orders* (1791) and *Letter to the National Convention* (1792), he propounded as the elemental axiom of the "science of liberty" the equal and inalienable rights of man. "Every man, as an individual, has a will of his own, and a manner of expressing it," he wrote. "In forming these individuals into society, it is necessary to form their wills into a government; and in doing this, we have only to find the easiest and clearest mode of expressing their wills in a national manner."[85] Yet Barlow drew upon the evangelical Christianity in which he had been trained in adamantly denying that private property formed the basis of political rights and republican government. "It is the *person*, not the property, that exercises the will, and is capable of enjoying happiness; it is therefore the person, for whom government is instituted, and by whom its functions are performed," he wrote, urging the extension of the suffrage to propertyless laborers and insolvent debtors.[86]

Like Niles, Barlow subordinated individual property rights to the supreme authority of society as a whole. "Society is the first proprietor, as she is the original cause of the appropriation of wealth, and its indispensable guardian in the hands of the individual," he argued. In a future "improved state of society," he imagined, "it shall be found more congenial to the social nature of man to exclude the idea of separate property, and with that the numerous evils which seem to be entailed upon it."[87] The revolutionary implications of natural right and social contract, both at the core of American political economy, appeared to lead him beyond the proprietarian premises of the classical social science itself.

Economic Development and Public Policy

The political-economic understanding of human nature and society largely defined the terms of debate over public policy in the new nation. As Barlow's defense of the dispossessed illustrated, the ideology of equal rights on the one hand and the identification of political rights with access to the means of production on the other fueled a growing struggle over social inequality. Immediately at stake was not inequality within the household, which remained largely beyond the bounds of mainstream political discourse, but inequality between households. More specifically, the paramount political issue in the early republic was the relationship between public policy and economic development.[88]

"Civil government," Smith had argued in his lectures on jurisprudence, "in so far as it is instituted for the security of property, is in reality instituted for the defence of the rich against the poor, or of those who have some property against those who have none at all."[89] In critical respects, Smithian political economy entailed an apology for economic inequality and the protection of the propertied against the propertyless in order to maximize societal wealth and social welfare in the long run.[90] In this spirit, American conservatives such as Noah Webster and John Adams contended that equality meant strictly equal protection for each individual's property, equal opportunity to make the most of what one already had. "[I]t must be remembered that the rich are *people* as well as the poor; . . . that they have as clear and as *sacred* a right to their large property as others have to theirs which is smaller," Adams reasoned.[91] The great danger to be guarded against in a republic, as Madison contended in the *Federalist*, was the tyranny of a jealous majority plundering the property of an outnumbered elite.[92]

Yet like Smith, Madison also held that public policy, while respecting the sanctity of private property, should favor a wide diffusion of wealth rather than its increasing concentration.[93] Even Adams agreed that the organization of political power invariably reflected the distribution of property, as Harrington had most famously shown, so that popular sovereignty depended upon a broad mass of self-employed citizens.[94] For more democratic writers in the aftermath of the Revolution, the preservation of the republic required more active governmental efforts to promote widespread ownership of productive resources, such as the Northwest Ordinance and later the Louisiana Purchase. "A republican, or free government, can only exist when the body of the people are virtuous, and where property is pretty equally divided," wrote "Centinel," one of the most widely read Anti-Federalist essayists, in 1787. " . . . [F]or when this ceases to be the case, the nature of the government is changed, and an aristocracy, monarchy or despotism will rise on its ruin."[95] Five years later, George Logan's *Five Letters to the Yeomanry* allowed that disparities of fortune naturally resulted from unequal talents but warned that excessive inequality was "the great malady of civil society." For as he noted, "The accumulation of that power which is conferred by wealth in the hands of the few is the perpetual source of oppression and neglect of the mass of mankind."[96]

The newly class-conscious politics of the Revolutionary Era reflected in part a set of contradictory changes in American class relations. As Allan Kulikoff, Christopher Clark, and James Henretta have shown, the yeoman farmers who, along with their dependents, made up the vast majority of the population throughout the colonial era were petty producers, relying overwhelmingly on family labor and consuming most of what they produced. In the mid-eighteenth century, rising demand for American foodstuffs overseas, along with a burgeoning domestic market for household manufactures, drew many farm families into producing a growing surplus for sale. By ending mercantilist restrictions on American industry and commerce, the Revolution offered new investment opportunities for seaboard wholesalers and inland retailers, while accelerating the development of ancillary urban trades and the emergence of a small but growing wage workforce in the Northeast.

Still, the family remained the basic unit of production in manufacturing as well as farming. Most households continued to rely primarily on informal barter with neighbors and friends in meeting their own needs, assiduously avoiding dependence on the market for their main livelihood.[97] "Corruption of morals," as Jefferson hardly needed to remind many readers, was "the mark set on those, who not looking up to heaven, to their own soil and industry, as does the husbandman, for their subsistence, depend for it on the casualties and caprice of customers."[98] American merchants naturally thought otherwise, but they continued to invest largely in expanding transatlantic trade rather than domestic industrialization. Meanwhile, the erasure of the British boundary of settlement in 1783 opened western, Indian-occupied territory to new generations of white homesteaders.

For rising numbers of frontier farmers, however, yeoman independence proved increasingly fragile or elusive. Eastern speculators consolidated control over larger and larger tracts of the most fertile western land, while hardscrabble settlers faced deepening destitution. Already in 1780, more than a third of the population of western Pennsylvania was landless, and dispossession claimed a growing share of new migrants in the coming years.[99] From Maine to the Carolinas, squatters and settlers had long battled large absentee landholders over title to backcountry farmsteads, through litigation as well as vigilante violence. But the Revolutionary War, while bolstering the political and economic position of the yeomanry in crucial ways, also sparked a wildfire of devastating debt all along the wide frontier. Chronically cash-poor farmers were suddenly saddled with unprecedentedly high and regressive taxes in order to pay the principal and interest on public securities issued to fund the war effort. At the same time, the exclusion of American merchants from the British West Indies, along with renewed dependence on British manufactures after the war, resulted in an enormous trade deficit. The new nation was swiftly drained of specie, setting off a chain of debt collection leading from coastal merchants to inland shopkeepers and finally to the farmer's door. Unable to pay their obligations in cash rather than kind, countless families faced foreclosure, impoverishment, and even debtors' prison, while their creditors amassed new wealth in public and private debt instruments. The searing political struggles of the 1780s manifested a widening social conflict between, on one side, smallholders demanding paper money and debt relief and, on the other, merchants and bankers insisting debts be paid in full and at face value.[100]

Political economy informed both sides in the emerging divide over economic development in the 1790s: those who favored the concentration of capital and the rise of a cash economy, foremost among them Alexander Hamilton, and those who favored the continuing diffusion of property and power within a growing yeoman republic, as Jefferson did.[101] Though they differed over whether public policy should support monied interests or smallholders, Federalists and Republicans alike promoted commercial expansion, and both championed private property as the bulwark of republican society.

Indeed, Adam Smith's iconoclastic critique of mercantilist policies that benefited wealthy merchants, financiers, and speculators at the expense of small farmers and petty proprietors found its most enthusiastic exponents in the Jeffersonian opposition to the Hamiltonian program, as Michael Merrill has argued.[102] Harrington's call for an agrarian law limiting the size of estates in order to prevent the monopolization of land by a privileged class, like Locke's stricture that ownership of land was a function of the labor that "improved" it, lent legitimacy to the mounting agrarian movement for relief from tax and credit policies threatening the family farm.[103] Jefferson could not condone the extralegal resistance seen in Shays' Rebellion and the Whiskey Rebellion. But neither could he dismiss the agrarian argument that property in productive resources was a basic human right, no less than property in one's own labor. "The earth is given as a common stock for man to labor and live on," Jefferson wrote to Madison in 1785. Though "for the encouragement of industry we allow it be appropriated," he contended, the social order must ensure "that as few as possible shall be without a little portion of land." "The small landholders," he argued, "are the most precious part of a state."[104] More radical writers on the left wing of the Republican opposition took the precepts of political economy still further in the direction of an assault on economic as well as political privilege.[105] "[E]very man is born with an imprescriptible claim to a portion of the elements; which portion is termed his *birth-right*," wrote Barlow. "Society may vary this right, as to its form, but can never destroy it in substance."[106] Paine's *Agrarian Justice* (1797) similarly observed that dispossession represented a denial of the individual's natural right to land, necessitating an elaborate scheme of redistributive taxation in order to compensate the landless for their lost inheritance.[107]

Having united Americans against Britain, eighteenth-century political economy provided an enduring incitement to class conflict in the new nation as well as a goad for nineteenth-century efforts to reconstitute the science of society itself. Beginning in the antebellum era, influential American writers joined their Romantic counterparts abroad in condemning classical political economy as an amoral, antisocial science of inhumanity rather than humanity, of crass materialism disguised as reason, of selfish individualism paraded as natural right.

The Romantic portrayal of "economic man" as a soulless automaton presented a devastating reflection of the emerging ethic of industrial capitalism, but it grossly caricatured the classical social science of the agrarian-commercial republic. The self-governing individual, endowed with the natural faculties of rational will and productive labor, entitled to the natural rights of property and popular sovereignty, indeed embodied male privilege, white supremacy, and the close identification of private wealth with public welfare. But under the banner of the "rights of man," schooled in the Smithian science of wealth, Americans also joined their Enlightenment counterparts in Europe in espousing a radically egalitarian understanding of human nature and society, premised upon the universal needs of security and subsistence along with the universal powers of ownership and self-governance. If political economy concealed essential aspects of social life, it also revealed the material basis of "commercial society" in ways that proved more effective in inciting rebellion than in promoting the harmony and stability of the new social order. Over the course of the nineteenth century, the incendiary implications of the classical social science brought forth a cultural counterrevolution, ultimately resulting in the breakup of political economy and the creation of a new master science of market society in its place.

CHAPTER TWO

Transcendental Psychology in Antebellum New England

Ralph Waldo Emerson, Horace Bushnell,
and Margaret Fuller

In the spring of 1837, a financial panic set off a sharp contraction of cash and credit. Mercantile establishments and banks went bankrupt, prices plummeted, textile mills idled, and tens of thousands of wage workers were laid off.[1] Influential observers in the financial and commercial center of New England viewed the panic as an ominous portent. The Whig opposition blamed Andrew Jackson and Martin Van Buren for impeding economic growth by dismantling the Bank of the United States and blocking federal subsidies for commercial and industrial development. Orestes Brownson, then a Unitarian minister, drew a different moral for his Boston congregation. Taking as his text, "Babylon is falling, and the merchants of the earth shall weep and mourn over her; for no man buyeth their merchandise anymore," Brownson interpreted the financial turmoil as a promising sign of the impending downfall of capitalism at the hands of the poor and oppressed.[2]

Amid the furor, the Congregationalist pastor Horace Bushnell proposed a prophetic alternative. In his August 1837 address to the Society of Phi Beta Kappa at Yale, "The True Wealth or Weal of Nations," Bushnell took aim at neither Jacksonian democracy nor industrial capitalism, but rather the social science derived from Adam Smith's *Wealth of Nations*. Decrying the nascent class politics that presumed money, commerce, and property to be the fundamental objects of public policy, he argued that the science of wealth had become woefully conflated with the public welfare. The true wealth or weal of a nation, he said, was "personal, not material": it lay in "*the total value of the persons of the people,*" of which political economy took no account. Invoking the civic republican ideal of public virtue, Bushnell called for a social science of character rather than wealth, of spirit rather than sovereignty. "I hope it may appear, that a ground is here open for the erection of a science more adequate, in some respects, than the science, so called, of political economy; and one that shall base itself on higher and more determinate principles," he said. "That the body and form of such a science can be developed in a single discourse, will not be supposed. If I am only able to open a passage, so that we may look in upon the field to be occupied, . . . my end will be answered."[3]

In the coming years, Bushnell took a leading role in staking out the field of the new science he envisioned—as did the Phi Beta Kappa speaker that year at Harvard, Ralph Waldo Emerson, whose address on "The American Scholar" issued a more celebrated call for a new kind of knowledge. The panic of 1837 was portentous indeed. A new society was being born in the financial crisis and the much deeper depression that followed in 1839, and the dawning industrial revolution inaugurated a century-long transformation in social thought. The 1830s, 1840s, and 1850s gave rise to a fundamental reformation of Protestant theology, articulated most importantly by Bushnell; a revolutionary departure in moral philosophy, led by Emerson; as well as a far-reaching revaluation of social relations that marked in many ways the birth of feminism in the United States, most expansively theorized by Margaret Fuller. In challenging conventional ideas about the relationship between nature and the supernatural, self and society, and male and female, these three New England theorists drew upon the work of their Romantic contemporaries in Germany and England to conceive a new, defiantly unscientific understanding of the human psyche. Valorizing what they described as the passionate and the intuitive, the "unconscious" and the "feminine," Bushnell, Emerson, and Fuller critically engaged the central assumptions about human nature and social relations that they identified with political economy's organizing principles of self-interest and social contract. Each found in the maelstrom of market society at once a demonstration of the perils of political economy and a warrant for ideological innovation. Their closely related yet divergent efforts to formulate a new psychology that transcended the political and economic conflicts associated with the origins of industrial capitalism are the subjects of this chapter.

In the first years of the nineteenth century, when Emerson, Fuller, and Bushnell were born, the port cities of New England were thriving upon trade with the warring nations of Europe. The growth of transatlantic commerce had boosted the fortunes of a small but powerful class of urban merchants while giving rise to a fledgling propertyless class of sailors, dockworkers, porters, clerks, and laborers. Yet the great majority of Americans, living outside the immediate orbit of the seaboard cities and away from navigable waterways, remained largely beyond the bounds of the world market and its cash economy. In the New England backcountry, as throughout the American interior, most people lived and worked on family farms, selling surplus crops or home manufactures for cash to buy new land or those few items that could not be produced locally, but mainly depending upon informal exchange with neighbors for whatever they did not make themselves. Even in the towns and cities, manufacturing was generally conducted by independent artisans and their families living and working in their own home workshops, along with apprentices and journeymen earning their keep while learning their trade. The independent household remained the dominant economic agent in commerce as in agriculture and industry.[4]

As Fuller, Emerson, and Bushnell were coming of age, two key changes in the world market were prompting Northeastern merchants to invest in expanding the domestic market for manufactures and railroads as well as farm goods. At the same time that the shipping trade was becoming less profitable with the end of the Napoleonic Wars, the demand for cotton to fuel the textile-led industrial revolution in England was soaring. The unprecedented profits from exports of southern cotton, along with the creation of a transportation and banking system, made possible the growth of domestic commerce in both Western foodstuffs and Northeastern manufactures. New England's wealth of savings institutions, banks, insurance companies, endowments, and trusts mobilized the capital to develop the textile industry in the region's multiplying mill towns, which in turn spurred the rise of the iron-casting, machine-tool, and metalworking industries. Amid the emerging national market, self-employed farmers and artisans either expanded their operations and hired additional laborers or were forced to sell their farms or shops and enter the labor market themselves. As in England, the rise of the factory system along with the transformation of craft manufacturing entailed the dispossession of independent family farmers and mechanics and the creation of a permanent class of propertyless wage earners.[5]

By the 1830s, when Bushnell, Emerson, and Fuller were beginning their public careers, the emergence of organized labor and working-class politics in the Northeast was making the reorganization of property and production a central social issue. In Philadelphia and New York City, journeymen demanded free access to land and denounced the monopolization of productive resources. Radical agrarians such as the New York City printer Thomas Skidmore drew upon the revolutionary tradition of Jefferson and Paine as well as the dark prophecies of Malthus and Ricardo in calling for a redistribution of property. Strengthened by the formation of Working Men's Parties in the late 1820s, journeymen organized more than sixty trade unions and more than a hundred strikes in the following decade. In New England, the predominantly female workforce of the textile mills struck repeatedly in the 1830s against wage cuts and rent hikes. The largely migrant and immigrant factory operatives of Rhode Island mounted a popular insurrection and briefly established a rival state government in 1841–42. As the franchise was gradually extended to propertyless white men, Jacksonian politics registered growing concerns about the demise of the agrarian republic and the widening class divide. Jackson's famous message vetoing the recharter of the Bank of the United States in 1832 issued a sweeping defense of a republic of freeholders and small producers against the encroachment of a predatory financial elite.[6]

In the United States as in England, the Romantic Movement in which Emerson, Fuller, and Bushnell participated presented a deeply ambivalent response to the advent of market society. Like the English writers William Wordsworth, Samuel Taylor Coleridge, and Thomas Carlyle, they reacted in large part against the increasing dominance of the market in social life and social thought that culminated in the commodification of labor, reducing personal relations to impersonal exchanges of material resources—a bushel of wheat, an ounce of gold, an hour of labor—conceived in the lowest common denominator of cash value. The Romantics deplored the crass materialism that robbed nature, especially human nature, of its intimate relation to the sublime or the divine, as a wilderness became so much lumber and fur, and a person became a machine. They were less concerned with the reorganization of production and property than with the closely related view of the world *as* solely productive property. They deplored the concomitant view of human nature as, objectively, the capacity for productive labor and, subjectively, the motivation to exploit such labor as well as natural resources in pursuit of wealth. Their complaint was less with capitalism itself than with the political economy that naturalized and rationalized it—the "dismal science," in Carlyle's enduring epithet, of "economic man."[7]

The alternative vision of human nature informing Emerson, Bushnell, and Fuller elevated the belief in innate intuition that formed half of the psychological dualism in the tradition of Descartes, Locke, and Scottish moral philosophy, while devaluing the empirical understanding that formed the other half. The Americans were inspired by Coleridge's creative adaptation of the Kantian dualism of "Reason" and "Understanding" in his avidly read *Aids to Reflection* (1825), published in the United States in 1829. Kant had posited an impassable divide between knowledge based on perception and deliberation, or the Understanding, and the innate or "transcendental" mental categories such as time and space and causality that make perception and deliberation possible, or the Reason. Coleridge, by contrast, described a tense working relationship between a kind of internal scientist and internal priest. The English writer's Reason was the emotional, intuitive wellspring of true faith as well as divine truth—the vital, creative, even heroic dimension of human nature, forever struggling for mental mastery against the pretensions of its more worldly, rational, fact-finding partner in the Understanding.[8]

For Coleridge's influential readers, the social conflict over the origins of industrial capitalism could be conceived as a psychological conflict between the head and the heart or as an ideological conflict between the social science of the Understanding, namely political economy, and the new psychology of Reason that Bushnell proposed. It was Coleridge who brought the word "psychological" into common English usage, along with "subjective," "intuitive," "self-conscious," and related terms, providing his American admirers with a new language with which to describe human nature and social relations.[9]

In a profound sense, the new understanding of subjectivity that Bushnell, Fuller, and Emerson explored was radically at odds with the logic of market relations, which defined selfhood in terms of independence and defined independence in terms of control of productive property. Yet in severing the bond between selfhood—or, in the language of the early republic, independence or liberty or virtue—and property, these writers did not necessarily call into question the transformation of self-employed farming and artisan families into propertyless wage earners. By identifying moral agency with the "inner self" rather than with political and economic sovereignty, they effectively redefined the founding ideals of freedom and democracy in ways that did not directly conflict with the revolution in property relations. Even as Jacksonian democrats, agrarian radicals, craft journeymen, and mill operatives invoked Jeffersonian political economy in their critiques of the emerging class society, the New England writers marshaled the language of Romantic psychology in framing a fundamentally different kind of critique, one that essentially dispensed with ownership and the political rights that accompanied it. Such a psycho-

logical critique could undermine the conventional rationale for market relations, founded in political economy, without challenging the changing material
basis for such relations in the rise of industrial capital.

Indeed, from the perspective of the new transcendental psychology, the separation of citizenship from ownership—by both the dispossession of the petty
proprietor and the enfranchisement of the wage worker—might pose not a
problem but a promise of emancipation from a social order predicated upon
property. Witness Henry David Thoreau's pity for the propertied, "whose misfortune it is to have inherited farms, houses, barns, cattle, and farming tools,"
and his celebration of the relative freedom of "the portionless, who struggle
with no such unnecessary inherited encumbrances," in *Walden* (1854).[10] The
decline of the household economy and the extension of market relations into
the home and work life of ordinary Americans might likewise appear not as a
threat to proprietary independence but as an opportunity for liberating the self
from its proprietary confines. The advent of industrial capitalism, then, could
be seen to make possible a new democracy of the psyche.

Conversely, by welcoming the demise of the agrarian republic as a fulfillment
rather than a betrayal of freedom and democracy, transcendental psychology
could be understood as less a fundamental critique than a newly legitimating
conception of market society. While insisting that the pursuit of happiness did
not mean the relentless pursuit of profit, the pioneers of modern American
psychological thought ironically took the ideological sting out of the emerging class divide. They repudiated the social-scientific basis of the critique of, as
well as the rationale for, class relations. Within that conflicted response to the
perceived failures of political economy in antebellum New England may be
found the origins of the main lines of modern American philosophy, theology,
and feminism.

Ralph Waldo Emerson's Psychology of Individualism

So much has been attributed to Emerson's influence that modern American
culture has sometimes seemed, in his own words, "the lengthened shadow of
one man."[11] That famous phrase recalls his most important legacy, the philosophy of individualism that his admirers as well as detractors have commonly
identified with the mainstream of American thought. The main currents of
earlier American thought, of course, had been individualistic in a certain sense:
the leading social theorists of the Founding Era had invested individual ownership of productive property with paramount significance, as the material

basis of virtue as well as liberty, of the republican state as well as the independent household. But the development and enfranchisement of a permanent working class made such proprietary autonomy an increasingly divisive ideal.

As a word and a concept, "individualism" arrived in antebellum America through the writings of European critics of liberal democracy and capitalism on both the right and the left, most notably Alexis de Tocqueville, who used the term to describe not property relations but popular mores. Like the Saint-Simonian socialists who had coined the term, Tocqueville lamented the breakdown of traditional authority and social bonds that resulted from the bourgeois political and economic revolutions, which he contended found their fullest cultural expression in the United States due to its lack of a feudal past.[12] Emerson (1803–1882), a scion of the Federalist Boston gentry with its lingering belief in social hierarchy and deference, shared Tocqueville's unease with the rise of popular politics and an avowedly self-interested bourgeoisie, and particularly with the convergence of the two in the 1820s and 1830s.[13] But Emerson was equally a product of Boston's proud Revolutionary Era heritage, with its reverence for independence as an individual as well as social ideal. His inspiration was to reconceive independence in terms of mental "self-reliance" instead of material self-employment, on the basis of a new transcendental psychology in place of political economy.[14]

To say that Emerson's was an individualism of the psyche rather than sovereignty, however, is not to say that he stood aloof or apart from the political and economic transformation of antebellum New England. It is rather to say that he was profoundly engaged with that transformation, which his work both responded to and helped to shape. For post–World War II "New Critics" dissatisfied with the seemingly inevitable advance of industrial capitalism and the conformity and banality of which Tocqueville had warned, Emerson represented the poetic escape from history and society that they deemed the enduring promise of the New World, a dream no less enchanting because it was never fulfilled.[15] Later writers, perhaps disillusioned with the romantic elements of the New Left, dismissed as delusional the same flight from life into art, the same emancipation from social institutions, that the New Critics had prized in him.[16] More recently, however, Emerson scholars informed by postmodern theory have called into question the sharp distinction between romance and reality that guided their predecessors, while reclaiming his work as a sustained response to, not a retreat from, his time and place.[17]

Central to his response to the advent of industrial capitalism was the psychological reconstruction of self and society elaborated in Emerson's seminal essays and addresses of the 1830s and early 1840s, when he was the leading figure in the Transcendentalist movement emanating from Boston.[18] His repudiation of "economic man" and his exploration of a new psychic realm of freedom and democracy were at the core of his rousing critique of the culture of the market in these early writings—as well as his frequently noted celebration of market relations, psychologically reconceived, in his later, more conservative works. His career neatly encapsulates the way in which transcendental psychology entailed at once a critique of the classic rationale for market relations in political economy and a new kind of rationale more appropriate for a society increasingly dominated by industrial capital.[19]

In rehistoricizing Emerson, recent scholarship reminds us that he was born not in 1832—when he quit his pulpit in the venerable Second Church of Boston to pursue his more personal faith, breaking a family tradition of New England clergy dating back seven generations—but in 1803.[20] By the time of that famed filial revolt, he had already found within his family, his church, and Brahmin Boston the financial as well as spiritual resources upon which he would draw in his new freelance career. Emerson and American Transcendentalism were children of the early-nineteenth-century "Boston reformation,"[21] the Unitarian movement in which his father and he took prominent part. Unitarian Christianity itself was the outgrowth of the rising fortunes of Boston's merchant elite and its representatives on the governing board of Harvard College. Harvard became a major beneficiary of private donations, and thus a major pool of investment capital for the market revolution, at the same time that it became the intellectual hub of liberal Protestantism. The Unitarian schism culminated more than a century of growing discord between the commercial and cosmopolitan aspirations of maritime Massachusetts, emboldened by American independence, and the humbling admonitions and enfeebling fatalism of provincial Calvinist orthodoxy. Liberal theologians led by the Rev. William Ellery Channing, whose iconoclastic sermons inspired the young Emerson, rejected the demeaning doctrines of innate human depravity and powerlessness in the face of an inscrutable, wrathful Lord. They proclaimed instead the essential likeness of God and humankind, indeed the innate human capacity to strive for godliness and grace through diligent "self-culture." Like their prosperous parishioners, Unitarian ministers such as Emerson's father combined a democratic faith in Lockean empiricism and Scottish common sense with a genteel disdain for the pietism and revivalism of evangelical Christianity, appealing as it did to those without education or refinement.[22]

The uneasy union of theological liberalism and social conservatism appeared in other aspects of Emerson's upbringing. Educated for eminence as the son of a prestigious minister, he nevertheless experienced real financial hardship after his father's death in 1811 left his mother unable to support her five sons, forcing them to move among their relatives in the manner of many artisan families struggling to cope with the expansion of market relations.[23] The striking disparity between his cultural privilege and his material privation provided a lasting lesson in the infinite promise of the life of the mind in contrast with the limits of economic livelihood. So too, Emerson's enervating battle with physical frailty and tubercular illness fostered a sense of his own inability to decide the course of his life, a tangible feeling of helpless drift jarringly at odds with the Unitarian gospel of free will and self-help.[24] He found solace for such feelings less in the supernatural rationalism of his father's church than in the passionate piety of his mother and particularly his otherworldly aunt, Mary Moody Emerson, whose religious writings profoundly affected her nephew.[25]

As an undergraduate at Harvard, Emerson joined a generation of young gentry uncomfortable with its place in the emerging market society, unfulfilled by its classical education in Enlightenment thought and rationalistic religion, and uncertain of how to reconcile its new knowledge with a sustaining faith in a Christian God and a moral order. Restive scholars turned with a sense of emancipation to the idealism of Kant and the spiritualism of Coleridge, to the enlivening revelation that the deepest truths were to be found not in logic or learning, not in science or society, but in the romantic spirit contained within each individual.[26]

The death of his first wife due to tuberculosis in 1831 seems to have "cut Emerson loose" from the conventions of his church and of Boston society more broadly, propelling him from Unitarianism in the direction of Romantic idealism, as Robert D. Richardson Jr. has written.[27] Financially as well as spiritually, the heartwrenching loss enabled Emerson's self-emancipation, as he successfully sued for his late wife's full inheritance, thereby securing an annual salary of about $1,200 and allowing him to resign his pastorate the following year. No longer would he work for someone else, as he had for the Second Church. In the coming years, he earned the remainder of his income as a popular lecturer in local lyceums, a new forum for paid public speaking, and as a freelance essayist. In this way, Emerson profited from the growing commercial market for oratory and literature while remaining beholden only to himself and his audience. Well might he imagine that his economic security depended upon his intellectual independence, rather than vice versa.[28]

By his thirtieth birthday, Emerson had secured the means as well as the motivation to expound a new vision of individual independence, or "self-reliance." But what was the self upon which he relied? This is the critical question, for especially in his early writings, Emerson must not be mistaken for a simple philo-sophical apologist of selfishness at the expense of social ties or obligations. To the contrary, his crucial innovation lay in his reconception of individual iden-tity in terms not of a pursuit of self-interest and provision for dependents, but of an explicitly noneconomic kind of psychological self-expression or self-re-alization deeply indebted to the Unitarian model of "self-culture."[29] He con-structed a new model of selfhood, and therefore of self-reliance, sharply in ten-sion with that of classical political economy. The first lines of *Nature* (1836), Emerson's spectacular philosophical debut, define the central problem he set for his readers: "The foregoing generations beheld God and nature face to face; we, through their eyes. Why should not we also enjoy an original relation to the universe?"[30] The universe, according to Emerson, comprised "Nature and the Soul." By "nature," then, he meant the entire material world, everything other than soul. His fundamental concern was the relationship between soul and na-ture, "ME" and "NOT ME," self and world. The problem he conceived was the disjuncture between these realms, dividing in two what was originally one.

In describing the alienation of soul from nature, Emerson responded to a pervasive concern in antebellum New England with the rupture of the con-ventional relationship between self and world due to the market revolution.[31] In the dominant liberal-republican discourse, that concern centered upon the transformation of property relations, the breakup of the unity of human labor and means of production (farmland, workshop) that formed the basis of indi-vidual agency (civic virtue as well as self-interest) in the early republic. Since individuality inhered in ownership of productive property, the emerging class divide between owners of labor and owners of capital represented to many ob-servers a division of the sovereign self, understood in essentially political and economic terms. Here lies the significance of Emerson's radical critique of ownership as the natural or normative relationship between self and world. What appeared in the light of classical political economy as the very essence of individual agency—mastery of productive property—was actually, he con-tended, the basis of the soul's alienation from nature.

Emerson's understanding of such alienation drew upon the Romantic ideal of "natural man" derived from Rousseau as well as the Neoplatonic concept of divine "correspondence" between human nature and the natural world identi-fied with the Swedish theologian Emanuel Swedenborg. The rightful relation-ship between self and world was one not of mastery, but of reflection: the ma-terial realm of nature mirrored the spiritual realm of the soul. To envision one's relation to the world in terms of ownership was to view nature as a resource to be claimed and exploited, and thereby to externalize rather than internalize it, to fail to realize the essential identity between soul and nature. "At present, man applies to nature but half his force. He works on the world with his understanding alone," Emerson wrote, using "understanding" in Coleridge's sense of intellect as opposed to intuition. "[Man's] relation to nature, his power over it, is through the understanding; as by manure; the economic use of fire, wind, water, and the mariner's needle; steam, coal, chemical agriculture," and so on, he explained. " . . . This is such a resumption of power, as if a banished king should buy his territories inch by inch, instead of vaulting into his throne."[32]

In place of such sovereignty, Emerson offered an alternative conception of property, defined by neither economic exploitation nor political right but by psychic identification. By immersing oneself in the natural world as a receptive soul rather than a commanding sovereign, he argued, the individual could claim "property" in a spiritual kingdom.[33] "[T]he universe is the property of every individual in it," he wrote. " . . . In proportion to the energy of his thought and will, he takes up the world into himself."[34] The soul who "takes up the world into himself" was a very different kind of proprietor than the sovereign self of political economy who exerted himself upon the world around him, establishing his independence through claims upon family labor and real property. Emerson's transcendent self established title to nature not through labor or law but sheerly through thought, which conferred a deeper claim. "The charming landscape which I saw this morning, is indubitably made up of some twenty or thirty farms," he explained. "Miller owns this field, Locke that, and Manning the woodland beyond. But none of them owns the landscape. There is a property in the horizon which no man has but he whose eye can integrate all the parts, that is, the poet. This is the best part of these men's farms, yet to this their warranty-deeds give no title."[35]

The contrast Emerson drew between what might be thought of as sovereign property, defined by legal right and economic use, and transcendental property, defined by perception, was crucial to his implicit critique of political economy. The proprietary individual of political economy united persons and property by claiming title to the land. Emerson's poetic "eye," by contrast, could "integrate all the parts" of the landscape by seeing it whole. The transcendent soul claimed its proper property in nature simply by seeing its surroundings in ideal rather than material form—as landscape rather than land. Property, like beauty, was in the eye of the beholder, not the deed of the proprietor. "The ruin or the blank, that we see when we look at nature, is in our own eye," Emerson wrote. " . . . The reason why the world lacks unity, and lies broken and in heaps, is, because man is disunited with himself."[36]

By uniting with himself, man could inherit his spiritual dominion, no matter how paltry or even nonexistent his material domain. "All that Adam had, all that Caesar could, you have and can do," Emerson reassured his readers. "Adam called his house, heaven and earth; Caesar called his house, Rome; you perhaps call yours, a cobbler's trade; a hundred acres of ploughed land; or a scholar's garret. Yet line for line and point for point, your dominion is as great as theirs."[37] In theory, Emerson's decoupling of selfhood from ownership extended the conception of moral agency to include wives, servants, and slaves, as well as dispossessed farmers and workers, though none of these were among his immediate audience in practice.[38] At the same time, he implicitly (and later explicitly) rejected the rising chorus of demands for political and economic power on the part of the propertyless. By denying the importance of property itself as it was commonly understood, he dismissed as well contemporary critiques of the reorganization of property relations entailed in the rise of industrial capitalism.

Yet in conceiving the relationship between self and world in thoroughly psychological terms, Emerson was deeply troubled by the expansion of market relations. In his renowned address to the Society of Phi Beta Kappa at Harvard, "The American Scholar," delivered amid the panic of 1837, he turned his attention directly to the alienating implications of the new market society. "Man," he told the scholarly society, "is not a farmer, or a professor, or an engineer, but he is all." Of necessity, he said, "in the *divided* or social state, these functions are parceled out to individuals." The sad result was that "this original unit, this fountain of power has been so distributed to multitudes, has been so minutely subdivided and peddled out, that it is spilled into drops, and cannot be gathered. . . . Man is thus metamorphosed into a thing, into many things. The priest becomes a form; the attorney, a statute-book; the mechanic, a machine; the sailor, a rope of a ship."[39]

Why was man-in-society, like man-in-nature, "disunited with himself"? Not because of wage earners' alienation from the products of their labor, for in fact, Emerson's audience of professors and priests did not work for wages. The division of labor that was transforming the industrial order was a division within the workplace, among wage workers performing different tasks in the production of a single commodity, and between labor and capital. But he only indirectly considered that distinctively capitalist division of labor. His critique rather centered upon the division of labor among people performing different services or producing different commodities in society as a whole.[40] What concerned Emerson was not the property relations governing production, but the ways in which individuals, abstracted from those relations, depended on others for things they might otherwise do or make for themselves. Every true man must be "priest, and scholar, and producer, and soldier," all at once, he argued.[41]

Emersonian "self-reliance" entailed an integrated, holistic spirituality or personality, a sense of psychic wholeness at odds with the specialization of knowledge as well as of labor.

The trouble with the division of labor, in other words, was fundamentally a problem of subjectivity or selfhood. Individuals mistakenly concerned themselves with the organization of economic and political power, according to Emerson, when the very nature of society itself was the root problem. "Men such as they are, very naturally seek money or power," Emerson wrote. " . . . Wake them, and they shall quit the false good, and leap to the true, and leave governments to clerks and desks." The problem Emerson posed could be surmounted only by a struggle within the individual for the "true," instead of a struggle within society for "money or power." The answer lay in the self, not in the social order. "The private life of one man," he wrote, "shall be a more illustrious monarchy . . . than any kingdom in history."[42] It was the same spiritual kingdom Emerson had referred to in *Nature*, the kingdom of the self.

In his first and second volumes of essays, published in the early 1840s, Emerson continued to map out the psychic realm he had defined in the previous decade. "What is the aboriginal Self on which a universal reliance may be grounded?" he wrote in his famed essay, "Self-Reliance." " . . . The inquiry leads us to that source, at once the essence of genius, of virtue, and of life, which we call Spontaneity or Instinct. We denote this primary wisdom as Intuition, whilst all later teachings are tuitions."[43] Here Emerson challenged the valorization of rational willpower that underlay political-economic thought. True to the spirit of his Romantic mentors in Germany and England, Emerson argued that rational will—whether in the form of conscience or self-interest—was a weak and unreliable guide. Instinct, by contrast, was an unfailing source of wisdom and power. "Every man discriminates between the voluntary acts of his mind, and his involuntary perceptions, and knows that to his involuntary perceptions a perfect faith is due," he wrote. "Voluntary acts" were the voice of the sovereign; "involuntary perceptions" were the voice of the soul. "My willful actions and acquisitions are but roving;—the idlest reverie, the faintest native emotion, command my curiosity and respect."[44]

In order to hear the voice of the spirit within, one had to "shun father and mother and wife and brother," to turn away from "the sour faces of the multitude," to "put off all foreign support," and to "stand alone."[45] But it was not only the voices of others that had to be stilled in order for the sound of the soul to be heard. One's own voice had to be silenced as well. Consciousness itself was the final obstacle to the inner self, the last barrier between the king and his throne. "[T]he man is, as it were, clapped into jail by his consciousness," Emerson wrote.[46] The soul, he explained, "is not the intellect or the will, but the master of the intellect and the will; is the background of our being, in which they lie." To be true to one's self meant to strip away what Emerson called "the façade" of everyday existence, to transcend not only the importunities of friends, family, and neighbors, but one's own reason and will. "What we commonly call man, the eating, drinking, planting, counting man, does not, as we know him, represent himself, but misrepresents himself," Emerson wrote in his essay on the "Over-Soul." The sovereign of political economy was a traitor and a fraud. "Him we do not respect, but the soul, whose organ he is, would he let it appear through his action, would make our knees bend." The inner self was the rightful king. The very thoughts and actions that constituted self-interest as well as the basis of moral action in political economy represented, to Emerson, self-deception. "[T]he blindness of the intellect begins, when it would be something of itself. The weakness of the will begins when the individual would be something of himself. All reform aims, in some one particular way, to let the soul have its way through us; in other words, to engage us to obey."[47]

What one obeyed, finally, was not the individual self or soul, but the collective soul or "Over-Soul," the transcendental God within. The "universal mind," according to Emerson, was "the only and sovereign agent."[48] Spiritual power, the only true power, coursed through souls like a current below consciousness, beyond human comprehension or control. Emerson's creed of self-obedience, as opposed to self-command, approached the most revolutionary—or rather, counterrevolutionary—principle of social psychology: the reconception of freedom as a function of submission rather than sovereignty. "[O]ur painful labors are unnecessary, and fruitless," he wrote in "Spiritual Laws." " . . . Place yourself in the middle of the stream of power and wisdom which animates all whom it floats, and you are without effort impelled to truth, to right, and a perfect contentment."[49]

What could such an inward-looking conception of selfhood mean for the social relations that Emerson dismissed as essentially trivial—for property and politics, capitalism and democracy? His scorn for the common culture and mundane pursuits of his contemporaries attracted him to New England reform, which reached high tide in the antebellum era. But the arch individualist never felt comfortable amid the army of advocates for abolition, temperance, social hygiene, and the sanctity of the Sabbath. In a series of addresses and essays in the 1840s, he embraced the spirit but spurned the substance of the reform crusade. The upsurge of reform activity, he said, came in response to a legitimate complaint: "the ways of trade" had "grown selfish to the borders of theft," while "the employments of commerce" were rife with "derelictions and abuses."[50] But Emerson hastened to add that the selfishness of trade and the derelictions of commerce were not the fault of traders and industrialists, nor did businessmen profit from greed. "I do not charge the merchant or the manufacturer. The sins of our trade belong to no class, to no individual," he said. "One plucks, one distributes, one eats," and all suffer equally from the sins of modern society.[51] The trouble with trade and commerce was not that one group preyed upon another. It was that society preyed upon its collective soul.

Emerson illustrated his argument with a parable. "You remember the story of the poor woman who importuned King Philip of Macedon to grant her justice, which Philip refused: the woman exclaimed, 'I appeal': the king, astonished, asked to whom she appealed: the woman replied, 'From Philip drunk to Philip sober,'" he recalled. "The text will suit me very well. I believe not in two classes of men, but in man in two moods, in Philip drunk and Philip sober."[52] What appeared at first as a conflict of power, pitting the sovereign against his subject, turned out to be a conflict of selfhood, pitting the false Philip against the true. So in society, Emerson contended, the apparent struggle between "two classes" concealed the real struggle between "two moods."

The false conflict was fueled by the false consciousness of those on both sides of the apparent class divide, according to Emerson. The prosperous, for their part, wrongly believed that selfishness paid. In truth, he argued, "The selfish man suffers more from his selfishness, than he from whom that selfishness withholds some important benefit."[53] Selfishness did not serve one person's interests at another's expense. It served the interests of the outer self, the "eating, drinking, planting, counting man," at the expense of the inner self. But affluent Americans unwittingly suffered from their prosperity in another way as well. While their outer selves luxuriated in the products made and the services performed by others, their inner selves atrophied from lack of the "education" that came with "stand[ing] in primary relations with the work of the world."[54] They forfeited their spiritual autonomy, the capacity to minister to their own needs and fulfill their own functions.

Emerson reconceived the value of labor in psychological rather than material terms. "[N]ot only health but education is in the work," he said.[55] Therein lay labor's true reward: not in its production of material wealth, but in its production of spiritual wealth, which resided in the creative process itself rather than in the finished product. In this light, the labor of wage workers and servants appeared as a kind of surplus that they kept for themselves and thereby denied to their deceptively prosperous employers and masters. "I feel some shame before my wood-chopper, my ploughman, and my cook," Emerson admitted, "for they have some sort of self-sufficiency" by virtue of having the skills and experience attached to manual labor. "[T]he whole interest of history lies in the fortunes of the poor," which were only mistaken for misfortunes, he said.[56] The dependence and poverty of the outer self was the "self-sufficiency" and "fortune" of the inner self.

But the poor, like the prosperous, mistook the fortunes of money and mastery for the true good. They too were easily led to believe that market relations pitted rich against poor instead of outer self against inner self. "In every knot of laborers, the rich man does not feel himself among his friends,—and at the polls he finds them arrayed in a mass in distinct opposition to him," Emerson observed. The mass of laborers gave their votes to "the ignorant and base," but only because "they were asked with the voice and semblance of kindness." Class antagonism resulted not from conflicting interests, but from conflicting sentiments. He therefore called for "the sentiment of love" to become the guiding principle of politics, binding rich and poor as it did men and women. "An acceptance of the sentiment of love throughout Christendom for a season, would bring the felon and the outcast to our side in tears, with the devotion of his faculties to our service," Emerson said. " . . . Let our affections flow out to our fellows; it would operate in a day the greatest of all revolutions." Genuine social change, he affirmed, must "proceed from the concession of the rich, not from the grasping of the poor."[57]

Emerson sympathized with many of the aims of the reform movement, including ending slavery, reforming marriage, and improving the conditions of labor. But he found that reformers did not practice what they preached. "The Reformers affirm the inward life, but they do not trust it, but use outward and vulgar means," he said. "They do not rely on precisely that strength that wins me to their cause; not on love, not on a principle, but on men, on multitudes, on circumstances, on money, on party."[58] Emerson singled out for criticism the two reform campaigns he most admired, associationism and abolitionism. He lauded New England's several experimental communities, modeled on the ideals of early European socialists, for "the idea of union." But while a community of affections would be admirable indeed, a community founded even partly on political and economic ties was dangerous if not deplorable. "[T]his union must be inward, and not one of covenants," Emerson declared. The campaign against slavery suffered from a related misconception of its mission, in his view. Abolitionists imagined that the evil of slavery consisted in its "circumstances"—that is, in the slavery of the body, not the slavery of the soul. "These benefactors," he said, "hope to raise man by improving his circumstances: by combination of that which is dead, they hope to make something alive. In vain.

By new infusions alone of the spirit by which he is made and directed, can he be re-made and reinforced."[59]

How were such spiritual "infusions" to be administered to benighted Americans? How could people be "re-made and reinforced," and freed from their mental chains? Real reform, according to Emerson, must respond to people's unconscious "wishes," not their conscious wills. "As every man at heart . . . wishes to be convicted of his error, and to come to himself, so he wishes that the same healing should not stop in his thought, but should penetrate his will or active power," he said. The "healing power" should vanquish the "active power," and the inner self triumph over the outer self. "What [every man] most wishes is to be lifted to some higher platform, that he may see beyond his present fear the trans-alpine good." What people feared was poverty and powerlessness, and their wills were guided by that fear. But what they "desired," deep down, was to yield to a greater power than themselves. Emerson translated the pursuit of individual and collective interest described by political economy into the wishes, desires, and fears of a new social psychology. In place of the liberal-republican valorization of ownership of productive resources as the foundation of independence, the basis of moral action as well as material welfare, he held out a profoundly psychological model of individuality based upon spiritual transcendence rather than political and economic power. "Here we are paralyzed with fear; we hold to our little properties, house and land, office and money," he said. " . . . We desire to be made great, we desire to be touched with that fire which shall command this ice to stream, and make our existence a benefit."[60]

Emerson recognized, however, that the mass of humanity was not to be reached through his own exhortations. Nor were most people, in his estimation, capable of the kind of psychic self-healing he exemplified. They required a firmer hand to make their existence a benefit. Government, he contended, should provide such a healing hand—though exactly what form such guidance should take he did not say. He suggested, however, that the state could fulfill this parental role only by psychologically redefining the nature of political authority. Just as Emerson articulated an individualism of the psyche rather than the sovereign, so he defined a new kind of statism, founded on a psychological conception of society instead of a political and economic conception of popular sovereignty.

Not surprisingly, he was dismayed by the Jacksonian uprising of popular politics, which set the "capitalist" against the "poor man," "those who have money" against "those who wish to have money."[61] Emerson's new statism went along with a subtly but sharply changed attitude toward economic as well as political power. By the mid-1840s, he had apparently transcended some of his earlier misgivings about the soul-dividing effects of the division of labor and the corrosive consequences of market relations. He had come to believe that the transcendent power that he had previously discovered in nature was also working wonders in trade and commerce, and that the growing spiritual force of market society promised to transform the role of government accordingly. "The history of commerce," Emerson told the Mercantile Library Association of Boston in 1844, was "the record of this beneficent tendency" that overpowered all attempts to stand in its way. Likewise, he said, "Trade is an instrument in the hands of that friendly Power which works for us in our own despite."[62]

Adam Smith, of course, had also seen an "invisible hand" at work in the free market: the pursuit of self-interest by competing individuals would tend to promote the productivity and progress of society as a whole. Emerson converted the invisible hand of political economy into a spiritual power that arose not from contractual relations among autonomous producers, but from the collective unconscious of society itself.[63] "That serene Power interposes an irresistible check upon the caprices and officiousness of our wills," he said of the market. " . . . We are very forward to help it, but it will not be accelerated. It resists our meddling, eleemosynary contrivances."[64]

The state must no longer aim to represent the "officiousness" of the popular will, said Emerson. Government in some form—he was weak on specifics—must become the spiritual guide of Americans' deeper desires rather than the blunt instrument of their superficial demands. "[I]n the scramble of parties for the public purse, the main duties of government [have been] omitted,—the duty to instruct the ignorant, to supply the poor with work and with good guidance," he said.[65] Though the poor had the benefit of the primary "education" that the struggle for existence afforded, as he had earlier observed, they lacked the higher knowledge of the spirit, which Emerson and his peers possessed. "Yes, Government must educate the poor man. Look across the country from any hillside around us, and the landscape seems to crave Government," he said.[66]

When Emerson had first surveyed the landscape in *Nature*, property lines had dissolved into a greater whole within the poet's eye. When he now took a second look at the landscape, with an eye toward common humanity rather than his own soul, he brought property back into play. It was not sovereign property, a legal claim upon the use and benefit of material resources. Nor was it transcendental property, the appreciation of nature as a reflection of the soul. It was yet a third, distinctively social kind of property: the property of society, of the overseer rather than the Over-Soul. "These rising grounds which command the champaign below, seem to ask for lords, true lords, *land*-lords," said Emerson. He chose his words, as ever, with care. Those who should govern the land were not mere owners, but "true lords," who understood "the land and its uses, and the applicabilities of men."[67]

In the late 1840s and 1850s, Emerson became increasingly concerned with grounding his philosophical ideals in contemporary social relations, and particularly in the rapidly changing world of work and wealth. In his lectures of the 1850s on the everyday ethics of industrial life, which formed the basis for the essays in *The Conduct of Life* (1860) and *Society and Solitude* (1870), he disavowed the kind of transcendental escape from market society exemplified by Thoreau at Walden Pond, as David M. Robinson has noted.[68] He rejected as well radical or utopian critiques of industrial capitalism as a whole. The rule of the market was the unappealable law of nature, which might be harnessed for good or ill, but could no more be transformed than transcended. Emerson aimed instead to spiritualize market relations themselves, to invest the pursuit of profit with the kind of mystical meaning that he had earlier ascribed to the primal reunion of human nature and the natural world. For, as he now contended, the fundamental human drive to unite the universe within the soul, to overcome the alienation of ME from NOT ME, was practically identical with the limitless desire for wealth. True wealth was no more nor less than the material embodiment of the ideal communion of mind and nature, a fulfillment of the innate human power to take the world up into the self.[69]

Rightly understood and properly practiced, trade as well as manufacture or farming, capital investment as well as wage labor, were manifestations of the psychic commerce of soul and world. "All things ascend, and the royal rule of economy is that it should ascend also, or, whatever we do must always have a higher aim. Thus it is a maxim that money is another kind of blood," Emerson wrote. " . . . The counting-room maxims liberally expounded are laws of the Universe. The merchant's economy is a coarse symbol of the soul's economy." Having earlier repudiated "eating, drinking, planting, counting man," Emerson now found that his own model of psychological man was equally at home in market society. "Political Economy is as good a book wherein to read the life of man and the ascendency of laws over all private and hostile influences, as any Bible which has come down to us," he wrote.[70]

Yet the political economy to which he returned looked strikingly different from the perspective of its new protagonist, the "inner self." Emerson envisioned a market society ruled by the pursuit of self-identity instead of self-interest, in which the fundamental social relationship was psychic community instead of productive property. That psychological reconception of market relations guided his continuing critique of "shallow Americanism," the race for riches as a means of social status rather than spiritual growth. "I fear the popular notion of success stands in direct opposition in all points to the real and wholesome success," he lamented. "One adores public opinion, the other private opinion; one fame, the other desert; one feats, the other humility; one lucre, the other love; one monopoly, and the other hospitality of mind."[71]

At the same time, however, Emerson's psychic self was blind to the class relations rooted in ownership of land, labor, and capital that the classical science of wealth had laid bare, and therefore to the source of the widening structural inequality between propertied and propertyless in industrial New England. "In a free and just commonwealth, property rushes from the idle and imbecile to the industrious, brave, and persevering," he wrote.[72] But his own erasure of political economy's core conceptual apparatus rendered the organization of property ultimately incomprehensible, and so too the freedom or justice of the commonwealth.

Horace Bushnell's Psychology of Christianity

Despite Horace Bushnell's contempt for the vulgar materialism of political economy, he too expressed an almost worshipful regard for the new wealth of New England. For the quarter-century from 1833 to 1859, Bushnell served as pastor to the merchants, bankers, and insurance executives of Hartford, Connecticut, assuring his parishioners that in making their city into a center of finance capital, they were doing the Lord's work. Ten years after the panic of 1837 occasioned his Phi Beta Kappa address on "wealth and weal," he was proclaiming prosperity to be a moral duty as well as virtue's reward, glorying in the transformative powers of trade. A decade later, amid another major financial crisis, he attributed godlike omniscience to the "credit system," urging his anxious listeners to keep faith in its ultimate beneficence.[73]

Like Emerson, Bushnell (1802–1876) descended from a long line of New England Puritans. The reorganization of political and economic power effected by the market revolution likewise prompted him to revise the tenets of Reformed Christianity in ways that at once challenged the traditional Protestant work ethic and provided a new spiritual license for the new worldly wealth. Though Bushnell preached and wrote from within the fold of Calvinist Congregationalism, his doctrinal innovations were sufficiently radical to force his prestigious North Church to withdraw from its consociation in order to prevent his trial for heresy and were influential enough to make him arguably the most important American theologian of the nineteenth century.[74] In sharp contrast to Emerson, he emphatically repudiated the individualistic elements of his Puritan heritage, elaborating instead the communitarian vision of church and state as a commonwealth of souls while decrying the impious illusions of social contract and natural right. Yet from his quite different religious perspective, Bushnell joined Emerson in dismantling the conventional model of individual ownership and popular sovereignty founded upon classical political economy, and in reconstructing that ideological framework upon the basis of a new psychology of unconscious influence and intuition. In his exaltation of psychic experience as opposed to church dogma as the standard of religious truth, and in his expansively social conception of the soul and deeply psychological conception of society, Bushnell followed Emerson in spiritually reconceiving the classical science of wealth, offering both a rebuke to vulgar materialism and a new rationale for market relations.

The need for such ideological revision was apparent in Bushnell's recollections of his boyhood on a family farm in the Litchfield hills of western Connecticut, where he was born in 1802. In a much-quoted address at the Litchfield Centennial Celebration in 1851, he lovingly remembered what he called the "age of homespun," a democracy of subsistence farmers as equal in political and economic status as they were in the eyes of God. "The house was a factory on the farm, the farm a grower and producer for the house. The exchanges went on briskly enough, but required neither money nor trade," he said. " . . . Harnessed, all together, into the producing process, young and old, male and female, . . . they had no conception of squandering lightly what they all had been at work, thread by thread, and grain by grain, to produce." With a guarded comparison to "men of patrimony in the great world," Bushnell noted that his homespun yeomanry was "too simple and rustic to have any conception of the big operations by which other men are wont to get their money without earning it, and lavish the more freely because it was not earned."[75]

Yet such "men of patrimony" became Bushnell's congregants in Hartford, and the gospel he gave them was, of necessity, far from the Arcadian ideal he described back home. His nostalgia was itself colored by the sweeping social changes he had felt even in his youth, when he had worked in his father's small wool-carding and cloth-finishing mill to supplement the family's income from farming. By the time he was twenty, the increasing encroachment of manufacturing upon the local homespun market had made it impractical to continue working with his father, so Bushnell had joined the local Congregational church and set off for Yale with plans to study for the ministry. But religious study did not come easily—"I was too thoughtful," he later wrote, " . . . expecting so intently to dig out a religion by my head that I was pushing it all the while practically away"—and he quickly lost what simple faith he had. After drifting discontentedly from schoolteaching to journalism to law school, Bushnell entered Yale Divinity School, the Congregationalist citadel then dominated by the "New Divinity" of Nathaniel W. Taylor. Like its Unitarian counterpart at Harvard, the New Divinity drew upon Scottish moral philosophy in endowing individuals with the ability to choose freely between sin and righteousness, thereby softening the orthodox understanding of innate depravity and divine determinism. Like Emerson, Bushnell absorbed the liberal critique of Calvinist orthodoxy while seeking to ground it in a religion of the heart rather than the head, to translate liberal theology into the terms of the transcendental psychology that he also learned from Coleridge. Late in life, he still considered Coleridge's *Aids to Reflection* the book that had most influenced him other than the Bible.[76]

In his widely read sermons and theological treatises of the 1840s and 1850s, Bushnell outlined a new Christian faith and theology inspired by the ideal of self-culture to which Unitarians and Transcendentalists alike subscribed. He shared Emerson's distaste for religious dogmatism and the endless debates it occasioned, and he too placed primary importance upon spiritual experience rather than doctrinal truth. Yet unlike Emerson, Bushnell conceived a new psychological rationale for Calvinist doctrine and Congregationalist practice.

In three seminal addresses delivered in 1848 at Yale, Harvard, and Andover Theological Seminary and published together as *God in Christ* (1849)—the work for which he was charged with heresy—he effectively reversed the received relationship between faith and doctrine, or between religious belief and religious truth. Faith, he contended, was not essentially a means of apprehending the truth of religious doctrine; rather, doctrine was fundamentally a means of fostering true faith. Christian teachings such as the fall of man, the gospel of Christ, the Trinity, sacrifice and atonement, or salvation and damnation were not to be understood as empirical propositions that literally described the course of events or the nature of God and his creation. Such doctrines were rather instruments designed to produce spiritual awareness in their believers—awareness not of the literal truth of the doctrines, but of the divine spirit within Christians themselves. The truth of doctrine, that is, resided in its subjective effect upon those who believed it, not in its objective description of the world they inhabited. Belief itself was the test of religious truth. Put another way, religious doctrines were external representations of internal states of mind. Christians found their personal experiences of God formally expressed in Scripture and sacrament.[77]

Bushnell's theology echoed the Romantic critique of Enlightenment ratio-nalism and materialism, and of political economy in particular, with the latter's scientific analysis of the ostensibly objective relations of property, class, and contract. In rejecting, as Emerson did, the tendency toward "supernatural ra-tionalism" within New Divinity Congregationalism as well as liberal Unitari-anism, Bushnell also undermined the conceptual basis of the strikingly unsen-timental science of wealth, at which he had taken aim in his Phi Beta Kappa address. His psychology of religious experience, strongly anticipating William James, marked a decisive step in the direction of making the Emersonian "inner self" the determinant of social as well as spiritual truth.

"[W]e must read [religious texts] by looking in their faces, as we do our friends," Bushnell wrote in *Christ in Theology* (1851), his answer to the charges of heresy. "We can not take them into our logical understanding and use them as the terms of a calculus. What they carry into our soul's feeling or perception, or awaken in it by expression, is their only truth, and that is a simple internal state of the soul itself."[78] Religious writings must be read figuratively or sym-bolically, with an eye to how they make one *feel* more than to what they make one *think*, much as one might read a poem. Spiritual or psychological insights, he explained, were inherently inexpressible in words, which were formal rep-resentations of what was fundamentally formless, undefinable, ineffable. Lan-guage, as a vehicle of human understanding, could never adequately contain or convey spiritual truths or states of mind, which were innately beyond the grasp of such understanding. Words could only ever act as signs or guideposts point-ing toward spiritual awareness.

Efforts to bring dogmatic precision or logical analysis to bear upon religious texts therefore mistook the forms of spiritual truths for the truths themselves. "The 'winged words' are required to serve as beasts of burden; or, what is no better, to forget their poetic life, as messengers of the air, and stand still, fixed upon the ground, as wooden statues of truth," Bushnell wrote.[79] What ap-peared in Scripture, taken literally, as a logical contradiction in terms—as in the representation of heaven as at once a garden and a city, or, more fundamen-tally, the representation of God as both a unity and a trinity—aptly evoked spiritual ideas beyond the bounds of language and logic. As Coleridge had written, "In a world, whose opinions are drawn from outside shows, many things may be *paradoxical,* (that is, contrary to the common notion) and never-theless true: nay, *because* they are true."[80]

Bushnell drew upon Coleridge as well as the biblical critic Josiah Willard Gibbs Sr., from whom Bushnell had learned at Yale, in elaborating a general theory of language on the basis of his ideas about the symbolic character of religious texts.[81] Following Gibbs, he contended that the origin of all words lay in the natural, sensible world of Coleridge's "Understanding." Only by analogy did such material terms come to denote the immaterial realm of the "Reason," of the psyche or the soul, as when "spirit" came to mean not breath or moving air but the unseen power of the divine. Invoking the Neoplatonic tradition also adopted by Emerson, Bushnell wrote that the correspondence manifested in language between the spiritual realm and the material realm revealed the intimate relationship between God and humankind, or between nature and the supernatural. God created the natural world as a formal expression or language for the spiritual insight, the knowledge of God, lodged in the human soul. "[T]he external grammar of creation answers to the internal grammar of the soul, and becomes its vehicle," Bushnell wrote. " . . . And if the outer world is the vast dictionary and grammar of thought we speak of, then it is also itself an organ throughout of Intelligence. Whose Intelligence?" That of "the universal Author," who communicated with humankind through the medium of nature.[82]

To think of the "outer world" as the poetic language of the soul was to conceive of religious experience as spiritual communication, as a process of expression and impression of divine thought. It was to see the soul itself as a product of such psychic exchange not only with God, but with other souls as well. As the religion scholar David L. Smith has shown, a theory of psychic communication was basic to Bushnell's understanding of nature and the supernatural, but also of selfhood and social relations.[83] Indeed, his insistence that the soul was a social as well as divine creation formed the core of Bushnell's most influential work, *Views of Christian Nurture* (1847), perhaps the most controversial American theological treatise of the nineteenth century.[84] In it, he offered not only a newly social view of the soul, but a newly psychological vision of society sharply at odds with the inherited tradition of American social science.

Bushnell joined the growing reaction among the merchant elite of the seaboard cities against the evangelical revivalism arising in the wake of the commercial transformation of the backcountry. Like high-church Episcopalians and liberal Unitarians, the members of his North Church frowned upon the swooning enthusiasm of the Second Great Awakening, with its egalitarian message that all were born in sin and each must undergo a soul-wrenching conversion in Christ. At the same time, many well-to-do Hartford churchgoers worried over the corrosive effects of urban growth and the breakdown of patriarchal authority upon patterns of deference and discipline within their own families. They were concerned, in other words, about the leveling implications of popular religion and the erosion of traditional social authority due to the onset of industrialization.[85]

Bushnell's work, like much contemporary literature, addressed the social problems posed by the market revolution through an analysis of the critical issue of child-rearing. Orthodox Calvinists had long struggled with the tension between their belief that children were born sinners whose only hope lay in redemptive conversion upon coming of age, on the one hand, and the need for early moral training in piety and respect for authority, on the other. Enlightened parents had increasingly abandoned the doctrine of original sin in favor of the Lockean understanding of the mind as a blank slate awaiting education, modified by Scottish philosophy's innate "moral sense," which likewise required careful cultivation by parents and teachers. Bushnell's *Christian Nurture* embraced the liberal emphasis on the nurture of Christian character, but it reconceived education in terms of his own ideas about spiritual communication. He too believed the soul to be a social as well as divine creation, the product of nurture as much as nature. But like contemporary writers such as Lydia Maria Child and the Transcendentalist Amos Bronson Alcott, Bushnell held that the path to the soul lay through the feelings rather than the intellect and, as he argued, through unconscious intuition rather than conscious instruction.[86]

In deliberate contrast to either the Unitarians or their Transcendentalist progeny, Bushnell cautiously maintained the principle of natural human depravity and the need for saving grace to rescue the soul from its fall. But he rigorously rejected the idea that such salvation could be sought only by means of the conversion of the repentant after a youth spent in sin. A Christian soul, he countered, must be fostered in the child from birth by parents serving as vehicles of God's grace. "THE CHILD IS TO GROW UP A CHRISTIAN," he wrote, " . . . to open on the world as one that is spiritually renewed, not remembering the time when he went through a technical experience, but seeming rather to have loved what is good from his earliest years."[87] Christian character required neither a mature understanding of church doctrine nor a willful disavowal of one's wayward youth, but rather an intuitive appreciation of God's loving spirit. Such spiritual awareness came most easily in infancy and childhood, "the ages most pliant to good." The child received grace not through dogmatic indoctrination in catechism or prayer book, but through the silent, psychic language of parental, especially maternal, affection. "[F]or the Christian scheme, the gospel, is really wrapped up in the life of every Christian parent and beams out from him as a living epistle, before it escapes from the lips, or is taught in words," Bushnell wrote. The most "plastic age" for Christian nurture came before the infant learned to speak, "the era of *impressions*, and these impressions are the seminal principles, in some sense, of the activity that runs to language, and also of the whole future character."[88]

In *Christian Nurture*, the dependent, unreflecting, suggestible child became the main model of human agency, supplanting the willful, rational, independent adult who was the agent of classical political economy. Bushnell's veneration of the divine force of parental influence formed the basis for his broader interpretation of social relations in general and for a fundamental critique of individualism. Long after the "era of impressions" was past, he argued, the individual remained largely a product of social influences involuntarily impressed upon the receptive soul. "We possess a mixed individuality all our life long," he wrote. "A pure, separate, individual man, living *wholly* within, and from himself, is a mere fiction. No such person ever existed, or ever can."[89]

In a suggestive 1846 sermon on "Unconscious Influence," Bushnell generalized the "law of social contagion" that he had earlier described.[90] Just as children learned deeper lessons from parents' spirit than from parents' words, so people always conversed in two tongues: one conscious and deliberate, the language of intellectual understanding; the other unconscious and involuntary, the language of "the sensibilities or affections," conveyed in tone and gesture and facial expression. While people generally were aware of how they were affected by the language of the head, they were all too unmindful of the far more powerful influence of the language of the heart. "The impressions they receive do not come through verbal propositions," he said, " . . . and therefore many think nothing of them. But precisely on this account are they the more powerful, because it is as if one heart were thus going directly into another, and carrying its feelings with it. Beholding, as in a glass, the feelings of our neighbor, we are changed into the same image, by the assimilating power of sensibility and fellow-feeling."[91]

Such psychic fellowship, according to Bushnell, pervaded society as a whole and indeed defined society itself. "And just so, unawares to himself, is every man, the whole race through, laying hold of his fellow-man, to lead him where otherwise he would not go. We overrun the boundaries of our personality—we flow together," he said. While the conscious, deliberate dimension of social communication underlay the "voluntary society" of autonomous individuals freely choosing the forms of their association—in other words, the social contract posited in one way or another by classical political economy and the liberal-republican thought of the Revolutionary Era—unconscious communication gave rise to the "involuntary society" of spiritual communion, "one consolidated social body, animated by one life."[92]

So Bushnell's psychological conception of religious and familial relations provided the model for his understanding of society and social order. His rejection of evangelical revivalism in favor of the Christian home as the "church of childhood" formed the foundation for a broader argument that the "law of organic connection" between parent and child—closely related to the "law of social contagion"—also governed relations among members of society or between the individual and the state. The revolutionary doctrines of natural right and social compact, he wrote in *Christian Nurture,* ran counter to the natural and supernatural social bonds into which individuals were born, and which defined their character in the same way that parental love fostered the Christian soul. Individuals' psychic ties to their church, their community, and their state were no more the products of conscious deliberation and willful choice than were children's ties to their parents. Society, like Bushnell's nurturing family, was ultimately grounded in a "common spirit" or "comprehensive will actuating the members, regarding also the common body itself, as a larger and more inclusive individual."[93] Here was a model of social life in which proprietary autonomy had no place, in which indeed dependence formed the organizing principle, and, consequently, in which the breakdown of the agrarian republic of independent households appeared fully in keeping with the dictates of God as well as humanity.

As early as the panic of 1837, Bushnell sensed the increasingly divisive implications of Anglo-American political economy and its conceits of independent proprietorship and popular sovereignty, and he called for a new social science of spiritual rather than political and economic relations. By the end of the Civil War, he was encouraged by the Union's victory to fully disavow what he called the "pernicious nostrums" of the Declaration of Independence, which he believed had prompted southern secession. In a telling Thanksgiving Day sermon for 1864, entitled "Popular Government by Divine Right," Bushnell argued that Revolutionary Era writers had arrogantly misconceived the justification for American independence as the right of self-government, when in truth their rebellion was founded in their divinely appointed destiny to found a great nation. "We revolted transcendentally, for reasons deeper than we conceived; such as we could only feel," he said. Nearly a century later, in his view, the "latent poison" contained in the doctrine of the consent of the governed was finally being purged on the battlefield, clearing the way for the consecration of the nation-state as the instrument of divine right rather than popular rule.[94] The great lesson of the Civil War, for Bushnell, was that the eighteenth-century ideals of early American political economy provided a better basis for rebellion than for rule, fostering social conflict rather than social order. His psychosocial reconstruction of sovereignty as well as spirituality, in other words, resulted in a Romantic nationalism that formed the conservative counterpart of Emersonian individualism, as Emerson's own later writings also revealed.[95] Bushnell's understanding of government as "the organic conscience of the State," conceived as the family writ large, effectively elided the economic basis of political authority as well as the political structure of economic relations that early American political economy had sharply illuminated.[96]

That familial conception of society also bolstered Bushnell's move toward a cultural and even racial nationalism characteristic of nineteenth-century American social psychology. For him, as for many later writers on social science, the notion of an organic polity, born not of declarations or constitutions but of spiritual solidarity, easily lent itself to racial and ethnic chauvinism. Where the leading American social theorists of the early republic had rooted their ideals of democracy and liberty in the model of a single-class society of self-employed citizens, Bushnell regrounded those fighting words in the model of an ethnically or racially homogeneous nation united by blood and spirit, if no longer by class.[97] Psychosocial kinship, rather than political and economic equality, formed the primary social bond. "A single family, proceeding thus from one parent stock, will suffice to people a nation," he wrote in *Christian Nurture.* " . . . Accordingly the very word *nation* implies a nascent order and growth."[98] Bushnell's decidedly racial hostility toward the growing Irish Catholic and black working class of Hartford, and his active concern with preserving the purity of Anglo-Saxon stock, were of a piece with his transcendental psychology and his rejection of political economy. As the centrality of class receded from view in his revision of social relations, race in the guise of nation came to the fore.[99]

So too, for related reasons, did an equally naturalized conception of gender come to the fore in the guise of the spiritualized "home" as opposed to the productive household. Bushnell's critique of individual rights and social contract and his defense of the family as an alternative model of social relations were predicated upon an explicitly sentimental understanding of marriage as well as parenthood. "[I]t is very true that the voters signify a trust in the men when they vote for them, and so does the woman signify a trust in the man, when she becomes his wife, but it does not follow that her act of trust makes him an agent and herself his principal, with a right to recall his trusteeship when she pleases," he said in his sermon on divine right. "Even God himself would, in this manner, be only our trustee and we his principals."[100] In disavowing the sovereignty of either a patriarchal God or a free, independent soul in favor of a notion of psychic identity between the human and the divine, he became an influential exponent of social interdependence modeled upon marriage as an "organic" rather than contractual relation.

Much as maternal affection was the primary vehicle of God's love in Bushnell's vision of Christian nurture, so the wife's devotion to her husband represented the supreme power of unconscious influence in its most precious form. "[T]here is nothing more beautiful, and more to be envied by the poets, than this same charm of power by which a good wife detains her husband," he wrote to his own wife in a letter of January 1844. "It is not an ambitious, noisy power; it is silent, calm, persuasive, and often so deep as to have its hold deeper than consciousness itself."[101] The spiritual power of the loving wife and mother, like that of the proud Anglo-Saxon stock, supplanted the political and economic power of the autonomous proprietor in Bushnell's Romantic psychology of the social soul. Marital devotion, racial identity, parental guidance—each formed an aspect of his vision of psychic kinship. His impressionistic social psychology drew a reassuring picture of social harmony for the members of Hartford's financial elite, struggling to reconcile the emergence of a class society with the ethical and spiritual precepts, the political economy and moral philosophy, inherited from the Revolutionary Era.

Margaret Fuller's Psychology of Gender

Bushnell's depiction of family relations highlights the close association of transcendental psychology with a deeply psychological understanding of the "feminine" that historians have described as the ideology of "domesticity."[102] It was not simply that Romantic writers defined "Woman" as the natural carrier of the qualities of passion, intuition, and spirituality that they exalted. In conceiving social life as spiritual communion, Bushnell and like-minded contemporaries portrayed the emerging industrial order as a whole in explicitly "feminine" terms, heralding what Ann Douglas has called "the feminization of American culture."[103] From their perspective, market society appeared less as an arena of competition and contract among autonomous proprietors, in the classically masculine terms of political economy, than as a tightly integrated organization of interdependent actors each fulfilling his or her part in a collective endeavor for common goals, a model commonly associated with the "feminine" attributes of mutuality, love, and sympathy—or, at least, that was what many imagined market society could and should be. Perhaps more than any other aspect of antebellum New England thought, the identification of the "social" and the "psychological" with the "feminine" reveals the struggles and contradictions within the Romantic response to the origins of industrial capitalism.[104] On the one hand, the partisans of "feminization" (or psychological socialization) critically contrasted their communitarian ideal with the greed, exploitation, and ruthless competition they found in the new industrial age, and they frequently called for major social reform. On the other hand, their own repudiation of the science of wealth in favor of a fledgling science of sentiment proved ironically compatible with profound political and economic inequality. Nowhere are the tensions between transcending and transforming the new market society more clearly confronted than in the meteoric career of Margaret Fuller (1810–1850), the first and foremost American theorist of feminine subjectivity, or of the complex connection between femininity and selfhood.

In little over a decade, from the first of her consciousness-raising "Conversations" with Boston women, in 1839, to the last of her newspaper dispatches from Europe, a few months before her death in 1850, Fuller came to represent for many both the living embodiment of the Romantic spirit in America and its greatest anomaly. She was at once the hub of the Transcendentalist circle and the consummate outsider who persistently stretched its limits.[105] If discoursing upon Greek mythology in Elizabeth Peabody's parlor represents one pole of her politics (and the beginning of her public career) and nursing the fallen fighters of the besieged Roman Republic the other (at the end), the critical midpoint is her *Woman in the Nineteenth Century* (1845), one of the first American feminist treatises.[106] Written on the cusp of her departure from Emerson's New England to become a literary critic in New York City, the text is a testament to the pivotal significance of gender in Fuller's understanding of the psychological dualism that informed both the American Romantics and their Revolutionary Era forebears: Understanding and Reason, tuition and intuition, prose and poetry. For Fuller, the basis of such distinctions lay in the fundamental divide between male and female, "the two sides of the great radical dualism."[107]

Like Emerson and Bushnell, she rebelled against the subordination of passion to intellect, of "harmony" and "beauty" to "energy" and "power," which she associated with the subordination of the feminine side of life to the masculine, and of women to men.[108] Yet unlike them, Fuller sought not to reverse the conventional relation between head and heart, but to bring them into balance, to reconcile the competing psychic imperatives of mastery and love, sovereignty and spirituality.[109] She identified the central social problem of the age, as Emerson and Bushnell did, as men and women's psychological alienation from their full, true nature. But her personal experience and journalistic career brought her to grapple on a theoretical as well as practical level, as they did not, with social inequality—between men and women, but also between masters and slaves, western Indians and white settlers, rich and poor, and even, uncertainly, bourgeois reformers, plebeian radicals, and the working poor. Ultimately, Fuller's widely noted struggle to harmonize the "masculine" and "feminine" principles within herself as in society reflected the deepening discord between her Enlightenment and Romantic allegiances, or between political economy and social psychology.[110] That ideological conflict as well as the emerging class divide upon which it was based were vividly displayed in the failure of the European revolutions of 1848, the climactic end of both Fuller's life and the age of republican revolution itself.[111]

The struggle that Fuller entered over the reconstitution of gender relations originated in the breakdown of the household economy, which had formed the basis of propertied men's political and economic "independence" as well as women's "dependence" in eighteenth-century thought.[112] The married women's property acts of the antebellum era, designed to protect propertied families against bankruptcy amid the vicissitudes of the new market economy, generally granted wives formal title to (though often not control over) their separate property, undermining the legal basis of women's disfranchisement in the common law of coverture.[113] Spurred by the economic and legal demise of the autonomous household with its male proprietor, antebellum feminists demanded for women the rights of ownership and citizenship enshrined in the founding texts of American political economy. "We hold these truths to be self-evident," stated the Seneca Falls Declaration of Sentiments in 1848, "that all men *and women* are created equal; that they are endowed by their Creator with certain inalienable rights."[114]

Yet even as the market revolution eroded the old basis of women's subservience in the male-headed household, the rise of wage labor represented a new kind of dependence for working women no less than men. As the value of labor, like that of other commodities, came to be measured by the price paid for it, women's unpaid housework was accordingly devalued—and this remained the great majority of the work women did. What Jeanne Boydston has called the "pastoralization of housework"—its redefinition as a labor of love rather than livelihood—bolstered the sexual division of labor within the paid workforce as well, where women earned far less than men.[115] As a result, the demand for women's economic independence and attendant political rights prompted leading feminists to attack not only the outdated doctrine of coverture, but the new logic of wage labor as well. As Reva Siegel has shown, the antebellum movement for women's "joint property" in household income and assets on the basis of their unpaid housework entailed a radical critique of the commodification of labor itself.[116] In this way, Fuller's feminist contemporaries demonstrated the explosive potential of classical political economy in the dawning industrial era.

Fuller felt the tension between the republican ideal of sovereign selfhood and the social dependency of women from an early age, and it shaped much of her mature thought.[117] As a young girl in Cambridgeport, Massachusetts, she was educated at home by her father, a Harvard-trained lawyer who had left behind the Federalism of his family to forge a successful political career as a Jeffersonian Republican in the state legislature and the U.S. House of Representatives. Timothy Fuller Jr. believed women deserved the same schooling as men, emphasizing rigorous indoctrination in the ancient history, Scottish moral philosophy, and classical political economy that formed the intellectual heritage of the American Revolution. From him, his gifted daughter learned to venerate the rational, willful, independent individual described by Jefferson, her political lodestar even in youth. She learned, too, the abiding admiration for the ancient Roman Republic that she would bring to the Risorgimento in later life. "Every Roman was an emperor," she recalled with reverence in an autobiographical essay written when she was 30.[118]

Yet the young Fuller was painfully aware of the seemingly unbridgeable gap between the enlightened public life for which she was trained and the limitations upon bourgeois women in the Age of Jackson. Timothy Fuller's own career in public service ended abruptly when she was twenty-two, due to his opposition to Jacksonian politics, which both father and daughter deemed a vulgar betrayal of the nobler Jeffersonian spirit. His sudden death from cholera three years later deepened her despair over her inability to fulfill the ideal of virtuous independence that he had upheld. The oldest of seven surviving children, she took charge of the Fuller household in his absence and supervised her siblings' education at great personal cost. But she was bitterly frustrated by her incapacity, as an unmarried woman, to assume legal title to the family estate or legal custody of the children, which devolved upon her uncaring uncle. Ann Douglas has justly argued that Fuller understood the legacy of the nation's founders to be "the struggle for independence, . . . and she expended her finest adult energies in rescuing it from obsolescence."[119]

If her youthful model of sovereign selfhood was informed by her father's Jeffersonian republicanism, however, she drew a different understanding of personal independence from the Emersonian Transcendentalism that she discovered in the disorienting aftermath of his death. Transcendentalism offered Fuller a means of support as well as a public identity—as a teacher at Bronson Alcott's Temple School in Boston and at a similar school in Providence, as the leader of the Conversations, and as the editor of the Transcendentalist journal, the *Dial*. But the movement and her mentors, Emerson and Goethe, gave her as well a new model of spiritual selfhood that stood in marked contrast to the Enlightenment ideal she had learned from her father. Transcendentalism afforded her employment commensurate with her talents, while her father's career in law and government was off-limits. So too, the Romantic realm of inspiration and intuition appeared to answer women's need for self-expression in ways the republican realm of property and politics did not.

Looking back upon her childhood in her "autobiographical romance" of 1840, Fuller found her father spiritually limited, consumed with the commonplace. "To be an honored citizen, and to have a home on earth, were made the great aims of existence," she wrote of him. "To open the deeper fountains of the soul, to regard life here as the prophetic entrance to immortality, to develop his spirit to perfection,—motives like these had never been suggested to him, either by fellow-beings or by outward circumstances." His ruthless instruction, she suggested, while overeducating her in matters of intellect, had severely stunted the growth of her affections, wreaking havoc with her delicate constitution. Her only refuge from his wholly "utilitarian" household she had found in that "emblem of domestic love," her mother's flower garden. "Here I felt at home," she wrote.[120]

To the dozens of women who enrolled in her three-month series of Conversations each year between 1839 and 1844, products of Brahmin Boston like herself seeking a wider field of endeavor than domestic life allowed, Fuller offered a Romantic education very unlike her father's. The method was carefully conversational in the manner of Alcott's school, designed to catch thought on the wing instead of pinning it down. The subject matter began with not Roman virtue but Greek myth, in which, as Fuller wrote in her memoir, "the law of life . . . was beauty, as in Rome it was a stern composure."[121] But the ultimate subject of study, in Transcendentalist fashion, was subjectivity itself—more particularly, feminine subjectivity, to which Fuller turned her complete attention in her best-known work, *Woman in the Nineteenth Century*.

The book grew out of an article she wrote for the *Dial* in July 1843, enigmatically entitled, "The Great Lawsuit.—Man *versus* Men; Woman *versus* Women." As she explained in the preface, the original title was intended to suggest her central argument: women's condition was not determined by any superficial social conflict with men. It was rather rooted in a deeper psychic struggle between men and women's perceptions of themselves, on the one hand, and their innate spiritual potential, on the other. Women's fundamental problem was their alienation from their true nature, which was men's problem as well.

"[W]hile it is the destiny of Man" to make his life "that of an angel or messenger," she wrote, "the action of prejudices and passions . . . is continually obstructing the holy work that is to make the earth a part of heaven. By Man I mean both man and woman; these are the two halves of one thought."[122] The faltering structure of gender relations reflected the gap between the conventional relationship of men and women, on the one hand, and the ideal union of "Man" and "Woman" on the other. "[T]he time has come," she wrote, " . . . when Man and Woman may regard one another as brother and sister, the pillars of one porch, the priests of one worship."[123]

Fuller conceived of the relationship between male and female ideals in terms of the transcendental psychology of Coleridge and Emerson. The dyad of Understanding and Reason became in her work the masculine and feminine dimensions of the human psyche.[124] "So far as these two methods can be distinguished, they are so as Energy and Harmony; Power and Beauty; Intellect and Love," she wrote. Woman's "especial genius" was "electrical in movement, intuitive in function, spiritual in tendency"; "her intuitions are more rapid and more correct"; and so on. The end goal of Fuller's feminism, accordingly, was not women's political or economic empowerment, "not money, nor notoriety, nor the badges of authority which men have appropriated to themselves," but psychic development. "What Woman needs is not as a woman to act or rule, but as a nature to grow, as an intellect to discern, as a soul to live freely," Fuller wrote. Such spiritual liberation, she suggested, would foster sexual harmony in place of strife. "Were [women] free, were they wise fully to develop the strength and beauty of Woman; they would never wish to be men, or man-like. The well-instructed moon flies not from her orbit to seize on the glories of her partner."[125]

Yet unlike Bushnell and other contemporary exponents of "woman's sphere," Fuller did not identify women solely with sentimental femininity.[126] Masculinity and femininity, she maintained, were not two classes of people, but two frames of mind—much like Emerson's "man in two moods." Though masculinity (or Understanding) predominated in men, and femininity (or Reason) in women, "they are perpetually passing into one another," she wrote. " . . . There is no wholly masculine man, no purely feminine woman." Further, some men were naturally more intuitive than rational, some women imbued with more military courage than maternal love. Women's feminine side, or "Muse," was but one aspect of their nature, along with their masculine side, or "Minerva."[127] Far from assigning to women one predetermined model of selfhood, Fuller aimed to open up for them the kind of free-ranging pursuit of individuality idealized by Emerson.[128] Still, while *Woman in the Nineteenth Century* refuses to confine women to a single psychological norm, its vision of women's liberation ultimately lies in the emancipation of the psyche from its mental as well as material fetters.

Unlike Emerson, however, when Fuller considered what stood in the way of women's self-culture or self-reliance, she confronted the political and economic as well as psychological bases of sexual inequality. If man, as she contended, had become woman's "temporal master instead of her spiritual sire," then her spiritual freedom required an end to his temporal mastery. "[I]n the present crisis," Fuller wrote, Minerva rather than the Muse must take the lead in women's self-defense, for women's immediate problems—if not their ultimate resolution—lay in the masculine realm of political economy.[129]

What constituted the "present crisis"? In part, she explained, it was women's lack of equal property rights, rendering wives and daughters dependent upon male proprietors, as Fuller knew from painful personal experience. Women's economic subjugation resulted as well from the conditions of industrial labor that already required many if not most to work for wages in order to support either themselves or their families. Fuller deplored in particular the "killing labors" of women textile workers in the North and slaves in the South, as well as the rise of prostitution along with urban poverty.[130] For many women, Fuller indicated, the greatest obstacle to self-development was their membership in the growing mass of the working poor. "We cannot expect to see any one sample of completed being, when the mass of men still lie engaged in the sod, or use the freedom of their limbs only with wolfish energy," she wrote. " ... While any one is base, none can be entirely free and noble." She decried, as well, the sexual division of labor within the paid workforce that severely restricted women's opportunities for economic advancement or self-support. "But if you ask me what offices they may fill, I reply—any. ... let them be sea-captains, if you will."[131]

Economic equality, Fuller clearly implied, required political equality. So long as women remained dependent upon men for just treatment, women's needs would never be adequately addressed. "[C]an we feel that Man will always do justice to the interests of Woman?" she asked. "Can we think that he takes a sufficiently discerning and religious view of her office and destiny *ever* to do her justice, except when prompted by sentiment—accidentally or transiently, for the sentiment will vary according to the relations in which he is placed?" Sentiment, she suggested, was an unreliable basis for social equality. Social equality, on the contrary, was the only firm foundation for the spiritual concord she espoused. Society would be ready for the millennial harmony of humankind that she envisioned only "when inward *and outward* freedom for Woman as much as for Man shall be acknowledged as a *right*, not yielded as a concession."[132] In this decidedly materialist spirit, Fuller persistently demanded women's "independence" from men. "Union is only possible for those who are units," she wrote, echoing Emerson. Woman, she wrote, "must be able to stand alone."[133] But whereas Emerson conceived of independence wholly in psychological terms, Fuller appeared to locate the *means* of transcendent freedom in political and economic rights.

The pervasive tension in *Woman in the Nineteenth Century* between the sentimental psychology of "Man" and "Woman," on one side, and the political economy of property, politics, and labor, on the other, reflected a broader ideological divide: the conflict between the classical science of society that Fuller had learned early on and the Transcendentalist philosophy that she had later ambivalently embraced. While she was eager to claim for women the spiritual self-reliance of Emerson's essays, her work betrayed a lingering allegiance to an earlier understanding of self-ownership, if only as a means to a loftier end. The text reflected the difficulty of reconciling that earlier ideal with not only the structure of gender relations, but the emerging class structure as well.

In this regard, Fuller's feminist treatise forms a revealing contrast with Catharine Beecher's trailblazing *Treatise on Domestic Economy*, published four years earlier in 1841.[134] The daughter of the leading figure in the evangelical wing of the Congregational Church, the Rev. Lyman Beecher—the young Rev. Emerson's crosstown rival—Catharine Beecher (1800–1878) had taken the evangelical emphasis on a religion of the heart rather than the head in a distinctly psychological direction, much as Bushnell had taken the tenets of liberal Congregationalism. Indeed her first book, *The Elements of Mental and Moral Philosophy* (1831), had anticipated Bushnell in uniting theology and psychology in a theory of the human mind as a mirror of God, as well as of other minds. In "the mutual relations of minds," Beecher had argued, lay true spirituality and the "highest kind of happiness."[135]

Ten years later, in her master work, Beecher mobilized her social psychology in essentially repudiating the revolutionary doctrines of natural right and human equality.[136] The deeper basis of democracy, she contended, lay not in equal rights, but in reciprocal relations between superiors and subordinates: between husbands and wives, parents and children, magistrates and subjects, employers and employees. Just as women were free to choose their husbands or remain unmarried, Beecher wrote, workers could choose their employers or remain unemployed. "No American woman, then, has any occasion for feeling that hers is an humble or insignificant lot," she wrote, clearly referring to the new order of class as well as gender relations. "The value of what an individual accomplishes, is to be estimated by the importance of the enterprise achieved, and not by the particular position of the laborer."[137] Her marital model of reciprocity within hierarchy offered a pointed response to the darkening specter of class strife. As the United States faced the prospect of the kind of "war of contending classes" that had torn apart the French nation in 1789, Beecher warned in an 1845 essay, "*it is in the power of American women to save their country*" by setting a different example of social relations.[138]

Beecher joined Bushnell in advancing a gendered psychology of voluntary subordination as a means of maximizing social harmony, in contrast to the utilitarian vision of social welfare as the sum of individual satisfactions. Fuller, by contrast, was far less willing to part with the ideals of equality and freedom rooted in classical political economy. In her extensive emphasis on women's need of political and economic as well as psychological "independence," as in her less probing but pointed consideration of class inequality, she remained faithful to the Jeffersonian politics that both Bushnell and Beecher disavowed.

As literary editor and social critic for Horace Greeley's *New-York Tribune* from 1844 to 1846, Fuller struggled to reconcile the pervasive social inequality she found in the burgeoning industrial metropolis with her dual allegiance to liberal-republicanism and Transcendentalism. Prostitutes, prisoners, mental patients, and paupers, as well as southern slaves and western Indians, drew her attention and sympathy, if not comprehension. She rested her hopes for moderate reform upon the wisdom of a philanthropic elite spreading the gospel of classification, education, and sanitation. But the condescension and contempt with which affluent New Yorkers regarded their working-class neighbors appalled her. Much as she had earlier described the Neoplatonic ideals of "Man" and "Woman," she drew for her readers "ideal sketches" of "The Rich Man" and "The Poor Man," united by their sympathetic psyches across the yawning class divide. Her "mercantile nobleman," like her humble but dignified pauper, appeared blessedly oblivious of politics and economics. "All depends on the spirit," she wrote. " . . . Yes, the mind is its own place, and if it will keep that place, all doors will be opened from it." Yet her columns evinced a growing awareness of the limits of such sentimentalism as well as charity along with a vague sense of the need for "radical reform" in the "present social system."[139]

Fuller's ultimate political awakening was yet to come. In 1846, she sailed for Europe, where she would spend her remaining four years chronicling the course of revolution for the *Tribune* and joining in the defense of the short-lived Roman Republic.[140] Stunned by the desperate poverty she came upon in the working-class districts of England and Scotland, she brought a new gravity to her increasingly urgent reports. Fuller was sickened not only by the degraded state in which she found the British working class, but by the monstrous luxury and stupefying indifference of the rich. "Poverty in England has terrors of which I never dreamed at home," she reported. "I felt that it would be terrible to be poor there, but far more so to be the possessor of that for which so many thousands are perishing." Visiting William Wordsworth, she was aghast to find the great Romantic poet "ignorant of the real wants of England and the world," deaf to "the voice which cries so loudly from other parts of England, and will not be stilled by sweet poetic suasion or philosophy, for it is the cry of men in the jaws of destruction." With initial horror, Fuller sensed that the laboring poor had been pressed to the edge of revolt, and she prayed "that the needful changes in the condition of this people may be effected by peaceful revolution which shall destroy nothing except the shocking inhumanity of exclusiveness, which now prevents [the treasures created by English genius, accumulated by English industry] being used for the benefit of all.— May their present possessors look to it in time!"[141]

As Fuller's political education continued in revolutionary Paris, her faith in both the idealism and the benevolence of an enlightened bourgeoisie was shaken if not destroyed. Close new friendships with the Italian patriot Joseph Mazzini, the Polish nationalist poet Adam Mickiewicz, and French socialists including George Sand drew her into the orbit of revolutionary politics. There she discovered with a shock of recognition the republican principles of liberty and democracy she had learned to cherish as a child.[142] She wrote sympathetically of the ideals of the French utopian socialist Charles Fourier, though she still regretted the "gross materialism" that marred what she took to be his altruistic philosophy. With rising enthusiasm, she embraced the call for revolution by "the people themselves," leaving behind her dread of popular uprising.[143]

Arriving in Italy, "those shores to which I had looked forward all my life," Fuller felt she had finally come home.[144] In the Italian revolution of 1848–1849, she found for the first time a social movement that matched the inspiring standards of freedom and equality she had learned from her father. She threw herself into the republican cause. In the 1848 New Year's Day issue of the *Tribune* —twelve days before Palermo rose in rebellion, swiftly igniting much of continental Europe west of the Turkish and Russian empires—Fuller identified the oncoming revolution with the highest ideals of both Europe and America, of both Christianity and Democracy. She recalled her country's founding "statement of the rights, the inborn rights of men, which, if fully interpreted and acted upon, leaves nothing to be desired." She bemoaned the betrayal of that revolutionary doctrine by "political ambition" and "boundless lust of gain" in the New World as in the Old—in the U.S. conquest of Mexico and the expansion of southern slavery as in the imperial oppression of Italy and Poland. And she heralded with hope "a new outbreak of the fire, to destroy old palaces of crime!"[145]

As the European "springtime of the peoples" turned increasingly radical, pitting emboldened peasants and workers against their bourgeois erstwhile allies, Fuller sided unambiguously with the forces of social revolution. She applauded the avowedly proletarian uprising of February 1848 in Paris, where "the political is being merged in the social struggle," urging her American readers to see their own cause in that of the French workers' republic. "You may learn the real meaning of the words FRATERNITY, EQUALITY . . . the needs of a true Democracy," she wrote. "You may in time learn to reverence, learn to guard, the true aristocracy of a nation, the only real noble—the LABORING CLASSES."[146] A fervent partisan of Mazzini's struggle for Italian independence, she nevertheless criticized her famous friend for confining his cause to "political emancipation" without the social and economic revolution espoused by French socialists and communists.[147]

How different was Emerson's response to his own tour of Europe on the eve of revolution, which impressed him far more with the progress and refinement of the ruling class than with the impoverishment and politicization of the laboring classes he disdained.[148] To be sure, Fuller hardly abandoned her earlier sentimentalism in adopting revolutionary politics. She rather joined in the prevailing Romantic ethos of 1848, identifying the cause of revolution with the heroic actions of a "natural nobility," the worldly vehicle of timeless ideals. The "beauty" and "genius" of the defenders of Rome recalled for her the novels of Sir Walter Scott. Her last dispatch from Europe, in January 1850, looked forward to the "next revolution" in defiantly utopian terms: "Men shall now be represented as souls, not hands and feet, and governed accordingly. A congress of great, pure, loving minds, and not a congress of selfish ambitions, shall preside."[149]

Yet Fuller's response to the revolution of 1848 owed as much, if not more, to the political and economic heritage of America's own revolution as it did to the Romantic Movement in which she took part. Inspired by the liberating potential of the transcendental identification of moral agency with the "inner self" rather than ownership or sovereignty, she was also increasingly attuned to the counterrevolutionary implications of that antipolitical ideal. In Fuller's writings on revolution, as in her work on feminine selfhood, the tensions within the Romantic response to the age of capital were brought to the fore, though they were never really resolved.

Conclusion

The market revolution and the emergence of industrial capitalism in antebellum New England reopened age-old questions about the relations between self and world, nature and the supernatural, and male and female. Transcendental psychology offered new answers: Emerson's "inner self," Bushnell's socialized soul, Fuller's androgynous psyche. In various ways, the new philosophy, theology, and feminism responded to a common ideological problem: the political-economic precepts of freedom and democracy, which had united the new nation in its first half-century, appeared increasingly incendiary amid the demise of the agrarian republic of independent households and the rise of a class-divided market society in its place. In reconstructing individuality in terms of psychic self-development instead of material self-rule, the American Romantics posed a utopian challenge to the hegemony of politics and economics in the new era. But in so doing, they also undermined the basis of contemporary agrarian and equalitarian critiques of the reorganization of property and production. They thereby provided ideological cover for class inequality even as they envisioned a society founded in spiritual rather than material relations. Unlike Emerson or Bushnell, however, Fuller maintained a tenuous commitment to the legacy of Jeffersonian political economy that led her alone to grapple with the troubling tensions between the utopian and ideological aspects of transcendental psychology.

Those tensions, between the critique of the culture of market society—the selfishness and materialism and strife—and the tacit acceptance or even outright approval of the emerging class divide, marked the rise of modern sociological thinking in the antebellum United States as well. Emerson, Bushnell, and Fuller challenged the model of selfhood at the core of classical moral philosophy and political economy, the valorization of "interests" over "passions," of reason over desire, and the possessive individualism that defined those values. Each explored the critical implications of their Romantic model of human nature for political, economic, and social relations, though none formulated a full-fledged alternative science of society. Such a thoroughgoing scientific reconception of society as a whole, closely related to the new psychology, appeared south of New England in these same years: in the emergence of the new science of sociology simultaneously in the Middle Atlantic and in the South, in defense of both of the rapidly expanding class systems of "free labor" and slavery.

CHAPTER THREE

Antebellum Origins of American Sociology

Henry C. Carey, George Fitzhugh, and Henry Hughes

orace Bushnell was not the only observer to call for a new social science to make sense of the new social order emerging in the antebellum era. In these same years, the revisionist political economist Henry C. Carey of Philadelphia joined the southern ideologists of slavery Henry Hughes and George Fitzhugh in repudiating the classical conceptions of property and contract in favor of a new model of modern society as an organic, familial whole. Their vision of psychosocial interdependence derived less from the tradition of German and English Romanticism that inspired the New England Transcendentalists than from the contemporary French discourses of utopian socialism and Comtean "sociology."

Alexis de Tocqueville, a scion of the aristocracy whose great-grandfather and many other family members had been executed in the French Revolution, looked to the United States as a society in which the "democratic revolution" overtaking Europe had reached its limit. Tocqueville was a cautious supporter of liberal democracy, but he dreaded the disintegrative social implications of political equality, which threatened to foment the kind of anarchy to which his relatives had fallen victim. "Abandoned to its wild instincts," he warned in his classic multivolume study of *Democracy in America* (1835–1840), democracy would degenerate into the despotism of an unthinking majority and the demise of rightful authority. New forms of social solidarity must therefore be found lest the new order follow the fate of the old regime. "The first of the duties that are at this time imposed upon those who direct our affairs is to educate democracy, to reawaken, if possible, its religious beliefs; to purify its morals; to mold its actions," he wrote. " . . . A new science of politics is needed for a new world."[1]

Tocqueville's misgivings about popular rule hardened in 1848, when he helped lead the bourgeois suppression of the Parisian workers' uprising and its radical assertion of the "right to work." In disavowing the republican language of natural right and social contract, even as working-class leaders shifted their allegiance from republicanism to socialism, he signaled the broader significance of the new social science he sought. Such a science, by advancing an alternative to the incendiary ideology of the Revolution, would counter as well the Revolution's proletarian offspring and its radical appropriation of the democratic ideal. Together with his countryman Auguste Comte, Tocqueville was the philosophical founder of what Robert Nisbet has called the "sociological tradition," which formed an enduring counterpart to the rival critique of classical political economy presented by Marxist socialism.[2]

Comte, like Tocqueville, left behind the monarchism of his family and became an early admirer of the American republic. Born in 1798, the son of a small-town clerk, his avid study of the American Revolution and its ideals of liberty and equality helped inspire his lifelong commitment to reconstructing society on a more rational basis. At 18, he seriously considered emigrating to the United States.[3] The intellectual origins of Comtean social science lay in the Enlightenment conception, central to early American social thought, of politics and history as rooted in particular forms of society or social relations, whose laws of motion might be discovered in the manner of the natural sciences.[4] But in his major works of the 1820s, 1830s, and 1840s, Comte defined his politics as well as his social science against the specter of social rebellion, which he identified with the destructive legacy of the political revolutions in which the French and American republics had been born.[5] Having served their proper purpose in bringing down the monarchy, he argued, the revolutionary principles of popular sovereignty and equal rights represented a continuing incitement to revolt and therefore an obstacle to the reconstitution of social order upon a higher foundation. Following his mentor, the Christian socialist Henri de Saint-Simon, Comte contended that the "great social problem" was the need to "ameliorate the condition" of the working class without "disturbing the general economy" or sparking "violent revolutions." Comte's solution was a massive "mental reorganization," which, "by habitually interposing a common moral authority between the working classes and leaders of society, will offer the only regular basis of a pacific and equitable reconciliation of their chief conflicts, nearly abandoned in the present day to the savage discipline of a purely material antagonism."[6]

The agents of such psychological socialization, in Comte's vision, would be social scientists such as himself, to whom would be entrusted society's "spiritual power," while its "temporal power" would "belong to the heads of industrial works." The basis of social scientists' new authority lay in their knowledge of the immutable laws that governed the progress of society from the "theological" stage of monarchy and war, through the "metaphysical" stage characterized by rude democracy and class struggle, to the "positive" stage ruled by science and industry. To such a spiritual science of social evolution, as opposed to either revolution or reaction, Comte gave the name, "sociology." This he designated the highest form of scientific knowledge, as industrial society represented the highest stage of civilization.[7] Originating like political economy in the Enlightenment project of studying the social basis of politics, the sociological tradition of Tocqueville and Comte disavowed the revolutionary implications of identifying the "social" with the play of competing class interests and redefined social science as the study of the "community of values and norms," in Göran Therborn's words.[8]

In the antebellum United States, Comte's work first attracted the attention of New England clergy, who generally opposed his scientistic assault on traditional "theological" and "metaphysical" ideas. He found a receptive reader, however, in the socialistic Unitarian minister William Henry Channing (nephew of the founder of Unitarianism), who read Comte's massive *Cours de Philosophie Positive* as it was being published in the 1830s and 1840s and shared what he learned with the Transcendentalist social reformers Orestes Brownson, George Ripley, and Theodore Parker.[9] But the first Americans to take up the new science of sociology themselves were southern writers who found in the "positive philosophy" support for their defense of slavery as a natural and just alternative to the system of wage labor developing in the North. In 1854, two proslavery polemicists produced the first American sociology texts, taking Comte's work as their point of departure: *Treatise on Sociology*, by Henry Hughes, and *Sociology for the South*, by George Fitzhugh.[10] Yet four years later, a sweeping reconstruction of American social science along explicitly Comtean lines appeared in defense of northern industrial capitalism: the three-volume *Principles of Social Science* (1858–59) by Henry Charles Carey, the nation's most renowned political economist.[11] Like his southern counterparts, Carey directed the brunt of his argument not against an opposing system of labor, but against an opposing science of society: classical political economy, to which all three writers attributed the ominous political and economic conflict dividing the nation.

How did Comtean sociology lend itself to both sides of the sectional divide? Why did Carey as well as Fitzhugh and Hughes base their respective arguments for "free labor" and slave labor upon a shared rationale for a new social science? The answer may be found in a deeper conflict underlying that of North and South: the intensifying conflict between the owners of productive resources, whether in southern plantations or northern mills, and the labor force upon which they depended, whether slave or free. In the wake of the industrial revolution and its grim reflection in the works of Thomas Malthus and David Ricardo, a critical political economy posited an inherent conflict of class interests that increasingly threatened northern manufacturers and financiers as much as it did southern planters and merchants. Just as French sociology offered an ideological response to the breakdown of republican unity amid class struggle, so its American counterpart provided a new social-scientific model of class harmony amid the widening divide between owners and workers on both sides of the sectional conflict. As was the case with the contemporary rise of transcendental psychology, the advent of sociological thought represented at once a utopian critique of the social struggle that was increasingly dominating American political and economic life, on the one hand, and a legitimation of the ultimate basis of such struggle in private ownership of productive resources, on the other.

Along similar lines, historians of "free labor" ideology such as David Brion Davis and Eric Foner have shown that the abolitionist critique of slavery—like Carey's quite different critique—entailed a defense of industrial wage labor.[12] In identifying the oppressive character of slavery with the extra-economic compulsion of labor by means of law and violence, leading abolitionists implicitly and often explicitly equated freedom as well as class harmony with contractual relations between labor and capital. They thereby disallowed the traditional identification, steeped in classical political economy, of freedom and class harmony with equal ownership of productive resources. They undermined as well the corollary charge of "wage slavery" leveled by both agrarian labor leaders and southern critics of northern capitalism. "Those who inculcate" the "pernicious doctrine" of a natural conflict between rich and poor "are the worst enemies of the people," wrote William Lloyd Garrison in his abolitionist newspaper, *The Liberator*, in 1831. "It is a miserable characteristic of human nature to look with an envious eye upon those who are more fortunate in their pursuits, or more exalted in their station."[13]

Conversely, southern apologists for slavery projected their fears of labor uprising onto northern society while denying the threat of class conflict within their midst. As John Ashworth has argued, the ideology of white supremacy denied the class basis of the racial divide, while more forthright advocates of class inequality—such as Fitzhugh and Hughes—found the basis of social harmony in the bonds of protection and loyalty fostered by slavery as opposed to the formal equality and competition of northern free labor.[14]

Both antislavery and proslavery ideology entailed withering critiques of aspects of the market revolution that gave rise to King Cotton as well as industrialization—as in abolitionists' denunciation of slaveowners' commerce in human life, and in southerners' attacks upon northern "wage slavery." So, too, antebellum American sociology, North and South, presented a thoroughgoing refutation of the received rationale for market relations in orthodox political economy. Yet it also entailed a less obvious but more fundamental erasure of the analysis of class relations—relations between landowners, workers, and capitalists, between "producers" and "non-producers," between "the many" and "the few"—at the core of the classical social science. In distinct yet parallel ways, the northern and southern pioneers of American sociological thought responded to the class conflict that underlay the sectional conflict by repudiating the science of class relations itself, and by constructing an alternative social science in which propertied independence yielded to psychic interdependence as the foundation of social order.[15]

Henry C. Carey and the Harmony of Interests

Rapid economic development in the wake of the market revolution occasioned an outpouring of antebellum writings on political economy, of which Henry Carey's were the most influential in the United States as well as abroad. American writers largely defined their work by reference to the emerging orthodoxy of British political economy established by the classic treatises of Thomas Malthus and David Ricardo, which appeared in the first two decades of the nineteenth century. Central to Ricardian economics in the United States, as in Britain, was the distribution of wealth, which was understood to be fundamentally determined by relations among the three great classes identified in Adam Smith's *Wealth of Nations* (1776): the respective owners of land, labor, and capital.[16]

For Smith, writing on the eve of the industrial revolution, the problem of distribution appeared secondary to the problem of economic growth. The wealth of nations, not of individuals, was his primary concern. Happily, he found individual self-interest to be naturally in harmony with national interest. The individual pursuit of wealth in a competitive market tended to maximize the aggregate wealth of society, Smith famously contended, while economic growth tended over the long term to raise the living standards of rich and poor alike. Yet the pursuit of wealth that Smith had in mind was not commerce or foreign trade, the centerpiece of mercantilist economics, but agricultural and industrial production, in which productive investment of accumulated capital appeared as the ultimate engine of growth. In arguing for the primary role of capital, he and his contemporaries pointedly differentiated the "profits of stock" accruing to productive capital from the wages of labor, and both of these from landowners' rent. These three distinct class incomes, based upon ownership of different factors of production, determined the distribution of wealth.

While the pursuit of self-interest by individual enterprises felicitously served the interests of society as a whole, no such harmony of interests governed the distribution of income. Landlords, capitalists, and wage-earners rather competed for their respective shares. Notably, Smith held that though the general welfare of society ultimately depended upon the accumulation of capital, the immediate interests of capital and labor were inherently opposed—and that employers generally exploited their superior position at workers' expense, preventing wages from rising much or long above the cost of a basic subsistence. "High wages of labour and high profits of stock," he wrote, " . . . scarce ever go together, except in the peculiar circumstances of new colonies."[17]

In the new United States, with its abundance of land, shortage of labor, and household economy, Smith's cautions about the competing class interests attendant upon capitalist development could easily be dismissed as inapplicable to American conditions. But in contemporary England, the industrial revolution and its creation of a mass wage-earning proletariat thrust the problem of distribution to the center of political economy at the beginning of the nineteenth century.[18] For Smith, the prospect of economic growth at least partly defused the danger of class conflict by promising an expanding surplus for all to share. For Malthus and Ricardo, by contrast, poverty seemed destined to overwhelm progress; in their view, the exponential growth of the laboring population would inevitably outpace the accumulation of capital and therefore the production of wealth.

The inverse relation of wages and profits, and of profits and rents, now took on the trappings of tragedy. For the disproportional expansion of the labor force, inexorably increasing the share of national wealth devoted to wages, would accordingly diminish the share remaining for profits, thereby eroding investment and depressing real per capita wages until both economic and demographic growth ground to a halt. At the same time, the growing share of the surplus reserved for rent, which likewise depleted profits, reflected the diminishing returns of agricultural investment and so the deepening disparity between mouths to feed and food to fill them. Landlords, laborers, and capitalists appeared locked in a struggle to the death over an ever-shrinking surplus, captives of a self-destructive spiral that could be forestalled only temporarily by technological advancement and entrepreneurial innovation.[19] Even in the United States, Ricardo and Malthus warned, the honeymoon of high profits and high wages that Smith had described must give way to falling profits and slowing growth along with mounting poverty, income inequality, and class antagonism.[20]

On both sides of the Atlantic, Ricardo's *Principles of Political Economy* (1817) established the framework within which mainstream political economists worked for roughly half a century. But Ricardian doctrine, with its recognition of rent as the price paid by the propertyless for access to productive property, its theory of exchange value as a measure of the labor embodied in commodities, and its related theory of the value or "natural price" of labor itself as a measure of the cost of subsistence, also lent itself to agrarian and socialist critiques of market society. In Ricardo's frank explication of class relations, intended as a defense of capitalist prerogative, partisans of the propertyless found a call to arms. Therefore, long before Marx extended the radical implications of Ricardian theory into an immanent critique of classical political economy itself as a rationale for private property in the means of production, bourgeois economists began distancing themselves from the divisive conclusions of Ricardian class analysis.[21]

American writers, schooled in the Jeffersonian understanding of the United States as a single-class society exempt from the class divisions and social inequality of the Old World, found the Ricardian depiction of class relations anathema to their most cherished beliefs. Agrarian radicals such as Thomas Skidmore, George Henry Evans, and Langton Byllesby highlighted the disparity between the class society that Ricardo described—and that their own society increasingly resembled—and the Revolutionary Era ideals of liberty and equality. But preeminent American political economists drew upon European contemporaries such as Jean Baptiste Say, Nassau Senior, and John McCulloch in "domesticating Ricardo," as Paul Conkin has aptly written. Writers such as Francis Wayland, the author of perhaps the leading American college text in political economy in the antebellum era, formed a broad consensus upon the principle of a "harmony of interests" governing not only the market in the products of industry and agriculture, but also the distribution of income among landlords, laborers, and employers, where even Smith had found a basic conflict of interests.[22]

Of all antebellum political economists in the United States and arguably in Europe as well, Henry Carey (1793–1879) formulated the most comprehensive case that capitalist development naturally led in the direction of class harmony rather than strife. Indeed, Carey contended that the free growth of market relations would result in the breakdown of class distinctions altogether, whether between master and slave or between employer and employee. In developing this influential position in his voluminous writings of the 1830s, 1840s, and 1850s, he was drawn into an increasingly complete disavowal of the starting assumptions of classical political economy—most importantly, a disavowal of the core concept that private property in productive resources, the basis of class relations, also formed the foundation of market society. In a momentous inversion of the embattled science of wealth, he ultimately suggested that property relations depended upon market relations, rather than vice versa—and therefore that a fully free market would bring emancipation from the bonds of property and class.

The agrarian vision of a single-class society of self-employed, independent proprietors appeared in Carey's revisionist political economy as the end result of, instead of the point of departure for, the market revolution. The true origin and basis of market relations themselves, he came to believe, lay not in class interests but in psychosocial "association," of which a cash and credit economy and corporate business enterprise represented the highest expressions. Inspired by the transcendental psychology of his friend, Emerson, as well as by utopian socialism, Carey finally made the pathbreaking move from political economy to Comtean sociology in his *Principles of Social Science*.[23]

Published shortly before the Civil War began, his master work culminated a quarter-century effort to chart a practical as well as theoretical way out of the escalating conflict between plantation slavery and wage labor brought on by the expansion of market relations.[24] From the start of his prolific writing career in 1835, Carey represented the entrepreneurial outlook of his native Philadelphia, the commercial entrepôt for the staple crops of West Indian plantations and Middle Atlantic farms as well as a national hub of manufacturing, mining, and banking. From his father, Mathew Carey—among the early republic's strongest proponents of the so-called "American System" of protective tariffs, a national bank, and state sponsorship of "internal improvements" to promote economic development—he inherited what was for many years the nation's largest publishing house, with interests extending from New England to the Lower South. At the age of 42, he was able to retire from the book business and support his family on income from investments in iron and paper manufacturing, coal mining, and real estate, allowing him to pursue his second calling as a political economist. Deeply rooted in the parochial interests of Pennsylvania venture capital, Carey nevertheless closely identified those interests with the progress and prosperity of the nation as a whole. He followed his father in tirelessly seeking to stake out a stable middle ground between the diverging political economies of North and South, even up to the brink of war.[25]

For Carey, as for many of his contemporaries, the basis of stability amid rapid growth lay in the liberal-republican model of a nation of petty producers like those that predominated in the Middle Atlantic region throughout the antebellum era.[26] The challenge was to reconcile this agrarian ideal with the rise of the factory system in New England, the expansion of the plantation system in the South, and the reorganization of craft manufacture in New York City and Philadelphia. His overarching project was to provide social-scientific support for the Whig and later Republican vision of industrialization without proletarianization, or of what Daniel Walker Howe has called a " 'middle state' between rural and urban life," reaping the rewards of capitalist development without the specter of class inequality.[27] Like most antebellum writers, he assumed that the United States might remain indefinitely immune to the mass poverty and social divisions of industrial England.

Yet, unlike those who found the reason for American exceptionalism in what Smith had called the "peculiar circumstances" of abundant land and scarce labor, Carey maintained that the basis of continuing—indeed increasing—social equality lay in the dynamics of market society. The English experience of widening inequality represented in his view the exception instead of the rule, the result of corrupting constraints upon market relations and not of the free market itself. In making this fundamental claim, Carey was forced to confront the central assumption of classical political economy, articulated most explicitly by Ricardo, that class divisions were integral to capitalist development, not accidental.

Carey's first work, the *Essay on the Rate of Wages* (1835), framed the essential problem to which he addressed virtually all his subsequent writing in one way or another. The rise of popular democracy, he wrote, had made the welfare of the laboring population and its relation to the propertied classes a central political question. The answer generally provided by classical political economy represented, as he recognized, a double-edged sword. On the one hand, political economists from Smith to Ricardo defined capital as the "stock" from which wages as well as profits were paid, and therefore maintained that the long-term fortunes of employee as well as employer depended upon capital accumulation. In the long run, according to orthodox theory, wages could be raised only by enlarging the "wages fund," which in turn could be accomplished only by increasing the productivity of labor and thereby increasing profits and productive investment as well. With this conventional conclusion encouraging workers to identify with their employers, Carey emphatically agreed.

Yet the flip side of the wages fund doctrine was the implication that any increase in the *share* of the surplus allocated to wages must come at the expense of profits, and vice versa. As Smith had indicated, labor and capital were united by their common ultimate interest in productivity and growth but divided by their competing immediate interests in the distribution of income. In the context of popular democracy and emerging industrialization, the inverse relation between wages and profits carried explosive potential. Carey concurred with the English economist Nassau Senior that Ricardian orthodoxy in this crucial respect prompted workers to combine forces against their employers in trade unions and strikes, inciting "the cry of *the poor against the rich*."[28] The critique of Ricardian economics as a provocation for class war became his guiding theoretical preoccupation, often repeated in his later works.[29]

In this first foray into political economy, Carey focused his criticism upon the disquieting idea, found in various forms in virtually all the classical writers, that wages naturally gravitated toward the cost of a basic subsistence for workers and their families. "The natural price of labour," as Ricardo wrote, "is that price which is necessary to enable the labourers, one with another, to subsist and to perpetuate their race, without either increase or diminution."[30] The concept of subsistence wages was a corollary of the fundamental postulate of classical political economy that the exchange value or "natural price" of any commodity, toward which its actual market price tended in the long term, was a function of its cost of production. As Ricardo's leading disciple, John R. McCulloch, explained in his 1826 treatise on wages, which prompted Carey's own essay on wages in response, "From whatever point of the political compass we may set out, the cost of production is the grand principle to which we must always come at last. This cost determines the natural or necessary rate of wages just as it determines the average price of shoes, hats, or anything else."[31] The exchange value of labor, accordingly, was determined by the cost of maintaining the wage workforce.

Smith, while acknowledging the tendency of wages to hover at the cost of subsistence in a static economy, nevertheless contended that in a growing economy, increasing demand for labor allowed wages to rise above their "natural" rate, so that the condition of the working class tended to improve.[32] But for Ricardo and Malthus, the rate of economic growth inevitably tended to fall over the long term, as the growth of the labor force outpaced that of the food supply. Declining profits due to rising rents and the multiplying total wage bill would reduce the aggregate demand for labor and so depress real per capita wages until they dropped below subsistence, at which point population growth would cease.

Together, the classical cost-of-production or labor theory of value and the principle of diminishing returns implied that real wages tended to sink to the bare minimum required for subsistence.[33] All of Carey's subsequent work may be seen as an effort to grapple with the disturbing ramifications of these two premises for the relationship between capitalist development and the condition of the working class. In several major treatises and many minor tracts and pamphlets over the next twenty-five years—including the three-volume *Principles of Political Economy* (1837–1840), *The Past, the Present, and the Future* (1847), *The Harmony of Interests* (1851), *The Slave Trade* (1853), and *Principles of Social Science*—he constructed a wide-ranging response that took him from political economy to the frontier of a whole new science of market society. Because these works form a generally coherent and consistent—if repetitive, rambling, and disorganized—whole, they may be best understood by analyzing Carey's central argument about class relations logically and in its entirety rather than following its development chronologically. The core of his defense of the cherished "harmony of interests" against the dire implications of Ricardian economics lay in two main theoretical innovations: a theory of increasing rather than diminishing returns from nature and a subtle but crucial revision of the cost-of-production theory of value. Together, these two revisionist premises overturned the Ricardian prediction of deepening poverty and inequality in favor of a reassuring vision of growing abundance, class harmony, and social equality.

Carey is perhaps best remembered as an early apostle of the gospel of American abundance later espoused by the economists Simon Nelson Patten, in the Progressive Era, and John Kenneth Galbraith after World War II. Classical political economy was dominated by the specter of scarcity, of limitless human needs and limited natural resources, which lay behind Smith's emphasis on economic growth as well as Ricardo and Malthus's darker picture of poverty and stagnation. The latter view was deeply colored by the presumption of diminishing returns from agricultural investment due to the exhaustion of soil fertility by farming and the necessity of cultivating less fertile land as richer land was used up. To Carey, the doctrine of diminishing returns appeared as the linchpin of the "dismal science," the source of political economists' dangerously misleading conjunction of poverty and progress. Defiantly inverting the so-called "iron laws" of population and rent decreed by Malthus and Ricardo, he contended that the natural tendency of social development was toward increasing abundance instead of scarcity. The growth of population and the division of labor, he held, would enable society to increase indefinitely the fertility of existing farmland through improved farming methods, while making possible the cultivation of progressively richer soils. In place of the Malthusian vision of mounting social conflict over increasingly scarce resources, Carey foresaw growing cooperation amid plenty. "Kindness and good feeling would take the place of jealousy and discord," yielding a "perfect harmony of interests."[34]

Yet his sunny forecast for an economy of abundance rather than scarcity did not directly address the more fundamental basis for the idea of subsistence wages in the cost-of-production theory of value, nor the broader understanding of competing class interests underlying it. Carey's deeper rationale for the harmony of interests lay in his critical modification of classical value theory. Labor was the central factor in the classical theory—commodities were valuable because they were products of human labor—though Smith and Ricardo differed over the specific role of labor in determining exchange value. Smith included profits and rent along with wages in the determination of "cost of production," and therefore exchange value, which he defined as the "quantity of labour" that a commodity enabled its possessor to "purchase or command."[35] Ricardo, by pointed contrast, defined exchange value in terms of the labor required to produce a commodity rather than the labor that a commodity purchased, and he maintained that value as such was not a function of factor prices —that is, profit, rent, and wages—but of productivity.[36]

Carey's revision of the renowned "labor theory of value" at the heart of classical political economy drew upon, while departing from, both Smith and Ricardo. The true basis of a commodity's value relative to other commodities, he found, lay in the labor that would have been required for its purchaser to reproduce it, not in the labor that actually had been expended upon its production in the first place. Value, that is, essentially represented a measure not of a commodity's cost to the producer but of its utility to the consumer, albeit utility measured in labor saved. A way station of sorts between the various cost theories of value in classical political economy and the utility theories of value that are basic to modern neoclassical economics, Carey's cost-of-reproduction theory held the key to his pioneering reconception of the distribution of class incomes, and therefore of class relations in general.[37]

He began from the relatively uncontroversial premise that the value of a commodity falls as productivity rises, since less labor is required for its production—or rather, as Carey would have it, its reproduction. He then applied his consumer-savings conception of value to the relation between labor and capital. Viewing the wage worker as essentially a petty proprietor engaged in buying capital and selling labor, he reasoned that in a free market, increasing productivity rendered capital itself, like any other commodity, less expensive to reproduce, therefore less valuable and cheaper for the laborer to purchase. Meanwhile, the more productive labor became, the higher grew its value to the employer, and the more the employer was compelled to pay for it. Oddly, Carey never quite explained why the value of labor did not fall along with the cost of reproducing the labor force, as his own theory as well as classical cost-of-production theory might suggest. He simply asserted that increasing productivity caused the value of "people" to rise and the value of "things" to fall under ideal free market conditions, so that more and more capital exchanged for less and less labor.

As a result, labor's share of industrial income grew along with productivity, enabling more and more wage workers to buy all the capital they required to become capitalists themselves. Capitalists, on the other hand, were more than compensated for their shrinking share of the social surplus by the increased profits due to gains in productivity. So as economic development netted ever-rising returns upon productive investment, as Carey's refutation of Malthus and Ricardo indicated, relations between labor and capital grew increasingly harmonious, with the position of the wage earner approximating that of the capitalist even as profits continued to climb.[38] "[T]he interests of the capitalist and the labourer are thus in perfect harmony with each other, as each derives advantage from every measure that tends to facilitate the growth of capital, and to render labour productive, while every measure that tends to produce the opposite effect is injurious to both," he concluded.[39]

So too, Carey claimed, landowning farmers in a fully free market saw the value of their property and its raw produce appreciate in relation to that of the tools and manufactured goods they purchased. The rising productivity of land, like that of labor, allowed the landowner, like the laborer, to become more and more a capitalist, as the value of capital declined while that of farmland grew. The sectoral divide between agriculture and industry, like the class divide between labor and capital, narrowed until the interests of each became those of all. "Such is the great law governing the distribution of labor's products," Carey wrote. "Of all recorded in the book of Science, it is perhaps the most beautiful—being, as it is, that one, in virtue of which there is established a perfect harmony of real and true interests among the various classes of mankind."[40]

Yet Carey's case for social harmony ultimately rested not upon this explicit empirical argument that class interests naturally converged over time, but upon an implicit theoretical elision of class distinctions to begin with. Class relations as he understood them were not determined by qualitatively different kinds of property in productive resources, as they were in classical political economy. Whereas classical economists considered the fundamental distinctions between class incomes axiomatic, he conflated rent with profit, and profit with wages. Land, as he described it, was essentially a form of capital, a "great machine" whose productive capacity derived from human improvements rather than natural endowments, and rent the price paid for the use of such landed capital.[41] Likewise, labor largely represented a fund of prior investment in education, skills, and training, and wages the price of human capital.[42]

In collapsing the property-based distinctions between classes, Carey conceived class relations as essentially relations of exchange among qualitative equals selling different commodities. Accordingly, the respective prices of land, labor, and capital—and not their intrinsic social bases—determined their relative positions. So the relationship between labor and capital depended upon the relative prices at which they exchanged for one another: as wages rose relative to profit, the worker accordingly approached the position of the employer. In this way, the problem of class resolved itself into a question of price determination under competitive market conditions. "In regard to no commodity, therefore, is the effect resulting from the presence or absence of competition so great, as in relation to human force [i.e., labor]," he wrote. "Two men competing for its purchase, its owner becomes a freeman. The two, competing for its sale, become enslaved. The whole question of freedom or slavery for man is, therefore, embraced in that of competition."[43]

The whole question of social equality, he might have added, was also embraced in that of the relative prices of land, labor, and capital, of raw materials and finished goods, of "people" and "things." In arguing that labor's share of the social surplus increased as the exchange value of capital fell while that of labor rose, Carey simply assumed that the laborer could claim the fruits of his or her increased output. If more and more capital accrued from less and less labor, the laborer could charge more for his or her services instead of having to produce more for the same pay.[44] By similarly setting aside the respective property rights of masters and slaves, he contended that slaves were likewise enriched and empowered by rising productivity, which heightened the value of slave labor no less than that of wage labor. "With every increase in the productiveness of labour, the slave must obtain an increasing proportion of the product, in the form of provisions, clothing, and shelter—constituting *wages*—enabling him to improve his physical and moral condition. With every such increase he must obtain, as he has obtained, increasing control over his actions, and over the produce of his labour, constituting improvement of political condition," Carey wrote.[45]

Carey's "great natural law" of distribution, according to which increasing productivity resulted in increasing equality, ostensibly obtained regardless of the property relations underpinning the system of production. As he explained in his 1853 treatise on the slave trade, "the more rapid the augmentation of wealth, the greater must be the demand for labour, the greater must be the *quantity* of commodities produced by the labourer, the larger must be his *proportion* of the product, and the greater must be the tendency toward his becoming a free man and himself a capitalist."[46] Just as the free market would make the wage worker a capitalist, so it would gradually emancipate the slave. "[T]he surest way to promote the freedom of the slave is to increase his value. *Every step that has a contrary effect is calculated to continue the system*," Carey wrote.[47] His abstraction of class relations from property relations enabled him to reconcile the interests of master and slave as well as those of employer and employee. By purportedly resolving the class conflict underlying both systems of labor, he claimed to have resolved the sectional conflict between the two as well. The free development of market relations, he promised, would transform both North and South into a single-class society of independent entrepreneurs.[48]

Sexual inequality, like inequalities of race and class, naturally diminished and eventually disappeared as market relations expanded along with productivity, according to Carey. The condition of women, like that of wage workers and slaves, was determined by the value of their services. Drawing upon the contemporary conventions of feminine domesticity, he presumed women's worth to differ from men's in that it measured not economic value, but moral value—the value of women's stewardship of the health, happiness, and virtue of home and family. But women's special value miraculously grew in tandem with societal wealth and prosperity, which enabled men to make increasing use of the "various powers of the weaker sex." "Brain then taking the place of mere muscle, the weak woman finds herself becoming more and more the equal of the man who is strong of arm—passing by slow degrees, from the condition of man's slave towards that of his companion," Carey explained. " . . . Woman's value grows with the growth of demand for her peculiar powers—that, too, growing with the growth of wealth. Capital is, thus, the great equalizer—the demand for female faculties growing in the direct ratio of the development of man's latent powers."[49] As he did with race and class, Carey abstracted from the property relations between men and women in envisioning equality as a matter of relative social value, and value as a function of consumer utility. If women were worth more to society, then men—considered as consumers of women's services—would value them more highly, and so women's condition would approach men's.

Like many contemporary critics, Carey assailed Ricardian political economy for its representation of social inequality as the inevitable consequence of the natural laws of population and commerce that governed economic development.[50] Yet his own counter thesis, in proclaiming ever-increasing social equality rather than inequality to be the "great natural law" of market society, no less effectively explained the distribution of wealth in terms of the seemingly impersonal and objective economic imperatives of demographic and commercial growth. Indeed, he went considerably further than the classical economists in naturalizing or depoliticizing the question of distribution. For Carey believed class relations themselves to be determined by the market forces of supply and demand, rather than by the extra-economic organization of property rights in productive resources that formed the social basis of the market.[51]

Nevertheless, Carey was far from a simple exponent of laissez-faire. Nor was he blind to the fact that the actual course of economic growth in the United States, as in England, appeared contrary to his happy prophecy of increasing harmony between labor and capital, agriculture and industry, slavery and wage labor. If, as he recognized, the expansion of market relations was accompanied by growing sectional, sectoral, and class discord, the reason must be found not in the intrinsic laws of motion of market society itself but in political transgressions that diverted capitalist development from its natural course. More specifically, Carey contended that the "British system" as much as the British science of political economy was to blame for the "constant war of classes" raging in England and threatening to engulf its American former colonies as well.[52] It was in order to guard the domestic market against the corrupting influence of British economic imperialism that Carey succeeded his father as the nation's leading advocate of protective tariffs in the 1840s and 1850s—not to constrain the operation of market forces as he understood them, but rather to free them from foreign interference. The panacea of protectionism, which he claimed would bring perfect peace and lasting prosperity, really reflected his total faith in the free market.[53]

In his persistent contrast between the true market society he envisioned and the pseudocapitalist "British system" he deplored lay the critical edge of Carey's work. The keywords of this distinction were "commerce" versus "trade." Instead of following the proper path of increasing commerce or direct exchange between the producers of different commodities, he charged, the British system promoted separation of the direct producers and expansion of the domain of "traders" who "perform exchanges *for* other men" rather than "*with*" them.[54]

Instead of fostering interdependence between industry and agriculture through regional development of small towns and family farms, the British system gave rise to huge industrial metropolises and vast agricultural hinterlands, each dominated by enormous enterprises capable of serving a national or international market, and each increasingly dependent upon the burgeoning network of merchants and transporters for trade with the other.

In the normal course of economic development as Carey described it, increasing commerce made possible increasing division of labor as well as cultivation of more fertile farmland, heightening the productivity and therefore the value of both labor and land.[55] But under the British system, "middlemen" thrived at the expense of "producers," who were compelled to devote a growing share of the social surplus to the transaction costs of buying and selling at a distance. Land became monopolized and labor proletarianized as the productivity and value of each declined. "The greater the power of the trader, the smaller must be commerce; whereas the more perfect the power of the principals, the greater must it be," Carey wrote. " . . . Trade tending necessarily towards centralization, every step in that direction . . . is an approach to slavery and death. Commerce, on the contrary, tending towards the establishment of local centres and local action,—every movement in that direction is an approach to freedom."[56]

Expounding an antebellum version of what Gerald Berk has termed "regional republicanism," Carey constructed a model of capitalist development purported to strengthen rather than undermine the eighteenth-century vision of a nation of self-employed petty proprietors.[57] As late as 1851, when he published his main work on protectionism, he called his ideal alternative to the British system, the "American system," in tribute to both the Whig program of the same name and the enduring predominance in the United States of relatively modest-sized, owner-operated, family firms.[58] But by the eve of the Civil War, he acknowledged that his own country appeared headed along the same path as Britain toward eventual impoverishment and enslavement of the working class.[59] Still, he insisted that widening inequality and social strife were not inherent in the system of private property in productive resources, nor the inevitable consequence of market development, as Ricardian economics suggested. To the contrary, the cause of conflict lay in wrongheaded public policies that stood in the way of free enterprise.[60]

Carey could therefore rail against the robbery of honest labor (and honest capital), as he did with growing fervor, while necessarily limiting his conception of exploitation to the toll taken by the state-sponsored gatekeepers of trade: the merchants, speculators, and moneylenders who profited from buying cheap and selling dear, capitalizing upon the time lag or geographic distance between production and consumption. Having theoretically elided the basis of class distinctions in the property relations framing the system of production, he excluded the possibility that exploitation might be rooted in those very relations.[61]

While, for Carey, market relations represented the solution to class division and exploitation rather than the problem, he had in mind a sharply different model of the market than that of earlier American writers informed by classical political economy. For the ideal market he envisioned was less a competitive arena of self-interested action by independent individuals than a realm of cooperation among closely knit producers working together to maximize societal prosperity and progress. The real meaning of commerce, as he understood it, was not competition but "association," the very embodiment of the ideal trumpeted by contemporary utopian socialists who imagined a society ruled by a spirit of commonality and mutuality rather than social struggle. Such would be the genial result not of any revolutionary reorganization of property, which Carey deemed unnecessary as well as misguided, but of the development of decentralized, economically diversified, relatively autonomous regional markets, minimizing the need for traders and merchants, maximizing the rewards of agriculture and industry, and nurturing voluntary cooperation among neighbors and coworkers in a common enterprise.[62] Such a cooperative capitalism, he emphasized, bore little resemblance to the selfishness and strife that prevailed in Great Britain and increasingly in the United States as well. "Buying and selling are an array of hostile interests,— excluding wholly the idea of harmony, sympathy, neutrality, partnership, or even equity of distribution," he lamented. "Not in any manner involving the idea of co-operation or organization, reference to the mutual life and health of the parties finds no place among its instincts."[63]

Carey's model of market society, then, was not finally founded upon private property in productive resources. For him, class relations were founded upon market relations, not the other way around. Market relations themselves, accordingly, were not determined by property-based class interests, as classical political economy presumed they were. Indeed, as early as his first work in 1835, Carey disparaged the centrality of economic self-interest to social science in terms evocative of Horace Bushnell and Emerson's attack upon vulgar materialism in these same years. He suggested that Adam Smith might have helpfully retitled his classic study, *The Happiness of Nations*, in order to indicate that social welfare entailed more than material wealth.[64] The implications of that position, and Carey's ongoing effort to articulate an alternative explanation of market relations not grounded in proprietary self-interest, led him beyond political economy into a new science of self and society in his *Principles of Social Science*. "Political-economical man," as he called the subject of the old science of wealth, represented to him only the lowliest aspects of human nature, those driven by the base instincts of self-preservation and procreation. "And what, we may ask, is the value of an analytical process that selects only the 'material parts' of man—those which are common to himself and the beast—and excludes those common to the angels and himself? Such is the course of modern political economy, which not only does not 'feel the breath of the spirit,' but even ignores the existence of the spirit itself," he wrote, quoting Goethe.[65]

"In common with all other animals [man] requires to eat, drink, and sleep," Carey continued, echoing Emerson's scorn for "eating, drinking, planting, counting man," "but his greatest need is that of ASSOCIATION with his fellow-men." Human nature was innately social. Individuals were fully human only in association with others. "INDIVIDUALITY"—as opposed to individualism— was humankind's second "distinctive quality," and it flowed from the first, deriving from "interdependence" rather than independence.[66] Drawing explicitly upon Comte's notion of a hierarchy of sciences, in which the science of society occupied the highest level, Carey went beyond even the French founder of "sociology" in applying the laws of nature to the social order. "Throughout nature, the more complete the subordination, and the more perfect the interdependence of the parts, the greater is the individuality of the whole, and the more absolute the power of self-direction," he wrote. " . . . So, too, must it be with society—its power for self-direction growing with the growth of interdependence among its various parts, and the latter becoming developed as the organization becomes more perfect, and the subordination more complete."[67] Social science, as Carey redefined it along Comtean lines, no longer denoted the study of political and economic interests, of their foundation in property relations, and of their articulation in the production, exchange, and distribution of wealth. Rather, his new sociology constituted "*the science of the laws which govern man in his efforts to secure for himself the highest individuality, and the greatest power of association with his fellow-men.*"[68]

Such a holistic science of society, highlighting the functional interrelation of individuals as parts of a single social organism, presented a powerful reproof to apologies for ruthless competition and greed predicated upon economic orthodoxy. At the same time, however, Carey found the material meaning of "association" and "individuality" within market relations themselves, not in opposition to them. He was perhaps the first in a distinguished line of American social scientists to suppose that the market itself might fulfill the socialist promise of a society governed by cooperation instead of competition, in which social conflict over scarce resources was supplanted by harmony and abundance, and in which each shared in the welfare of all. Long before the French sociologist Émile Durkheim argued that the division of labor gave rise to "organic solidarity," Carey conceived the elaboration of market relations in similarly organicist terms.[69]

As acerbically as Carey denounced the monopoly power of the railroad trusts, he nevertheless virtually sanctified the modern business corporation as the institutional expression of his associationist ideal. "The principle upon which they are based is a plain and simple one," he wrote of industrial corporations, "that of the unity and identity of social interest; or in other words, the brotherhood of man translated into the partnership of business."[70] Likewise, much as he inveighed against financial profiteering by merchants and moneylenders at the expense of "producers," Carey exalted free banking as the engine of commerce and a free-flowing currency as its fuel. On no issue did he more explicitly break with Smithian as well as Ricardian economics than in his contention that money itself represented far more than "dead capital," a mere means of exchanging wealth, not producing it. Rather, money embodied the bountiful wealth-creating force Carey attributed to commerce itself, making possible limitless abundance through endless exchange of goods and services, dissolving class differences through the alchemy of association. The greatest "labor-saving machinery in use among men," the very "instrument of association," money represented nothing less than the power of society, manifested in market relations.[71]

Little wonder that after the Civil War, Carey became a leading theorist of the greenback campaign for a fiat currency, which would allow the money supply to grow along with the economy, and that his vision of "association" became the movement's cross-class gospel. For even as the currency crusaders decried the "money power" in the name of the "producing classes," they implicitly embraced Carey's assumption that the fundamental power over the distribution of wealth lay in the system of exchange, not the system of production—or rather, that control over the means of production could be secured through control over the medium of exchange. For Carey as for his many admirers, commerce appeared as the solvent of class inequality.[72]

The Civil War ushered into public policy key elements of Carey's political agenda: permanent protective tariffs, escalated industrialization, and the first national paper currency, the "greenback." Yet the postbellum United States, with the rise of big business and the expansion of wage labor to encompass the vast majority of Americans, was a far cry from the model of decentralized, cooperative capitalism that he envisioned. Carey's intellectual legacy, like that of the modern American social science he helped to inform and inspire, was at once a utopian critique of and an ideological rationale for the emergence of industrial capitalism from the womb of the agrarian commercial republic. In the name of the independent petty proprietor and a single-class society, he ultimately helped to legitimate the breakdown of the household economy and the rise of a class-divided social order. Such was the significance of his fundamental revision of the analytic core of classical political economy and his construction of a new sociology in its place.

Henry Hughes, George Fitzhugh, and the Sociology of Slavery

As Carey perceived, the prevailing ideology of the Revolutionary Era required fundamental rethinking in order to comport with the emergence of industrial capitalism in the antebellum Northeast. For his southern contemporaries, the task of ideological reconstruction was no less formidable. Southerners had struggled since the Revolution to reconcile the principles of liberty and equality with the institution of slavery. But capitalist development in the North and in England, and the concomitant expansion of the slave-based economy of the South, prompted southern writers in the 1830s, 1840s, and 1850s to formulate a far more systematic defense of slavery as the natural and proper foundation of society.[73] Spurred by the rise of northern "free labor" ideology, proslavery theorists were forced to grapple with the tension between the Jeffersonian ideal of a self-employed yeomanry that reaped the fruits of its own labor and the reality of a master class that grew rich upon the labor of an enslaved workforce. More starkly than the nascent system of industrial wage labor, the expanding system of agricultural slave labor confronted its advocates with the problem of class exploitation—a problem that classical political economy, despite the best efforts of its leading exponents, did more to reveal than conceal.

Many proponents of slavery denied any irreconcilable conflict between their belief in freedom and democracy and their ownership of slaves. Defining slaves as essentially property rather than people, such southerners excluded them from membership in human society on the grounds of racial inferiority, while championing the rights of slaveholders on the grounds of private property and free enterprise. Other proslavery writers, however, deeming slavery inherently incompatible with the philosophy of natural rights and social contract, abandoned their Jeffersonian heritage in whole or in part. They articulated instead an unequivocal justification of social inequality, deference, and duty as opposed to equal rights, often drawing upon European conservative thought rooted in the defense of nobility and aristocracy as opposed to the Enlightenment tradition born of the rise of bourgeois democracy. Historians have long debated whether the southern master class was at bottom more liberal and democratic or more aristocratic and paternalistic in its ideology.[74]

But scholars on both sides of the issue generally identify the classically liberal-republican argument for slavery with the party of progress, while associating the disavowal of Lockean liberalism or "possessive individualism" in favor of social organicism with the party of reaction. According to this common historical view, to justify slavery on the basis of private property, the pursuit of self-interest, and laissez-faire (along with white supremacy) was to join the victory train of capitalist development. To justify slavery instead on the basis of the reciprocal obligations of different social classes, the rights of society as opposed to those of the individual, and social interdependence as opposed to individual autonomy, was to turn backward toward feudalism rather than capitalism. From this perspective, the paternalist position, however dominant or eccentric it may have been in the Old South, seems in retrospect anachronistic and ultimately doomed—"a dying philosophy, not an emerging one."[75]

The contemporary critique of classical political economy emerging in the antebellum North, however, calls into question any easy identification of Enlightenment ideology with capitalist progress.[76] The agrarian ideal of a freeholder republic posed a profound challenge for the proponents of wage labor as well as for those of slavery. In framing a modern version of premodern social organicism, wedding Burkean conservatism with the imperatives of profit-driven production and commercial competition, southern critics of liberal-republican dogma joined a transatlantic Romantic Movement that was as progressive as it was conservative. Like their northern and European counterparts, the Romantic apologists for slavery ratified class inequality and capital accumulation even as they denounced the reign of market man. To be sure, they styled themselves a new nobility and scorned the leveling pretensions of plebeian democrats as well as the rude cash culture of market society.[77] Yet in drawing inspiration from the tory socialism of Thomas Carlyle and the utopian socialism of Charles Fourier, the proslavery paternalists appear not as quixotic reactionaries but as participants in an antebellum avant-garde heralding a new social consciousness. Their sharp criticisms of "free society"—like those of Emerson, Bushnell, Fuller, and Carey—aimed less at capitalism itself than at the philistine philosophy of political economy. In defense of slavery, they sketched out a new social science that ironically provided a more progressive and enduring rationale for market society.

So while ostensibly more "liberal" southern writers such as Jacob Cardozo and James De Bow strained to find support for unfree labor within the Smithian science of wealth, more "conservative" thinkers such as Joseph Le Conte and George Frederick Holmes turned to Comte's novel system of "sociology." Foremost among the small circle of "southern Comteans" were George Fitzhugh (1806–1881) and Henry Hughes (1829–1862), who together introduced American readers to the new science of society in their corresponding 1854 texts on the subject.[78]

Fitzhugh, the best-known of the proslavery paternalists among historians, is commonly regarded as the most rigorously reactionary, largely for his thorough repudiation of liberal rationales for slavery as well as northern arguments for free labor and free trade—along with his unflinching case for the enslavement of workers everywhere regardless of race.[79] Descended from a long line of Anglo-Virginian gentry, he admiringly recalled his first American ancestor's patrician contempt for "the rabble" as "only made to be taxed and whipped," and he passionately identified with the defense of aristocratic and ecclesiastical prerogative by the contemporary partisans of "Young England." Yet having seen his father's plantation sold at auction when Fitzhugh was 19, he became a largely self-taught lawyer and a leading supporter of efforts to revitalize the Virginia tidewater through scientific agriculture, educational reform, and local development of railroads, banking, industry, and small towns. His vision of economic diversification and regional growth, along with his opposition to free trade, closely resembled that of Carey, who may have influenced Fitzhugh's thinking.[80] His *Sociology for the South*, based upon articles he wrote for the South's largest newspaper, the *Richmond (Va.) Examiner*, reflected the appropriation of traditionally conservative ideals in the service of political and economic progress, a stance characteristic of modern sociology and social psychology. As C. Vann Woodward has observed, "Fitzhugh's approach was not political, or economic, or legalistic, but sociological and psychological—both with an antique flavor, and yet more attuned to the modern than to the eighteenth- or nineteenth-century mind."[81]

Born twenty-three years later to a cotton merchant in the boom country of the Mississippi delta, Hughes shared little of Fitzhugh's reverence for the traditions of the Old South or the Old World. Hughes venerated modern science and emulated Francis Bacon's polymathic mastery of the natural and social realms, excelling in the study of history, philosophy, languages, and rhetoric along with geology, anatomy, chemistry, mathematics, and engineering. Like Fitzhugh, he admired most the social criticism of Carlyle and Fourier, but he devoured as well the political economy of John Locke, Jeremy Bentham, and

John Stuart Mill. Like Emerson, whom he also read, he identified with Carlyle's iconoclastic model of the heroic scholar who created a new world through the omnipotence of his imagination. In his messianic view of his intellectual powers, Hughes rivaled even Comte, envisioning himself as both prophet and emperor of a new South, ushering in a new age. Ever restless in his law practice, at 25 he published his *Treatise on Sociology*, which remained the standard textbook in southern social science courses until the 1890s—and which anticipated the twentieth-century structural-functionalist sociology of Talcott Parsons in central respects, as Stanford M. Lyman has noted.[82]

Because they wrote in defense of slavery, Fitzhugh and Hughes's combined works form a largely forgotten first chapter in the history of American sociology.[83] Yet the very connection between their sociology and slavery makes their texts significant, by illuminating the distinctive ideological nature of the Comtean critique of market society—and, more profoundly, of classical political economy. Both writers based their sociology of slavery upon their assessment of the fundamental failings of the Revolutionary Era social science. The attributes that elevated man above the beast, they believed, were missing from political economy's sovereign self. These same, distinctively human qualities—leisure rather than labor, propriety rather than property, sentiment rather than sovereignty—were the very things that southern society boasted in abundance. Fitzhugh's attack upon Benjamin Franklin's model of bourgeois virtue echoed Carey and Emerson's caricatures of "economic man." "His sentiments and his philosophy are low, selfish, atheistic and material," Fitzhugh wrote. "They tend to make man a mere 'featherless biped,' well-fed, well-clothed and comfortable, but regardless of his soul as 'the beasts that perish.'"[84] Nor did Fitzhugh spare any sympathy for his native Virginian heritage of Jeffersonian agrarianism, with its abiding ambivalence about slavery lending strength to the abolitionist cause. His frontal attack upon Jefferson sparked a firestorm of counterrevolutionary sentiment among proslavery writers.[85] The Declaration of Independence and the Virginia Bill of Rights, he charged, were highfalutin frauds. "[M]en are not born physically, morally, or intellectually equal, . . . [and] their natural inequalities beget inequalities of rights," Fitzhugh wrote. "The weak in mind or body require guidance, support and protection; they must obey and work for those who protect and guide them—they have a natural right to guardians, committees, teachers or masters." He flatly denied that men were born with equal and inalienable rights. "It would be far nearer the truth to say, 'that some were born with saddles on their backs, and others booted and spurred to ride them,' and the riding does them good."[86]

The problem with classical political economy, as Hughes and Fitzhugh saw it, was not only the political conceits of liberty and equality, but their philo-sophical foundation in contract and consent as the basis of social order. Social relations, according to Hughes, were not acts of free will, but acts of duty. In-dividuals entered into society not as independent sovereigns, but as born sub-jects of the natural or divine law of "association," he wrote, much like Carey. "Society substantially, is therefore, not from compact or agreement. The sub-stance of society is perfunctory,—every individual is under an obligation to as-sociate, for the existence and progress of himself and others," Hughes wrote. "Dissociation is immoral and unnatural. Isolation is injury."[87] Fitzhugh em-phatically agreed. "Man is born a member of society, and does not form soci-ety," he insisted. "Locke's theory of the social contract" he assailed as the great-est "heresy in moral science," for it gave rise to the insidious individualism that crippled both democratic politics and capitalist economics. Fitzhugh lay the blame squarely on the shoulders of political economy itself. "The first principles of the science of political economy inculcate separate, individual action," he wrote. But "man isolated and individualized is the most helpless of animals."[88]

Perhaps the most radical element of Hughes and Fitzhugh's sociology was their outright rejection of the Lockean principle that the basis of private prop-erty lay in individuals' ownership of the fruits of their labor. As Eugene Gen-ovese has argued, such an individualistic ideal proved difficult to reconcile with a social system in which the direct producers possessed no rights to their own labor or its fruits. Southern courts, along with social theorists such as Fitzhugh and Hughes, gravitated toward a reconception of labor and property rights as originating with society rather than the individual.[89] Like contemporary expo-nents of "associationism," the nation's first sociologists envisioned labor as a social resource rightly commanded by society as a whole. "The association of labor properly carried out under a common head or ruler, would render labor more efficient, relieve the laborer of many of the cares of household affairs, and protect and support him in sickness and old age," Fitzhugh wrote, drawing what seemed to him the only reasonable conclusion: "Slavery attains all these results. What else will?"[90]

Fitzhugh accordingly disclaimed the conception, central to the tradition of political economy, of personal wealth as a reward for work. One's needs, not one's efforts or powers, determined one's just deserts, he contended. "It is a beautiful example of communism," he wrote of slave society, "where each one receives not according to his labor, but according to his wants."[91] "The com-fortable livelihood of all," Hughes concurred, was the "societary reality" to which the South aspired. "None are in want," he wrote of his slave-based utopia. "The children do not cry because they lack. The cruse of oil is never empty. The meal never shows the bottom of the barrel. Instead of meat, three times a week; there is meat three times a day. The old people are fat: there is a chicken in every man's pot."[92]

When the sociologists of slavery overturned labor power as a natural endowment and natural right inhering in individuals, they overthrew individual willpower as well. They denied the capacity of slaves for rational will, not by excluding black people from the human species, but by redefining human nature itself.[93] Fitzhugh and Hughes were pleased to report that individuals were by nature neither rational nor willful. Rationality was a delusion that drew people into unnatural isolation and conflict. Human nature was rather passionately social, manifested in the loyalty of slaves and the benevolence of masters, in the love of men and women, the devotion of parents and children, and the honor of southern society. The natural social order, and the most humane, was not one that reduced people to calculating machines, but one that gave greatest expression to human feeling. "The institution of slavery gives full development and full play to the affections," Fitzhugh wrote. "Free society chills, stints and eradicates them. . . . Love for others is the organic law of our society, as self-love is of theirs." Free society went awry because it overlooked humankind's true capacities and instead attributed to individuals a "right of Private Judgement" that was merely a figment of Enlightenment imagination. "The right of Private Judgement, naturally enough, leads to the right to act on that judgement, to the supreme sovereignty of the individual, and the abnegation of all government," Fitzhugh wrote.[94] "A man has not a right to use his mind and body as he will," Hughes agreed.[95]

In place of judgment or willpower, Fitzhugh and Hughes argued for the primary place of irrational desire in governing human affairs. "Desire and fear are the springs of human action," Hughes wrote in a passage that easily could have appeared in any standard textbook of social psychology fifty years later. "By ordering these, men are ordered. By these, they are associated, adapted, and regulated. Desires are economic, political, hygienic, esthetic, philosophic, moral and religious. That is their objective nature. Their modifications are appetites, sentiments, and affections."[96] By ordering desires, men would be ordered: a profound and enduring program. "Appetites" and "affections" became the bedrock of human nature in the sociology of slavery, supplanting labor power and willpower. "Association" and "adaptation" took the place of ownership and rulership as the fundamental social relations. Indeed, ownership and rulership themselves took on essentially new meanings in the new social science.

Private property, Hughes and Fitzhugh contended, constituted not an individual entitlement but a public trust, properly managed by individual proprietors in the interests of society as a whole. "Say the Abolitionists—'Man ought not to have property in man.' What a dreary, cold, bleak, inhospitable world this would be with such a doctrine carried into practice," Fitzhugh wrote. "Men living to themselves, like owls and wolves and lions and birds and beasts of prey? No: 'Love thy neighbor as thyself.' And this can't be done till he has a property in your services as well as a place in your heart." Fitzhugh thus made the crucial link between what he took to be the fundamental psychic and social relation, namely love, and the political economists' fundamental political and economic relation, namely contract. The political-economic relation, the "property in your services," was to be redrawn along the lines of the psychosocial relation, the "place in your heart." "[T]he great truth which lies at the foundation of all society," he declared, was "*that every man has property in his fellow-man!*"[97]

Hughes put the same point rather differently. "Property in man, is absurd," he wrote. "Men cannot be owned."[98] How then to explain the relationship between master and slave? Hughes did so by denying that the slaveholder either owned or ruled the slave. Rather, he argued, both master and slave were servants of the social order. Society entrusted the slaveholder with certain responsibilities, such as supervision and planning, and the slave with other responsibilities, such as menial labor. Their relationship was defined by their respective functions, not by their respective rights. In order to dispense with the misleading language of political economy, Hughes renamed the southern system, "warranteeism," and renounced "slavery" itself.

In one sense, by defining "warranteeism" against actually existing slavery, his work may be read as a utopian critique of southern society, much as Carey's archetype of cooperative capitalism represented a utopian critique of competitive capitalism. But in a deeper sense, Hughes, like Carey, envisioned not an alternative social order, but an alternative social science, in which the political-economic conflict between owners and workers was reconceived as psychosocial harmony without necessitating any fundamental reorganization of political and economic relations themselves.[99] "Warranteeism therefore, is not 'an obligation to labor for the benefit of master, without the contract or consent of the servant.' That is not it. That is slavery," Hughes explained. "Warranteeism is a public obligation of the warrantor and the warrantee, to labor and do other civil duties, for the reciprocal benefit of, (1) the State, (2) the Warrantee, and, (3) the Warrantor." What appeared from the perspective of political economy as a relationship of authority between master and slave was refigured in Hughes's sociology as a relationship of "reciprocity" between "warrantor" and "warrantee," on the one hand, and society (represented by the state) on the other. "The obligation is public; there are three parties to it; reciprocity is its essence."[100]

Reciprocity did not mean equality. The former meant a balance of obligations, while the latter meant a balance of powers. Just as responsibilities were to be "reciprocal"—based on respective duties or functions—so too were rewards to be reciprocally distributed. Neither Hughes nor Fitzhugh thought that the wealth produced by southern society should be distributed equally among its members, any more than natural endowments or social responsibilities were evenly apportioned. Each would rather receive, as Fitzhugh decreed, according to his "wants." Both slaves and masters, or warrantees and warrantors, were seen to possess a property right of sorts in the plantation and its produce. "Every Southern slave has an estate . . . in the lands of the South," Fitzhugh wrote. "If his present master cannot support him, he must sell him to one who can. Slaves, too, have a valuable property in their masters." Slaves were entitled to "a *fair* proportion of the profits in the community of property which grows out of the institution of domestic slavery." Fitzhugh left the determination of that "fair proportion" up to the master, just as the master was responsible for apportioning his property among his family members and livestock. "A man's wife and children are his slaves, and do they not enjoy, in common with himself, his property?" he wrote. " . . . Look to a well ordered farm and see whether the cattle, the horses, the sheep, and the hogs, do not enjoy their full proportion of the proceeds of the farm. Would you emancipate them too?"[101]

Clearly the slave's "property" was of a different order than the master's. Property apparently conferred upon its owner not an equal right, but a reciprocal right with every other proprietor, a right tailored to each individual's obligations and wants. The property of the slaveholder made him a trustee of society and a warden of his extended family—of his wife, his children, his animals, and his slaves. The property of the slave, by contrast, made him or her a ward of the master, entitled to care and support. "The right of property, is warranted to warrantees," Hughes wrote, referring to slaves. "Warrantees therefore, have always the tenant-right of a comfortable dwelling; and the family-right of a comfortable sufficiency of food, fuel, raiment, and of medical and other necessities."[102]

When Hughes and Fitzhugh discussed "rights" in general, as when they referred to "property" in particular, they meant something far different from what those terms denoted in political economy. The model of the social order upon which the notion of right rested in political economy was that of ownership and rulership, or sovereignty. But in the sociology of slavery, "right" resided in a field of "appetites, sentiments, and affections," in Hughes's words.

One obvious model for such a field of feelings was the family. Slaves, like children, could be seen as objects of love. The "negro," according to Fitzhugh, was "but a grown-up child, and must be governed as a child, not as a lunatic or criminal"—governed not adversarially, but paternalistically. "The master occupies toward him the place of parent or guardian."[103] Fitzhugh drew upon the patriarchal philosophy of Locke's contemporary, Robert Filmer, in arguing for a social order founded on the model of the family.[104] Both Fitzhugh and Hughes embraced the sentimental vision of domesticity as a model of hierarchical harmony, ostensibly founded upon familial affection rather than property and power, much as Bushnell did.[105] But Filmer's quaint familial ideal was, in important ways, unsuited to the big business of antebellum cotton production, which more closely resembled the factory than the family. The northern model of domesticity, likewise, could not adequately describe a social system in which the separation of home and work effected by the rise of wage labor had not occurred.[106] The sociologists needed a vision of social relations based on sentiment rather than sovereignty, yet appropriate for plantation-style agribusiness.

Hughes, in his idiosyncratic language, suggested something new. The rights of warrantees, unlike those of their warrantors, were "associationally exercised." Slaves were essentially "associates" in the plantation, responsible for carrying out its labor. The "head of the association" was responsible for transacting the plantation's business. "In the division of labor, that is his function. He aliens, purchases and administers for all. This conforms to the law of adaptation. Warrantees therefore, have the right of property, in association," Hughes wrote.[107] He was groping toward a model of labor relations that replaced the authority of ownership with the authority of management.

Hughes and Fitzhugh's creation was not just a science of slavery. It was a "sociology for the South," a science of social relations among rich and poor, gentry and commoner, as well as master and slave. Just as they strove to justify the master's authority over the slave in new terms, so they sought to lend scientific sanction to the great wealth of the planter class amid the relative poverty of many other southerners. Fitzhugh, especially, argued for the continued concentration of wealth in the hands of a privileged few families. His repudiation of the concept of private property as an inherent human right prevented him from defending private fortunes in terms of the rightful claims of the individual. Instead, Fitzhugh grounded wealth in general, as he did slave labor in particular, in social sentiment rather than individual sovereignty. "Property," he wrote, was "too much interwoven with the feelings, interests, prejudices and affections of man, to be shaken by the speculation of philosophers." The passing on of wealth from one generation to the next, according to Fitzhugh, promoted "learning, skill, and high moral qualifications." By contrast, "too much insecurity of property invites to extravagance and speculation, and prevents refinement and progress." Finally, he asserted that the existing distribution of wealth rendered both rich and poor suitably content, whereas any redistribution would result in turmoil and distress. "Those accustomed to poverty, suffer little from it," he wrote. "Those who have been rich, are miserable when they become poor."[108]

Fitzhugh managed to make his case for inherited and unequal wealth without any reference to the rights, privileges, or powers associated with ownership in political economy. Having dispensed with sovereignty, he could stake his social vision on cultural and sentimental grounds. He therefore could contend that the difference between an equalitarian society and an aristocratic one was really the difference between savagery and civilization. A "community of property" in which individuals claimed an equal right to common lands was workable only in "the savage state," according to Fitzhugh. The slaveowning South represented the civilized alternative. "This latter kind of community of property," he wrote, "exists where separate ownership having been acquired in the soil of a State, those who own that soil also own those individuals who cultivate it." The North, of course, was as far as possible from a community of property of any kind. When Fitzhugh compared southern society to a different sort of "communism," as he put it, he had in mind not northern capitalism, but the utopian vision of the European socialists of his day, including Fourier and Robert Owen. Sociology, Fitzhugh explained, prescribed a different cure than the socialists did for the same "disease" of "free society."[109] Aiming to socialize people instead of property or power, the "new philosophy" was essentially a socialism of the psyche rather than of sovereignty. It was a philosophy that ostensibly divorced power from ownership and rulership, vesting it instead within a psychic and social hierarchy of human affections and desires.

Slavery embodied that philosophy in its finest form. "[S]lavery," Fitzhugh wrote, "is a form, and the very best form, of socialism." Like utopian socialism, the sociology of slavery purported to solve free society's problem of class power. Those who owned the soil, as Fitzhugh explained, also owned those who worked it. "Every social structure must have its substratum," he wrote. "In free society this substratum, the weak, poor and ignorant, is borne down upon and oppressed with continually increasing weight by all above. We have solved the problem of relieving this substratum from the pressure from above. The slaves are the substratum, and the master's feelings and interests alike prevent him from bearing down upon and oppressing them."[110] Because the master actually owned—or, as Fitzhugh and Hughes would have it, superintended—his slaves' labor, he could regard them with the same concern for their health and welfare that free laborers felt for their own well-being. The conflict of interests between the good of the employer and that of the employee was thus ended—or so said the sociology of slavery.

Hughes died of rheumatism while serving in the Mississippi Guards in 1862—late enough to savor the Confederacy's centralization of economic power in accord with his expansively statist politics, but early enough to miss the emancipation of four million slaves.[111] Fitzhugh, however, survived the war and swiftly transformed himself from a diehard defender of slavery into an enthusiast of southern capitalism. By 1869, he had abandoned any lingering reservations about bourgeois depravity and conferred upon wealthy employers the mantle of paternalism formerly reserved for the defeated master class.[112] In important respects, as other scholars have argued, the demise of slavery rendered the proslavery critique of classical political-economic principles irrelevant and quickly forgotten, "without a basis in social reality."[113] Yet the increasing predominance in the postwar period of social-scientific concepts such as those first formulated in the United States by Fitzhugh and Hughes suggests that their sociology reflected the ideological inadequacy of classical political economy as a rationale for northern wage labor no less than southern slavery.[114]

The origins of American sociology, in the South as in the North, lay less in the contrasting methods of exploitation peculiar to each section than in the common conflict between the owners of the means of production and the direct producers, and in the potential of political economy to reveal the competing interests at stake. The Comtean critique of the revolutionary social science in the antebellum South therefore mirrored essential elements of the emergence of sociological thought in the industrializing North: the espousal of "associational" conceptions of property and power along with social interdependence as opposed to individual autonomy, and most importantly, the recourse to psychosocial sentiment as opposed to political-economic sovereignty as the foundation of social order. Carey, like Fitzhugh and Hughes, ultimately elided the basis of earlier understandings of class power in political economy, enabling him, like them, to identify a class-divided social system with the dawning ideal of socialism. With the North's victory clearing the way for the full development of industrial capitalism, the project of ideological reconstruction begun by Fitzhugh, Hughes, and Carey as well as by Emerson, Bushnell, and Fuller would reach fruition as well.

CHAPTER FOUR

The Postbellum Crisis of Political Economy

Henry George and
William Graham Sumner

When the Civil War began, William Graham Sumner (1840–
1910) was a 21-year-old undergraduate at Yale College, a humble mechanic's son from Hartford following Horace Bushnell's footsteps into the ministry. "It seemed to me then," as
Sumner told a biographer many years later, recalling ideas first recorded in his
college compositions, " ... that the war ... must certainly bring about immense
social changes and social problems, especially making the rich richer and the
poor poorer, and leaving behind us the old ante-war period as one of primitive
simplicity which could never return."[1] Across the country in San Francisco,
Henry George (1839–1897) was just a year older with a similar background, the
child of a struggling book dealer in Henry Carey's Philadelphia. Having quit
school at the age of 13, George had headed for California on his own a few years
later. He spent the war bouncing between odd jobs and frequent unemployment, barely getting by. George was painfully aware, as he later wrote, that
while wartime mobilization was creating "monstrous fortunes," it was also giving rise to enormous poverty, a "degrading and embruting slavery" that betrayed the war's fitting legacy in the emancipation of labor.[2]

Along with the abolition of chattel slavery, the most enduring economic
consequence of the Civil War indeed proved to be the redistribution of wealth

into the hands of financiers and manufacturers who largely bankrolled the spectacular industrialization of the postbellum era.[3] At the same time, the rapid growth of the working class brought the tension between the agrarian ideals of American political economy and the realities of proletarianization to the forefront of national attention. The dissolution of the household economy and the rise of a new industrial order changed the status of labor in thought and culture as well as in factories and fields.

The wrenching class struggle that marked the protracted depression of the 1870s, 1880s, and 1890s threw political economy itself into crisis, as evidenced in the dueling polemics of the best-known contemporary writers on social science, namely George and Sumner. George's classic, *Progress and Poverty* (1879), became an unofficial manifesto for many American workers and their bourgeois allies in the nascent labor movement, while Sumner's *What Social Classes Owe to Each Other* (1883) and his widely read essays in the following years made him "the schoolmaster," as it has aptly been written, of the ascendant leadership of big business.[4] Yet even as George and Sumner pulled political economy in opposite directions, their strikingly parallel revisions of the embattled science of wealth signaled the rise of a different kind of social science, affording a new ideological basis for class harmony in the age of industrial capitalism.

In responding to the new context of postwar industrialization, they and contemporary social theorists were forced to confront the same ideological inadequacies of classical political economy that had appeared to avant-garde thinkers such as Emerson and Fuller, Carey and Fitzhugh, in the antebellum period. Like those earlier writers, George and Sumner helped to redefine the Revolutionary Era ideals of individual autonomy and popular sovereignty in newly psychosocial terms—in terms of the romantic self and organic society of nineteenth-century social psychology instead of the sovereign self and contractual society of eighteenth-century political economy.

Currency Reform and the American Social Science Association

The first signs of the approaching crisis of political economy appeared even as the great crisis of the Union was drawing to a close, with the emergence of the greenback movement and the American Social Science Association. In the aftermath of Appomattox, each arose in response to widening economic inequality. Each drew upon the transcendental psychology and Comtean sociology of the antebellum era in seeking a new rationale for class concord amid the demise of the household economy. Together, the currency reform movement and the host of organizations and institutions spawned by the American Social Science Association set the stage for the reconstruction of political and economic thought encapsulated by Sumner and George.

The popular demand for a growing money supply dated to the colonial era, and currency concerns had become especially pressing for yeoman farmers during the cyclone of debt and dispossession following the Revolutionary War. But the explosive expansion of wage labor in the 1840s and 1850s, along with the swift proliferation of banks and banknotes in those same years, conferred newfound significance upon monetary policy. Soon the "money question" came to center upon the national currency system established during the Civil War.

The issuance of $400 million in legal tender Treasury notes, or "greenbacks," the first national paper currency in the United States, fueled a cash-starved economy and enabled many northerners of modest means to provide the mass market for government bonds, which largely subsidized the war effort. At the same time, the centralization of finance capital in the urban Northeast underwrote the nation's first large-scale securities market, through the rise of modern investment banking and the creation of the National Banking System, whose pyramidal structure funneled financial resources from the hinterland to New York City.[5] On the one hand, the newly created national banks and their bank notes, backed by government bonds ultimately payable in gold, came to symbolize for postbellum Americans the "money power" of wealthy speculators and financiers. On the other hand, the U.S. Treasury and its greenbacks, secured solely by government fiat, came to represent "the people's money"— "that money which saved the country in war and has given it prosperity and happiness in peace," in the words of Benjamin Franklin Butler, the famed Civil War general and later U.S. representative, governor of Massachusetts, and presidential candidate for the Greenback-Labor Party. "To it four million men owe their emancipation from slavery; to it labor is indebted for elevation from that thrall of degradation in which it has been enveloped for ages."[6]

Butler's paean to paper money was emblematic of the identification of a free-flowing currency with the freedom of labor in the postwar greenback movement, which opposed the contraction of the currency and the return to a specie standard. In the name of the "producing classes," the soft money cause mobilized popular resistance to the monopoly power of finance capital, while uniting organized labor with entrepreneurial industrialists in staking out a new monetary foundation for economic democracy and labor-capital harmony. The preeminent theorist of the currency crusade was Henry Carey. Carey's creative amalgamation of the utopian socialist ideal of "association" with faith in private property and the free market found its most influential advocate within the postbellum labor movement in Alexander Campbell, a onetime iron manufacturer, coal promoter, and Illinois state legislator often considered the "Father of the Greenback Party."[7]

Campbell's short book, *The True American System of Finance* (1864), provided the basic platform for the National Labor Union, which arose in part from the labor strife of 1867 in the coal fields of his home district of La Salle County. "The design of the Fathers of the Republic was ... to secure to each the fruits of his own labor or talents," Campbell conventionally began. "It cannot be denied that labor is the wealth-producing power of the nation, and it is equally true that as a whole the laborers are poor. Some cause has been operating with continual and growing effect, to separate production from the producer." The cause of this inequity, he quickly concluded, was not to be found in the relationship between wage labor and industrial capital, for "the interests of employer and employee" were "mutual," warranting "no agrarian or other distribution of property, nor any interference in contracts between capitalists and laborers."[8] Rather, the source of the separation of wealth from work lay in the relationship between both the employer and the employee, on the one hand, and the financiers who held the purse strings of production, on the other.

Drawing extensively upon the pioneering exponent of fiat currency, Edward Kellogg, whose 1849 work was tellingly entitled, *Labor and Other Capital,* Campbell anchored his analysis of exploitation in a fundamental reconception of economic value.[9] He rejected outright the classical axiom that a commodity's exchange value emerged from the process of production, as he moved beyond Carey's revisionist "cost-of-reproduction" theory to argue along with Kellogg that such value actually measured a commodity's utility to its consumer. "The value of property is estimated by its usefulness, and not by its cost of production," Campbell wrote, summarily dismissing the basic distinction between "use value" and "exchange value" in classical political economy.[10]

At the same time, he identified another kind of value that represented the price of access to the market itself, or the cost of exchange rather than the cost of production: the value of money, the medium of exchange. Like other commodities, he explained, money derived its value not from the cost of its production but from its utility, reflected in the rate of interest paid for its use. It was the interest rate, the access price of the means of exchange rather than that of the means of production, that governed the distribution of income between the "producing classes"—whether employees, employers, or self-employed— and the moneylenders who served as the gatekeepers of the market. By artificially constricting the money supply and inflating the rate of interest, according to Campbell, bankers and financiers reaped a windfall at producers' expense. But unlike the value of other commodities, the interest rate as well as the money supply were established by law rather than by the market itself. Simply by declaring the currency redeemable not in specie but in government bonds earning an annual interest rate of 3 percent, which he calculated to be the approximate rate of economic growth, the "legal value" of money could be pegged to popular demand and the expropriation of wealth from its creators effectively ended.

Campbell's (and Kellogg's) "interconvertible bond" scheme, offering an apparently cost-free, legislative means of ameliorating economic inequality while avoiding the supposedly self-destructive spiral of conflict between owners and workers, formed the centerpiece of the labor reform movement in the 1860s and 1870s.[11] The Populist campaign for the free coinage of silver in the 1890s, while abandoning the radical attack upon the specie standard, revived the reassuring promise that a plentiful common currency could afford the basis of a new commonwealth.[12] Like their agrarian ancestors, the partisans of greenbacks and silver insisted that wealth remained the natural reward of work and that money remained essentially a mere medium of exchange. Yet in finding the origin of economic value as well as exploitation in the process of exchange rather than the process of production, they shifted the struggle over the distribution of wealth, however unintentionally or unwittingly, onto a new terrain defined by access to financial resources instead of productive property. In this way, the currency crusades framed the crisis of classical political economy that gave rise to neoclassical economics, which took the utility theory of value as its starting assumption and purchasing power rather than labor power as its central concern.

The vision of cross-class cooperation at the heart of the greenback movement was informed as well by the principles of the American Social Science Association. The Association was founded in 1865 as an organization of largely New England lawyers, physicians, ministers, and academics committed to the dual advancement of social science and social reform.[13] As was true of currency reform, the roots of the Association lay in the formation of a new urban working class during the long economic boom beginning in the late 1840s, fueled by labor migrations from the countryside and from abroad as well as by the transformation of the craft system in manufacturing.[14]

For bourgeois reformers, the most immediate problem presented by the new workforce was the crushing burden it placed upon the aging system of public and private poor relief, especially in the seaboard cities. The American Social Science Association grew directly out of the Massachusetts Board of State

Charities, which was established in 1862 as the first of many state investigatory commissions charged with systematizing and centralizing the provision of aid to the urban poor.[15] Unavoidably coupled with the problem of "charities," from the perspective of reformers, was that of "corrections," to which the American Social Science Association dedicated itself as well, along with the related concerns of public health and education. As the Massachusetts Board of State Charities stated in its circular convening the first meeting of the new Association, "Our attention has lately been called to the importance of some organization in the United States, both local and national, whose object shall be the discussion of those questions relating to the Sanitary Condition of the People, the Relief, Employment, and Education of the Poor, the Prevention of Crime, the Amelioration of the Criminal Law, the Discipline of Prisons, the Remedial Treatment of the Insane, and those numerous matters of statistical and philanthropist interest which are included under the general head of 'Social Science.'"[16]

Like their British counterparts in the National Association for the Promotion of Social Science, founded in 1857, the leaders of the American Social Science Association recognized in the growth of poverty and pauperism the signs of a fundamental shift in the social order, necessitating a basic revision of social science. "The problems presented in 1865, following the close of the Civil War . . . were more numerous, novel, and difficult than any existing here since the first great reorganization of order and liberty . . . from 1776 to 1789," wrote Franklin Benjamin Sanborn, the Association's founding secretary and leading figure.[17] A veteran of Emerson's literary circle as well as of the antislavery movement, Sanborn epitomized what Thomas L. Haskell has called the "abolitionist as transcendentalist," with his faith in the emancipatory power of the heroic scholar — "the man," as Emerson famously said, "who must take up into himself all the ability of the time, all the contributions of the past, all the hopes of the future," to become a "university of knowledges."[18] Drawing upon the organicist understanding of society in Comtean sociology, the members of the Association envisioned a natural harmony of individuals, classes, races, and sexes, in need only of proper coordination by an educated elite. Like Carey as well as Fitzhugh and Hughes, they valorized social "interdependence" as much as individual autonomy, championing the ideals of integration, symmetry, and equilibrium within society as a unified whole.

In so doing, the members of the American Social Science Association did not simply recognize and sanction the transformation of the American economy from an agrarian republic to industrial capitalism. As William Leach has emphasized, they also ideologically interpreted the disintegration of agrarian independence as a movement toward increasing mutuality and reciprocity in social relations, rather than toward the widening dependence of the dispossessed and heightening class conflict as a result.[19] In reconceiving the interdependence of market society on the basis of reciprocal roles rather than individual ownership of productive resources, the American Social Science Association offered a deliberately constructed alternative to the looming threat of class politics, which directly prompted the Association's successful campaign for civil service reform. "Social Science is not Socialism," the Association proclaimed in the introduction to the first issue of its house organ, the *Journal of Social Science*, in 1869. " . . . It is essentially constructive, and aims at strengthening, rather than undermining, the constitution of society. Again, Social Science is not Radicalism in the common sense. . . . It is essentially conservative, not of the evil, but of the good which society contains, and which can be developed only by gentle and discriminating treatment."[20]

The pioneers of postbellum social science defined their field in this way by reference to radical socialism—presumably of the kind broadly represented by the International Workingmen's Association (later the "First International"), which was organized by Karl Marx and other European radicals in 1864 and swiftly gained an eclectic following in the United States—rather than to the radical agrarianism that had provided the foil for antebellum political economy.[21] While earlier writers on social science had found in market society the fulfillment of the agrarian ideal of propertied independence, the American Social Science Association and its professional progeny tended to find within industrial capitalism the fulfillment of the socialist ideal of cooperative interdependence. Like the greenback movement with which it was intellectually allied, the Association occupied a transitional position. It combined a new commitment to scientific expertise with a traditional faith in the lay knowledge of the learned gentry, and it united an embrace of the power of society as an organic whole with a lingering belief in the self-governing individual.[22]

That dualism of neorepublican and protoprogressive principles also characterized the network of professional organizations to which the American Social Science Association directly or indirectly gave rise in the 1870s and 1880s, including the National Conference of Charities and Correction, the American Public Health Association, the American Historical Association, the American Economic Association, and the American Bar Association.[23] Even as the emerging "culture of professionalism" sanctified the specialized knowledge of university-trained experts, it envisioned the burgeoning power of the professional as providing a new basis for individual autonomy and equality, or "academic freedom" and meritocracy.[24] So too the modern research university, the most enduring legacy of the reorganization of knowledge that the American Social

Science Association helped to chart, provided a new institutional home for the social sciences, one founded upon the dual ideals of specialized graduate training and broad undergraduate education in "liberal culture." Led by Association members such as Charles W. Eliot at Harvard, Daniel Coit Gilman at Johns Hopkins, and Andrew Dickinson White at Cornell, the research university was born of the new industrial and financial capital created in the Civil War era. But it was inspired as well by the Romantic ideal, closely associated with Bushnell, of education as a realm of timeless culture that transcended the market society it inhabited, affording a new foundation for intellectual and spiritual unity amid growing political and economic division.[25]

In the late 1860s and early 1870s, the vision of social solidarity that the currency reform movement and the American Social Science Association jointly articulated drew strength from the stunning growth of output and employment throughout the industrializing economy, from manufacturing to mining to transportation and communication. But in the mid-1870s, the rapid expansion of regional, national, and international markets propelled the capitalist world into a quarter-century crisis. Cutthroat competition sent prices plummeting and set off a tidal wave of bankruptcy, disinvestment, and unemployment. Employers' feverish efforts to reduce wages or increase productivity through mechanization and reorganization of the productive process met mounting resistance from an increasingly organized and restive working class.[26] Amid the great strikes of miners, textile operatives, and railroad workers that attended the nation's first truly industrial depression, the greenback alliance of the "producing classes" gave way to increasingly intractable conflict.[27] The genteel reform and "scientific charity" promoted by the American Social Science Association in the name of class harmony took on the trappings of class war, as bourgeois reformers decried the onslaught of the "dangerous classes" in the wake of the Paris Commune.[28]

Pauperism and Poverty

"I affirm that the questions on which our national future to-day depends are questions of political economy, questions of labor and capital, of finance and taxation," William Graham Sumner instructed his new students at Yale in 1873, the year of the international financial collapse, having returned to teach at his alma mater the previous year.[29] Like Henry George, Sumner identified the first great crisis of industrial capitalism as a critical challenge to the science of political economy itself, in which they both believed the salvation of the strife-torn republic must be found.

Despite their opposing political perspectives, recent scholarship has examined the remarkably similar ways in which Sumner and George grappled with the profound tension between the old science of wealth and the new industrial order. While historians have effectively undermined the "Social Darwinist" label with which Sumner was too easily dismissed by earlier writers, they have shown that he struggled to reconcile competing commitments to the independent, proprietary individual of classical political economy and moral philosophy, on the one hand, and to the interdependent, acculturating society of modern anthropology and sociology, on the other.[30] Several studies of George's writings and of his leading role in the great labor uprising of the 1880s have similarly highlighted a central, productive tension between the pastoral republic that he mourned and the urban utopia that he envisioned.[31]

Convinced that the crisis of political economy held the key to the crisis of capitalism, George and Sumner both set out to reconstruct the tottering social science by discovering within it the cause of the rising economic inequality that increasingly imperiled the social order. George called the problem "poverty" and Sumner called it "pauperism," but each described it as a new form of slavery that threatened to bring on a new civil war. Poverty was the dividing line for Sumner and George in several ways: the historical boundary between the Jeffersonian republic of self-employed farmers and artisans and the emerging industrial society, the rising wall between what George called the "House of Have" and the "House of Want," and the battle line between him and Sumner. For George, the poor were the workhorses of the new age, poverty the "unpitying machine" that robbed them of their rightful rewards.[32] For Sumner, by contrast, the pauper appeared in the saddle, riding the hardworking, smallholding taxpayer enslaved by a new industrial despotism.[33] Both understood, as Alexander Campbell did, that the vital bond between production and distribution had been broken: those doing the work were no longer reaping the wealth. But from their crucial difference over the significance of the new poverty, they took the science of agrarian capitalism in opposite directions. George's advancement of the rights of the propertyless led him to leadership in the cause of organized labor, while Sumner's defense of the rights of the propertied made him a champion of industrial capital. In turning political economy into a domain of class war (despite their protestations), they staked out the opposing extremes between which their contemporaries sought to establish a new social psychology of common desires and shared social norms.

At the same time, Sumner and George themselves pointed the way out of the thickets of political economy and onto the ideological terrain of modern American social science. Even as they sought to defend the market republic of autonomous individuals, they each turned to repudiate a central feature of classical political economy and its embattled ideal of propertied independence. Sumner rejected the revolutionary principles of natural right and natural liberty in favor of a deeply organicist, historicist vision of freedom, in keeping with the general turn toward the ideology of interdependence advanced by the American Social Science Association. For his part, George overthrew not only the doctrine of natural scarcity so vital to the classical tradition of Ricardo and Malthus, as Carey had done, but likewise the natural wealth-producing powers of land and labor. These he replaced with a thoroughly social conception of what makes land and labor productive to begin with: namely the market itself, conceived, as in greenback ideology, no longer as a neutral arena of trade between independent economic agents, but as the very source of the value being exchanged.

For George as for Sumner, the sphere of social exchange—in other words, the market—came to determine the distribution of both liberty and property, of both rights and rewards. Ultimately, both men came to conceive of this newly powerful social realm not in the traditional terms of political economy, of natural right and social contract, but in the terms of a new social psychology. Whereas George made the movement out of political economy only haltingly and uncertainly in his idiosyncratic urban utopia, Sumner crossed over more completely in his final, landmark work on *Folkways* (1906).[34]

George's Problem of Poverty

The problem of poverty came as a revelation to George. His father failed in the book business and struggled to support a large family on a clerk's salary, yet the Georges were never truly poor, and they were rich in the craftsman spirit of laboring Philadelphia, the legacy of Ben Franklin and Tom Paine. But after brief stints as a ship's cabin boy and a printer's apprentice, young George headed west amid the brief economic downturn of 1857 only to find hardship rather than fortune in the California gold country.[35] Desperation drew out his prophetic voice, and the evangelical Christianity with which he had been reared gave it words. "How I long for the Golden Age—for the promised Millennium," he wrote his sister from San Francisco, " . . . when the poorest and meanest will have a chance to use all his God-given faculties, and not be forced to drudge away the best part of his time in order to support wants but little above those of the animal."[36]

George found his chance in journalism, but he found his calling in the dreadful juxtaposition of luxury and squalor that he observed on a business trip to

New York City in 1869. "And suddenly there came to him—there in daylight, in the city street—a burning thought, a call, a vision," George's son recalled. "Every nerve quivered. And he made a vow that he would never rest until he had found the cause of, and if he could, the remedy for this deepening poverty amid advancing wealth."[37] The answer came in another revelation shortly thereafter in the foothills overlooking San Francisco Bay, where a teamster told him land was selling for a thousand dollars an acre. "Like a flash it came upon me that there was the reason of advancing poverty with advancing wealth," George later wrote. "With the growth of population, land grows in value, and the men who work it must pay for the privilege. I turned back amidst quiet thought, to the perception that then came to me and has been with me ever since."[38]

Awestruck, he quickly wrote a 48-page booklet entitled *Our Land and Land Policy* (1871). Eight years later he published *Progress and Poverty*, "the oak," in his son's words, "that grew out of the acorn" of the earlier essay. With a sense of deliverance, George sent a copy to his father, writing him: "It will not be recognized at first—maybe not for some time—but it will ultimately be considered a great book, will be published in both hemispheres, and be translated into different languages."[39] His faith was soon rewarded. The book swiftly outsold any previous work of political economy and the most popular novels in the United States and England, making it second only to the Bible in nineteenth-century readership and its author the most influential American economist worldwide.[40]

The millennial vision of the Golden Age that inspired *Progress and Poverty* reflected George's firsthand observations of pioneer California. In the mining district of the Sierras, he witnessed the passing of what he would describe as "the natural order": a state-sponsored system of common property without official titles, allowing every man to claim only so much territory as he could mine himself, and only so long as he mined it. As an editorial writer and later a newspaper editor in Sacramento and San Francisco, George watched with rising rage as government surveyors parceled out private plots, mining companies patented mineral rights, and speculators sent land values soaring. At the same time in the farmlands of the interior valleys, millions of acres of the public domain were sold off largely to wealthy investors amassing huge holdings, creating, in Donald Worster's words, "a society of vast estates, world markets, bare, makeshift, sunbleached houses, and armies of tramps on the road looking for work between harvests."[41]

To George, California's rapid progress appeared distinctly unnatural, and so did the poverty it brought. Simply by seeing poverty as unnatural, he marked a decisive departure from the conventional wisdom that held want to be the curse of the weak in a social order conceived as harsh and unforgiving, yet brutally fair. He rejected the social science of the contemporary "scientific charity" movement, with its argument for systematic "discrimination" between the few "deserving" recipients of assistance and the "undeserving" many. For George, poverty was not a subject of charity; it was, he repeatedly insisted, "a degrading and embruting slavery," a more "insidious and widespread form" of bondage than chattel slavery itself.[42] He rested this claim upon the traditional Lockean conception of freedom, championed by the antislavery movement, as the right to the fruit of one's own labor, or "the right of each to the free use of his powers in making a living for himself and his family," as George explained in a series of articles written for *Frank Leslie's Illustrated Newspaper* in 1883. Slavery, conversely, meant "the robbery of labor," he argued. "It consists in compelling men to work, yet taking from them all the produce of their labor except what suffices for a bare living."[43]

George's radical move was to argue that poverty forced people to choose between such slavery and starvation. "Unable to employ themselves," he wrote, "the nominally free laborers are forced by their competition with each other to pay as rent all their earnings above a bare living, or to sell their labor for wages which give but a bare living." As "thousands and thousands of men" were rendered homeless and hungry, they were left no alternative but to surrender their rightful earnings and work for merely "board and clothes . . . the wages of slaves."[44] Yet George's notion of "slave wages" differed fundamentally from the charge of "wage slavery" advanced by contemporary labor leaders and socialists, who contended that the wage system itself was a form of unfree labor. To the contrary, he crucially maintained that there was no intrinsic difference between being an employee and being self-employed. "The gold washed out by the self-employing gold digger is as much his wages as the money paid to the hired coal miner by the purchaser of his labor," he wrote in *Progress and Poverty*.[45] The sinful secret of poverty lay for George not in wage labor—nor in exorbitant interest, as Campbell contended. Poverty was rooted in rent, the unearned increment that landowners accrued by charging others for access, which forced the poor to work for the "bare living" they could get instead of the larger living they earned.

Sumner's Problem of Pauperism

Sumner was in a sense poverty's warmest admirer. No one argued more forcefully that the suffering of the poor was a blessing for society. "A drunkard in the gutter is just where he ought to be," he famously wrote, for "Nature has set up on him the process of decline and dissolution by which she removes things which have survived their usefulness."[46] But while such remorseless logic accounts for his reputation as the leading American "Social Darwinist," it does not explain what made Sumner as fearful for the nation's future as George, nor what drove him to develop an equally elaborate critique of the postwar order. Sumner matched George in freedom-fighting zeal, and he set out to destroy an opposing system of "slavery" that he found arising alongside poverty.

He also shared George's sense of prophetic mission. As the newly ordained Episcopal rector of the Church of the Redeemer in Morristown, New Jersey, the 30-year-old Sumner summoned his parishioners to war against the legions of Christ's enemies.[47] Eager for a wider arena of battle, he left the clergy two years later to take up the chair of political and social science at Yale, where his fighting spirit gained him a following. "He had the air of a conqueror," one of his students recalled. " . . . He came stamping into the classroom, glared at us, ripped his notes out of the leather receptacle (it certainly was his old sermon-case, my father had one just like it), and the fight was on. We undergraduates had ringside seats."[48]

In the opposite corner of the ring, Sumner faced his lifelong imaginary adversary, the demon from which his father had fled. His parents came from artisan families in Lancashire, England, the cradle of industrial capitalism, where the rise of the factory system had brought unemployment and poverty. Two years after the Poor Law Reform Act of 1834 virtually ended outdoor relief, Sumner's father emigrated to the United States in order to avoid the poorhouse, but he never finally escaped the threat of pauperism, and he died nearly as poor as when he had arrived. The moral keynotes of Sumner's upbringing in Hartford were hard work and self-reliance; the first book he owned was entitled, *Self-Dependence*.[49] But the books that sparked his youthful interest in social science and, by his own account, shaped his enduring understanding of the subject were Harriet Martineau's *Illustrations of Political Economy* (1834).[50] From the renowned English writer's popular primers on classical political economy, published at the time of the poor law reform, he learned that "all arbitrary distribution of the necessaries of life is injurious to society, whether in the form of private almsgiving, public charitable institutions, or a legal pauper-system," and that "the pauper system must, by some means or other, be extinguished."[51]

In Martineau's "pauper system," Sumner found his foe. His first major work, *What Social Classes Owe to Each Other*, began as a critique of "the State," particularly the newly powerful national government's pretension to represent "All-of-us" when in truth, he contended, it was only a means by which some

Americans made claims upon others.[52] But the real villain of the piece, lurking behind the shield of the state, was quickly revealed to be the pauper. "A pauper is a person who cannot earn his living; whose productive powers have fallen positively below his necessary consumption; who cannot, therefore, pay his way," Sumner wrote. " . . . He drops out of the ranks of workers and producers. Society must support him. It accepts the burden, but he must be canceled from the ranks of the rulers likewise."[53] Yet instead of being excluded from citizenship on these classically liberal terms, according to which the body politic was limited to economically "independent" individuals, the pauper had effectively assumed a new kind of political authority to appropriate the earnings of taxpaying citizens, much as lords and kings had once lived upon others' labor.

Sumner voiced the widespread sense of siege among propertied Americans of the Northeast and the Midwest, who saw the enormous rise in public spending and public debt during and after the war as a revolutionary expropriation of their savings to benefit a handful of heavily subsidized industrialists and a rapidly multiplying mass of propertyless urban workers. Indeed, as C. K. Yearley has shown, skyrocketing state and local property taxes largely funded the creation of a vast urban infrastructure to meet the needs of the emerging manufacturing empire and its increasingly immigrant workforce. New tax revenues paid the salaries of public employees and the benefits of public relief recipients in return for electoral support. While much of the wealth of manufacturers and financiers arose in intangible forms of property that the tax code left untouched, a growing majority of Americans owned virtually no property at all, leaving the shrinking minority of middling property holders to bear the financial burden of the growing public sector.[54]

Sumner's conception of the "pauper system" extended far beyond the relative pittance spent on poor relief. His "pauper" was the figurehead of a new polity, comprising not self-supporting proprietary individuals but a panoply of economic actors dependent upon taxpayer support, whether in the form of protective tariffs, paper money, public works, or the dole.[55] Like leading contemporary jurists such as Stephen J. Field and Thomas M. Cooley, Sumner regarded the redistributive use of taxation to benefit certain individuals or classes, whether at the top or the bottom of the social order, as a violation of the basic principles of free enterprise and the neutral state.[56] Such "socialistic measures," he warned, would destroy the agrarian basis of economic equality by systematically exploiting and ultimately ruining the narrowing "middle class" of freeholders, creating instead a class-divided society of "paupers" and "plutocrats" whose common ground was not the market republic but the welfare state.

Like George, Sumner drew upon the Lockean ideal of "free labor," elaborated by antebellum abolitionists, in advancing the radical argument that the emerging class society was founded upon a new system of slavery. "The notion of civil liberty which we have inherited is ... *that each man is guaranteed the use of all his own powers exclusively for his own welfare*," he wrote. Conversely, "a man whose labor and self-denial may be diverted from his maintenance to that of some other man is not a free man, and approaches more or less to the position of a slave."[57] Such was the situation of Sumner's famed "Forgotten Man," the working man of little means who struggled to support himself and his family without public assistance, much as Sumner's father had. In the postbellum political order, the Forgotten Man was compelled to surrender his earnings for others' support; in Sumner's words, "his chief business in life is to pay."[58] He was the slave of the pauper system.

George's Critique of Natural Scarcity

In framing their parallel critiques of poverty and pauperism, George and Sumner both began from the conventional notion, articulated most famously by John Locke and Adam Smith, that wealth was rightly owned individually by those who produced it or paid for it. George, no less than Sumner, defined freedom in terms of free labor and free trade and opposed on principle the fiscal machinery of tariffs and taxes that increasingly mediated market relations.[59] But both men perceived that the growing divide between propertied and propertyless Americans had thrown the classical political economy based upon an earlier stage of economic development into crisis. "[P]olitical economy, as at present taught, does not explain the persistence of poverty amid advancing wealth in a manner which accords with the deep-seated perceptions of men," George wrote in *Progress and Poverty*. As a result, the aging social science was "spurned by the statesmen, scouted by the masses, and relegated in the opinion of many educated and thinking men to the rank of a pseudo science."[60] Like Sumner, he was convinced that a lasting solution to the deepening social crisis could only be found by redressing the inadequacies and anachronisms of the Smithian science.

By his own account, George's original insight into the cause of poverty was not informed by any previous study of Adam Smith or the other founders of political economy.[61] But in *Progress and Poverty*, he engaged extensively with the classic British texts of Smith, Ricardo, Malthus, and John Stuart Mill, and he discussed the striking similarity of his own conclusions to those of the French philosophe François Quesnay, whose disciples had formed in a sense the first full-fledged school of political economy in the 1760s. Called "Physiocracy," meaning "rule of nature," Quesnay's visionary model of agrarian capitalism had been founded upon the idea that the social order should maximize the natural wealth-producing partnership of productive labor and fertile farmland by securing the natural rights of private property and free trade. From this premise, the Physiocrats had derived the first theory of capital accumulation or surplus value, which they had rooted in the natural fertility of farmland, the object of their proposed "*impôt unique*," or single tax, on ground rent.[62] From the theory of rent as the value of fertility, in turn, Ricardo and Malthus had formulated the "iron laws" of natural scarcity, of the growing gap between diminishing natural resources and increasing human needs, which had provided the orthodox explanation of rising poverty. "The niggardliness of nature," in Mill's words, "not the injustice of society, is the cause of the penalty attached to overpopulation."[63]

To George, this conventional connection between scarcity and poverty flatly contradicted the "great enigma" he had set out to solve: the rise of poverty amid plenty. The burning truth, scarcely explained by the principle of diminishing returns, was that many Americans were growing poorer even as their nation grew richer. George's approach to this critical theoretical problem began from the classical understanding of the paramount importance of land, by which he meant natural resources of any kind, and which he conceived as the essential requirement for all productive labor.[64] He adopted as well the Ricardian model of the inverse relationship between "wages," the reward of productive labor, and rent, the price paid for natural resources. That price, he agreed with his orthodox forebears, was set by the ratio of the population to the means of subsistence, or demand to supply. An abundance of free and fertile land, such as Americans had long enjoyed, kept wages relatively high; workers would sell their labor for no less than they could earn on their own homesteads. But the "enormous common" of free soil that for centuries had set the New World apart from the Old was about to end, George wrote (predating Frederick Jackson Turner's "frontier thesis" by more than a decade).[65] As a result, Americans faced for the first time on a nationwide scale high rents, low wages, and rapidly spreading poverty.

Contrary to orthodox teaching, however, George did not view rising rent as the natural consequence of population growth outpacing the availability of fertile land. It was rather the result of the conversion of the public domain into a system of private property that allowed wealthy investors to monopolize the natural resources upon which everyone else depended. Since no one could earn a living without access to land, rent became the price the propertyless were forced to pay landowners for life itself. "For as labor cannot produce without the use of land, the denial of the equal right to the use of land is necessarily the denial of the right of labor to its own produce," George wrote. "If one man can command the land upon which others must labor, he can appropriate the produce of their labor as the price of his permission to labor." Over time, private ownership of land inevitably forced the landless to pay an increasing share of their earnings in rent, until they were left with only the bare necessities of life.[66] "I assert that the injustice of society, not the niggardliness of nature, is the cause of the want and misery which the current theory attributes to overpopulation," he wrote, deliberately inverting Mill's words.[67]

Yet in arguing that poverty was due to private property in land rather than to natural scarcity, George remained faithful in crucial respects to the spirit of classical political economy. Carey and other earlier writers had challenged the presumption of diminishing agricultural returns on empirical grounds, but George found such arguments unpersuasive and misplaced.[68] More profoundly, founding theorists beginning with Locke and his seventeenth-century contemporary, James Harrington, had recognized that the engrossment of land by a privileged class threatened the natural rights of those left landless. The critique of the landed aristocracy had given the classical tradition culminating in Ricardo its radical edge. Even Mill had acknowledged that land was ultimately the common inheritance of all, and that it was only provisionally made the private property of each.[69] In claiming equal access to natural resources as a natural right, George followed in a distinguished line of agrarian radicals including Paine, Jefferson, and the New York City workingman's advocate Thomas Skidmore. His proposed panacea, the famed 100 percent "single tax" on ground rent, was practically identical to that of the Physiocrats. Like other radical Ricardians, George found the basis of a revolutionary critique of class privilege within political economy's linked analysis of the production and distribution of wealth.

Like many others as well, he realized that the basis of class privilege had fundamentally changed with the advent of what contemporaries were calling the "industrial revolution."[70] But it was in his innovative analysis of the nature of class privilege in industrial society, rather than in his related explanation of the cause of poverty, that George made his truly pathbreaking revision of the science of wealth. Unlike writers from Smith to Marx who presumed that industrial capital replaced agricultural land as the primary productive resource within modern manufacturing, George contended that land remained the main means of production—but that land itself had been transformed into a new kind of resource, with a new kind of wealth-producing power in partnership with productive labor. He argued that land's productive capacity now derived not from its natural fertility, but from the function it performed in facilitating the exchange of goods and services as well as art and ideas. Land had become the material basis for the market, to which George attributed a new productive power. Rent, then, was the value of this distinctively social rather than natural resource, which rightly belonged to no individual, but to society as a whole.

Therein lay the reason that rents rose (as did poverty) most steeply in the city: not because of "the natural qualities of the land," but because of its "mere quality of extension," its "superficial capacity" to provide a setting for social exchange. While land's natural fertility might decline as the population dependent upon it grew, its social fertility would rise due to the "increased powers of co-operation and exchange" that the city afforded.[71] "With no greater agricultural productiveness than it had at first, this land now begins to develop a productiveness of a higher kind," George wrote. "To labor expended in raising corn, or wheat, or potatoes, it will yield no more of those things than at first . . . but the artisan, the manufacturer, the storekeeper, the professional man, find that their labor expended here, at the center of exchanges, will yield them much more than if expended even at a little distance away from it."[72] What made labor so rewarding and land so valuable where population was most dense, he explained, was not simply the productive power of the factory system. It was, more importantly, the unparalleled opportunities to buy and sell in the metropolitan market, which gave rise to intellectual and cultural exchange as well. "Here, if you have anything to sell, is the market; here, if you have anything to buy, is the largest and the choicest stock," he wrote. " . . . Here are the great libraries . . . the learned professors . . . museums and art galleries . . . great actors, and orators, and singers, from all over the world. Here, in short, is a center of human life, in all its varied manifestations."[73]

In his analysis of poverty, George drew upon the agrarian understanding of land as a limited natural resource, properly claimed by individuals as a corollary of their natural right to the use and benefit of their natural capacity for productive labor. But in repudiating the myth of natural scarcity, he moved beyond the agrarian critique of land monopoly to reconceive land itself as a potentially limitless social resource, deriving its productivity from "co-operation and exchange" instead of natural fertility. Such social fertility would expand infinitely along with market relations, knitting individuals ever more tightly together, multiplying their wants as well as their abilities, turning land from a source of scarcity into a means of ever-increasing abundance.

By the same token, George reconceived the productive power of labor, the other parent of wealth in classical political economy. In place of the natural capacity traditionally attributed to individuals, he described a new kind of labor power that flowed from the market relations of exchange and consumption. Even as he defended labor's traditional property in the wealth it produced, he redefined that claim in terms of labor's "effectiveness" in creating consumer demand, or in terms of its purchasing power.

In what sense did labor "yield" more "at the center of exchanges" than elsewhere? George explained that while "a settler and his family may raise as much corn" on a remote farmstead as in "a populous district," in the latter they would be richer, "because in the midst of a large population their labor would have become more effective; not, perhaps, in the production of corn, but in the production of wealth generally—or the obtaining of all the commodities and services which are the real objects of their labor."[74] These "real objects of their labor" were not what working people directly produced, but what they purchased and thereby indirectly produced through the medium of the market. So too, he wrote, the industrial wage worker "virtually produces the things in which he expends his wages."[75] In other words, "The common expression, 'I made so and so,' signifying 'I earned so and so,' or 'I earned money with which I purchased so and so,' is, economically speaking, not metaphorically but literally true. Earning is making."[76] Labor's right to its "products," accordingly, was essentially a claim upon what it bought rather than what it built. Workers, in other words, had a right to a fair share in the value created by society as a whole rather than to the whole of what they individually produced. In establishing on a new basis labor's right to land, George joined, largely unintentionally, in the momentous shift of the center of economic analysis from the realm of production to the realm of exchange.[77]

By redefining land and labor as social rather than natural resources, George ultimately reconceived the third and most elusive factor of production in the social science of capitalism, namely capital itself, which he began by defining in commonsense fashion as "wealth devoted to procuring more wealth." In an older agrarian society, he contended, capital had relied upon "the reproductive or transforming forces of nature" to create new wealth from old. But in modern industrial society, the main mechanism of capital accumulation was the market. "Production includes not merely the making of things, but the bringing of them to the consumer," he wrote. "The merchant or storekeeper is thus as truly a producer as is the manufacturer, or farmer, and his stock or capital is as much devoted to production as is theirs." The consumer market, that is, was as productive as the natural transformation of seeds into crops, so that capital was more precisely defined as "wealth in course of exchange."[78]

George made his case for conceiving capital in terms of relations of exchange in the process of elaborately refuting the orthodox "wages fund theory," which held that wages were determined by the ratio between the number of laborers and the amount of capital available for their payment. Closely related to the theory of natural scarcity, which indicated that workers' welfare was determined by the ratio of labor to land, the wages fund suggested that workers could gain collectively only by enlarging the total pool of capital relative to their numbers. Had he conceived of capital as the means of industrial production, much as land was the means of agricultural production, George logically would have argued that capital was made scarce artificially rather than naturally by private ownership, and that workers without access to capital, like those without access to land, were thereby obliged to pay "rent" for the use of their own labor. But he explicitly rejected such a Marxian critique.

The very terms with which George championed labor's traditional claim as the creator of wealth denied not only the wages fund theory but the more basic idea that labor was as dependent upon industrial capital for industry as it was upon land for agriculture. What modern industry really depended upon, his work suggested, was the "co-operation and exchange" that conferred market value upon land, purchasing power upon labor, and reproductive capacity upon capital. Market society appeared to possess the power to produce wealth from social exchange itself, raising the possibility that such a society could transcend the class divisions defined by ownership of land, labor, and capital as these factors of production were classically conceived.

Sumner's Critique of Natural Liberty

Like George, Sumner rejected the conventional notion that wages and profits came from a common fund. But while George maintained that labor produced its own wages, Sumner made the converse argument for capital's production of profits. "In no sense whatever does a man who accumulates a fortune by legitimate industry exploit his employés, or make his capital 'out of' anybody else. The wealth which he wins would not be but for him," he wrote in *What Social Classes Owe to Each Other*.[79] Accordingly, Sumner defined his "Forgotten Man" not as a laborer or landowner, but as "a capitalist, though never a great one."[80]

Despite Sumner and George's shared belief in the common interests of labor and capital, the two men took opposing sides in the developing class struggle of the late nineteenth century.[81] During the decade after their first major works were published, George became a leading standard-bearer for organized labor's massive political mobilization, while Sumner became the fighting priest of organized capital. In 1886, George was narrowly defeated in his campaign for New York City mayor as the candidate of the newly formed United Labor Party, while labor leaders ran for public office in thirty-four states and nearly two hundred cities. That same year saw more strikes than any previous year in American history and a crescendo of labor-led boycotts as well as the Haymarket Square bombing, which sparked a nationwide employer backlash against the rising labor movement.[82] The general upheaval prompted Sumner, who was renowned for his libertarian defense of laissez-faire, to reconsider and elaborate his ideas about the meaning of freedom in the context of class conflict. *The Independent*, a New York weekly founded before the Civil War as a platform for evangelical Congregationalism and antislavery polemic, provided a fitting forum for a long series of articles between 1887 and 1890 in which he sought to place the ideal of liberty on a new social-scientific foundation.[83]

The old foundation, as Sumner described it, comprised the social science of the French and American Revolutions a century earlier. In seeking to bring the social order into conformity with the "natural order," revolutionary political economy had conceived of liberty as a natural human endowment and birthright that free society must respect—a conception essentially compatible with the free labor ideology of the abolitionist movement and not unlike Sumner's own in *What Social Classes Owe to Each Other*. By the late 1880s, however, he recognized that the rise of industrial capitalism appeared to many laboring Americans to betray the revolutionary ideal of a republic of independent freemen and to render them rather the servants of capital. The popular epithets of "debt-slavery," "wages-slavery," and "tenant-slavery," he wrote, were inspired by the romantic myth of freedom as the natural, presocial state of man, which gave those bound by modern economic constraints a dangerously misguided sense of outraged entitlement. In a sense, the myth of natural liberty was for Sumner what that of natural scarcity was for George: a pernicious misconception concealing the greater truth within the science of wealth. By it, he believed, the venerable precepts of free labor and private property had been perverted into a renewed rationale for social revolution and a warrant for the sort of "socialistic measures" that he equated with pauperism, the very opposite of the true spirit of political economy.[84]

Sumner's ideological reconstruction of liberty betrayed a profound tension between the Lockean individualism of his earlier work and an increasingly conservative defense of social order and organization at the expense of individual freedom and proprietary independence. On the one hand, he deplored the vision of state socialism advocated by the Prussian monarchist Johann Karl Rodbertus, whom he oddly deemed "the master" of contemporary socialist thought, and who, he wrote, "defines liberty to be a share in the power of the state" rather than freedom from state control.[85] Yet at the same time, Sumner was deeply distressed by what he considered the "anarchistic" implications of the agrarian critique of land monopoly and/or wage labor trumpeted in various forms by American labor leaders, farmers' advocates, currency reformers, and avowed anarchists like those arrested in the Haymarket affair. So he strenuously rejected the argument of the Belgian political economist Emile de Laveleye that since liberty was a natural right, and since liberty required property in land or industrial capital, then such property in productive resources was itself a natural right to which all were equally entitled. Liberty, Sumner countered, was not something one was born with but something one "acquired" through effort and industry—and so too was property.[86]

Similarly, amid rising calls from the Knights of Labor and others for the abolition of the wage system, he lamented that the classical conception of economic independence had fostered false expectations concerning the relationship between liberty and labor. Labor, he wrote, was inherently a form of servitude rather than freedom, "a thraldom from which there is no escape." Implicitly departing from his earlier insistence that freedom meant working for oneself, Sumner wrote: "The term 'labor' cannot be taken in any narrower sense than that of contributions of any kind to the work of society, and, in that sense, we see that when we labor we set aside our liberty for the sake of some other good which we consider worth more to us under the circumstances." While acknowledging that the development of industrial capital and wage labor had "forced higher and more stringent organization" upon the workforce, entailing "in some respects more irksome restraints on individual liberty," he argued that such narrowing limits on the worker's freedom were necessary "in order to acquire greater power and win more ample sustenance for society." Those who deplored "wages slavery" wrongly imagined that liberty was rooted in individual human nature, timeless and inalienable. "But we have seen that liberty is not, and never can be, anything but an affair of social institutions, limited by their scope, and never reaching into any field of poetry or enthusiasm," he wrote.[87]

Sumner's defense against the increasingly militant critics of industrial capitalism moved him to disavow the traditional identification of freedom with independence, which he traced to the Rousseauian "notion that liberty was a primitive endowment of the race." Quite the opposite, he argued: the lone savage, "instead of furnishing a notion of liberty, furnishes an ideal of non-liberty; and liberty, instead of being a status at the beginning of civilization, appears rather to be a description of the sense and significance of civilization itself."[88]

Like the members of the American Social Science Association and other contemporary social critics across the political spectrum, he turned away from what C. B. Macpherson has called the "possessive individualism" of classical political economy and toward an organic vision of social order that viewed the individual as inherently a creature of social norms.[89] Sumner's earlier emphasis on laissez-faire therefore gave way to the organizational imperatives of "discipline," "responsibility," and liberty under law. "Men increase their power indefinitely by co-operation and organization, but in order to co-operate they must make concessions," he wrote.[90]

The organization Sumner had in mind, of course, was industrial capitalism. Capital accumulation, as he had written in *What Social Classes Owe to Each Other*, was "the reason why man is not altogether a brute," or what distinguished modern man from the savage.[91] In his essays on liberty, he identified capital more fully with the "co-operation and organization" that formed the foundation of modern civilization; capital appeared as a means of interdependence rather than independence. "We cannot get our living unless we get into the organization; when, however, we once get into it, it is ruin to fall out, but if we stay in, we must submit," he wrote. " . . . Where is there any liberty, in the sense of unconstrained self-will, for the civilized man? The declaimers about the ills of civilization are not astray in their facts; the civilized man is the slave of the industrial organization, of contracts, of the market, of supply and demand—call it what you will, it is after all, only the weight of existence."[92]

George's critique of natural scarcity carried him from an agrarian argument for labor's right to the use of land into a novel formulation of labor's primary claim upon the "co-operation and exchange" of the consumer market. In parallel fashion, Sumner's critique of natural liberty transformed his libertarian defense of the petty proprietor into an innovative case for capital's central stake in the "co-operation and organization" of industrial society. At the same time that they helped define the opposing parties in the class politics of the Gilded Age, they separately staked out the terrain of a classless new polity, a new social realm to be settled by modern American social science.

George's Cooperative Capitalism

"What I have done in this book," George wrote in *Progress and Poverty*, " . . . is to unite the truth perceived by the school of Smith and Ricardo to the truth perceived by the schools of Proudhon and Las[s]alle; to show that *laissez-faire* (in its full true meaning) opens the way to a realization of the noble dreams of socialism."[93] Like the French anarchist Pierre-Joseph Proudhon and the German social democrat Ferdinand Lassalle, as well as Henry Carey, though in very different ways, George envisioned a cooperative capitalism guided by the mutualist ideals of utopian socialism yet founded upon private property and free enterprise.[94]

Though his critique of land monopoly inspired the founding theorists of British socialism, and though American socialists supported his 1886 mayoral campaign, George swiftly dissociated himself from them after the election and denounced the idea of abolishing private property as vigorously as Sumner.[95] Not surprisingly, Marx dismissed George's work as a reactionary effort "to *save capitalist domination* and indeed to *establish it afresh on an ever wider basis* than its present one."[96] The American socialist Laurence Gronlund similarly argued that the socialization of rent would simply shift the distribution of capitalist "fleecings" from landlords to employers and financiers, while doing nothing to alter the fundamental exploitation of labor by capital. "George would, if he could, separate the Individual entirely from Society," Gronlund misleadingly wrote in an 1887 critique of the single tax. "But Society is an organism, whose members are interdependent even now to a much greater degree than it seems."[97]

To characterize George as an old-fashioned individualist, however, is to overlook his expansively cooperative vision of capitalism. No less than Gronlund, he embraced what he too called the increasing "interdependence" of industrial life, in which "the individual [becomes] more and more subordinate to society."[98] For George, the means of interdependence was the market, the social source of the productive power of land, labor, and capital as he reconceived them. Market society was not simply a neutral arena of contract, competition, and trade between independent producers, but a "collective power which is distinguishable from the sum of individual powers," a "social organism" or "Greater Leviathan" with its own will and force.[99] It was property in this distinctively social power, not in the material means of production, that he sought to socialize through the public appropriation of ground rent. After all, in his view the rising value of land derived from the limitless growth of societal cooperation and exchange, not from natural fertility or individual labor.

This new social sovereign that worked its will through market relations was the antithesis of the "invisible hand" that Adam Smith had described as the regulative resultant of individuals' competing self-interests. In language steeped in the liberal Christian faith in human holiness, George righteously rejected the idea that human nature was essentially selfish and that market society was necessarily predicated upon that principle. "Self-interest is, as it were, a mechanical force—potent, it is true; capable of large and wide results. But there is in human nature what may be likened to a chemical force; which melts and fuses and overwhelms," he wrote in *Progress and Poverty*. " . . . Call it religion, patriotism, sympathy, the enthusiasm for humanity, or the love of God—give it what name you will; there is yet a force which overcomes and drives out selfishness; a force which is the electricity of the moral universe; a force beside which all others are weak."[100] In the spirit of Auguste Comte's "Religion of Humanity" and its apostles in postbellum American social science, George found the wellspring of this "force of forces" in what he variously called "association," "integration," and "co-operation," a psychic fellowship that grew deeper and broader as the market expanded the sphere of social exchange outward to connect communities and inward to encompass every aspect of personal life. "[A]ssociation in equality is the law of progress," he wrote, echoing the Careyite gospel of "association" espoused by the greenback movement, which likewise seated this new socioeconomic power in the means of exchange. "The mental power," he continued, "which is the motor of social progress, is set free by association."[101] The emancipation of this psychic or spiritual force flowing from social exchange, rather than that of the "mechanical force" of self-interest, was what George meant by the "full true meaning" of laissez-faire.[102]

Poverty, as he ultimately conceived it, was not the slavery of individuals deprived of the full use of their labor power, but the slavery of society deprived of the full use of the psychosocial power of association. For poverty was the sole basis of self-interested individualism, the sole obstacle to the deeper human drives of sympathy and cooperation. "But an equitable distribution of wealth, that would exempt all from the fear of want, would destroy the greed of wealth," he wrote, still a materialist of sorts. In such a free society, "[w]ant might be banished, but desire would remain."[103] Liberated desire, George believed, would foster humanity's true social nature, replacing competition with cooperation and dissolving social conflict in spiritual solidarity. By freeing individuals from "want and the fear of want," he argued, the social appropriation of rent would bring an end to the myriad forms of oppression that stemmed from selfishness and would usher in the millennial age of eternal peace and plenty, in which society would reach unimagined heights of material as well as spiritual abundance. "For, greatest of all the enormous wastes which the present constitution of society involves, is that of mental power," he wrote. No longer compelled to "wast[e] their energies in the scramble to be rich," individuals would be able to develop their higher creative faculties. "Talents now hidden, virtues unsuspected, would come forth to make human life richer, fuller, happier, nobler."[104]

Finally freed from natural limits, society would feed on itself, prospering upon its limitless powers of association. "There would be a great and increasing surplus revenue from the taxation of land values, for material progress, which would go on with greatly accelerated rapidity, would tend constantly to increase rent," George wrote. " ... [W]e could establish public baths, museums, libraries, gardens, lecture rooms, music and dancing halls, theaters, universities, technical schools, shooting galleries, play grounds, gymnasiums, etc. Heat, light, and motive power, as well as water, might be conducted through our streets at public expense; our roads be lined with fruit trees; discoverers and inventors rewarded, scientific investigations supported; and in a thousand ways the public revenues made to foster efforts for the public benefit."[105]

George's cooperative utopia formed a revealing contrast with his picture of poverty. He envisioned emancipation not simply from exploitation, but from need, indeed from the pursuit of self-interest itself, the very standard of freedom and equality in the scarcity-minded science of political economy. His luxuriant vision of true progress was premised upon a science of social abundance instead of natural scarcity, of sympathetic association instead of self-interested independence, of boundless desire in place of the prisonhouse of want. Even as he deplored increasing economic inequality in traditional terms, George redefined those terms with reference to a new social psychology that echoed the themes of transcendental identity and social organicism in the American Romantics and their Comtean contemporaries. Like his antebellum predecessors, he subtly but decisively shifted the stakes of struggle over industrial capitalism from individual ownership and popular rule to participation in a socioeconomic mainstream. As property in productive resources became increasingly unequal, George pointed to a new kind of psychosocial power in which all might share alike, and he identified that power with market society itself.

Sumner's Social Psychology

On the opposite side of the ideological divide, Sumner's movement from political economy into social psychology was far more deliberate and complete.[106] Even before leaving the clergy, Sumner was captivated by Herbert Spencer's founding essays on sociology, and in 1876 he introduced the nation's first university course in the subject, with Spencer as his controversial text.[107] Sumner was quick to sense the significance of his English mentor's reconstruction of associationist psychology and Comtean sociology as a conservative new framework for economic individualism.[108] "What political economy needs in order to emerge from the tangle in which it is now involved," Sumner wrote in 1881, " ... is to find its field and its relations to other sciences fairly defined within the wider scope of sociology."[109] But it was not until a mental breakdown in

1890 left him permanently weakened that he ceased writing and teaching political economy and turned his entire attention to what he termed "the science of society," or what his students came to call "Sumnerology."[110]

Sumner's increasing identification of market society with "co-operation and organization," prompted by the class politics of the 1870s and 1880s, took new social-scientific form in light of the definitive advent of corporate capitalism in the 1890s and 1900s. The rise to economic dominance of giant, oligopolistic manufacturing firms through vertical integration and merger depended upon concurrent transformations in jurisprudence and social theory that endowed the modern business corporation with the constitutional rights of life, liberty, and property, rights formerly limited to individuals.[111] In a 1902 article for *The Independent*, Sumner embraced corporate consolidation as part of "a grand step in societal evolution," and he explained its importance in distinctly sociological terms. "[I]t is essential to recognize the concentration of wealth and control as a universal societal phenomenon, not merely as a matter of industrial power, or social sentiment, or political policy," he wrote. "Stated in the concisest terms, the phenomenon is that of a more perfect integration of all societal functions. The concentration of power (wealth), more dominant control, intenser discipline, and stricter methods are but modes of securing more perfect integration."[112]

In a celebrated lecture the following year, Sumner drew upon recent field studies in the young discipline of anthropology to argue that the "group" rather than the "individual" was the basic agent or "ultimate unit" of all social relations; the competition and struggle he had originally located among individuals was now revealed to take place primarily among groups.[113] Like other contemporary "group theorists" such as John Dewey, Charles Horton Cooley, and George Herbert Mead, Sumner indicated that individuals were essentially products of the social groups to which they belonged, rather than vice versa.[114] His earlier critique of natural rights gained newfound support from an emerging social psychology that dismissed the autonomous individual of classical political economy as an anachronistic myth. Seen in this way, corporate capitalism appeared to comport with the newly discovered nature of society itself: by socializing production, the concentration of capital was progressively reconstituting market society as a realm of social selfhood instead of proprietary independence.

Individuals' primary allegiance, Sumner now suggested, was not economic self-interest but "patriotic" identification with their families, communities, nations, and cultures. "The sentiment of cohesion, internal comradeship, and devotion to the in-group, which carries with it a sense of superiority to any out-group and readiness to defend the interests of the in-group against the out-group, is technically known as ethnocentrism," he wrote.[115] Cultural or "ethnic" affinity rather than common interest was the fundamental social bond, which began with the family and extended to the nation—a "peace-group" bound by "concord and sympathy," as Sumner called it, comparing the United States with the clan, tribe, or confederation of aboriginal peoples.[116]

Largely on this ethnocultural basis, he opposed the U.S. takeover of the former Spanish colonies in Cuba, Puerto Rico, and the Philippines. "The attempt to absorb into the body politic of the United States communities of entirely foreign antecedents, nationality, religion, language, *mores*, political education, institutions—in short, of a different culture and social education from ours" violated Sumner's growing sense of cultural solidarity, as he wrote in a series of articles on imperialism. Further, conceiving of both "industrialism" and "militarism" as cultural traits, he contended that the American military conquests in the Caribbean and the Pacific really represented the *cultural* conquest of the industrious United States by Spanish-style imperialism.[117] His opposition to imperialism marked his entrance into an anthropologically informed discourse of cultural identity, which redefined politics and economics in "ethnic," familial, or racial terms.[118]

Sumner's migration from political economy to a new master science of American society culminated in his monumental treatise of social psychology, *Folkways: A Study of the Sociological Importance of Usages, Manners, Customs, Mores, and Morals* (1906). Twenty years earlier, struggling with the incendiary implications of classical political economy's ideal of freedom, he had described "the family" as a sphere of unique social responsibility in which conventional notions of liberty had no place, and "monogamic marriage" as a "great monopoly" in which the usual rules of the competitive market did not apply.[119] By the early twentieth century, the exception had become the rule. Monopoly capital dominated the market, and Sumner accordingly expanded his vision of familial relations into a model of market society as a whole.

Much as many Progressive social scientists envisioned the burgeoning "social realm" as an extension of the "domestic sphere" of marriage and family, he reconceived society in terms of the emotional ties and mutual responsibilities commonly attributed to family life. His conventional interpretation of the sexual division of labor, in particular, provided the lens through which he viewed economic relations in general. "The sexes differ so much in structure and function, and consequently in traits of feeling and character, that their interests are antagonistic. At the same time they are, in regard to reproduction, complementary," Sumner wrote. Such "antagonistic cooperation," he contended, "presents us the germ of the industrial organization."[120] That is, industrial relations were patterned upon the reciprocal roles and complementary functions of the marital relation. Sexual difference provided Sumner with a paradigm for understanding social conflict as a manifestation of individuals' differing "societal functions" and accordingly conflicting "traits of feeling and character," while finding the basis of social unity in an increasingly "integrated" economy. The "antagonistic cooperation" that he had earlier grounded in the competitive market found a new home in his familial conception of the corporate order.[121]

In this way, Sumner charted an alternative to the ideological battleground of political economy, entailing a fundamental redefinition of the core concept of class. Rather than ownership of labor, land, or capital, "class" denoted individuals' "classification" according to their ever-changing position in the statistical distribution of "self-realization" or "societal value," meaning their "intellectual, moral, economic, and physical" capacities relative to a societal norm. "Each individual falls into his place by virtue of his characteristic differences," Sumner wrote, so that classification established a new basis for individuality as well as for class. "Two things result," he noted. "(1) The classification gives us the notion of the relative position of one, or a subdivision, in the entire group. This is the sense of 'class.' (2) The characteristic differences furnish the notion of individuality and personality."[122] Such progressive "differentiation" of individuals along a bell curve of social value formed the statistical counterpart of his organicist model of market society, and together they supplanted the earlier understanding of class relations.[123]

The central importance of statistical normality in *Folkways* led Sumner to introduce a new prototypical American, a successor to the "Forgotten Man" of his earlier work: the "common man," whom he also called the "man on the mode," the "average man," and the "man in the street."[124] The common man was defined not by petty proprietorship, but by his membership in what Sumner now called the "masses," the broad middle stratum of American society whose principal asset was no longer productive property but social norms. "The masses are the real bearers of the mores of the society," he wrote. "They carry tradition. The folkways are their ways."[125] In his seminal theory of folkways, Sumner described in detail the psychosocial power that coursed through the corporation, the group, the mass, and the average man. "[T]he folkways are the widest, most fundamental, and most important operation by which the interests of men in groups are served. . . . The life of society consists in making folkways and applying them. The science of society might be construed as the study of them," he wrote.[126]

He coined the term "folkway" to describe "habits of the individual and customs of society" that originated in "primitive notions," such as "goblinism" and "demonism," that eventually became "regulative for succeeding generations" and that gradually assumed "the character of a social force." This force was irrational, instinctive, even unconscious; the folkways were "not creations of human purpose and wit."[127] The "mores," according to Sumner, were simply folkways with the added sanction of ethical value and an added imperative to obey. Among them were social institutions ostensibly based on affection or devotion, such as marriage and religion, as well as political and economic institutions such as private property, free enterprise, and representative government. "We learn the mores as unconsciously as we learn to walk and eat and breathe," he wrote. "The masses never learn how we walk, and eat, and breathe, and they never know any reason why the mores are what they are. The justification of them is that when we wake to consciousness of life we find them facts which already hold us in the bonds of tradition, custom, and habit."[128]

Sumner's description of the unappealable authority of the mores echoed his wistful comments many years earlier about the power of industrial organization. "The most important fact about the mores is their dominion over the individual," he wrote. " ... If he submits and consents, he is taken up and may attain great social success. If he resists and dissents, he is thrown out and may be trodden underfoot."[129] The reigning power in market society, Sumner suggested, was not property or production, not competition or contract, the keywords of classical political economy. It was "suggestion," the irresistible force of public opinion, the power of social psychology. The invisible hand was giving way to the mass mind.

Conclusion

While George and Sumner represented the opposing sides of the class politics of the late nineteenth century, they were united by a shared belief in the fundamental identity of interests between labor and capital in a market society. That common interest of the "producing classes" was originally rooted in early American political economy and the agrarian republic it described, in which ownership of labor and capital were typically united in the same household. As American society came to be dominated by wage labor and industrial capital as separate classes, the agrarian ideal of a nation of independent proprietors appeared to bolster the conflicting claims of both sides in the spiraling conflict. In that context, their common commitment to market society as the basis of class harmony rather than strife led both Sumner and George to make a double movement away from classical political economy.

First, they each shifted away from the classical model of the market as a neutral arena of contract, competition, and commerce among autonomous producers and toward a vision of market society as a wellspring of cooperation and organization that delegated its power to individuals rather than vice versa. Second, they defined the bountiful social force of market society in the terms not of political economy but of modern sociology and psychology. In other words, they reconceived the individual's relationship to society not in terms of ownership of productive resources but in terms of participation in a mainstream of guiding desires and compelling social norms. They both described a socialism of the psyche that appeared to transcend the very basis of class conflict in political economy and to rest upon a new master science of American society, affording a new foundation for social harmony. In so doing, they helped to reestablish the parameters of political debate upon a new terrain of socialized desires and needs, instead of individual rights and powers.

Sumner's and George's parallel movements from the tradition of political economy to the frontier of social psychology heralded not an end to the ideological struggle over power and wealth in the emerging industrial era, but a new set of stakes. Like many contemporary partisans of the propertyless, from trade unionists to free-silver Populists to Progressive social scientists and social reformers, George translated traditional agrarian claims upon productive resources into new terms. The natural right to the products of one's labor, and the corollary right to farm one's own land, were transformed in his work into a newly "social" right to a decent standard of living, to a consumer's stake in the cultural and intellectual as well as material abundance made possible by market society itself. Similarly, Sumner ultimately joined the effort by enlightened capitalists and their managerial allies to recast the earlier faith in economic individualism and the competitive market. The defense of the acquisitive entrepreneur's private profits yielded, in Sumner's later work, to a rationale for corporate reorganization as a means of socializing people as well as property, in order to maximize the productivity and prosperity of society as a whole. Together, Sumner and George represent a momentous shift by both the right and the left wings of American social thought onto a new ideological battleground, marked less by the old struggle over property in land, labor, and capital than by a new contest over the management of the corporate economy and the consumer market.

In viewing the transition from agrarian to industrial capitalism as a call for a new science of market society, they provided a bridge between the antebellum innovations of Transcendentalist and Comtean writers and the postbellum emergence of professional, academic social science. With the rise of the modern disciplines of sociology and psychology around the turn of the century, and with the accompanying breakup of political economy into the technical fields of political science and economics, the Romantic reconstruction of selfhood and society moved from the margin to the mainstream of American social thought.

CHAPTER FIVE

The "New Psychology" of the Gilded Age

William James, John Dewey, and G. Stanley Hall

How selfish soever man be supposed, there are evidently some principles in his nature, which interest him in the fortune of others, and render their happiness necessary to him, though he derives nothing from it, except the pleasure of seeing it." So wrote Adam Smith in *The Theory of Moral Sentiments* (1759), in words that gained new significance for American social scientists amid the industrial strife of the late nineteenth century.[1] As the pursuit of self-interest that formed the beneficent basis of the *Wealth of Nations* increasingly represented an incitement to class war, liberal social theorists rediscovered Smith's earlier work, with its exaltation of the natural human propensity for sympathy and the paramount desire for social esteem.[2] If, as the preeminent theorist of "economic man" himself had written, "it is chiefly from this regard to the sentiments of mankind, that we pursue riches and avoid poverty," then the draconian dictates of political economy might be appealed to the higher tribunal of social psychology. The "invisible hand" of the market might yield to what Smith called the "impartial spectator" of conscience, the emissary of society "within the breast," whose sentiments formed the ultimate object of sympathy and the basis of self-esteem.[3]

For Smith and his contemporaries on both sides of the Atlantic, the science of sentiment and the science of wealth were adjoining aspects of a single moral philosophy predicated upon the revolutionary principle of autonomous self-hood, or mental as well as material "self-command." The "prudence" with which the independent proprietor looked after the interests of his household enabled, though it did not ensure, his regard for others' rights and needs, in a free society ostensibly ruled by the common sense of reason and the common law of property.[4] The Smithian vision of reason as the mastery of one's passions and of property as the mastery of one's labor and land provided a fragile basis for societal cohesion in the early American household republic.

By the nation's centennial, however, the agrarian model of self-command at the base of the *Theory of Moral Sentiments* as well as the *Wealth of Nations* appeared dangerously divisive to the pioneers of modern American social science. As the competitive market opened a widening divide between ownership and productive labor, economic writers such as Henry Carey and Henry George embraced the independent spirit of the classical science of wealth while radically revising the core concepts of value and class. The Gilded Age inheritors of Scottish "mental philosophy" or "psychology," as it had come to be called, confronted a related divide between the individual moral agency they cherished and a material world that seemed increasingly governed by the impersonal laws of supply and demand and survival of the fittest.[5] The "labor question" that concerned Carey and George appeared to leading American mental philosophers as a question of willpower rather than labor power, much as it had in Emerson's Romantic psychology of self-reliance. The crisis of capitalism manifested for them a deeper crisis of autonomous selfhood. But like their contemporaries in political economy, the philosophical founders of the "new psychology" invoked the spirit of Smithian science even as they fundamentally reconstructed the model of mental self-mastery at its heart.

Two of the foremost theorists of the new field around the turn of the century—William James, whose *Principles of Psychology* (1890) remains the single most important American treatise on the subject and the point of departure for virtually all subsequent work, and his leading disciple, John Dewey, whose pathbreaking exploration of the social dimensions of the Jamesian psyche made him the most influential exponent of modern American social psychology—are now better-known for their subsequent work in formulating the philosophy of Pragmatism. A third pioneering psychologist of far less renown today, G. Stanley Hall, often considered the founder of educational as well as child psychology in the United States, is similarly remembered for his broadly philosophical writings on mental growth in individuals and in the human species. While all three were acknowledged leaders in the establishment of an experimental psychology newly distinguished from philosophy, their common reliance upon armchair psychologizing in framing many of their main ideas quickly became outmoded in the scientific discipline they helped to create.[6] So too, succeeding generations of American psychologists abandoned or reduced to narrowly technical terms the central philosophical issue to which James, Dewey, and Hall addressed their psychological work—the problem of human will—much as mainstream twentieth-century economists were able to leave behind the "labor question" that preoccupied their nineteenth-century forebears.[7]

The relationship between willpower and labor power, the fundamental faculties of human nature in early American political economy, holds a key to the breakdown of the classical social science and the emergence of modern social psychology as a new master science of self and society. So while their combined effort to reconceive the bond between labor and will, or body and soul, has rendered James, Dewey, and Hall of more historical interest than continuing relevance to psychologists, that shared enterprise gave them a leading role in the transformation of American social science and social thought in the late nineteenth century. From their common reconception of Smithian self-command, they derived an enduring understanding of the meaning of freedom, best articulated by James; of the meaning of democracy, most fully developed by Dewey; and of the nature of historical development or progress, described most clearly by Hall.

The Problem of Willpower

Much as others sought to redefine the embattled ideal of economic autonomy, so James, Dewey, and Hall aimed to reconstitute the Enlightenment faith in free will in response to the new challenges of the industrial age. Chief among those challenges, from their perspective, was the heightening tension between Christian faith and evolutionary science. They traced the roots of that cultural conflict to the distinction between spirit and substance, or subjective and objective phenomena, that had framed Enlightenment philosophy from René Descartes to Immanuel Kant. Revolutionary Era writers had united virtue and wealth, moral philosophy and political economy, in the figure of the sovereign self, whose command of his passions as well as his labor embodied the uniquely human conquest of mind over matter. But as the social basis of the republican synthesis appeared to collapse under the weight of market society in the nineteenth century, the Cartesian dualism came to inform two rival psychological traditions.[8]

The English empiricist school of Hobbes and Locke, with its model of the mind as a blank slate upon which sensory data were inscribed and "associated," inspired radical hopes for social engineering in the new nation.[9] But in the mid-nineteenth century, "associationist" writers drew upon studies in psychophysiology and neurology in reducing mental phenomena to brain states or reflexive responses to physical stimuli, relegating consciousness to a marginal role.[10] In the Revolutionary Era, the competing Scottish rationalist tradition of faculty psychology likewise bolstered radical notions of natural right and self-evident truth. But in the nineteenth century, American colleges joined Scottish "common sense" and Kantian transcendentalism in promulgating an increasingly dogmatic defense of religious faith.[11]

By the time James, Dewey, and Hall began writing in the late 1870s, both psychological traditions were running up against their limits. Neurologists' inability to identify the somatic cause and cure of many apparent mental ailments contributed to the rise of new psychotherapies that shared a more holistic approach to mind and body and a new scientific respect for the power of the unconscious.[12] At the same time, the aging faculty psychology proved unequal to the challenge of Darwinian evolution, prompting a group of recent Harvard graduates—James among them—to forge their own innovative accommodation between faith and science. Accepting the argument of the Scottish philosopher Alexander Bain, the leading contemporary associationist, that beliefs were essentially tendencies to respond to stimuli in certain ways, these scholars reasoned that the validity of beliefs—whether religious or scientific—consisted in the success of their corresponding behavior. In terms that echoed the logic of natural selection, the members of what came to be called the "Metaphysical Club" contended that the fittest beliefs were those with the best practical results, much as liberal theologians like Horace Bushnell defended the instrumental validity of faith in enabling believers to lead godly lives.[13]

To James, Dewey, and Hall, the contemporary debates over neuropathy and mental illness, belief and behavior, cast the hoary mind-body problem in a new light, centered upon the nature of human will. They extended the associationist argument—advanced in turn by David Hume, Bain, and the English neurologist David Ferrier before them—that the conventional image of the mind's power over the body was largely illusory. Virtually all action originated not in any mental effort or command, but in an unthinking, automatic response, the only difference between "voluntary" and "involuntary" behavior being that the former was immediately triggered by force of habit rather than simple reflex. But they emphatically rejected the associationist conclusion that the mind was essentially a passive spectator, consciousness a mere shadow play projected by muscles and nerves. Embracing instead the Kantian conception of an active ego that conferred sense and structure upon the world, they argued that the real role of the will lay in focusing attention upon certain ideas, certain habits or beliefs, rather than others—in deliberately "dissociating" discrete thoughts from the senseless, seamless jumble of experience, not just mechanically "associating" separate sensations. Though individuals could not directly decide what they did, they could control what they thought, knowing that their beliefs tended to mold their automatic actions.

The new meaning of self-command lay in what James famously called the "will to believe," the central premise of his psychological reconstruction of freedom as a matter of habit and faith rather than property and "prudence." That changed understanding of willpower similarly informed Dewey's redefinition of democracy in terms of common identity rather than collective interest, as well as Hall's picture of societal progress as a process of mental maturation instead of individual competition or class struggle.

For the architects of the new psychology as for the framers of political economy a century earlier, free will was not just a philosophical abstraction. It was a practical principle of everyday life, whose significance derived from its concrete consequences for individuals and society. The hallmarks of the new model of the mind were action, practice, and willpower, lending psychological sanction to the Metaphysical Club's "pragmatic maxim" that the meaning of ideas lay in the tangible results of believing them. In its conflation of faith and works, the new psychology earned the allegiance of Progressive reformers, who found in it scientific support for the new social gospel, along with the lasting disdain of romantic critics such as Lewis Mumford, who viewed its philosophical offspring in Pragmatism as the epitome of crass American utilitarianism, sacrificing higher truth and culture on the altar of industry.[14]

What sharply distinguished the new notion of willpower from the old, however, was the flip side of the identification of thought with action: the psychologizing of action itself. If beliefs were measured in behavior, so too the sole "significance" of behavior lay in the beliefs it entailed. If the new psychology identified instincts and ideas, faith and feeling, with what James called their "cash value" in material terms, it conversely reconceived material relations, private property, and social power, wholly in terms of their psychological value or mental meaning. While Adam Smith's analysis of self-interest as a means of self-esteem in *The Theory of Moral Sentiments* echoed in the new psychology, his understanding of interest itself as a matter of legal and economic right yielded to the conception of interest as mental "attention," or subjective rather than objective value.[15] The principle that practice was the test of truth took on new meaning when practice was identified with the psychological effect or significance of activity.

Seen in this way, the proof of the new psychology itself ultimately resided in the psychological results of living by its precepts. James, Dewey, and Hall each described his work as a personal liberation and resolution of psychological conflict, which they—like many later scholars—took to be representative of a collective crisis of identity afflicting American society. Their new model of selfhood, they believed, held the remedy for the inner turmoil that had given rise to widespread social unrest. The therapeutic character of the new psychology has long attracted critical scrutiny from historians as an opiate of the bourgeoisie, enabling anxious intellectuals to avert their eyes from the alienating effects of industrialization, and as a straitjacket for the masses, compelling individual adjustment instead of collective resistance.[16] In recent years, however, more sympathetic scholars have highlighted the ways in which the search for psychic well-being dovetailed with Progressive efforts to humanize and harmonize the new economic order, to make industry fit for humanity instead of the other way around.[17] More generally, the neopragmatist renaissance in intellectual history, as in many other fields, has tended to displace the New Left critiques of "corporate liberalism" or "social control" with a renewed appreciation for the "lost promise of Progressivism" as well as the social science that informed it.[18]

To be sure, the "will to believe" was meant as a call for enlightened action, not an open warrant for wishful thinking, despite what many of its later apostles as well as detractors read into it. Yet the psychologizing of action itself at the heart of the new psychology can help explain why the philosophical liberalism and egalitarianism of thinkers such as James and Dewey proved in many ways compatible with the benevolent dictatorship of capital and its army of experts envisioned by more administratively minded Progressive reformers such as Hall.[19] Like the Transcendental tradition upon which it built, the new psychology betrayed a profound tension between utopian dissent and ideological apologetic. At their most ambitious, its founding theorists sought to refashion political and economic relations in the image of social psychology, an image of liberated desire in place of pressing need, of social sentiment instead of selfishness. But by redefining freedom, democracy, and progress in terms of self-expression instead of self-interest, they reconceived the very categories of political economy—labor and property, value and class—in essentially psychological rather than material terms as well. As a result, even as they emphatically identified thought with practice, they reconciled mental autonomy with material dependence in ways the Cartesian science of mind over matter never could. Therein lay the ironic secret of the new psychology's success, and therefore its pragmatic validity, in a nation dominated by wage labor and finance capital.

William James's Psychology of Freedom

In the celebrated psychodrama of his life and work, William James (1842–1910) exemplified the ambiguous relationship between mental and material freedom described by the new psychology. Blessed by his illustrious family with financial independence as well as unbounded educational and vocational opportunity, he was famously cursed by neurasthenia, depression, and crippling self-doubt, along with a host of psychosomatic ailments. Little wonder that he came to regard himself as his own worst enemy, or that his triumph over psychological debility represented for him a new model of self-command.[20]

At the same time, the healing power with which James saved himself gave him a mental Midas touch, casting the material misfortune of others in a liberating new light. He "would lend life and charm to a treadmill," wrote his younger sister, Alice James, whose own chronic nervous condition left her an invalid for much of her 43 years.[21] Like its creator, James's psychology bestowed the spirit of free agency upon the quickening treadmill of industrial life— upon the specialization of knowledge, the socialization of industry, the dispossession of labor, and the consolidation of capital that spelled the demise of the autonomous individual conceived in classical political economy. In so doing, his work encapsulated both the emancipatory promise and the ideological accommodation entailed in the new social science.

Long regarded as an essentially apolitical thinker, James has been rediscovered in recent years by scholars who have found particularly in his later writings, after his main contributions to psychology, the emergence of a political vision variously identified with Progressivism, anarchism, socialism, or populism.[22] But his psychological studies of the late 1870s and 1880s, culminating in the *Principles of Psychology*, carried a profoundly political burden that anchored his subsequent work in Pragmatism, "radical empiricism," and cultural criticism. The psychological reconception of freedom at the base of his earlier writings informed his later understanding of a wide range of social issues, from mental hygiene to imperialism to class relations.[23]

James's warm sensitivity to psychological issues derived, in turn, from his brilliantly self-absorbed family—especially from his sister, whose posthumously published diary and letters sparkle with introspective insight; from his younger brother, the expatriate novelist Henry James Jr., who took consciousness as his central subject; and above all from his father, the eccentric theologian Henry James Sr., to whom he once wrote he owed his whole "intellectual life."[24] A prolific writer of little-read treatises on the relationship between society and spirituality, James Sr. supported his family on his inheritance from his own father, a wealthy merchant, banker, and landowner whose values of capitalist accumulation and Calvinist morality he rigorously repudiated. Much like his friend Emerson, James Sr. declared that "the curse of mankind is its sense of selfhood," more specifically the ideal of proprietary independence that made "a man feel that he has an absolute or independent selfhood."[25] He drew upon the teachings of the Swedish scientist-prophet Emanuel Swedenborg as well as the early socialist Charles Fourier in exalting self-expressive rather than self-interested labor, for its spiritual rather than economic value, and in likewise disavowing "any special system of social organization" in favor of "a perfect fellowship or society among men."[26] Yet he attributed his main inspiration not to other writers, but to his spiritual rebirth, sparked by an episode of sudden, soul-shattering terror.[27]

The elder James's account of his idiosyncratic conversion was eerily echoed in William James's renowned description, in *The Varieties of Religious Experience*, of his own traumatic experience as a young medical student. Exempted from the Civil War draft on account of physical frailty, James had drifted disconsolately from an early interest in painting into the Lawrence Scientific School and finally into Harvard Medical School, from which he had graduated in 1869. Plagued by deepening depression and thoughts of suicide, he had retreated to his parents' house, where he soon suffered the "panic fear" that ultimately propelled him into academic psychology.

"[S]uddenly there fell upon me . . . a horrible fear of my own existence," he recalled. The immediate cause was the memory of an epileptic patient he had seen in a mental asylum, whom he described as "entirely idiotic" and motionless as a mummy. "*That shape am I*, I felt, potentially," he wrote. " . . . It was like a revelation; and although the immediate feelings passed away, the experience has made me sympathetic with the morbid feelings of others ever since." That same year, Henry George's shock at the opulence and indigence of New York City prompted his mystical revelation of the cause of poverty amid progress. But the "sick soul" in which James saw himself posed a starkly contrasting dilemma: material wealth could not ensure mental health. "Nothing that I possess can defend me against that fate," he wrote, "if the hour for it should strike for me as it struck for him." James's paralyzing dread of the mental patient seemed to demonstrate that mental morbidity, like physical mortality, was ruthlessly egalitarian. Faith alone, in "scripture-like texts" of divine salvation, kept him from going "really insane."[28]

The kernel of Jamesian psychology lay in his ensuing discovery that the saving power of faith arose from the mind itself. In his graduate studies at Harvard and for eighteen months in Germany, James had learned biology from Louis Agassiz, physiology from Hermann von Helmholtz and Claude Bernard, pathology from Rudolf Virchow. But his central psychological principle drew less from his scientific study of the body than from the faith in the mind that he took from the French philosopher Charles Renouvier, as James's biographer Ralph Barton Perry has shown.[29] A leading theorist of the new liberalism of the Third Republic in the 1870s, Renouvier had renounced an early commitment to utopian socialism after 1848, turning his attention to devising a philosophical alternative to the discredited republican radicalism of the French Revolution. His Kantian vision of freedom through faith inspired the fin-de-siècle French sociologist Émile Durkheim as well as James, for whom Renouvier was as much savior as mentor.[30] "I think that yesterday was a crisis in my life," James wrote in his diary in April 1870. "I finished the first part of Renouvier's second 'Essais' and see no reason why his definition of Free Will—'the sustaining of a thought *because I choose to* when I might have other thoughts'—need be the definition of an illusion. . . . My first act of free will shall be to believe in free will."[31]

To act freely was to think freely, to choose to believe. That was the radical insight upon which James built the towering edifice of the *Principles of Psychology* over the course of a dozen years, while teaching the subject at Harvard and writing articles for the *Journal of Speculative Philosophy*, founded by the leading American philosopher William Torrey Harris, as well as Alexander Bain's journal, *Mind*, along with occasional pieces for *Scribner's Monthly* and other periodicals. While drawing extensively upon the faculty psychology upheld by Harris as well as upon the associationist school represented by Bain, James sharply departed from both traditions in developing his psychology of free will, much as he later founded his version of Pragmatism upon a simultaneous reconciliation and rejection of "tender-minded" ("idealistic," "religious") and "tough-minded" ("materialistic," "irreligious") philosophy.[32]

To act freely, he agreed with Bain and other exponents of "sensori-motor" neurology, did not mean to direct one's body with one's mind. "[T]he only *essential* point in which 'the new psychology' is an advance upon the old, is . . . [the] notion, that all our activity belongs at bottom to the type of reflex action," James wrote.[33] All bodily action was essentially automatic. The "feeling of effort" associated with such action derived not from the mind's mastery over the muscles, but from the sensation of "tense muscles, strained ligaments, squeezed joints, fixed chest, closed glottis, contracted brow, clenched jaws, etc., etc.," unintentionally responding to external stimuli.[34] In this respect, the feeling of effort was no different than any other feeling associated with bodily expression, as James argued in his well-known analysis of emotion. In every case, the feeling actually registered the physical reaction, rather than vice versa. "[T]he more rational statement is that we feel sorry because we cry, angry because we strike, afraid because we tremble, and not that we cry, strike, or tremble, because we are sorry, angry, or fearful," he explained.[35]

Once an external stimulus became associated with a particular response, however, the mere memory or idea of the original cause tended to reproduce the same sensori-motor reaction—just as the thought of the epileptic patient brought on James's panic attack. Likewise, the "anticipatory image" of a remembered reaction would cause a person to act in the same way without external prompting. The "voluntary" element of such habitual action, as opposed to "involuntary" reflex, consisted not in any active mental command over the body, but in the mind's passive "consent" to recall a certain action and so cause it to recur.[36]

Hence the premium that James placed upon habit formation as the main means of acting in accord with one's designs. "The great thing . . . is to *make our nervous system our ally instead of our enemy*," he wrote. "It is to fund and capitalize our acquisitions, and live at ease upon the interest of the fund."[37] In characteristically appropriating the language of the market, James did not reduce mental philosophy to political economy, as antimodern critics like Mumford have charged, so much as he reconceived political-economic dynamics as psychological phenomena. In place of the rational pursuit of self-interest, he urged self-training in healthy habits. Instead of the social contract, he described habit as the foundation of social order and class harmony. "Habit is thus the enormous fly-wheel of society, its most precious conservative agent," he wrote. "It alone is what keeps us all within the bounds of ordinance, and saves the children of fortune from the envious uprisings of the poor. It alone prevents the hardest and most repulsive walks of life from being deserted by those brought up to tread therein."[38]

Yet the behavioral treadmill that James described was enlivened by a new psychic freedom. People were not merely creatures of habit, contrary to the arguments of Hume and Bain. As adamantly as Christian theologians and their philosophical allies, James denied that humans were soulless automatons whose "thoughts" were simply chains of physical sensations. He drew on the English idealist Thomas Hill Green's critique of Humean skepticism in arguing that mental life did not comprise discrete sensory "atoms" or "*separate* parts" mechanically combined in the nervous system, but rather formed a continuous "stream of consciousness," in James's famous phrase. "The traditional psychology talks like one who should say a river consists of nothing but pailsful, spoonsful, quartpotsful, barrelsful, and other moulded forms of water," he wrote. "Even were the pails and the pots all actually standing in the stream, still between them the free water would continue to flow. It is just this free water of consciousness that psychologists overlook."[39] In James's view, the distinguishing feature of the human mind was its capacity to select particular elements from the stream of inchoate consciousness and so form intelligible thoughts out of an otherwise meaningless whirl. "My experience is what I agree to attend to," he wrote. "Only those items which I notice shape my mind—without selective interest, experience is an utter chaos."[40]

In this psychological sense of selective attention, "interest" formed the essential instrument of free will in James's work. While behavior was controlled by reflex or habit, thought was governed by force of will. Free will figured not in the body's obedience to the dictates of the mind, but in the mind's ability to think as it willed. "*To sustain a representation, to think,* is what requires the effort, and is the true moral act," he wrote.[41]

Though he repudiated the Cartesian dualism of mind and body in his treatment of behavior, he conceived of free will in explicitly mental *as opposed to* physical terms. Just as behavior entailed no exercise of willpower, willpower required no bodily manifestation. "Now notice in all this, whether the act do follow or not upon the representation is a matter quite immaterial as far as the *willing* of the act represented goes," he wrote. " . . . [V]olition is a psychic or moral fact pure and simple, and is absolutely completed when the *intention* or *consent* is there. The supervention of motion upon its completion is a supernumerary phenomenon belonging to the department of physiology exclusively, and depending on the organic structure and condition of executive ganglia, whose functioning is quite unconscious."[42] His reconception of human willpower and the freedom it conferred as matters of belief rather than behavior underlay the converse claim, in his classic essay on "The Will to Believe" and in *The Varieties of Religious Experience*, that belief was essentially a matter of will.[43] As he concluded in *The Principles of Psychology*, "Volition is primarily a relation, not between our self and extra-mental matter (as many philosophers still maintain), but between our self and our own states of mind."[44]

James's depiction of the will as a relation between "self" and "states of mind" underpinned a new model of selfhood itself in his *Principles*. Just as he adopted the empiricist account of feeling as a function of behavior, so he conceived "self-feeling," or the sense of oneself, as an "empirical and verifiable thing" rather than a "pure principle" or transcendental ego.[45] "*In its widest possible sense,*" he wrote, " . . . *a man's Self is the sum total of all that he* CAN *call his,* not only his body and his psychic powers, but his clothes and his house, his wife and children, his ancestors and friends, his reputation and works, his lands and horses, and yacht and bank-account."[46]

In identifying the "empirical self" with health, wealth, and social status, James subtly but sharply transformed the model of proprietary autonomy in classical social science. Much as he described behavior as the result of reflex or habit instead of conscious effort, so he envisioned the empirical building blocks of selfhood as objects of unconscious instinct rather than deliberate design. "Egoistic interests" in one's body, one's family, and one's property, no less than loftier human desires for social esteem and spiritual fulfillment, derived alike from "blind impulse." "[A]ll the shiftings and expansions and contractions of the sphere of what shall be considered me and mine, are but results of the fact that certain *things* appeal to primitive and instinctive impulses of our nature, and that we shall follow their destinies with an excitement that owes nothing to a reflective source. These objects our consciousness treats as the primordial constituents of its Me," he wrote. "Our *interest in things*" referred not to ownership but to the "attention and emotion which the thought of them will excite."[47]

In his analysis of the relationship between self and world as well as that of mind and body, James, like Emerson before him, disavowed what the philosopher Charles Taylor has called the "instrumental stance" from which both labor and wealth conferred power upon the possessor.[48] In place of active, intentional appropriation or ownership in a political-economic sense, James described a process of passive, involuntary identification of the self with its material constituents. "It appears as if all our concrete manifestations of selfishness might be the conclusions of as many syllogisms, each with this principle as the subject of its major premise, thus: Whatever is me is precious; this is me; therefore this is precious," he wrote.[49]

Yet in the same way that James banished free will from the realm of behavior but reincarnated it in the realm of belief, he undermined the older mental as well as material meaning of self-ownership only to redefine it in exclusively psychological terms. As in his discussion of volition, his treatment of "consciousness of self" reintroduced a Kantian distinction between the objective, unconscious "empirical self," or "Me," instinctively identified with worldly goods, and a subjective, deliberate "Thinker," or "I," which selectively claimed the objects that made up the empirical self as parts of a single identity. Here too, he took up where Emerson, who had replaced the Cartesian dualism with a new relation between "me" and "not me," left off. Over and beyond what James called the sense of "sciousness," the intuitive identification of self and world, humans uniquely possessed the "conscious" ability to choose which objects of their instincts to mentally focus upon and which to overlook, just as the will chose to attend to certain thoughts rather than others. Though James rejected the notion of a static, metaphysical soul or ego in favor of a continuous "stream of thought," he nevertheless endowed the "passing Thought" itself with the capacity not only to "remember those which went before" but also to "emphasize and care paramountly for certain ones among them as '*me*,' and *appropriate to these* the rest."[50]

Once again, the element of free choice shifted from the appropriation of "extra-mental matter" to the appropriation of "states of mind." The act of ownership, like that of will, mediated not between self and world or mind and body, but between the "I" and the "Me," or "the empirical person and the judging Thought."[51] "It seems as if the elementary psychic fact were not *thought* or *this thought* or *that thought*, but *my thought*, every thought being *owned*," he wrote.[52] More broadly, humans enjoyed the fundamental freedom to choose which elements of their "empirical selves" to develop and which to let go. Neither innate instincts nor their natural objects were for individuals to decide, according to James, but "personal identity" as well as beliefs were products of free will. Self-determination meant determining one's identity, and in this the mind was basically free. "So our self-feeling in this world depends entirely on what we *back* ourselves to be and do," he wrote. " . . . Once more, then, our self-feeling is in our power."[53]

James was not unmindful of the need for material objects for those instincts with which individuals chose to identify, and of the resulting potential for material deprivation to hinder the exercise of psychic self-determination. Though he noted that "self-esteem" could be enhanced as easily by reducing one's "pretensions" as by increasing one's "success," he allowed that "a sort of starvation of objects" might prove an insuperable obstacle to mental health. "Compare the accomplished gentleman with the poor artisan or tradesman of a city: during the adolescence of the former, objects appropriate to his growing interests, bodily and mental, were offered as fast as the interests awoke, and, as a consequence, he is armed and equipped at every angle to meet the world," James wrote. " . . . Over the city poor boy's youth no such golden opportunities were hung, and in his manhood no desires for most of them exist. . . . [P]erversions are too often the fruit of his unnatural bringing up."[54] The problem of poverty was not the slave wages for which it forced people to work, as Henry George held, but rather the damage it did to their identity or "psychic constitution," and the different danger it therefore posed to the "mental hygiene" (as his concern came to be called) of society as a whole. James's psychology did not render invisible the broader problem of social inequality at the center of American political culture at the time he wrote, but it provided a new way of understanding what was at stake.

In a talk to college students in the 1890s revealingly entitled, "What Makes a Life Significant," James offered his only explicit psychological exploration of class relations.[55] He began with a rhapsodic description of the "middle-class paradise" to be found in the vacation resort on Chautauqua Lake in upstate New York, with its fine homes and model schools, its freedom from poverty, crime, and disease. "You have the best of company, and yet no effort," he wrote, and that was the trouble. With no need of invigorating struggle, no bounty of hardship, the fantasyland of "bourgeoisie and mediocrity" appeared limp and lifeless, all head and no heart.[56] There was of course another America, James reminded his privileged audience, where the heroism of hard work yet reigned. It was the "daily lives of the laboring classes," in which "the demand for courage is incessant; and the supply never fails." What the middle class wanted in strength, however, the working class lacked in "inner *ideal[s]*" to imbue their struggles with "significance." "The barrenness and ignobleness of the more usual laborer's life consist in the fact that it is moved by no such ideal inner springs," he said.[57]

The union to which James was leading his listeners was a match made in two different heavens and two different hells: in the bourgeois paradise, devoid of heroic effort; and in the working-class crucible of courage, devoid of ennobling ideals. "We are suffering to-day in America from what is called the labor-question," he said. But beneath the superficial social conflict between labor and capital lay an essentially psychological struggle, in need of psychological resolution. "[T]he unhealthiness consists solely in the fact that one-half of our fellow countrymen remain entirely blind to the internal significance of the lives of the other half."[58] If only they could look beneath the "external situation" that divided them, each class would find its necessary fulfillment in the other. Instead of opposing interests, they would discover their mutual need. "The significance of a human life . . . is thus the offspring of a marriage of two different parents, either of whom alone is barren," James said. The means of reuniting labor and capital were to be found in the psychic interdependence of manly virtue and feminine ideal.[59]

Such a panacea for deep-seated social conflict appears naïve compared with his profound psychological reconstruction of free will and self-command. So too, the glib gospel of mind-cure self-help with which he leavened his popular essays and talks lends itself easily to caricature, concealing the deeper inquiry upon which it depended. James's larger psychological legacy resides less in the cookbook therapies and "healthy-minded" faith that won his sympathy (but not his allegiance) than in his searching reconsideration of the mental meaning of freedom. Nor can that message rightly be reduced to a simple rationalization of the new ethos of corporate capitalism and consumerism, for his normative as well as descriptive insistence upon the freedom of the individual meant much more than "cash value" in economic terms. Indeed, in redefining freedom in terms of belief and identity instead of ownership and rulership, James implicitly (and later explicitly) challenged its contemporary invocations on behalf of imperialism and the rule of might makes right, whether in religion, politics, business, or the professions.[60] Yet that same psychologizing of free will and self-determination for which he was the most eloquent American exponent played a critical role in reconciling the capitalist reorganization of ownership and rulership with the nation's founding ideals. In that fundamental sense, James shares responsibility with Dewey, Hall, and other leaders of the transformation of social science for helping to radically redefine, and so ultimately displace, the "labor question" along with the political economy that informed it.

John Dewey's Psychology of Democracy

What James did for individual liberty, John Dewey (1859–1952) did for social equality: he regrounded the aging ideal in a new psychology that aimed, by transcending the philosophical dualisms of mind and body, faith and science, to overcome the political divide between individual and society itself. From James's *Principles of Psychology*, Dewey derived much of the approach to thought and ideas that informed the functionalist psychology as well as the Pragmatist philosophy he developed, first at the University of Chicago and then at Columbia University, along with James Rowland Angell, George Herbert Mead, James Mark Baldwin, and James McKeen Cattell.[61] For Dewey, as for James, what counted as thought was "practice." But while the practical character of James's work lay largely in its therapeutic value for individuals, Dewey viewed philosophy and psychology as practical responses to problems facing society as a whole, and therefore each of its members. It was in this doggedly social spirit that Dewey insisted, in a debate with his Columbia colleague William Pepperell Montague in 1939, that his life's work was devoted not to "practicalizing intelligence" for the benefit of philosophers, but to "intellectualizing practice" for the good of society.[62]

Those words, however, suggest something more than he may have intended, namely Dewey's distinctively "intellectual"—or "ethical" or "psychological," as he elsewhere put it—conception of social practice itself. Long after he had left his formal psychological work behind at the turn of the century, his enduring psychological understanding of social relations helps account for his bafflingly abstract and ethereal manner of writing about even the most mundane or material affairs, and for his paradoxical aloofness from the concrete political and economic issues that all his philosophy was theoretically intended to address.[63] "He is as complete an extrovert as ever lived, but the extroversion all takes place inside his head," observed the editor and poet Max Eastman, who was once Dewey's student. "Ideas are real objects to him, and they are the only objects that engage his passionate interest."[64]

Only Emerson, who was his predecessor in psychologizing political and economic relations, compares with Dewey in the status accorded him by American writers as well as foreign observers as the philosophical exemplar of American culture. Dewey's "*divinely* average" background, in Eastman's words, as the child of an entrepreneurial grocer and his evangelical wife in Burlington, Vermont, may have enabled him to become what the eccentric James never fully could: a representative American, commonly identified by admirers and critics alike with the supposedly distinctive features of American society and social thought, often in implicit or explicit contrast to European Marxism and Soviet Communism.[65] After his death in 1952, Dewey's iconic stature was seriously eroded both by the belated advent of analytical philosophy in the United States and by the demise of the notion of a unitary and unique "American Mind" that he had once embodied.[66] In recent years, though, his reputation has enjoyed a resurgence, reclaimed for their own diverse purposes by leading philosophers including Richard Bernstein, Richard Rorty, and Jürgen Habermas as well as by historians who have found in his vision of "deliberative democracy" an egalitarian alternative to the capitalist technocracy that triumphed among Progressive reformers.[67]

Yet a careful reconsideration of Dewey's early career as a pioneer of the new psychology in the Gilded Age, before his more acclaimed works of philosophy and social theory, indicates a more ambivalent relationship between his social psychology of democracy and the political economy of corporate capitalism.[68] For to claim, as he repeatedly did, that "psychology is the democratic movement come to consciousness," was to redefine not only psychology but democracy as well, and to do so in ways that challenged the limits of liberal-republican ideology while effectively evading the republican challenge to plutocracy and proletarianization.[69] It was to hold that democracy depended less on the institutional organization of property and government than on the psychic identification of each individual with the larger society or "Great Community," and vice versa.[70]

Such an affirming sense of spiritual solidarity was distressingly lacking in Dewey's childhood. "[T]he sense of divisions and separations that were, I suppose, borne in upon me as a consequence of a heritage of New England culture, divisions by way of isolation of self from the world, of soul from body, of nature from God, brought a painful oppression—or, rather, they were an inward laceration," he recalled many years later.[71] Though he described the problem in characteristically philosophical terms, as the dehumanizing expression of Cartesian culture, his youthful alienation appears to have been related to two more immediate concerns. His mother Lucina Rich Dewey's puritanical piety, her strict censure of dance and drink and games, her persistent demand, "Are you right with Jesus?", all helped instill in young Dewey the unstable compound of awe and disbelief that fueled much of his innovative early work.[72] At the same time, his booming hometown of Burlington saw the tradition of township democracy rocked by rapid industrialization, immigration, and a searing class divide that long tore at him as well, as Alan Ryan has noted.[73] If the writings of William, Alice, and Henry Jr. all in different ways reflect the psychic hothouse in which the James siblings were reared, so Dewey shared with his older brother a lifelong productive tension born of New England's divided heritage of democracy and industry. Chair of economics at the Massachusetts Institute of Technology and longtime editor of the *American Economic Review*, Davis Rich Dewey inherited the mantle of charity reform from the American Social Science Association as an expert on poverty, employment, and public relief in Massachusetts.[74] For John Dewey, however, the class question was less political or economic than spiritual or psychological. The conflict of democracy and capitalism, as he came to conceive it, posed essentially the same problem as the conflict of faith and doubt that he likewise took from his childhood, rooted in the same misguided metaphysics.

At the University of Vermont, where he enrolled at age 15, Dewey responded with appropriate enthusiasm to Samuel Taylor Coleridge's Transcendentalist handbook, *Aids to Reflection* ("our spiritual emancipation in Vermont," as he aptly called it). He was captivated by Auguste Comte's *Positive Philosophy*, with its sweeping indictment of Western individualism and its call for a new science as well as religion of society.[75] But he seized upon the elegant model of organic interdependence and functional coordination that he found in his junior year physiology textbook, by Darwin's disciple Thomas Henry Huxley, as an answer to the alienation he felt in himself and his world. "Subconsciously, at least, I was led to desire a world and a life that would have the same properties as had the human organism in the picture of it derived from the study of Huxley's treatment," he later wrote.[76] Like Huxley, Dewey found in Darwinian evolution an organic alternative to the mechanistic model of humanity inherited from the Enlightenment.[77]

The functional approach and experimental method of physiology sparked Dewey's entrance into scientific philosophy, or physiological psychology, which he studied at Johns Hopkins University under the direction of G. Stanley Hall.[78] In his first essay in the new field, a paper entitled "The New Psychology" and read before the university's metaphysics club in 1884, he declared "the general failure of the eighteenth century in all but destructive accomplishment"— an astonishing claim for an American writer outside the Old South—singling out for derision the rival traditions of faculty and associationist psychology to which the Revolutionary Era gave rise.[79] Seconding James and Hall's dismissal of "autonomous faculties" as well as separate and "distinct ideas," he similarly described mentality as an "organic unitary process" rather than a "compartment box" of discrete thoughts, feelings, and actions.[80]

But Dewey quickly signaled the distinctive direction in which he would take the Jamesian paradigm. "Along with this recognition of the solidarity of mental life has come that of the relation in which [the individual] stands to other lives organized in society," he wrote, emphasizing that "the idea of environment" formed the necessary counterpart to "the idea of organism."[81] The dynamic unity of mental life that James posited for the individual, Dewey envisioned for the social "environment" as an organic whole, identifying self and society in the same way that James identified thought and action.

For his understanding of the social nature of psychology and the psychological basis of society, Dewey turned to German Idealist philosophy, which he studied under the noted neo-Hegelian George Sylvester Morris.[82] Kant's belief that the transcendental ego was inaccessible to experimental investigation had led him to call for an "anthropological" psychology akin to earlier works in historical jurisprudence and ethnography. Wilhelm Wundt, often considered James's German counterpart in founding experimental psychology, pursued a Kantian "Völkerpsychologie" of language, custom, and myth alongside his better-known laboratory studies of reaction time.[83] But it was Georg Wilhelm Friedrich Hegel's awesome vision of the collective "Absolute Mind" in which all individual minds found their ultimate "actualization" that gave Dewey the synthesis for which he had been searching, connecting his personal and professional life, much as Renouvier had done for James. Answering "a demand for unification that was doubtless an intense emotional craving," Hegel's work brought Dewey "an immense release, a liberation," as he later recalled.[84]

Categorically rejecting the individualistic ideals of natural right and social contract, which inevitably resulted in the antisocial anarchy that Hegel associated with the Terror of the French Revolution, the German philosopher valorized instead the fundamental human need for social "recognition," the sole basis of "self-consciousness." Such awareness came not from seeing oneself objectively as if through others' eyes, so as to differentiate self from not-self, as in Smith's *Theory of Moral Sentiments*. For Hegel, recognition meant seeing one's identity fully reflected in that of the group and the group's social spirit wholly manifested in oneself, thereby transcending the very divide between self and other that formed the basis of Smithian autonomy. The Hegelian "Personality" afforded a new basis for Dewey's faltering faith: not the "moral sense" or independent ego of each individual, but the singular spirit of society.[85]

"The individual consciousness is but the process of realization of the universal consciousness," Dewey wrote in *Mind* in 1886, defining what he called "the psychological standpoint."[86] That cryptic conceit guided his foundational work in the new psychology between his graduation from Johns Hopkins and his subsequent appointment at the University of Michigan in 1884, and his move from Ann Arbor to Chicago ten years later, including several influential articles and an acclaimed textbook, *Psychology*.[87] His point of departure, like James's, was the Kantian insight that consciousness did not consist of a series of disconnected sensations, but rather comprised the inherent relations that the mind perceived as part and parcel of its sensory impressions, enabling humans to decipher the intelligible order encoded in the world around them. "What is perceived is, in short, significance, meaning," Dewey wrote in an 1887 article.[88] As he explained in his *Psychology*, "The isolated, the separate, is never the object of knowledge. . . . Relationship is the essence of meaning."[89]

But unlike James, Dewey followed T. H. Green's further argument that the ultimate thinker was a macrocosmic intelligence of which each individual represented an organ or microcosm.[90] The Jamesian stream of consciousness appeared to the young Dewey as the Hegelian Absolute, uniting individual minds as well as experiential data in a single "system" or "*uni-verse*, one world, in which order, connection, is the universal rule."[91] Just as the ordering connections that conferred meaning upon otherwise senseless sensations were essentially psychological, so the bond among individuals was fundamentally mental or spiritual as well. "[R]elations are thoroughly *ideal*," Dewey wrote, and knowledge was "a process of idealization"—of recognizing the ideal meaning of empirical facts in relation to the cosmic system that comprised them, and of seeing one's own significance within the collective Mind.[92]

Such self-realization, according to Dewey, was as much a matter of intuitive emotion as of deliberate intellect. In Jamesian fashion, he deemed "knowing" and "feeling" alternative aspects of a unitary mental experience rather than separate parts or powers of consciousness. But Dewey differed from James in conceiving of "subjective" feeling, no less than "objective" knowing, as a process of identifying one's individual experience with the universal experience of which it was a part. The fundamental social relation was therefore a special kind of "interest," which Dewey, like James, defined in terms of psychological "attention" rather than ownership: interest in the feelings of others, or "sympathy." Much as the ability to attend to certain thoughts formed the essence of free will for James, so the innate human capacity to feel what others felt represented for Dewey the social equivalent of gravity.

Like knowledge, feeling deepened as it widened, sympathetically surmounting distinctions of "social rank, wealth, or learning, or anything that tends to cut off one person from another," culminating in "a completely developed personality, a personality which has become absolutely universal."[93] The apotheosis of sympathy was "religious feeling," in which "we recognize the worthlessness, the *nullity*, of this private separate self, and surrender ourselves wholly to the perfect personality, God."[94] Self-interest, as it had been conceived in political economy, appeared in Dewey's early work as a pathological self-conflict that pitted the unrealized "ideal self" against the constricted "actual self."[95]

The basic presumptions of the new psychology continued to inform Dewey's work for many years after he explicitly disavowed the hybrid of Christian faith and Hegelian idealism that guided his first decade of writing. His understanding of "self-expression" in terms of the individual's progressive identification with a universal consciousness shaped the analysis of political and economic relations in his writings of the 1880s and 1890s on ethics, education, and "social practice," even as he transferred his faith from the Absolute to "democracy." In overturning the traditional dichotomy of self and society, as he came to argue, the new psychology formed a profoundly "political science," advancing a new "conception of democracy" itself.[96]

He inaugurated his career as a social theorist with a broad programmatic statement, "The Ethics of Democracy," published as a University of Michigan Philosophical Paper in 1888.[97] To Dewey, as to many contemporary observers, the Enlightenment ideal of popular sovereignty appeared in crisis, imperiled on the one hand by the class politics accompanying the rise of industrial capitalism, and on the other by the growing disaffection of Anglo-American political theorists. His immediate target was the English jurist Sir Henry Maine, whose widely read diatribe on *Popular Government*, published two years earlier, charged that the dependence of democracy upon public opinion rendered it volatile, self-destructive, and reactionary.[98] The source of the contemporary crisis, as Dewey saw it, lay in the anachronistic definition revealed in the two words of Maine's title: in the common assumption that democracy meant a form of government, namely government by popular majority. Such a conventional conception derived in the first instance from the Hobbesian model of the social contract, the political bond that united otherwise autonomous individuals as well as rulers and ruled, enacted by law and enforced by the coercive power of the state. The Lockean principle of majority rule, in Dewey's view, simply took the misguided individualism underlying the social contract to its logical conclusion, conceiving the sovereign as the sum of its citizens.

But to imagine democracy as an aggregate of individuals, "as sovereignty chopped up into mince meat," was to define it as the "abrogation of society, as society dissolved, annihilated."[99] For, as he had learned from Hegel and Huxley, society consisted in the organic interrelation of individuals bound by a common consciousness, so that "the individual is society concentrated, . . . the localized manifestation of its life." Democracy, from this psychosocial perspective, meant far more than the rule of a putative majority. "In conception, at least, democracy approaches most nearly the ideal of all social organization; that in which the individual and society are organic to each other," Dewey wrote. In a democracy, unlike any other social order, every individual fully "participated" in the "common will," and society conversely found expression in each of its members.[100] Government itself was no "external power formed by a process of delegation" but rather an internal power formed through the process of identification and self-realization described in Dewey's psychology. "Democracy is a form of government only because it is a form of moral and spiritual association," he wrote.[101]

Such association emphatically did not mean the subordination of the individual to society, but rather the replacement of the "numerical individualism" associated with utilitarianism with an "ethical" or psychological individualism that enabled everyone to realize his or her "personality" or social self to the greatest extent. Just as James rested his psychology of freedom upon the individual will to believe, so Dewey's participatory democracy depended upon individuals to find their respective "functions" in the "social organism" for themselves. "[T]he spirit of personality indwells in every individual," he wrote, " . . . and the choice to develop it must proceed from that individual."[102] So long as any individual was spiritually alienated from state and society, personality as well as the red-letter ideals of "liberty, equality, fraternity" remained unrealized, and democracy incomplete.

What this millennial vision required for its achievement was not immediately clear. But Dewey gave a general indication in his concluding discussion of the significance of participatory democracy for modern industry. Inspired in part by the economist Henry Carter Adams at the University of Michigan, he noted that the truly social democracy he envisioned embraced economic as well as political relations, entailing a "democracy of wealth" as well as of government. But he was careful to distinguish his notion of industrial democracy from more materialist demands for redistribution of property. In calling for "industrial relations" to be ruled by "the law of personality" rather than the pursuit of private profit, he specifically proscribed "numerical identity" or equality of ownership as a retrograde reflection of the kind of utilitarian thinking that was anathema to his psychosocial ideal.[103] Deweyan democracy, at least at this early stage, meant both more and less than economic equality, holding society to a higher standard of participation and integration while not necessarily requiring a fundamental reorganization of property rights as they were traditionally conceived.

Ten years later, in 1899, Dewey's presidential address to the American Psychological Association on "Psychology and Social Practice" afforded an opportunity to elaborate his psychological approach to industrial relations. Wrongly conceived as a question of profits and wages, of property in the productive process and the income it generated, what he called "the industrial problem" inevitably fostered the kind of intractable class conflict that had plagued the preceding decades. The fundamental problem, however, lay not in the property relations between owners and workers, but rather in the psychological relationship between individual laborers and the broader productive system, according to Dewey. Workers' psychic alienation from the industrial organism, their inability to identify in a Hegelian sense with their respective functions, resulted not from the growing gap between labor and capital, but from that between modern engineering and modern social science. Technological development had rendered the aging political economy obsolete and necessitated a new social psychology that comprehended industry as an organic system.

"The question of the amount of wages the laborer receives, of the purchasing value of this wage, of the hours and conditions of labor, are, after all, secondary. The problem primarily roots in the fact that the mediating science does not connect with his *consciousness*, but merely with his outward actions," Dewey wrote. "He does not appreciate the significance and bearing of what he does; and he does not perform his work because of sharing in a larger scientific and social consciousness. If he did, he would be free."[104] To be free, in other words, no longer meant to own the means of providing for oneself and one's dependents and to exercise reason in pursuit of enlightened self-interest—an increasingly unattainable ideal for most working people. Freedom rather meant the ability to find psychic and spiritual fulfillment in the recognition of one's role in society as a whole—a power that remained within ordinary Americans' grasp.

The total identification of the individual with the social process that Dewey had in mind was not accomplished when people worked solely for a wage, with no psychic stake in the work itself. But neither did it inherently entail a propri-etary stake in productive resources, as the older understanding of economic democracy did. Rather, Deweyan industrial democracy depended primarily upon the kind of holistic education for which he became famous in the field of pedagogical reform and which he outlined in *The School and Society*, published the same year as his presidential address. Psychologically reconceived, educa-tion became the vehicle for the kind of psychic socialization that he counter-posed both to the reactionary individualism of laissez-faire and to contempo-rary calls for the socialization of property from the left wing of organized labor. "The world in which most of us live is a world in which everyone has a calling and an occupation, something to do. Some are managers and others are sub-ordinates," he explained. "But the great thing for one as for the other is that each shall have had the education which enables him to see within his daily work all there is in it of large and human significance."[105] Dewey's vociferous resistance to narrow vocational training in a particular craft or skill, his insis-tence upon a broad education in the significance of labor and industry in gen-eral, reflected his aim of enabling workers, managers, and owners alike to real-ize themselves in the productive system as a whole.

His fullest consideration of the relationship between the new psychology and the older science of political economy came in a series of lectures on "psycho-logical and political ethics" that Dewey delivered at the University of Chicago in 1898. As Donald F. Koch, who edited the lectures for publication many years later, notes, they form a critical bridge between Dewey's early career as a psy-chologist and his better-known works of social and political theory.[106] Survey-ing the spectrum of modern social thought from Hobbes and Locke to John Stuart Mill, Dewey noted the common reliance upon the outdated psychology of the atomistic individual, itself in turn philosophically founded upon the Cartesian divide between self and world.[107] The new psychology had discred-ited both the independent transcendental ego of moral philosophy and the au-tonomous empirical actor of political economy, supplanting them, as he contended, with a wholly social self continuously evolving in response to its psychosocial environment.[108]

In traditionally political terms, the new psychology effectively replaced the social contract with what Dewey called "social consciousness" as the basis of a newly socialized "sovereignty," democratically diffused throughout society rather than concentrated in the state, and relying upon individuals' psychic identification with the social order in place of the threat of physical force.[109] In so conflating self and society, he crucially denied not only individual self-interest, but class interests as well. Just as the fixed mental "structures" or faculties of thought, feeling, and action dissolved and flowed together in the Jamesian stream of consciousness, so the new psychology signified "the breakdown of all rigid, fixed separations within the social organization," whether defined by caste or class, according to Dewey. "[I]f any individual is taken as a member of a limited social group, we cannot have and historically did not have any psychology as psychology," he told his students, welcoming the emergence of "the individual as an object of psychology" as a sign of the growing freedom and fluidity of modern social relations. "The distinctions of classes become . . . simple functional distinctions" in the mainstream of social consciousness, he said.[110]

The line between prescription and description likewise disappeared as Dewey moved seamlessly from articulating the promise of a psychosocial society freed from the confines of class to describing current political and economic relations as if that promise was already being realized. The attainment of the participatory democracy he envisioned, it seemed, called for nothing so much as a proper appreciation of the direction of societal evolution in its full psychological significance. As the class structure of political economy gave way, the course of economic development appeared to Dewey as "the evolution of wants into effective demands on one side and the evolution of nature into serviceable commodities on the other"—or the ebb and flow of supply and demand, conceived not as distinct interests but as "objective" and "subjective" aspects of a single organic coordination.[111] Economic value, accordingly, was not conferred upon commodities by either individuals' labor or their self-interested needs and desires, but rather by the same dynamic of self-realization through social recognition that Dewey originally had learned from Hegel. "[T]he essential meaning of the industrial process," Dewey wrote, "is that it is one by which the agent is brought to consciousness of his own activity in the form of wants, and that instead of these wants having at the outset a fixed scale of value, this economic process is the process by which he learns to value his wants."[112] Like Henry George, whom he much admired, he joined neoclassical economists in dispensing with classical theories of "natural price" and reconceiving value as entirely a function of market exchange, even as he conceived market exchange itself in cooperative rather than competitive terms.

In this way, Dewey's social psychology presented a double-edged challenge to contemporary economic thought. By insisting upon the thoroughly social rather than individual determination of economic value, he offered an explicit rebuttal to the "hedonistic psychology" that still informed mainstream neoclassical economics, with its utilitarian calculus of individual desires.[113] At the same time, his critique of the labor theory of value seemed to him to reveal a fatal "weakness in all socialistic plans" based upon an equally reactionary calculus of work and wealth, or class distribution of income. In imagining "too immediate a relationship between the matter of social service and the return which society makes to the individual," he argued, socialism overlooked the "automatic interplay" that determined the larger psychic returns individuals drew from their efforts, the broader significance they derived from fulfilling their respective functions. "It fails to notice the number and the kind of factors which influence the values which the individual can really get out of what is physically given back to him; how much it depends upon his education, upon the consciousness of power, of initiation, and of self-direction," he explained.[114]

More fundamentally, in calling for the socialization of productive resources, socialists took for granted the existence of the same competing interests between individuals and classes posited by classical political economy, which Dewey's entire psychological corpus denied. "[S]ocialism as an end insists upon existing actual diversity and opposition of interests," he noted. It "paints the picture of existing society" first sketched in Hobbes's state of nature, "when the hand of every man is turned against every other man." But if that portrait was false, if society was in fact as well as in theory founded upon a collective consciousness rather than competing interests, then the path of progress lay not in a revolutionary socialization of property, but in an evolutionary socialization of the psyche.[115]

Dewey's notion of social evolution was in many ways opposed to the Darwinian defense of laissez-faire issued by the young William Graham Sumner, or even to the sociological conservatism of Sumner's later writings on mores and folkways. In common with contemporary American socialists such as Eugene V. Debs and Daniel De Leon, Dewey and like-minded Progressives drew upon the Romantic tradition in proclaiming sympathy and solidarity rather than selfishness to be the most basic attributes of human nature, and in heralding the triumph of cooperation over competition as the natural destiny of human progress. Yet he defined his own ideal of social consciousness against both the individual consciousness presumed in different ways by classical political economy and its neoclassical inheritors, on the one hand, and the social property variously envisioned by the partisans of Debs and De Leon, on the other. In conceiving democracy in terms of psychic "participation" and social "significance" and in viewing his own society accordingly as a developing "personality" rather than an arena of class struggle, Dewey presented a profoundly psychological alternative to revolutionary socialism, much as he and many of his followers claimed. But contrary to those who have seen him as the spokesperson for an enduringly exceptional American political culture born of the Revolution, his critique of political economy entailed a far-reaching revision of the democratic promise of the early republic. Even as he planted the seeds of a new psychosocial egalitarianism, Dewey uprooted an older democratic radicalism dispossessed of its material basis in household production.

G. Stanley Hall's Psychology of Progress

Dewey's vision of an evolutionary movement from the reign of capital to that of consciousness reflected a rising neo-Hegelian faith in history that was shared by European revisionist socialists such as Eduard Bernstein, Jean Jaurès, and Beatrice and Sidney Webb, as the historian James Kloppenberg has shown.[116] Informed by neoclassical as well as Marxist economic theory, they embraced the Enlightenment promise of progress but disavowed the mechanism of revolutionary struggle championed by Jefferson and Paine no less than Marx. Deweyan democrats found in capitalist development itself the force effecting an inevitable fading of class distinctions and a gradual transition to social democracy, abetted by a growing cross-class alliance for reform in the interests of society as an increasingly unified whole. Like Henry Carey before them, they reclaimed Smith's "invisible hand" in a neosocialist guise, shorn of the troublesome association with individual competition and class conflict.

For such serene trust in the benevolent course of economic evolution to emerge from a quarter-century of unprecedented depression and industrial warfare required a Jamesian will to believe, in more ways than one. The reassuring belief in "revolutionary evolution" entailed a basic rethinking of the dynamics of social revolution, a reconception of progress itself, in which the new psychology played a defining part. Much as James's individualistic psychology called for the new understanding of society developed by Dewey, so Dewey's social psychology implied the changed view of history elaborated by his graduate mentor, Granville Stanley Hall (1844–1924).[117]

The stream of consciousness that united mind and body for James, self and society for Dewey, represented for Hall the temporal course of progress, binding the mental maturation of each person to the psychosocial development of civilization. Evolutionary science, which shaped James's functionalist view of free will and Dewey's organicist conception of democracy, informed Hall's developmental psychology of both the individual child and the whole human race. His model in this regard was the biological theory that the growth of an organism "recapitulates" the evolution of its species. Liberal theology, which bolstered James's defense of personal faith as well as Dewey's belief in social consciousness, similarly inspired Hall's case for "conversion." Through conversion, the child came to identify with the race and vice versa, each overcoming its alienation from the other in a psychological reenactment of the Christian Gospel. The reconciliation of scientific materialism and religious idealism at the heart of the new psychology took form in Hall's magnum opus, *Adolescence* (1904), as a peaceful passage from childhood to adulthood, from the agrarian republic to industrial capitalism, and from the self-centered egotism of early moral philosophy and political economy to the social or "race" consciousness of modern social science.[118] His was ultimately a psychology of the Gilded Age itself, seen as a collective coming-of-age.

The Cartesian divide between mind and matter that the new psychology sought to transcend accordingly appeared to Hall as a fundamentally historical problem: namely, the separation of mental from manual work manifested in the specialization of academic expertise, on the one hand, and the homogenization of industrial labor, on the other. At the same time, Hall confronted the turn-of-the-century "crisis of work" as an issue of personal development. He identified the natural bond between rational willpower and productive labor with his childhood in western Massachusetts, and with the nine generations of New England farmers on both sides of his family dating back to the first English settlers.[119] His parents valued education and briefly taught school themselves, and his father was a local leader in the advancement of scientific agriculture who "lectured his son on what he called 'putting brains into all our work,'" as Dorothy Ross has written.[120] In a speech at the county fair on the eve of the Civil War, recorded in Hall's autobiography, his father chided farmers who were slow to learn the value of new developments in science and technology, but he gently mocked as well "those who are farmers in theory only," "authors, editors, lawyers," and others who performed but "half the work, that is, the head work," instead of uniting "virtue and intelligence with physical and moral strength."[121]

The lesson was not lost on the young Hall, who pointedly noted in *Adolescence* his knowledge of bookbinding, glassblowing, shoemaking, plumbing, smithing, and other crafts, adding, "I can still mow and keep my scythe sharp, chop, milk, churn, make cheese and soap, braid a palm-leaf hat complete, knit, spin and even 'put in a piece' in an old-fashioned hand loom, and weave frock-ing."[122] Yet in another respect he seemed to feel that he fell short of his father's model of manly virtue, having been exempted from military duty in the Civil War ostensibly on account of a sprained knee—but in truth, as Hall later con-fessed, due to a cowardly heart. This "very sorest of all my memories," he wrote in his *Life and Confessions of a Psychologist* (1923), "has also been a tremendous stimulus to atone by service, so that it is not too much to say that there has been something like a penance *motif* in all my efforts ever since."[123] A similar sense of obligation and determination derived from his subsequent decision against a career in either farming or the Congregationalist clergy in favor of grad-uate work in philosophy. "Now Stanley wherein is the great benefit of being a Ph.D.," his mother wrote him at the time. " . . . Just *what is* a Doctor of Philos-ophy? and wherein would it give you *credit, influence,* or usefulness?"[124]

Hall came to see his own effort to fashion an academic alternative to the re-publican ideal of productive labor informed by practical knowledge as em-blematic of his age, in the double sense of the Gilded Age and early adulthood. More specifically, he identified with the challenge facing young scholars in the postbellum era who were seeking to claim for the new university-based disci-plines the sense of higher calling long associated with the older professions of law, medicine, and ministry, as well as the practical importance previously ac-corded to knowledge of a special skill or trade.[125] But the underlying problem posed by the specialization of knowledge, for Hall, was the danger of unnatu-rally divorcing intellect from willpower, thought from feeling, empirical learn-ing from spiritual development, and thereby stunting the psychological growth both of individual scholars and of the society that depended for its progress upon their expertise. "In academic isolation from the throbbing life of the great world," "[w]ith little experience in willing and far less with the floods of feel-ing that have irrigated the life of the man in the past," as he wrote in the preface to *Adolescence*, "the sedentary and mentally pampered thinker has lost reality and devotes himself to a passionate quest of it as if it were a Golden Fleece or a Holy Grail."[126] So too, he argued, modern America had sacrificed the heart for the head, a deeper soul-life for shallow sophistication. "What we have felt is second-hand, bookish, shop-worn, and the heart is parched and bankrupt."[127]

Yet Hall found the antidote for such hyper intellectualism not in any Ro-mantic return to an antediluvian past, but in the new university system itself, as exemplified by the great universities at Berlin and Leipzig where he studied with such masters in their respective fields as Adolf Trendelenburg in philosophy, Emil du Bois-Reymond, Carl Ludwig, and Hermann von Helmholtz in physiology, and Wundt in psychology. In the German academy—"the freest spot on earth," as it seemed to him—with scientific philosophy at its core, he saw research and education anew, embodying no merely cerebral endeavor but a second Reformation, "a new dispensation of religion itself," as he wrote in an 1891 article on "Educational Reforms."[128] The proper study of modern philosophy and psychology, he explained in an 1885 article on "The New Psychology," provided college students not simply intellectual enlightenment, but the depth of spiritual experience otherwise lacking in their cloistered academic careers, offering "aid through what are now unmistakably recognized as adolescent crises and readjustments."[129] Further, graduate research, the special province of the modern university, afforded the newborn scholar an "epoch making experience in the growth of any soul," the glorious "sensation of discovery," fulfilling the primal need of "mastery and power." "Specialization is now the best of all modern refuges of individuality," Hall wrote in 1901. "Here personality culminates and finds often its most distinctive expression and here celebrates its chief triumphs in the modern world."[130]

His Germanic appreciation of the role of scientific philosophy in fostering the spiritual growth of individuals as well as society guided Hall's leadership in the professional development of psychology itself. He received the first Ph.D. in psychology granted by an American institution, under James's direction at Harvard; became one of the first two students to work in Wundt's famous Leipzig psychological laboratory, generally considered the first of its kind in Europe; returned to found one of the first two such laboratories in the United States, at Johns Hopkins University; created the nation's first independent department of psychology, at Clark University, where he was also the school's first president; established both the *American Journal of Psychology* and the American Psychological Association; and directed more than half of the fifty-four American doctorates in the new discipline admitted by 1898, including those of such leading figures in their own right as Dewey, James Cattell, and Joseph Jastrow.[131] Much as Dewey identified individual self-fulfillment with the psychic growth of society, so Hall understood professionalization in both individual and collective terms: psychology as a discipline evolved in tandem with the professional development of each of its practitioners. Through the medium of the psychological profession, which he did more than any other American to bring into being, the developmental needs of young scholars ostensibly merged with those of society as a whole, reuniting work and will on a new psycho-evolutionary basis.

The flip side of the problem of disembodied knowledge presented by the rise of academic expertise was the problem of mindless labor created by the accelerating mechanization of industry and homogenization of wage work. In his early pedagogical writings of the 1880s as well as his later study of adolescence, Hall contrasted the character-building routines of farm work and handicrafts in the New England of his childhood with the enervating experience of modern factory operatives. "Work is rigidly bound to fixed hours, uniform standards, stints and piece-products, and instead of a finished article, each individual now achieves part of a single process, and knows little of those that precede or follow. . . . Personal interest in and the old native sense of responsibility for results, ownership and use of the finished products, which have been the inspiration and soul of work in all the past, are in more and more fields gone," he wrote.[132] "Work, as too often conceived, is all body and no soul, and makes for duality and not totality," he concluded.[133] If the "academic isolation" of the modern scholar formed a distinctively bourgeois predicament, the degradation of manual labor posed an equal and opposite challenge for the emerging working class, whose weaker members, he wrote, "drop limp and exhausted in body and soul" into indigence and squalor.[134]

Like James, and like Emerson earlier, Hall viewed the widening class divide as the superficial manifestation of a deeper psychological alienation common to bourgeois professionals and wage laborers alike. Industrial labor severed the traditional bond between intellect and will much as academic expertise did from the other side, alienating workers less from the material means of production than from the spiritual means of selfhood. Hall followed James and Bain in attributing behavior to automatic muscular action rather than the dictates of an incorporeal mind, and in consequently conceiving the willful element of behavior in terms of habit instead of deliberate intention.[135] So the problem of enlightening labor lay in the challenge posed by modern industry to the formation of healthy habits, which had previously arisen from the errands, chores, and skills that formed the school of the soul in an agrarian age. No longer did work provide its own reward by fostering willpower; industrial life enfeebled rather than strengthened body and soul. Historical change, as Hall described it, had given rise to an essentially developmental dilemma: how to provide young workers, like young scholars, with the "education of the will" formerly afforded by apprenticeship in the family farm or craft workshop.

To the historical problem of industrial labor, like that of academic expertise, Hall accordingly proposed a developmental solution. For him, as for Dewey, the "labor question" resolved itself into a question of education. What the modern university provided young scholars in the form of research and professional development, the common schools were to supply young workers in the form of "muscle-culture," or habit training. An enthusiast of Emerson while in college, Hall became during his graduate career a great admirer of Otto von Bismarck and the German "educational state," whose military and industrial might rested in Hall's view upon the rigorous "moral discipline" effected through compulsory schooling.[136] As new modes of work and leisure undermined the earlier pattern of learning by doing, he wrote in 1882, the responsibility for such psychic socialization increasingly fell upon the common school system. Like the university, the primary school must fill the psychological void left by the demise of the household republic, by fostering spiritual as well as intellectual growth. "Indeed the intellect may be so trained as to enfeeble and dissipate the will," Hall warned, urging educators instead "to moralize as well as to mentalize children."[137]

Uniting the Romantic pedagogy that Bushnell also drew upon with the Jamesian psychology of habit-formation, he argued that education should focus less on children's conscious interests and deliberate actions than on their unconscious spiritual needs. Less committed to liberal and democratic ideals than James or Dewey, he found in the new psychology a warrant for a new paternalism, a pedagogical "despotism . . . if need be," even as he trumpeted the blessedness of childhood. "For most of us the best education is that which makes us the best and most obedient servants," he wrote.[138] "When things are mechanized by right habituation," as he explained in *Adolescence*, the ultimate goal of general education was achieved. "The person who deliberates is lost, if the intellect that doubts and weighs alternatives is less completely organized than habits. All will culture is intensive and should safeguard us against the chance influence of life and the insidious danger of great ideas in small and feeble minds."[139]

Hall's developmental approach to the "labor question" pivoted upon his broader conception of adolescence as a dual coming-of-age, from childhood to adulthood and from savagery to civilization. For the individual, adolescence represented a mental rebirth, "the infancy of man's higher nature," in which the "floodgates of heredity are thrown open again" admitting newer, more civilized impulses and passions to displace the older, more primitive instincts inherited at birth.[140] "The whole future of life depends on how the new powers now given suddenly and in profusion are husbanded and directed," Hall wrote. Properly channeled, the civilizing force of "higher and more completely human traits" gently guided adolescents over the rocky passage and prepared them to accept their new duties and responsibilities. But as Hall gravely observed, "The momentum of heredity often seems insufficient to enable the child to achieve this great revolution and come to complete maturity, so that every step of the upward way is strewn with wreckage of body, mind, and morals."[141]

The further society advanced in its own development, the greater the leap adolescents needed to make from savage instinct to civilized habit, and the deeper the danger that they would fall by the wayside between the two. The quickening pace of industrial life posed unprecedented challenges for urban youth, unmoored from the traditional bonds of church and home life and disoriented by a bewildering array of new choices, temptations, and potential pitfalls. "Never has youth been exposed to such dangers of perversion and arrest as in our own land and day," Hall wrote.[142] Two closely related developmental hazards merited special concern in modern America: "precocity," due to inadequate preparation for adult interests and activities, and "delinquency," resulting from the abrupt loss of earlier ways of expressing childlike impulses and needs. "In this environment our young people leap rather than grow into maturity," Hall wrote. As "our vast and complex business organization . . . absorbs ever more and earlier the best talent and muscle of youth . . . we are progressively forgetting that for the complete apprenticeship to life, youth needs repose, leisure, art, legends, romance, idealization," along with proper training in modern science and industry.[143] The proliferation of "juvenile faults, immoralities, and crimes" testified to "the great difficulty which youth finds in making adjustment" to "the new conditions of industrial life."[144]

Political enthusiasms of all kinds similarly tempted impressionable adolescents, who seized upon radical dissent as a lifeboat in stormy seas. "The young man finds the world out of joint and would reform the church, school, perhaps social and family life; . . . is fired at the tyranny of wealth or trusts, and would himself reconstruct by doubting, casting out everything which does not seem to his own fledgling intelligence good, true, and beautiful." Carefully directed, such youthful idealism developed into a mature Aristotelian temperance, moderation, and appreciation of received truths and "established institutions," according to Hall.[145]

If the pace of societal development exacerbated the travails of adolescence, modern society's own growing pains were rooted in the new challenges of socializing its youth. For Hall, as for contemporary social theorists such as Van Wyck Brooks and George Santayana, the extraordinary economic volatility and unrest of the Gilded Age were symptoms of a quintessentially "precocious" social order.[146] "No country is so precociously old for its years," Hall wrote. Suddenly catapulted into the vanguard of industrial progress, the United States found itself psychically unprepared for the jolting transition from agrarian republic to industrial commonwealth. "In a very pregnant psychological sense ours is an unhistoric land," he explained. " ... [W]e have had neither childhood nor youth, but have lost touch with these stages of life because we lack a normal developmental history."[147]

Like the university student in need of spiritual as well as intellectual nourishment, the young factory operative in need of "will-culture" as well as industrial training, and the juvenile delinquent in need of romance and repose as well as excitement and opportunity, American society required both deeper ancestral roots and stronger progressive branches in order to naturally mature. Americans needed to reach at once backward, as Hall did in tracing his family tree to the Puritan settlers, and forward, as he did in pioneering the development of professional psychology, in order to negotiate the tortuous passage from a republican to an industrial order. "[T]he child and the race are each keys to the other," he wrote. " ... Along with the sense of the immense importance of further coordinating childhood and youth with the development of the race, has grown the conviction that only here can we hope to find the true norms against the tendencies to precocity in home, school, church, and civilization generally."[148]

The research university and the common school served as the main institutional instruments for coordinating personal with societal development in Hall's pedagogical psychology. But the ultimate unification of the child with the race transcended any material or institutional expression. Like Dewey's identification of self and society or James's identification of mind and body, the ideal union of personal growth and societal evolution that Hall envisioned entailed a formative act of faith, the developmental analog of the "will to believe." Noting that his own survey of evangelical denominations revealed adolescence to be the preeminent age of religious rebirth, he contended that "the chief fact of genetic psychology is conversion, a real and momentous change of unsurpassed scientific and practical importance and interest." Inspired in part by the German theologian Friedrich Ernst Daniel Schleiermacher, Hall depicted conversion as the natural consummation of adolescence, when the self-centered child gave itself over to the service of the human race. "Complex as the process is, a pivotal point is somehow discernible where the *ego* yields to the *alter*," he wrote. "Normal and imperceptible as this evolution is ideally, the transition is in fact the chief antithesis in the human cosmos."[149] Viewed from the perspective of developmental psychology, the Christian Gospel appeared as the archetypal coming-of-age narrative, the classic "dramatic representation of ... the most critical revolution of life," the primal passage from the "lower selfish self" to "a new and higher life of love and service."[150]

As a "true philosophy of human history," Hall's psychology of conversion represented a reconception of the historical ideal of social revolution inherited from the Revolutionary Era. "[Adolphe] Quetelet sagely says that the best measure of the state of civilization in a nation is the way in which it achieves its revolutions," he wrote, citing the nineteenth-century Belgian astronomer and mathematician who originated the concept of the "average man," defined as a statistical aggregate, as opposed to the individual "man of reason." "As it becomes truly civilized they cease to be sudden and violent, and become gradually transitory without abrupt change. The same is true of that individual crisis which physiology describes as adolescence, and of which theology formulates a spiritual aspect or potency called regeneration and conversion."[151]

Conversion and adolescence, in other words, represented in psychological terms the revolution-by-evolution posited by Progressive thinkers as a way of describing the capitalist transformation of political and economic relations as well as the related reconstruction of political economy itself. The commodification of labor and the consolidation of capital, the decline of the autonomous household and the rise of the modern business corporation, appeared to Hall and many of his colleagues to be as natural (and as heartrending) as the end of childhood, as divinely ordained (and as soul-wrenching) as the triumph of faith. So too, the counterrevolution in social science, from the social contract among proprietary individuals to the social organism in which individuals found their true function, reflected the predestined progress of market society. The new psychology no less than the new order it described was to be understood as the product of inevitable evolution, not revolutionary struggle. Hall's wistful lament for the lost innocence of the nation's youth was therefore fully compatible with his commitment to progress, psychologically reconceived.

CHAPTER SIX

The Sociological Turn in Progressive Social Science

Simon N. Patten and Thorstein Veblen,
Lester F. Ward and Edward A. Ross

T
he year after G. Stanley Hall's *Adolescence* appeared and the year before William Graham Sumner's *Folkways*, the first chair of sociology at the University of Chicago heralded a new "social philosophy" born of the union of Hall and Sumner's respective fields. "Psychology and sociology are the most important media through which this new thought is finding expression," wrote Albion W. Small in 1905. " ... [P]sychology and sociology, both immature, are together formulating a 'world-consciousness' in a way which must surely set off the epoch upon which we have entered from all the thought-eras that have preceded."[1] What distinguished the new psychology and the new sociology from their predecessors, demanding "a general rethinking of all our theories, from our most concrete economic and political and legal policies, to our logic and our theologies and our metaphysics," was also what bound the two disciplines together in a hybrid social science of modern America.[2]

The pioneers of the new psychology defined their field against the older rationalist and empiricist traditions by insisting that "faculties," "sensations," and "ideas" had no meaning outside of the ceaseless cycle of thought and action they called "practice." This pragmatic principle drew Jamesian psychology away from the autonomous individual innately endowed with conscience as well as prudence, toward the intrinsically social self theorized by Dewey, and toward the total identification of individual development with societal evolution entailed in Hall's account of adolescence. Such a social psychology necessitated a new science of modern society to describe the concrete social relations within which selfhood emerged, even as it required that social practices be conceived in terms of their mental meaning or significance.

"Psychology is the science of the *mechanism* of the social process," Small wrote. "Sociology is the science of the mechanism of the *social process*."[3] For the new sociology as for classical political economy, the "social process" took the form of market relations. But early American political economy had described an agrarian society in which the realm of the market remained loosely circumscribed by geography as well as by older forms of household production and family or slave labor. By the late nineteenth century, in contrast, Americans struggled to make sense of a fully capitalist economy in which the market knew no sectional or sectoral bounds and appeared increasingly coextensive with society itself.

Neoclassical economists like John Bates Clark viewed the growing universality of market forces as a license to largely abandon the classical concern with the objective distribution of productive resources. Such writers rather derived all economic relations, including the distribution of wealth and income, from the subjective decisions of individual buyers and sellers. Contemporary "social economists" and sociologists found a different but related lesson in the increasingly absolute dominion of the market. Convinced that economic needs and desires arose from the "social process" of market relations itself, social scientists turned to the new psychology for an understanding of how individual choices depended upon social norms. For if individuality emerged only through interpersonal exchange, then the notion of a social contract between self-directed individuals with predetermined interests appeared absurd.

Carrying to its logical conclusion the neoclassical disavowal of any objective basis for economic interests beyond or beneath the market, the founders of modern sociology described the fundamental social relationship as not "contract" but "contact," in Small's words: an unconscious, involuntary exchange in which individual agency was more consequence than cause.[4] The expansively "social" vision of market society articulated earlier by Henry Carey and Henry George thus proved compatible with the new naturalization of market relations entailed in neoclassical theory. Precisely because it rejected the proprietary individualism of classical political economy, the sociological turn in economic thought resulted in the ultimate science of market society, identifying "market" with "society" more completely than its eighteenth-century ancestor.[5]

Unlike the new psychology, born of Emerson's New England, the new sociology had its roots in the burgeoning hinterland of Chicago, the great new market metropolis of the Gilded Age.[6] This chapter considers the work of four sons of the Middle Border who defined the sociological turn in Progressive social science: the social economists Simon N. Patten and Thorstein Veblen, the leading theorists of what came to be called "consumer society"; and the sociologists Lester F. Ward and Edward A. Ross, who charted the political dimensions of the new social realm in their pathbreaking writings on "assimilation" and "social control." Together they reconceived market society as a powerful circuit of social conventions, common customs, and shared desires, not unlike the circuit of sensations, volitions, and actions described in the new psychology. Old divisions between the owners of land, labor, and capital yielded to new divides between insiders and outsiders, between those fully plugged into the powerhouse of psychic commerce and those hampered by weak connections. As social power increasingly appeared to emanate from social exchange itself, freedom and equality became redefined in terms of access to what Small called the "alternating current of influence," or the means of exchange instead of the means of production.[7] Exploitation and oppression were accordingly attributed to the engrossment of this quintessentially social resource by unsocialized individuals, rather than the monopolization of the material resources of land and capital goods.

In their parallel efforts to define the psychosocial mainstream that united modern Americans as well as divided them, these writers betrayed a central tension that underlay modern psychology as well. James, Dewey, and Hall conceived theirs as a "pragmatic" science, anchoring mind in body, belief in behavior. Yet by conversely conflating action with thought, material relations with mental meanings, the new psychology detached the inherited ideals of liberty, equality, and progress from their political-economic basis in property and sovereignty, redefining self-ownership and self-rule in psychological terms. Patten and Veblen, Ward and Ross, similarly wrote in revolt against static and asocial models of human nature along with the related concept of the social contract. Like George Fitzhugh, Henry Hughes, and Horace Bushnell before them, they proclaimed the primacy of social norms in constituting individuals instead of vice versa. Yet in insisting that human needs and wants, interests and values, were wholly cultural constructs, they concluded that identity or selfhood was not a product of individual volition or consent. The social realm as they conceived it comprised the unconscious habits, unspoken ideals, and unquestioned standards, the "folkways" of Sumner's title, which people shared less by choice than by social instinct. The ultimate subject of the new sociology was the common spirit that Emerson called the "Unconscious," Dewey called "social consciousness," and Hall called "the race," the master creation of the German Romantic tradition that inspired much of the transformation of American social science.

The cultural determinism of modern American sociology (as well as anthropology) was tied in complex ways to the transatlantic racial nationalism of the turn of the century, galvanized by the mass movements of labor and capital across national borders.[8] Even as the founders of the field commonly rejected biological or naturalistic explanations of social relations, they conceived capitalist culture in distinctly racial or ethnic terms. Their organicist understanding of the market as a mainstream of values and norms shared by a nation or people, rather than a neutral arena of exchange among autonomous proprietors, thus tended to naturalize market relations in new ways. Sociologically conceived, old debates over self-ownership and self-government gradually gave way to new debates over participation and exclusion, cultural assimilation and cultural pluralism.[9]

Social Economy and National Culture in Germany and the United States

As founding chair of the nation's first department of sociology as well as founding editor of the *American Journal of Sociology*, Albion Small was also among the first historians of the new social science.[10] In an introductory text and three subsequent historical studies, he traced the origins of his field to the sweeping economic upheaval of the late nineteenth century: "The production of wealth in prodigious quantities, the machine-like integration of the industries, the syndicated control of capital and the syndicated control of labor, the consensus of interests in production and the collision of interests in distribution, the widening chasm between luxury and poverty," and related developments, he wrote, had given rise to "the well-nigh universal instinct that there is something wrong in our social machinery and that society is gravitating toward a crisis."[11] That impending crisis, according to Small, pitted a "bastard individualism" grounded in laissez-faire economics against a "Marxian socialism" that turned conventional economic wisdom on its head. "Modern sociology protests against the tendency at either extreme to treat the question as an issue to be settled by measure of strength between classes," he wrote. "It is a question of social economy in the deepest sense. It is a question of the ways and means of allowing all human interests to realize themselves most harmoniously."[12]

"Social economy," as Small explained in his 1907 study, *Adam Smith and Modern Sociology*, bore an ambivalent relationship to both classical political economy and contemporary socialism.[13] He and other Progressive social scientists generally embraced the paramount concern with the spiritual and material welfare of society as a whole, common to both eighteenth-century moral philosophy and the social democratic wing of the growing socialist movement. In providing scientific sanction for the contemporary social gospel movement, Small invoked the early church of Smithian political economy, with its message that wealth was the means rather than the ends of human endeavor.[14] Against the single-minded pursuit of profit in modern business, he endorsed the basic socialist demand for "a more inclusive and secure democracy," entailing "the equalization of social relations."[15] "If Adam Smith had lived until today," Small wrote, " . . . he would be classed as a socialist, without benefit of clergy."[16]

Yet, like Henry George, Small found a fundamental flaw in Smith's system as well as the "systematic socialism" to which it unintentionally led: namely, the theory of economic value as a reflection of labor cost. By overlooking the "subjective and social factors in value," the labor theory represented a purely materialist measure of wealth and welfare, along with the basis for believing that the distribution of productive resources determined the distribution of income.[17] This producerist understanding informed the merciless Ricardian law of rent and the corollary "wages-fund doctrine," according to which rent inevitably rose and wages fell with the ratio of the total population to the means of subsistence. While the classical model indicated a long-term common interest in economic growth, it revealed a more immediate conflict of class interests in distribution. By identifying wealth with work, as Small further noted, the labor theory provided critics of capitalism with a dangerous weapon to use against "non-producers."

On both sides of the Atlantic, the attack on the labor-cost theory of value and the class theory of distribution had begun in earnest in the 1830s. It came particularly from writers such as Carey who combined a genuine antipathy to class privilege disguised as natural law with an equally fervent belief in the socializing and harmonizing capacity of market relations, properly fostered and channeled. But the producerist principles of classical political economy proved more resistant to reform in the United States than in Britain, due in large part to the political and economic resilience of the agrarian household and the enduring promise of limitless expansion.[18] Not until the last quarter of the nineteenth century, with the transcontinental development of industrial capitalism and the closing of the frontier, did mainstream economic writers, led by Francis Amasa Walker, reject the wages-fund doctrine. In so doing, economists theoretically decoupled the distribution of income from the class relations inhering in ownership of land, labor, and capital.[19]

Walker and others maintained that wages, profits, and rents were not shares of a divided surplus, but independently earned rewards of the respective factors of production, each separately determined by the forces of supply and demand. In analyzing factor prices independently of the original distribution of factors, the new economic model dovetailed with the so-called "marginalist revolution" in Europe, which similarly derived the value of commodities solely from the subjective decisions of buyers and sellers. The new "neoclassical economics" abstracted individual expenditures and revenues from class relations, applying instead a universal calculus of "marginal utility" or "marginal productivity" to every transaction.[20]

By dispensing with the classical distinctions between class incomes, neoclassical writers provided a new rationale for capitalist profit in particular and market relations in general. Yet by divorcing the allocation of income from the division of productive resources, they also helped legitimize contemporary public efforts to redistribute income, since such measures no longer appeared to threaten capitalist relations of production. Moderate downward redistribution even appeared beneficial to influential neoclassical thinkers who reasoned that increased income would bring a higher marginal utility to those with little to start with than to those with a lot.[21]

By cutting individual market actors loose from the objective class interests that governed their decisions in classical political economy, the marginalist revolution rendered such "choices" or "preferences" wholly subjective.[22] "*The phenomena of the market are at the same time phenomena of the mind, and they must be explained accordingly*," Small wrote, summarizing his understanding of the central premise of neoclassical economics. "To that extent," he observed, the marginalists "began the development of modern sociology."[23] Indeed, the neoclassical focus upon individual subjectivity in the context of market society provided an important point of departure for Max Weber, Georg Simmel, and other leading European sociologists, for whom sociology was virtually synonymous with "subjective economics."[24]

Yet the new economics largely retained the material as well as mental individualism of the classical tradition, reducing market relations to the resultant of rational, self-interested decisions by autonomous individuals. Even as the marginalists severed the classical bond between work and wealth, namely the core concept of a "natural price" of commodities based upon the cost of production, they held that the distribution of income remained in principle proportional to individual output. Contemporary critics of industrial capitalism such as Henry George, however, argued that since the very value of productive contributions derived from the market, the rents that individuals charged for their services were ultimately tolls upon social exchange rather than the rewards of individual productivity.[25] In a similarly social spirit, sociological thinkers drew upon the new psychology in contending that economic interests were no more inscribed in human nature than in the organization of productive resources, but rather emerged from market relations. Freed from the invisible hand of preordained interests, market society took on a mind of its own, which itself determined individual needs, desires, and decisions.

Seeking a new understanding of market society as a psychic whole, leading American economists broke with British orthodoxy to embrace the rival tradition of the German Historical School in which Weber and Simmel were also trained.[26] The source of that tradition lay in the rise of cultural, economic, and political nationalism in Germany between the breakup of the Holy Roman Empire by Napoleon and unification under Bismarck. The construction of a German *Volksgeist*, or national culture, rooted in a common language and folklore went hand-in-hand with the creation of a national economy governed and protected by a strong interventionist state. Inspired by the vision of a new market society bound by the distinctive history and traditions of the German nation, historical economists established the *Verein für Sozialpolitik*, or Society for Social Policy, in 1873. Leading the charge were Small's teachers at the University of Berlin, Adolph Wagner and Gustav Schmoller. Nicknamed "*Kathedersozialisten*," or "socialists of the chair," members of the *Verein* called for the new German nation-state to mediate disputes between employers and employees, sanction trade unions, regulate labor conditions, and enact redistributive policies such as workers' pensions in order to foster class harmony.[27]

In the United States, the development of a truly national market and a powerful federal government in these same years provided the context for the establishment of the modern research university and professional social science on the German model. The *Verein* set the explicit example for the formation of the American Economic Association (AEA) in 1885. The AEA, in turn, spawned similar organizations in Britain and other capitalist countries, as well as the American Sociological Society in 1905 and the American Political Science Association in 1909.[28] In their quest for the psychosocial unity underlying the growing political and economic divisions of the postbellum era, American social scientists across a wide range of disciplines turned for guidance to the cultural nationalism of their German mentors. The founders of American political science, chief among them Francis Lieber in the antebellum era and John

W. Burgess later in the century, took as their central subject the Germanic notion of a "nation" as a racial or ethnic unity, as opposed to the liberal Anglo-American model of a "people" as an aggregate of individuals bound essentially by social contract. "A nation is a nation only when there is but one nationality," as Lieber wrote in 1868.[29]

Similarly, the founders of modern American economics and sociology regarded the market itself as a living, growing, thinking organism, in which individuals were joined not by rational choice but by the shared customs, traditions, values, and beliefs that constituted the German model of national culture. Not surprisingly, the new social sciences betrayed elements of the racism and authoritarianism that colored the broader milieu of historical economics in its homeland. Yet the complex cultural organicism that shaped the origins of modern social science cannot be reduced to simple racial chauvinism. Indeed, a sociological understanding of cultural identity—whether racially, ethnically, or nationally defined—motivated cultural pluralists like Jane Addams no less than assimilationists like Simon Patten or nativists like the young Edward Ross.[30] A psychosocial conception of racial difference informed Booker T. Washington's celebration of "imitativeness" as the chief asset of the "Negro race" in white America, as well as the "Chicago School" of sociology led by Washington's onetime secretary, Robert E. Park.[31] But W. E. B. Du Bois's romantic portrait of "the souls of black folk" was equally indebted to the new psychology he learned from William James and the new sociology he learned from Wagner and Schmoller.[32]

In reconceiving market society as a culture rather than a contract, modern social economics and sociology set the stakes of a new kind of social struggle: a struggle over inclusion instead of independence, over self-identity instead of self-interest. The old ideal of a commercial republic united by a common class of self-employed households, steeped in the political economy of the Revolutionary Era, slowly lost ground to the new vision of an industrial order united—or divided—along racial, ethnic, and national lines, a vision steeped in the social psychology of the Progressive Era.

The Culture of Consumption:
Simon N. Patten and Thorstein Veblen

The *Verein für Sozialpolitik* actually inspired two different proposals for an American organization in 1885, as A. W. Coats has noted. First came a plan for a Society for the Study of National Economy, put forward by Edward J. James and Simon N. Patten at the University of Pennsylvania, a bastion of economic nationalism in the tradition of Carey. Calling for extensive state planning and regulation of economic development, the Pennsylvania platform seemed far too disrespectful of private property to many of James and Patten's peers, who approved instead the more moderate alternative of the American Economic Association, proposed by Richard T. Ely of Johns Hopkins University.[33] For most American social scientists, the national culture that bound a truly social economy was not ultimately embodied in the central state, as it was for their German counterparts.

The American *Volksgeist* resided instead in the social process that created individual needs and desires through the medium of the market: the culture of consumption. The moral heart of Adam Smith's philosophy, as Small and others described it, lay in the ethical standards that directed the consumption of wealth, not in the property relations that controlled its production. For Smith, as for the social economists and sociologists who were his rightful heirs, wrote Small, "The center of interest is the nation of consuming persons."[34] Franklin H. Giddings, an economist active in the formation of the AEA who went on to chair the department of sociology at Columbia University, described mass consumption as the basis of a new "consciousness of kind," or "Social Personality." In his 1911 presidential address to the American Sociological Society, Giddings observed that the increasing division of labor and diversity of the workforce were counterbalanced by the "assimilative force" of standardized consumption. "As consumers of wealth we exhibit an amazing mental and moral solidarity," he said. "We want the same things."[35]

The most influential theorists of the newfound culture of consumption were Simon Nelson Patten (1852–1922), the prophet of the "pleasure economy" and pioneer of both the modern business school and the profession of social work; and Thorstein Veblen (1857–1929), the arch critic of "conspicuous consumption" and founder of "institutional" or "evolutionary" economics in the United States. Though Patten is commonly remembered for his utopian vision of socialized desire, and Veblen for his dystopian depiction of barbaric gluttony, each was deeply ambivalent about the consumer society they both described. Like Henry George and William Graham Sumner, they took up opposing positions upon a shared ideological ground, together defining the terms of an enduring debate over "consumerism," one much rehearsed in recent historical scholarship.[36] Patten and Veblen agreed that market relations were no longer rooted in the Hobbesian drive for self-preservation and the resulting struggle over scarce resources described in classical political economy. Both conceived instead a contest for the mental rather than material rewards of wealth. They viewed ownership as a means of self-esteem and social status, not of self-ownership and self-rule. The consumerist "standard of living" they each envisioned was rooted not in self-interest, but in social norms, which individuals obeyed out of instinctive imitation rather than rational calculation. Such a psychosocial competition implied a new foundation for cooperation as well, based upon shared habits and standards instead of common political and economic interests.

Born five years apart in the 1850s, they both grew up on prosperous pioneer farms in the long shadow of Chicago. Patten's parents moved from upstate New York to found a homestead on the Illinois prairie. In the rich black soil they struck paydirt, and the barns overflowed with crops and livestock. Patten's father seemed always one step ahead of nature, the first farmer in De Kalb County to tile his land so as to avoid flooding, the first to install a windmill as well. When the Illinois Central Railway built its road from Chicago to New Orleans, Patten's father made sure it passed through the local trading post, turning the town of Sandwich into a thriving commercial hub. The son, a pensive, withdrawn boy who preferred sitting alone in the milkhouse to working the fields (his father called him "lazy"), never lost the faith in nature's generosity instilled in him by the farm. The city man of few passions or pleasures whom he later became retained a lifelong love of plowed land and fast trains, the hallmarks of prosperity remembered from his youth.[37]

Veblen came from a hard-working, plain-living family like the Pattens, and they too found good fortune on the Midwestern prairie. But they traveled a rougher road to get there. His Norwegian parents were themselves the children of dispossessed peasants, and they twice lost all or part of their land in their adopted country before acquiring a self-sufficient farmstead on the Wisconsin coast of Lake Michigan. There Thorstein, the sixth of their twelve children, was born. Eight years later they moved to a larger farm in Minnesota, where their hostility toward bankers, land speculators, and other land-hungry city folk was only deepened by the Scandinavian farming community's disdain for its town-dwelling Yankee neighbors. When their fiery fellow Minnesotan, Ignatius Donnelly, chief lecturer for the Patrons of Husbandry ("the Grange"), urged farmers to unite in defense of "economic independence" against the "possessors of great wealth," he found an enthusiastic audience in the Veblen household. And he found a kindred spirit in the sharp-tongued teenager who was already honing the erudition and wit that would make for a scathing satire of the leisure class.[38]

At the age of 17, Veblen and Patten were each sent off to study for the ministry, as befitted farmers' sons with intellectual aspirations. Both chose to pursue graduate study in social science instead. Both returned to their families' farms without much hope of putting their doctoral degrees to work. But they saw their surroundings anew.

Patten came back with a mysterious ailment of the eyes that shrouded him in a dark fog for nearly three years, but with his mind's eye he perceived the secret of his father's success. Having joined the rush of young American men to German universities, Patten had studied with Professor Johannes Conrad of Halle, one of the crusading social economists who were following Wagner and Schmoller's lead and a specialist in agricultural statistics. Patten had been impressed by the prodigious progress of German farming and convinced by Conrad's argument that the new empire had ushered in a new age, in which social abundance was rapidly overtaking natural scarcity. As Conrad saw it, the social power responsible for the empire's emancipation from natural limits was the central state, to which he was an adviser. But back home, Patten found that an equally miraculous power, consumer demand, had transformed De Kalb County from a backwater of log cabins and yeoman farms into a busy district of frame houses and cash crops.[39]

It was the growing power of the mass market for agricultural as well as industrial goods that was turning the prairie into a factory of foodstuffs. The rise of the railroad, along with the creation of the commodities exchange and new technologies for shipping, preserving, and packing meat and grain, made it possible for Midwestern farmers to reach a national market. But in order for that market to continue to grow, Americans accustomed to a locally limited diet would have to change their eating habits. To that end, giant food firms such as Swift, Heinz, Nabisco, and Kellogg arose in the 1880s and began aggressively seeking to create consumer demand for new products, like breakfast cereal, as well as for old products that were newly available nationwide and year-round, like granulated sugar and garden vegetables. Their main challenge was surplus, or "overproduction," rather than scarcity. From the perspective of agribusiness, the market, rather than the land, now needed to be "cultivated."[40]

That was Patten's perspective as well. It was the source of his central insight, which he revealed in a stunning series of writings—chief among them, *The Premises of Political Economy* (1885), *The Theory of Dynamic Economics* (1892), and *The Theory of Social Forces* (1896)—that took him from obscurity to leadership of the Wharton School at the University of Pennsylvania.[41] In the increasing variety of the American diet, he found the secret not only of farmers' success, but of societal prosperity. Like George and Carey, Patten rejected the principle of natural scarcity that condemned society to an ever more bitter battle over diminishing resources. But the social force that Patten believed could free society from such struggle was his own discovery: the force of socialized consumption.

The "iron law" that there would always be more mouths to feed than food to fill them, he argued, assumed that people subsisted upon a few basic foods available in their region, and that those staples were in short supply. But if people learned to eat foods that were naturally more abundant, the struggle for existence would be softened accordingly. If, in addition, with the extension of agricultural trade routes over longer distances, people came to eat a little of each of a wide variety of foods instead of a lot of just a few, then fewer foods would grow scarce to begin with, and there would be more of everything for all.[42] To Patten, eating seemed the most basic form of consumption, and it provided the model for a wholesale revision of political economy based on the power of consumption rather than production. The more that people learned to consume those things of which nature provided a plentiful supply, and the more they came to consume many things in moderation rather than a few things to excess, the further they would progress from natural scarcity to social abundance.[43] The iron laws of production gave way in his work to a "primary law of social progress," which decreed: "*[S]ociety progresses from a simple, costly and inharmonious consumption to a varied, cheap and harmonious consumption.*"[44]

"Harmony" was as important as variety in Patten's theory of consumption, for peace and prosperity were intertwined in his social vision. Such harmony depended, in part, upon how well the consumption of any particular commodity accorded with that of others. Those goods that enhanced the enjoyment of—or in other words, expanded the market for—other goods, were in Patten's scheme truly "social." Those commodities, on the other hand, that "shut out the enjoyment of other pleasures and reduce[d] the number of goods from which enjoyment may be had," were to be "ejected."[45]

Taking his cue from the marginalist revolution in economic thought, Patten reasoned that market exchange, by fostering increasing variety and harmony in individuals' habits of consumption, could actually "raise the margin of consumption" for society as a whole, reversing the law of diminishing returns. "*The essence of social progress lies not in the increase of material wealth but in a rise of the margin of consumption,*" he wrote. Such socialization of consumption represented a marked departure from the liberal individualism entailed in the classical preoccupation with maximizing production. "The increase of wealth demands a merely negative attitude. . . . The *laissez faire* policy must be supreme," Patten wrote. "On the other hand, endeavors to raise the margin of consumption, demand that the instincts, habits, and education of all the people should be the same. Social feelings arise which insist that every individual make his consumption conform to the best interests of society."[46]

Veblen was equally convinced of the central importance of socialized consumption, but far less sanguine about what it meant. Like Patten's native Illinois, the Minnesota to which Veblen returned with his Ph.D. from Yale was a boom country, having absorbed a massive migration of fortune-seeking farmers from eastern states and northern Europe after the Civil War and having quickly become, along with the neighboring Dakota Territory, the nation's leading producer of wheat. With a new milling process that allowed the mass production of white flour, which had traditionally been reserved for the rich, firms such as General Mills and Pillsbury were making Minneapolis the world's capital of flour manufacturing.[47]

But when Veblen came home in 1884, Minnesota was a bust country as well, where the price of wheat had plummeted to the lowest level since 1869, and where most of the revenue from the sale of the crop went to pay the high price of shipping. Eighteen eighty-four also marked the beginning of the agrarian uprising that dominated the seven lean years during which Veblen remained in the region, unable to find a teaching job. From the perspective of the Northwestern Farmers' Alliance, food handlers with "sticky fingers"—railroad operators, flour millers, commodities dealers, big food firms, and others involved in transporting, storing, processing, and distributing foodstuffs—were like the gluttonous grasshoppers that devoured the farmers' livelihood. The cruel combination of booming agribusiness and deepening depression appeared to be the result not of "overproduction," but of a feeding frenzy. It seemed a sign not of surplus, but of waste.[48]

That was Veblen's perspective as well. Long after he married the daughter of a railroad magnate and went to teach at John D. Rockefeller's new University of Chicago, he retained the Middle Border farmers' sinking suspicion that riches had become the reward of greed rather than industry. But Veblen cast the agrarian critique of earning without working in a radically new mold. In a series of groundbreaking articles around the turn of the century and three major books—*The Theory of the Leisure Class* (1899), *The Theory of Business Enterprise* (1904), and *The Instinct of Workmanship* (1914)—he challenged the basic assumptions underlying the traditional "producerist" understanding of unearned income, founded as it was upon classical political economy. Like Patten, Veblen took issue with the Ricardian model of a struggle over scarce material resources, though for different reasons.

The hallmark of the classical school, Veblen noted, was the idea that the market mediated a natural relationship between "man" and "nature," population and subsistence. Exchange relations were rooted in humans' natural needs and natural interests, on the one hand, and commodities' natural capacity to meet those needs and serve those interests, on the other. But in fact, Veblen argued, market relations had little or nothing to do with the innate qualities of either individuals or the goods they exchanged. The market value of commodities, he agreed with his neoclassical contemporaries, was not tethered to any "natural price" determined by the cost of production; it depended entirely upon the subjective choices of buyers and sellers. Yet neither were those subjective decisions guided by the intrinsic usefulness of commodities in meeting individuals' natural needs or desires, as neoclassical economists tended to assume. Veblen rejected the utilitarian psychology that attributed to individuals a natural propensity to maximize pleasure and minimize pain, and that informed classical and neoclassical economics alike.[49]

Drawing upon both modern psychology and anthropology, Veblen held that market relations were regulated solely by the distinctively social value of commodities as status symbols, signifying the relative fortune and prestige of their owners. The value of goods was entirely unrelated to their intrinsic, material attributes. Veblen's concept of "invidious distinction" as the basic motive of market exchange underlay his famed analysis of "conspicuous consumption" as an end in itself, whose main purpose was to advertise the relative wealth of the consumer. "Under modern conditions the struggle for existence has, in a very appreciable degree, been transformed into a struggle to keep up appearances," he wrote.[50] Such a limitless contest for status, rather than for limited material resources, was the real reason for economic competition as well as accumulation. "If, as is sometimes assumed, the incentive to accumulation were the want of subsistence or of physical comfort, then the aggregate economic wants of a community might conceivably be satisfied at some point in the advance of industrial efficiency," Veblen wrote. "[B]ut since the struggle is substantially a race for reputability on the basis of an invidious comparison, no approach to a definitive attainment is possible."[51]

In his theory of business enterprise, Veblen likewise contended that the pursuit of invidious distinction motivated competition among firms, with virtually no regard for what was actually being produced and consumed, bought and sold. The value of tangible assets bore little relation to their productive capacity, just as the market value of consumer goods was essentially independent of their use values. Business owners, in Veblen's view, were no more "utilitarian" or "hedonistic" in the conventional sense than consumers were. "The hedonistically presumed final purchase of consumable goods is habitually not contemplated in the pursuit of business enterprise," he noted in a critique of marginalist as well as classical utilitarianism. "Business men habitually aspire to accumulate wealth in excess of the limits of practicable consumption, and the wealth so accumulated is not intended to be converted by a final transaction of purchase into consumable goods or sensations of consumption."[52] Moreover, the core of the modern firm's capital lay not in tangible assets, however valued, but in "intangible assets": in the firm's "good will" or reputation itself, and in franchises, trademarks, patents, "customary business relations," and the like, whose sole value lay in the "preferential advantages" they conferred. The income-producing capacity of such "immaterial wealth," Veblen explained, was a matter of purely "pecuniary" rather than "industrial" value, bearing no essential relation to the production or consumption of material wealth.[53]

Indeed, Veblen archly suggested that the market value of consumer goods as well as business assets was in many ways inversely related to their material "serviceability." The more useless the commodity, the better it demonstrated the consumer's capacity for "waste" rather than work, he wrote, effectively turning the labor theory of value on its head. So too, business enterprise commonly capitalized upon its capacity for "disservice" rather than "service," as in producing military armaments, or in restraining output, efficiency, or trade in the interests of maximizing profit at the expense of product.[54] The socialization of desire that Patten celebrated as a recipe for abundance, Veblen debunked as a formula for waste.

Patten, too, saw potential peril as well as promise in the new economy. Like Veblen, he dissented from the vulgar utilitarianism that informed much of neoclassical as well as classical economic theory and which implied that all consumers derived essentially the same satisfactions from the same commodities. "Subjective standards being once introduced," Patten wrote, "it is no longer possible to assume that the pleasures and pains which one man obtains from given objective relations or goods, are equal to those which other men obtain from the same sources."[55] The "theory of prosperity" he espoused therefore required a new social psychology to make sense of the social mechanism of desire itself. Overturning the classical political-economic premise that the supply of goods inevitably creates the demand for them ("Say's Law"), Patten offered a psychological explanation for what seemed painfully clear to manufacturers and retailers amid the great depression of the 1890s: mass production and distribution did not in fact ensure mass consumption. "It is not the increase of goods for consumption that raises the standard of life, but the mental state of a man after the order of his consumption has been changed so as to allow a greater variety," he wrote. "The standard of life is determined, not so much by

what a man has to enjoy, as by the rapidity with which he tires of any one pleasure. To have a high standard means to enjoy a pleasure intensely and to tire of
it quickly."[56]

To have a low standard, conversely, meant to gorge oneself continually on a
few goods instead of savoring small portions of an ever-growing smorgasbord.
Those consumers whose tastes widened along with the market became progressively socialized by cultivating new habits, increasingly developing desires
in harmony with the greatest good of society as a whole. But those who retained their more primitive, homogeneous appetites amid the cornucopia of
mass consumption inevitably sunk into gluttony, addiction, and vice, becoming drags upon social progress. Like G. Stanley Hall and other writers who
viewed contemporary social strife in developmental terms, Patten warned of a
perilous transition from the "pain economy" described in classical political
economy to the emerging "pleasure economy." "Where economic goods are
abundant, any strong desire for single articles will lead to an excessive consumption, and the tempted individual will in time suffer from disease or fall
into vice," he wrote. The danger to modern society then arose not from the
struggle between individuals and classes in response to increasing scarcity, but
from the psychological struggle within individuals in response to growing
abundance. "[W]hen men are transferred to a pleasure world their evils are internal. They are their own foes," Patten wrote. "They want relief not from per-
secution, but from temptation."[57]

In such a society, the distribution of wealth and income came to depend
upon the distribution of the "mental qualities" or "economic instincts" that governed individuals' consumption, instead of upon the distribution of the means
of production.[58] The old "conflict theory of distribution" based upon competing class incomes must yield to a new "diffusion theory of distribution" in
which class lines dissolved as consumption became progressively socialized.
"Harmony results and conflict ceases," Patten wrote, echoing Carey, "for the
play of economic forces grinds to powder the old social classes with their
conflicting interests, and builds up a single type with a greater productive
power and a higher standard of life. In a truly economic world there is no marginal man."[59]

Unlike Patten, Veblen retained a sharp sense of class division and even class
conflict. But he redefined the category of class itself in essentially psychological
and cultural terms. The classical political-economic conception of class, as a
function of the objective interests flowing from property in productive resources, seemed flawed to Veblen in two ways. First, as he argued in an extensive critique of Marxism that echoed Dewey's contemporary writings, the con-

ventional understanding of class interest depended upon the same outdated utilitarian psychology that informed mainstream marginalist economics, wrongly presuming that individuals naturally tended toward the rational pursuit of their material self-interest. In truth, as revisionist Marxists increasingly acknowledged, economic behavior was essentially irrational and "unhedonistic," motivated by unthinking habit rather than deliberate calculation.[60]

"Without reflection or analysis, we feel that what is inexpensive is unworthy," he wrote.[61] Americans did not come to prefer white flour because of its aesthetic appeal or nutritional value, but because of its value in social esteem due to its traditional association with affluence. The vicissitudes of business activity were "in great measure a question of folk psychology," subject to the "largely instinctive, shifting movements of public sentiment and apprehension."[62] The allegiance of the leisure class to its senseless standards of consumption was likewise "instinctive, and does not rest primarily on an interested calculation of material advantages," as was the equally unreasoning regard for riches among the poor.[63] Even socialistic agitation among the working class stemmed not from objective oppression or exploitation, but from the habitual envy and veneration of wealth that formed the common culture of modern market society.[64] More fundamentally, the culture of consumption itself arose from the "instinct of emulation," Veblen's version of the concept of social selfhood at the core of modern American social science: individual identity was a product of social norms, rather than vice versa.

The second problem with the materialist concept of class that derived from classical political economy, according to Veblen, concerned the understanding of property and productive resources that it entailed. Just as the "pecuniary" or market value of commodities was essentially independent of the material wealth it ostensibly represented, so the "industrial" or productive worth of land, labor, and capital goods did not inhere in their physical, intrinsic attributes. What made these inert resources into dynamic factors of production was the "immaterial equipment" of technological knowledge, inhering in the communal wisdom, usages, and "habits of thought" conveyed from one generation to the next via "tradition and habituation."[65] The source of capitalists' power in modern industry lay not in their control of the material means of production per se, but in their resulting ability to engross the "usufruct of . . . commonplace knowledge," the mental means of production. Henry George's argument that private property in land enabled landlords to monopolize the fruits of social exchange seemed to Veblen to touch upon a broader truth: the value of productive resources, like that of pecuniary assets and consumer goods, derived from society as a psychic whole. The source of laborers' power similarly lay in their knowledge of "ways and means"—in the technical skill that capitalists, better acquainted with the ways and means of pecuniary "business," required to run their enterprises.[66]

The conception of individual income as a return for individual output, commonly espoused by agrarian and socialist agitators as well as by neoclassical apologists for profit and rent, made no sense in light of Veblen's self-styled "technological view" of capitalism. Class struggle appeared as a conflict not over competing claims upon material resources, but rather over competing "habits of thought" and their underlying economic "instincts." For while business was based upon the competitive culture of consumption and the instinct of emulation, industry was based upon the communal culture of technology and the "instinct of workmanship" from which it grew. While both rich and poor tended to be more attuned to pecuniary emulation or conspicuous consumption, the semiskilled and skilled working class and the emerging stratum of engineers were the natural bearers of technological expertise.[67] For Veblen as for Patten, older social divides rooted in rational self-interest gave way to new social divides rooted in instinct and habit.

To view the epochal economic strife of the Progressive Era from such a psychosocial perspective was not to depoliticize the crisis of capitalism, but rather to reconceive what was politically at stake. Patten's vision of increasing harmony and abundance via the socialization of desire depended upon the triumph of "skilled and intelligent" over "ignorant and inefficient" consumers— or of "surplus earners" over "social debtors," "citizens" over "dependents." Because the difference between insiders to the emerging consumer culture and outsiders appeared rooted in rival habits, instincts, and social standards, he predictably drew upon racial and ethnic stereotypes in identifying poor consumption with more "primitive" cultures and peoples. "[E]ach class or section of the nation is becoming conscious of an opposition between its standards and the activities and tendencies of some less developed class," Patten wrote. "The South has its negro, the city has its slums, organized labor has its 'scab' workman, and the temperance movement has its drunkard and saloon-keeper. The friends of American institutions fear the ignorant immigrant, and the workingman dislikes the Chinese. Every one is beginning to differentiate those with proper qualifications for citizenship from some class or classes which he wishes to restrain or to exclude from society."[68]

Joining the rising rhetoric of biological degeneration with the prevalent nativism of leading sectors of organized labor, he warned that low-grade consumers could enjoy an ominous advantage in an unregulated struggle for economic survival because their lesser wants enabled them to accept lower wages.[69]

Society must therefore enforce progressive standards of consumption in the interests of safeguarding the general welfare against retrograde economic individualism. Such enforcement entailed a positive obligation to promulgate healthy habits and social desires among the "dependent classes." "A progressive society must integrate its parts," Patten wrote. "Isolation and conflict produce stagnation and decay."[70] The central challenge was not poverty or material deprivation per se, but "misery," a "state of mind . . . due to a misuse of goods, not to a lack of them." "The gap is not between effort and goods, but between goods and enduring satisfactions," he wrote. " . . . The task [of ending misery] involves the whole complex problem of adjustment, and not the simple one of production."[71] Nor was adjustment simply a matter of adapting individuals to a rapidly changing social environment. It equally entailed reforming the social environment itself. Social settlements, playgrounds, parks, amateur sports, and cheap amusements, along with shorter work hours, higher wages, and improved living conditions, all fostered the kind of psychic socialization Patten envisioned.[72]

Yet he insisted that such efforts to integrate those on the margins of market society must not be based upon older ideals of blind "justice" or political "equality," but rather upon a new ideal of "social solidarity." The basic principles of social solidarity, Patten explained, were three. First, "no appeal should be made" to the new ideal "except when the claimant plainly lacks some of the common qualities possessed by the typical man." Second, such claims were to be made "against society and not against individuals," for "inequity is due to defects in the regulations or activities of the state, and if these defects are not remedied the state should bear the burden." Third, "the right of the social debtors to some share in the social surplus does not carry with it the right to determine the form in which they shall receive it. . . . Society is the sole judge of these matters."[73] Underlying these avowedly illiberal principles, which echoed the authoritarian "socialism" of George Fitzhugh and Henry Hughes in the antebellum South, was Patten's support for what he called American-style "altruistic" or "sentimental" socialism, as contrasted with European-style "revolutionary" or "scientific" socialism. "This desire of upper-class men to improve the conditions of the lower classes is a radically different phenomenon from the pressure exerted by the lower classes for their own betterment. The lower class movement stands for the control of the state by themselves in their own interests. The upper class movement directs itself against the bad environmental conditions preventing the expression of character," Patten wrote. He concluded: "Our foes are not groups of antagonistic men, but incompetence, mismanagement and maladjustment."[74]

In his own way, Veblen emphatically agreed. The struggle he foresaw over the future of market society lay not between rival interests that derived from ownership of different productive resources, but between rival instincts that derived from greater or lesser acquaintance with the "machine process" of modern industry—or, more precisely, with the "habits of thought," the culture of workmanship, embodied in modern science and technology. "It is now not so much a question of equity in the distribution of incomes, but rather a question of expediency as regards the . . . management of productive industry," he wrote in his last major work, *Absentee Ownership* (1923). " . . . What the material circumstances are bringing to men's attention is a question of how to get the work done rather than of what to do with the output."[75]

Though Veblen subjected Patten's beloved consumer culture to its sharpest critique, the alternative technological culture he seemed to sanction was likewise indebted to the new psychology of social selfhood. Like Patten, he repudiated the ahistorical model of "economic man." But Veblen's understanding of the competing instincts of emulation and workmanship as the basis of economic behavior led him to a similar reliance upon prevailing ideas about the primacy of race and ethnicity, whether biologically or culturally conceived. For Veblen even more than for Patten, the roots of market society ultimately lay in natural history: in the development of the "Aryan culture," both "pecuniary" and "industrial," embodied in the evolution of the "dolichocephalic [long-skulled] blond race."[76] Much as Patten depicted an evolutionary struggle between civilized and primitive consumers, so Veblen described an anthropological conflict between the "barbarian" and "archaic" culture of the competitive market and the "modern," "scientific" culture of mechanical technology.

In the end, Veblen's answer to the crisis of capitalism also entailed a combination of technocracy and cultural eugenics characteristic of the sociological tradition of Comte as well as the German Historical School. In the "evolutionary" as opposed to "revolutionary" socialism he appeared to endorse, "the mechanical exigencies of the industrial system must decide what the social structure is to be," as interpreted by those "designing engineers" most fully acculturated by the machine process. Property would be effectively abolished rather than redistributed, for property itself—the bedrock of classical political economy—was ultimately a construction of barbarian culture, with no place in the technological culture of modern industry.[77] If Veblen offered a far more radical socialist vision than Patten's, his was nevertheless likewise a program of ethnocultural assimilation rather than class struggle. For both men, a racialist version of national culture supplanted the social contract of classical political economy along with its proprietarian ideals of individual liberty and social equality.

Solidarity and Assimilation in
France and the United States

The "new economy" heralded by Patten and Veblen arose alongside a "new republic" theorized by modern sociology, in which notions of racial solidarity and psychic assimilation played a similarly key role. While American social economy was modeled upon the German example, the inspiration for the sociological rethinking of political theory in the United States came especially from the French Third Republic, where a similar reconstruction of the heritage of the Revolutionary Era was underway. In the wake of the revolution of 1848 and the Paris Commune of 1871, French theorists faced the breakdown of the republican ideology that had united their nation's founders. Alexis de Tocqueville declared the annulment of the social contract amid the fighting between Parisian workers and their erstwhile bourgeois allies at midcentury, and he called for the regrounding of governmental assistance to the working class in Christian morality rather than natural right.[78] The self-styled "liberal republicans" who took power in the 1870s after roughly seventy-five years of royalist rule were disillusioned about the prospects for preserving liberty along with equality and fraternity, the trio of French revolutionary ideals. The uprootedness of peasants and the militancy of workers contributed to bourgeois intellectuals' increasing distrust of the French citizenry, as the pervasive public discussions of "degeneration" and "crowd psychology" in the 1880s and 1890s attested.[79]

Like their American counterparts, French social scientists sought to rebuild republican politics upon a sturdier theoretical foundation, safe from class conflict and revolutionary upheaval. The ideologists of the Third Republic called the social theory they devised for their new order "solidarity," by which they meant a spiritual bond that held modern society together much as the bonds of family and community had united people in the past. Solidarity gained currency as a new basis for republican rule in the 1880s, but it received its most complete elaboration in the sociology of Émile Durkheim, beginning with his classic work on the "social division of labor" in 1893.[80] Durkheim echoed Comte in arguing that the expansion of market relations entailed a treacherous passage from the "mechanical solidarity" of the peasant community to a new "organic solidarity" born of increasing economic interdependence. To curb the reckless individualism and ameliorate the alienation or "anomie" endemic to this transition period, he called for educational programs and occupational as-sociations that would bring to collective consciousness the solidarity inherent in market society as a moral community rather than a neutral playing field for self-interested action.[81]

Yet Durkheim's vision of organic solidarity essentially preserved the Carte-sian model of "reason" taming "desire," or of "society" regulating the "individ-ual." More in tune with the new psychology of the neo-Kantian philosopher Charles Renouvier and his American admirer, William James, was the fin-de-siècle social psychologist Gabriel Tarde, who became a major influence upon many of the founding thinkers of modern American social science, including James, Dewey, Albion Small, Franklin Giddings, Lester Ward, and Edward Ross.[82]

Tarde drew upon both the psychological concept of "attention" (what James termed the "will to believe") and the marginalist concept of subjective economic value in formulating his theory of "imitation," the "transmission" of desire or belief, as "the elementary and universal social fact."[83] His vision of sociology as "inter-mental psychology" collapsed the Cartesian dualism of individual and society, desire and reason, much as James and Dewey did, providing at once a more "solidarist" model of society than Durkheim's and yet one more easily reconciled with American social scientists' reluctance to vest moral authority in a powerful central state.[84] For individuality was stifled when social standards were imposed upon individuals from a single source, according to Tarde. "But when, instead of patterning one's self after one person or after a few, we borrow from a hundred, a thousand, or ten thousand persons, . . . the very nature and choice of these elementary copies, as well as their combination, expresses and accentuates our original personality," he wrote in his best-known work, *The Laws of Imitation*, published in French in 1890 and in English in 1903. "And this is, perhaps, the chief benefit that results from the prolonged action of imitation."[85]

For Durkheim, as for Smithian political economy, the solidarity of market society was based upon the division of labor. Tarde's more thoroughly psycho-logical conception of interdependence, by contrast, was rooted in the socializa-tion of consumption rather than production. As Rosalind H. Williams has noted, Durkheim's more producerist sociology was predicated upon societal restraint of individual desire, in the tradition of eighteenth-century moral philosophy, whereas Tarde's consumerist social psychology aimed to liberate desire instead. "The consumer . . . determines more and more how he is to be served, and when he is to be served," Tarde wrote. "He determines to make everything cater to his momentary desires, no matter how fleeting and extravagant they may be. This is called, in high-flown language, the emancipation of the individual."[86]

Tarde's understanding of the supremacy of the consumer provided a new model of democracy as well as liberty, in which popular sovereignty consisted in psychological "assimilation" rather than political and economic rights. Indeed, he argued that inequality of power and wealth would inevitably widen even as "social dissimilarity" narrowed with the advance of "international *assimilation*."[87] By enabling the lower classes to assimilate the standards of the higher, the progress of imitation led to the eventual erasure of social divisions, the "gradual suppression of caste, class, and nationality barriers."[88] With the rise of modern technology allowing for "instantaneous transmission of thought from any distance," the spiraling "social force" of shared ideas would overwhelm all other forces, and the "purely spiritual collectivity . . . of individuals who are physically separated and whose cohesion is entirely mental" would replace all other social groups.[89]

Ultimately, Tarde envisioned the emergence of a global community, or world market, of shared desires, values, and norms. "And so the imitative passivity of mankind has had the happy result of multiplying the commercial and political and intellectual ties of human groups and of effecting or preparing their fusion," he wrote. "[T]he widespread propagation of a single language, of a single religion, of a single governmental authority, or of a single body of laws, [is] the first and preliminary condition of a great . . . civilisation. . . . [and] the widespread propagation of the same . . . wants and tastes, or, in a word, of the same individual *usages*, is the first and preliminary condition of great wealth and of a great industrial system."[90] This ideal of shared "wants and tastes" was the ultimate meaning of social democracy for Tarde. In the subsequent work of American social scientists, the concepts of imitation and assimilation formed the basis of a subtle but thoroughgoing reinterpretation of collective self-rule.

Assimilative Democracy:
Lester F. Ward and Edward A. Ross

The "universal consciousness of kind" that mass consumption made possible, according to Franklin Giddings, supplanted a more parochial consciousness akin to what Durkheim called "mechanical solidarity," or what the contemporary German sociologist Ferdinand Tönnies called "community" as opposed to "society." In the United States as in Europe, the founders of modern sociology were centrally concerned with identifying a new basis for collective consciousness amid the emergence of industrial capitalism.

Edward Alsworth Ross (1866–1951) was acutely conscious of his kind. For much of his career, he thought of little else. The report on "anthropometric data" that Ross appended to his autobiography, *Seventy Years of It* (1936), in order to certify his credentials as a long-headed, fair-skinned representative of the "Nordic type," entitle him to his historical distinction as "one of the most race-conscious of American social scientists."[91] But race was not the only way that he defined his kind. A childhood spent on a string of farms in Illinois, Iowa, and Kansas had made him, he wrote in his memoirs, "a farmer for life . . . more concerned with the lot of farmers than with that of any other class."[92] Ross was equally proud of his roots in his race and his roots in his land.

Yet he had been permanently uprooted from both ancestry and agriculture by the time he turned twenty. His mother died when he was six years old and his father followed her two years later, leaving their only child to be passed around among various families until he was old enough to take over his father's land. Ross severed his sole remaining tie to family and farm by selling the inheritance in order to pay for college and graduate school. "Entering college I became my own master," he wrote in his autobiography. " . . . How I reveled in this freedom—*and ever since I have been free!*"[93]

If his sense of self-mastery was peculiarly at odds with his sense of roots, the reason lay in the new sense of himself that Ross fashioned as a social psychologist. By the time he began his career in social science, he had a new consciousness of kind to add to the old. "No longer could I respect those whose behavior reflected jangling selves; no 'split-personality' for me!" Ross recalled. "The man I wanted to be must be carved, as it were, from a single block." In this aspiration for psychic health, Ross judged himself to have been a complete success, and it formed the recurrent theme of his life's story: "I cannot bear to have to do with persons who are 'off-center'"; "I never acquired an inferiority complex"; "Never having felt foiled and frustrated I am free from 'blues'"; "I am a stranger to compunction, remorse and repentance"; "The dark forces must have overlooked me when I was conceived"; and so on. Along with the appendix of anthropometric data, he included a report by a psychiatrist attesting that Ross was free of "oddities," "very sane," and in sum, "merely normal."[94]

Clearly he was not carved from a single block, but from at least two: the Nordic farmer that he was born to be and the social scientist and "normal" man that he became. This movement from one consciousness of kind to another, from blood and soil to expertise and normality, framed his scientific understanding of society as well as of himself. Unlike Patten and Veblen, Ross never returned to the farm, and by the end of his career he had "lost faith in Race" as well.[95] But the fate of the farmer or "sturdy backwoodsman," like that of the "restless, striving, doing Aryan," was the central problem considered in his first and most famous book, *Social Control* (1901), and it remained his life-long concern.[96]

In a sense, Ross identified two kinds of "common stock": the land and the people from which he came. The material and mental resources that he prized were "common" in the old sense of being bestowed as a birthright upon each individual. But in Ross's sociological writings, he described a new kind of commonality: material and mental resources that arose out of social interaction itself. Such "social" resources formed the basis of what Ross described as the modern equivalents of the land and the people: the "corporation" and the "crowd" of metropolitan America. These two kinds of social stock posed a new problem addressed in Ross's work, the problem of "social control." His solution was a theory of assimilation and public opinion, which he laid out in what he professed to be the "pioneer treatise in any language" on *Social Psychology* (1908).[97]

Contrary to his claim of originality, the latter work was "probably the most important single vehicle for the diffusion of Tarde's thought in America," according to a Tarde scholar.[98] But Ross was even more deeply influenced by his long association with Lester Frank Ward (1841–1913), having studied Ward's truly pioneering works, *Dynamic Sociology* (1883) and *The Psychic Factors of Civilization* (1893), as a graduate student and young professor; having married the niece of Ward's wife; and having corresponded extensively with Ward while preparing his own main writings.[99]

Ward's *Dynamic Sociology* was, as Gillis J. Harp has written, "probably the most successful attempt to 'republicanize' the Comtean system for Gilded Age Americans."[100] His *Psychic Factors*, in turn, rooted the new republic firmly within the social psychology of desire and the social economy of consumption, just as Tarde did.[101] Like Tarde, Ward spent virtually his entire career working in government and finally became a professor only after completing all of his important research and writing.[102] His greatest service to government, like Tarde's, was his theoretical reconstruction of the republican system, which formed in important ways what Henry Steele Commager has called "the philosophy of the welfare state."[103]

Ross's work likewise shaped the thinking of such makers of the modern American state as Theodore Roosevelt, Oliver Wendell Holmes Jr., and Walter Lippmann.[104] Ward and Ross may be seen as the respective authors of the first and second parts of a single story, chronicling the fall of political economy and the rise of social psychology as the scientific basis of Progressive political theory. Ward's work ended where Ross's began, with the problem of assimilation.

But Ward started out with a different problem, which had been central to the revolutionary republic: the problem of equality. What Ross conceived as the threat to blood and soil, as "race suicide" and the fading frontier, Ward originally perceived as a transformation of the mental and material means of popular sovereignty. The story of American social democracy thus begins with Ward and culminates in Ross, with assimilation forming the overarching ideal that connects the two.

For the orphaned Ross, ancestry was a racial abstraction, an imaginary family. By contrast, Ward was the youngest of ten children, with strong ties to his siblings and with roots reaching back to one of the founders of colonial Connecticut. His father received a quarter-section on the Iowa frontier for service in the War of 1812, and the Wards raised their children to be loyal to the nation and steadfast for freedom. At the age of 21, Ward took up the cause by enlisting as an infantryman in the Union Army. At the war's end he claimed his reward, a clerkship in the Treasury Department in Washington, D.C., the first of his many government jobs.[105]

His oldest brother, Lorenzo, inherited the family farm in Iowa and went on to edit *The Farmers' Alliance*, an agrarian newspaper calling for "Labor for the Landless, Money for the Moneyless, Homes for the Homeless."[106] Another brother, Cyrenus, took on another of their father's many trades by becoming a wheelwright and later a master machinist, as well as an organizer in New York City socialist politics and the author of a major history of labor and socialism.[107] Though Lester Ward's works also became popular reading in socialist circles, his philosophy of "sociocracy" emerged from his identification with not the working class but the governing class — the class of civil servants in which he made his career.[108]

The growing army of clerks had as yet no real rights, he believed, but it held the keys to two rising sources of power: the power of the national government and the power of expertise. The first of these forces had been amply demonstrated by the abolition of slavery and the program of Radical Reconstruction, of which Ward was an active supporter as well as an outspoken advocate of black and woman suffrage. But the retreat from Radicalism and the continuing oppression of the former slaves, as well as of women and workers, indicated to him that the emancipatory power of popular government was limited by the lack of proper direction for popular sentiment. "No people ever were free to act until they were first free to think. Our people are not, however, by any means free of the fetters of the mind," Ward wrote in an 1871 editorial on "Mental vs. Physical Liberty" in *The Iconoclast*, the newspaper of a secret society of government clerks called the National Liberal Reform League. " . . . The religious character of the women make them the willing slaves of their 'lords' whom they worship while imagining they love. The struggle just now commencing between labor and capital shows the weakness of the former to lie in its *reverence*, and the strength of the latter to lie in its *authority*. In other words, the hands of labor can never be unfettered till its brain is disenthralled."[109]

Ward spent the 1870s writing an endless manifesto provisionally entitled, "The Great Panacea," which called for public education as the key to equality. At the same time, he was educating himself with a prisoner's fury for the saving truth, piling up degrees in law, botany, chemistry, and anatomy, founding societies for the study of biology, anthropology, and philosophy, all while serving as the official librarian of the Bureau of Statistics.[110] In 1875 he read Comte's system of "positive philosophy" for the first time in the original. So captivated was Ward by the French visionary that he decided to rewrite his entire manuscript within the framework of the science of society, and to rename it, with words taken from Comte, *Dynamic Sociology*.[111]

"All civilization is artificial," Ward wrote in the encyclopedic two-volume treatise that Albion Small called general sociology's Tower of London.[112] Like Carey and George, Ward sought to dispel the myth that human affairs were governed by "natural law," but, unlike them, he drew extensively upon natural science in doing so. Following the school of evolutionary biology associated with the eighteenth-century French naturalist, Jean-Baptiste Lamarck, he argued that the course of humankind's development was not determined by natural selection, or in Spencer's famous phrase, "survival of the fittest." Progress was guided rather by the deliberate design of the social order, by conscious cooperation instead of unconscious competition.[113] The significance of Ward's work lay in his changing conception of the basis for such cooperation—in his movement from an egalitarian faith in education to a later belief in expertise and assimilation.

The modern legacy of natural law was what Ward called the "Law of Acquisition," according to which individuals instinctively sought to acquire as much personal wealth as possible, wealth being the societal equivalent of the means of survival in the natural world. But while the " 'money-making' faculty of the human mind" continued to prove of use to individuals, it had become increasingly detrimental to society as a whole. This was so because of what Ward, anticipating Veblen, called the growing "antithesis between *getting* and *producing*" wealth. Modern "money-making" entailed not the production of wealth, but its acquisition from others.[114] Acquisitiveness not only retarded social progress; it also made for an increasingly unjust distribution of wealth. "Instead of [the] equitable distribution [of wealth] in proportion to the amount each contributes to its production, it tends to concentrate in the hands of those who produce least," he wrote.[115] Like his socialist and Populist brothers, he railed against the exploitation of "producers" by "parasites."

The same capacity of "intelligence" that enabled people to exploit nature also allowed them to exploit each other, Ward contended.[116] "In a word, the entire anomaly—the evil itself—is due to the inequality which exists in this power of acquisition, in this cunning, or shrewdness—this mental force," he wrote.[117] While inborn intellectual differences were not insignificant, according to Ward, the great cause of differences in "this mental force" was "the inequality in the distribution of knowledge."[118] Moreover, those in power used their higher education and greater knowledge to move from raw competition to "cooperation," which he deemed the inevitable "result of superior intelligence." Cooperation, in turn, provided the basis of yet more power.[119]

An equal distribution of knowledge would bring an end to the inequities born of unequal intelligence, chief among them the self-destructive competition of workers. The state, as Ward envisioned it, would then become the highest expression of both universal education and universal cooperation. Government would be "transformed into a central academy of social science, which shall stand in the same relation to the control of men in which a polytechnic institute stands to the control of nature."[120]

This vision of an academic state had much in common with the educational ideal long espoused by major theorists of Anglo-American political economy, such as John Stuart Mill and Thomas Jefferson.[121] The republican realm of political economy had also assumed an informed citizenry. Ward's goal of awakening women and workers to their true interests presumed that they were endowed with the requisite reason and willpower to make use of their new knowledge.[122] Yet at the same time, he challenged the very notion of free will, the premise underlying self-government as well as self-ownership in political economy. "The illusion consists in supposing that our will is subject to our orders, that it is in any sense free," he wrote.[123] But the real "mental force" lay in "feelings" rather than in deliberation or decision-making. "Intellect is not an impelling but a directing force. Feeling alone can drive on the social train," he wrote.[124]

Ten years later in his *Psychic Factors of Civilization*, Ward drew upon the insights of the new psychology in examining more carefully the mental motor of the "social train." Following James, Dewey, and Hall, he argued that earlier writers had focused exclusively upon the intellect at the expense of "desire," which he defined as a "true natural force," indeed "the all-pervading, world-animating principle, the universal *nisus* and pulse of nature, the mainspring of all action, the life-power of the world."[125] The power of desire could not effectively be governed by reason or rationality, as political economists had imagined willpower to be. It was regulated instead by the "omitted factor" in political economy's model of the mind: "intuition." Intuition meant the distinctively human ability to pursue desires "indirectly" instead of blindly following instincts.[126] The omission of intuition was "the vice of the old political economy."[127]

The social psychology of desire and intuition marked a departure from the political economy of rationality and willpower. But it also represented a revision of the central concerns of Ward's earlier work, namely acquisitiveness and education. In *Psychic Factors*, he moved away from the emphasis in *Dynamic Sociology* on restraining acquisitiveness toward a newly articulated interest in harnessing desire. Likewise, he shifted from tuition to intuition, from exposing exploitation through education to channeling instincts in social directions. "The forces of nature are good or bad according to where they are permitted to expend themselves," he wrote. "And so it is with the passions of men as they surge through society. Left to themselves like the physical elements they find vent in all manner of ways and constantly dash against the interests of those who chance to be in their way. But like the elements they readily yield to the touch of true science, which directs them into harmless, nay, useful channels, and makes them instruments for good."[128] The goal of the "social physics" that Ward here laid out was "lessening social friction."[129]

By 1900, Ward's towering influence in American sociology was on the wane. Yet on the first day of the new century, Ward convened what he called "a small company of the *élite* of the National Capital" to discuss his plan for a second "system of sociology," a New Testament to complete the work begun in *Dynamic Sociology*.[130] The resulting two volumes on *Pure Sociology* (1903) and *Applied Sociology* (1906) reflected the new authority of his scientific field and his class of expert civil servants, now in control of such institutions as the United States Geological Survey, the Library of Congress, the United States Commission on Labor, and the National Zoological Park, all of which were represented at Ward's auspicious book-launching.[131] The self-styled "iconoclast" had become a self-styled "sociocrat." The historical interest of these two works lies in how Ward adapted his ideas to suit the emerging governmental and academic establishment.

In *Dynamic Sociology*, he had written that "the practical work which sociology demands is . . . the *organization of feeling*."[132] In *Psychic Factors*, he had indicated that the primary feeling to be organized was "desire." In his last works, Ward spelled out how desire was organized in modern America. "Consumption," he wrote, represented the social "satisfaction of desire." It was the "dynamic element" missing from the old social science, but central to the new. "If political economy has nothing to do with consumption, sociology has everything to do with it."[133] Ward now embraced "the law of marginal utility," according to which people naturally sought to maximize the utility they derived from their purchases.[134] Instead of the taming of acquisitive instincts, social progress now came to mean what Patten said it meant: the development from a "pain economy" to a "pleasure economy," allowing "the maximization of pleasure."[135]

"There is scarcely any limit to the possible increase of production," Ward explained, citing both Patten and John Bates Clark for support. With natural limits effectively overcome, the only remaining restraint upon progress was limited consumption due to untapped or unchanneled desires. "There would be no object in the increased production unless there was correspondingly increased consumption. In the language of 'political economy,' positive ethics demands an enormous rise in the standard of living," he wrote. " . . . It demands the creation of new wants and the satisfaction of these."[136]

Returning to his old interest in the relation between wealth and knowledge, he portrayed the public as a market for intellectual commodities as well as consumer goods. His earlier commitment to the equal distribution of knowledge yielded to a new problem, the lack of a sufficient "market for the products of genius." The creations of science, technology, philosophy, and literature were as limitless as the production of wealth, according to Ward. "But for all this, as for the necessaries of life, there must be a market. It is of no use to cast pearls before swine," he wrote. Education, once the key to equality in his thinking, had become finally the means of creating a demand for art as well as expertise. "The conditions to increased achievement imply and involve its assimilation," he wrote. Science and the humanities would progress only so long as ordinary people were sufficiently educated to appreciate the products of higher learning.[137]

Assimilation was the dominant theme of Ward's late works, and it was shaped as much by the onrush of immigration and the United States' imperial expansion into Asia and the Caribbean as it was by the rise of consumer capitalism. Desire, which had appeared in his previous works as the universal "mental force" of humankind, was attached in his revised sociology not only to the force of mass consumption but also to that of "Western civilization." In a racial theory absent from his earlier writings, Ward wrote that "the inhabitants of southern, central, and western Europe" and their descendants were the torch-bearers of "social energy" itself, manifested in the "vigorous push" of the West into the cultural wastelands of the East.[138] For Ward as for Tarde, international "social assimilation" was the final force of emancipation, freeing "savage races" from the "abject slave[ry]" of "primitive society."[139]

While assimilation offered the ultimate answer to the problem of inequality for Ward, it posed a new problem for Ross, his closest follower. Ross identified the problem as the search for "order," as would many American social scientists and historians to come.[140] By it he meant the breakdown of the personal bonds of church, family, and community in the emerging society of strangers, creating the crisis of social order that formed the leitmotif of modern sociology. Ross was among the first to find the solution to that distinctively modern problem in what he called "social control," which became for many writers the fundamental way of conceiving the organization and exercise of power in American society.[141] Always an elusive concept, social control meant essentially a system of power founded upon control of human instincts, desires, and habits rather than upon ownership and rulership as they were conceived in political economy.

In his major work, *Social Control: A Survey of the Foundations of Order*, Ross defined his task in terms of the contrast between Western and Eastern civilization, which Ward described similarly in his later writings. "[S]ocial order, even among the passive, unambitious Hindoos, presents a problem for solution," Ross wrote. "But it is a much more serious problem among the dolichocephalic blonds of the West," with their "daring and disobedient" spirit. That problem grew more serious still when the West met the East, as it did in the 1890s in California, where Ross was teaching at Stanford University while he wrote *Social Control*. In the "composite society" being born, he wrote, "the need of control is most imperative and unremitting." On the Pacific Coast, he believed, the old frontier ended and a new one began. "Natural order" made way for "social order."[142]

His vision of the natural order was as harmonious as Ward's was harsh, and it was brightly colored by Ross's early enthusiasm for Henry George.[143] For Ross, as for George, the golden age was the California gold rush. "The order of 1848 was literally a natural order," "an order without design or art," Ross wrote. Two "favoring circumstances" allowed the gold miners to coexist peacefully without benefit of church, family, or state. First, they were "picked men," a self-selected population of industrious, independent individuals. "They were at first chiefly Americans, and hence not without some training in self-control," he wrote. Second, they lived of necessity in rough "economic and social equality." For "all came to labor," and "no man was allowed to hold more ground than he could work."[144] In other words, the early miners were blessed with two kinds of "common stock," a common people and a common land, much like the twin blessings he attributed to the farmers of his native Midwest.

Ross witnessed firsthand the breakdown of that natural order amid the development of industrial capitalism. Fresh from graduate study in political economy with Richard Ely, whose expertise in socialism had spurred Ross's thinking about economic inequality, he plunged into laborite political activism at Stanford. California politics, as he later recalled, was then dominated by the warring forces of organized labor and the Southern Pacific Railroad, which was headed by the university's founder, Amasa Leland Stanford, until his death in 1893.[145] Ross's outspokenness on the loss of both kinds of common stock— calling for the exclusion of Asian immigrant workers as well as for municipal ownership of utilities—ultimately led to his resignation from Stanford under pressure from the widow of its founder.[146]

But it was his active opposition to the gold standard that decisively shaped his thinking about economic issues and that marked most dramatically the end of California's golden age. Recognizing that the case for free silver was built upon a utility theory of value, as discussed in Chapter 4 above, he disavowed the labor-cost theory of classical political economy and embraced purchasing power instead of labor power as the true measure of value.[147] The shift in his concern from labor to consumption, along with his reading of Ward's works, turned Ross from political economy to sociology—the science, as he put it in his sociology textbook, of "the main stream of desire." "When economics comes to treat of the consumption of wealth," he explained, "it . . . quickly loses itself in sociology."[148]

In *Social Control*, he described the "socialization" of the common people and the common land of the old frontier. The great wave of immigration from southern and eastern Europe and Asia—"alien ethnic elements introduced among a people, one in blood and culture"—was but one of several changes breaking down the natural bonds among Americans, according to Ross. Equally significant was the growth of cities, in which the "circle of kindred and friends" was eclipsed by the wider sphere of strangers, and in which "natural communities" were swallowed up in "artificial societies."[149]

At the same time, "the equality that gives homesteaders or golddiggers a few Arcadian days" was rapidly yielding to "the steepest inequalities in reward, possession, and inheritance." In particular, "private ownership of income-producing property, such as land and capital" was destroying the independence that had united prospectors, pioneers, and yeoman farmers. "As we cease to be so much a farming people, and as in almost every branch of industry the independent producer gives way to some Titanic organization," Ross wrote, "the sense of dependence on the business magnate, the employer, and the capitalist [increases accordingly]."[150]

He presented his work as a modern version of Machiavelli's *The Prince*, offering a dispassionate exposition of the bases of "social" rather than sovereign authority. Modern society, according to Ross, required a new kind of control rooted in the command of psychic rather than physical force. He addressed himself "to teachers, clergymen, editors, law-makers, and judges, who wield the instruments of control."[151] Those instruments included the traditional tools of the state and the law. But the burden of his argument was that even those venerable institutions would only continue to be honored to the extent that they made use of modern methods of "social control," or "control through the feelings" instead of "control by sanctions."[152]

Popular sentiment, not popular sovereignty, was the true source of democratic authority. The new basis of republican rule was "prestige" and "public opinion" rather than representative government, or the "confidence" of the people rather than their consent.[153] "With a democratic, forward-looking people like ours, opinion, no longer split up into small currents by class lines or broken in force by masses of family, sect, or caste tradition, the débris of the past, acquires a tidal volume and sweep," he wrote. " In such a stream all oaks become reeds. The day of the sturdy backwoodsman, settler, flat-boatman, or prospector, defiant not alone of law but of public opinion as well, is gone never to return. We are come to a time when ordinary men are scarcely aware of the coercion of public opinion, so used are they to follow it. They cannot dream of aught but acquiescence in an unmistakable edict of the mass."[154]

In other words, modern Americans by and large adopted their "opinions" unquestioningly from the "mass" of their fellow citizens. Expert "opinion-makers" could steer such sentiment in a progressive direction, but common people could hardly be expected to think for themselves. The political principle of Ross's social psychology was that the vast majority of people were neither rulers nor subjects in a sovereign sense; they were participants at best, followers at worst, swimmers in the mainstream. What did Ross's conception of this psychosocial stream mean for popular sovereignty? How, in the end, did Ross reconceive political agency? In a series of books published in the aftermath of Social Control—Foundations of Sociology (1905), Sin and Society (1907), and Social Psychology (1908)—he centered his analysis upon two forms of psychosocial democracy, or what he called the "edict of the mass." These were the crowd and the corporation, or "mob mind" and "corporate association." They represented social thought and social property, the social equivalents of common people and common land.

The common people that Ross repeatedly described, often in racial or ethnic terms, were united by their spirit of industriousness and independence, of restless "striving," self-assertion, and "self-control." Members of a crowd were united by just the opposite quality: a readiness to surrender themselves to the mass.

Unlike the "individual self," according to Ross, the "crowd self" was "credulous," "suggestible," "irrational." "A *one-mindedness*, therefore, the result not of reasoning or discussion or coming together of the like-minded, but of *imitation*, is the mark of the true mob," he wrote.[155] The modern "public" was similarly bound by ideas and opinions absorbed without deliberation or even awareness of the quiet coercion taking place. "Many a man thinks he makes up his mind, whereas, in truth, it is made up for him," Ross wrote.[156] Modern Americans were the unwitting consumers rather than the willful producers of their own thoughts.

Likewise, whereas the common land of "homesteaders or golddiggers" was the foundation of propertied independence, the corporate economy was dominated by propertied "interdependence," in Ross's words. "Nowadays the water main is my well, the trolley car my carriage, the banker's safe my old stocking, the policeman's billy my fist," he wrote. " ... I let the meat trust butcher my pig, the oil trust mold my candles, the sugar trust boil my sorghum, the coal trust chop my wood, the barb wire company split my rails."[157] The danger was that the corporation, like the crowd, would represent the lowest common denominator rather than the highest collective ideal. The "beak-and-claw struggle, renounced as between individuals" could continue between corporate entities— by which he meant unions and political parties as well as business corporations —wreaking havoc on a societal scale.[158] Like the members of a crowd, corporate owners, directors, and employees could not be held individually responsible for their collective crimes. The corporate criminal was more often than not "a buyer rather than a practitioner of sin," "a consumer of custom-made crime."[159]

Yet as consumers of thought as well as wealth, Americans could in theory assert a new kind of social power, according to Ross. They could "rationalize public opinion" and regulate corporate conduct, turning their dependence upon common knowledge and consumer products into a position of popular authority. But Ross offered little guidance as to how ordinary Americans might truly take charge in the "era of publics" that he, like Tarde, heralded.[160] In the meantime, he showed more confidence in Ward's expert elite than in common citizens or their elected officials, the agents of an older republic. "Social defense is coming to be a matter for the expert. The rearing of dikes against faithlessness and fraud calls for intelligent social engineering," he wrote. "If in this strait the public does not speedily become far shrewder in the grading and gulling of sinners, there is nothing for it but to turn over the defense of society to professionals."[161]

CHAPTER SEVEN

Corporate Capitalism and the Social Self

Thomas M. Cooley and
Charles H. Cooley

C harles Horton Cooley (1864–1929), one of the founding theorists of American social psychology, was prodigiously self-conscious. That is, he was extraordinarily conscious of what he imagined others thought of him, and his enduring contribution to American social thought was the idea that that was what self-consciousness, or even selfhood, meant. Cooley called this concept the "looking-glass self." "As we see our face, figure, and dress in the glass, and are interested in them because they are ours, and pleased or otherwise with them according as they do or do not answer to what we should like them to be; so in imagination we perceive in another's mind some thought of our appearance, manners, aims, deeds, character, friends, and so on, and are variously affected by it," he wrote in 1902. " . . . We always imagine, and in imagining share, the judgments of the other mind." His pathbreaking studies of such "imaginative sociability" entitle him to primary credit for that master creation of modern American social science, the "social self."[1]

Along with the other original theorists of social selfhood, foremost among them John Dewey and George Herbert Mead, Cooley formed the intellectual vanguard of what James Livingston has aptly called the "cultural revolution" of the late nineteenth and early twentieth centuries, in which an older understanding of self and society was decisively undermined.[2] That earlier conception, itself the product of the political and economic revolutions of the late eighteenth and early nineteenth centuries, was of a society of essentially autonomous households whose political rights and responsibilities derived from their independent ownership of productive resources—of their own farms, shops, or mercantile enterprises. What might be termed the "sovereign self" had its roots in the classically "republican" ideal of the virtuous citizen as well as the classically "liberal" ideal of the self-interested freeholder. But by the late nineteenth century, as business corporations had increasingly monopolized productive resources, earlier ideas about economic independence and the political rights that went with it had become closely identified with the property claims of corporate capital. "Nearly all enterprises requiring for their successful prosecution large investment of capital are conducted by corporations," Supreme Court Justice Stephen J. Field wrote in 1890. "They, in fact, embrace every branch of industry, and the wealth that they hold in the United States equals in value four-fifths of the entire property of the country."[3]

The modern business corporation had its roots in the early republic, when state legislatures granted special charters for the provision of public necessities entailing large and long-term investment, such as transportation, banking, water, and insurance.[4] With the widespread enactment of general incorporation laws in the antebellum era, incorporation was transformed from a special grant awarded to a select few into a basic right available to all qualified investors. The midcentury railroad boom, which gave rise to the nation's first truly big businesses, employing a mass workforce supervised by salaried officials, depended upon both generous public subsidies and the development of an extensive private securities market centered in New York City.[5] Yet outside of the railroad and textile industries, the prevailing form of business organization in the postbellum period remained the family firm or partnership, owned and operated by its founding entrepreneurs, mainly financed internally from its own profits, engaged in specialized production for a local or regional market.[6]

The completion of the national rail network provided the opportunity to produce for a mass market as well as the imperative of heightened competition, which compelled manufacturers to keep up with falling prices by slashing labor costs. As profits plummeted amid the deepening struggle between organized workers and employers, leading industrialists in oil, steel, farm machinery, and other fields turned to mechanization and merger as means of reorganizing production and gaining control over the shop floor. Antitrust legislation and related court rulings prohibiting collusion among firms made outright combination an increasingly attractive alternative. At the same time, the overbuilding and diminishing returns of the railroads drew financial investors into a growing market for industrial stocks and bonds during the depression of the 1890s. The tidal wave of corporate consolidation between 1898 and 1902, involving between one-fourth and one-third of the nation's entire manufacturing plant, culminated twenty-five years of intense intercapitalist as well as class conflict. From the social crisis over Gilded Age industrialization arose a new economic order in which the large business corporation, owned by absentee shareholders, managed by a hierarchical bureaucracy, producing a diverse and integrated array of goods and services for a national or international market, reigned supreme.[7]

Charles Cooley's father, Thomas McIntyre Cooley (1824–1898), was a leading exponent of the federal judiciary's sustained effort to apply the classical principles of private property and free enterprise to a society increasingly dominated by corporate capital.[8] As one of the most influential jurists and legal scholars in postbellum America, the elder Cooley joined Justice Field as a principal author of the doctrine of "substantive due process," by which the constitutional protections of life, liberty, and property formerly reserved for individuals were gradually conferred upon business corporations. By extending preexisting constitutional restrictions on the public appropriation of private property, Thomas Cooley's widely read writings on the related doctrine of "public purpose" drew critical new limits upon the states' power to tax corporate earnings. Spurred by revisionist studies of Cooley and Field, legal historians in recent years have shown that the "laissez-faire constitutionalism" of the late nineteenth and early twentieth centuries was guided not simply by sympathy for big business, as earlier scholars contended, but by a deeper allegiance to the Jacksonian ideology of the free market and the neutral state.[9] The sovereign self, torn from its roots in the early republic of freeholders, found a new home in the synthesis of economic individualism and corporate property that is the enduring legacy of Thomas Cooley and his contemporaries on the bench.

As the traditional ideal of the independent proprietor was transformed into a defense of the rights of corporations, Charles Cooley and like-minded social scientists constructed a rival model of the relation between self and society, predicated upon the principle of "interdependence," as opposed to independence. More than an attack upon the tradition of "possessive individualism" definitively described by C. B. Macpherson, their critique of "economic man" entailed a rigorous repudiation of the Enlightenment social science of political economy and its core concepts of self-interest and social contract, along with a sweeping reconsideration of its epistemological and ethical underpinnings. In sharp contrast to the logic of laissez-faire and the competitive market, the younger Cooley and his cohorts envisioned a society bound not by contractual relations among property owners but by a common current of desires, values, and ideas that he called the "stream of communication," a kind of socialism of the psyche. By elaborating a psychosocial conception of selfhood, he joined in the Pragmatist movement that provided the philosophical framework for Progressive reform.[10]

In striking ways, the two Cooleys appear to articulate the central ideological divide in modern American social thought between a corporate conservatism informed by neoclassical economics and a reformist liberalism guided by the communitarian vision of the founders of social psychology.[11] A rereading of their work, however, reveals fundamental continuities underlying the apparent conflict between them. To begin with, the concentration of capital and the expansion of wage labor in the postbellum era prompted Thomas Cooley to disavow the older, liberal-republican precepts of natural right and social contract. Much like his younger contemporary, Oliver Wendell Holmes Jr., the elder Cooley found in the Anglo-American common law tradition an organicist vision of a society founded upon common customs, habits, and values.[12] From it, he derived a new, sociological basis for the regulatory state, of which he was both a preeminent theorist and, as the first chair of the Interstate Commerce Commission (ICC), a leading practitioner. Thomas Cooley's expansive formulation of the state's "police power" to regulate corporate conduct formed the essential counterpart of his recognition of new corporate property rights, and it marked a pivotal departure from the individualistic conceptions of property and society in classical political economy.

Charles Cooley began his career by working at the ICC under his father, from whom he inherited the theoretical challenge of reconceiving the relationship between self and society in the emerging corporate order. The younger Cooley's doctoral thesis in political economy led him into the emerging field of social psychology, in which he elaborated his father's late organicist ideas into a whole new theory of social selfhood during his distinguished career at the University of Michigan. By envisioning a "democracy of sentiment" instead of an oligarchy of property, a society governed by "self-expression" rather than "self-interest," he issued a sharp cultural critique of the "pecuniary values" of American capitalism, and he insisted that such values were rooted not in human nature, but in society. Yet in so doing, he also deliberately shifted the stakes of social struggle away from political and economic rights and toward psychosocial norms, desires, and needs, away from proprietary claims upon productive resources and toward cultural claims upon selfhood and moral agency. The social self that he created was therefore ironically compatible with wage labor and corporate capital in ways that the sovereign self it supplanted was not. Much as

Thomas Cooley's common-law rationale for the regulatory state was integrally related to his constitutional legitimation of corporate property, so Charles Cooley's social psychology was wedded in complex ways to the logic of corporate capitalism. Together, Thomas Cooley's reconstruction of property and sovereignty along with Charles Cooley's reconstruction of selfhood encapsulated the broader shift from political economy to social psychology as the master science of American society.

Thomas M. Cooley and Corporate Property

The elder Cooley's *Treatise on the Constitutional Limitations Which Rest Upon the Legislative Power of the States of the American Union* (1868), published just two months after the Fourteenth Amendment was ratified, became the definitive work on "America's second constitution" and the most widely read book on American law in the late nineteenth century.[13] "Eighteen sixty-eight marks a turning point in American constitutional law," Benjamin R. Twiss wrote in 1942. "In that year laissez faire capitalism was supplied with a legal ideology in Thomas M. Cooley's *Constitutional Limitations* almost as a direct counter to the appearance a year earlier of Karl Marx's *Das Kapital*." For Twiss and like-minded contemporaries, Cooley's treatise represented the point of departure for a judicial counteroffensive on behalf of propertied interests against the on-slaught of popular democracy. In the half-century beginning around 1890, the argument went, the courts had successfully stymied legislative efforts to bring privately owned business under public control, until the "constitutional revolution" of 1937, coinciding with Twiss's work, had reopened the door to economic democracy.[14] Thirty years later, Alan Jones challenged Twiss's influential interpretation by convincingly demonstrating that Cooley's constitutional defense of corporate property had been rooted in the antebellum politics of Jacksonian democracy, with its populist hostility toward economic privilege, rather than in conservative allegiance to a propertied elite.[15] More recently, Gerald Berk and other scholars have highlighted Cooley's increasing sympathy for public regulation of corporate conduct, distinguishing him from more laissez-faire Gilded Age jurists such as John Dillon, Stephen Field, and David Brewer.[16]

As a small-town lawyer, journalist, and ardent Democrat on the Michigan frontier in the antebellum era, Thomas Cooley voiced the egalitarian demand of aspiring artisans and yeomen for an end to "special privilege," meaning state sponsorship of select industrialists and financiers in order to promote economic development. His democratic suspicion of the entanglement of government with private business led him to support general incorporation laws and bolstered his belief in the developing legal doctrine of "public purpose," which strictly limited the use of the state power of eminent domain—the power to appropriate private property for public use—on behalf of private economic interests such as canals, toll roads, and railroads.[17]

Cooley brought the Jacksonian distinction between "public purpose" and private interest to the new Department of Law at the University of Michigan, where he taught for twenty-five years beginning in 1859, and to the Michigan Supreme Court, to which he was elected in 1864. In his most famous ruling, *People v. Salem* (1870), he rejected a railroad's contention that it was serving a "public purpose" and could therefore demand issuance and enforcement of public bonds to finance the railroad's construction, once such subsidies had been promised. Contradicting the prevailing opinion of state courts, Cooley sided with a town board that argued that its predecessors had acted unconstitutionally in pledging taxpayer support. Railways, he wrote, "are not, when in private hands, the *people's highways*; but they are private property." The danger was the familiar bugbear of special privilege, for "when the State once enters upon the business of subsidies, we shall not fail to discover that the strong and powerful interests are those most likely to control legislation, and that the weaker will be taxed to enhance the profits of the stronger."[18]

In his master work, *Constitutional Limitations*, Cooley turned the state court doctrine of "public purpose" into a guiding principle for the federal judiciary in interpreting the Fourteenth Amendment's sweeping mandate that no state be allowed to "deprive any person of life, liberty, or property, without due process of law."[19] "[T]here is no rule or principle known to our system under which private property can be taken from one man and transferred to another for the private use and benefit of such other person, whether by general laws or by special enactment," he wrote. "The purpose must be public, and must have reference to the needs of the government."[20] In this and his subsequent *Treatise on the Law of Taxation* (1876), Cooley specifically proscribed the use of the power of taxation to assist certain persons or classes at the expense of others, at a time when states and municipalities were relying upon skyrocketing property taxes to subsidize railroads, financiers, and manufacturers. "However important it may be to the community that individual citizens should prosper in their industrial enterprises, it is not the business of government to aid them with its means. Enlightened states leave every man to depend for his success and prosperity in business on his own exertions," he wrote.[21]

For Cooley, as for a majority of the Supreme Court after the 1880s, "due process" was more than a procedural guarantee of fair consideration before the law; it was a substantive right not to be deprived of one's property for any other than "public purposes."[22] But the principal beneficiaries of such "substantive due process," far from the petty proprietors who had been the dominant economic agents before the Civil War, were the giant, oligopolistic corporations that came to control the great majority of the nation's railroads, manufacturing, mining, and banking in the postwar era.[23] In this rapidly changing context, Cooley's strict construction of property rights and his opposition to redistributive taxation crucially contributed to the emerging jurisprudence of corporate property. Even as the federal judiciary continued to espouse the traditional conception of property rights rooted in classical political economy, it expanded the definition of property to include expected income from stockholdings and other intangible assets and to encompass the rights of corporate "persons" as well as individuals.[24]

Cooley viewed the awesome growth in corporations' power over the American economy with dismay, particularly because it was predicated upon the doctrines of private property and "public purpose" that he himself expounded. "It is under the protection of the decision in the Dartmouth College Case," he wrote in the second edition of *Constitutional Limitations* (1871), referring to the landmark Supreme Court ruling of 1819 that corporations were not simply instruments of government, "that the most enormous and threatening powers in our country have been created; some of the great and wealthy corporations actually having greater influence in the country at large and upon the legislation of the country than the States to which they owe their corporate existence."[25] In an 1883 article entitled "State Regulation of Corporate Profits," he noted that private corporations had assumed responsibility for providing such basic public services as transportation and communication, clean water and gas lighting, which would otherwise be the responsibility of government. Without adequate public regulation of such businesses, he wrote, "we may find . . . that [the State] has bartered away a large part of its ability to be useful to the people, and that, instead of existing for the equal and common good of all, it has built up privileged classes to whom the functions of government have been granted or pledged."[26]

A deeper danger, as he saw it, lay in the growing political power of the mass of propertyless wage workers that arose alongside corporate capital. "Property is safe when it is generally possessed, so that the people can perceive that they participate in the benefits of existing institutions; and it is not safe otherwise," Cooley wrote in an 1884 article entitled "Labor and Capital Before the Law." "Persons who are both idle and needy may be thinking dangerous thoughts," condemning "all that have capital as robbers and plunderers," regarding "the Constitution itself" as "an instrument whose office is to protect the rich in the advantages they have secured over the poor," he warned. In such a class-divided society, popular sovereignty would come to threaten rather than strengthen the constitutional protection of private property that formed the substance of "substantive due process." Surveying the polarized class politics of the 1880s, Cooley found the regime of private property in unprecedented peril. "[T]he best security for capital is in cordial relations between those who possess it and those whose labor gives it satisfactory employment," whereas the mounting conflict between organized labor and corporate capital tended to bankrupt employers, pauperize employees, and undermine the social basis of private property itself, he wrote.[27]

How was the government to defend private property against the class conflict brought on by corporate consolidation without, in so doing, trampling upon corporate property rights? Cooley's widely followed response to that problem made him one of the foremost theorists of the so-called "police power," which came to be recognized in the postbellum era as a fundamental power of American government along with, for example, the powers of taxation and eminent domain. In eighteenth-century European and American social thought, "police" had denoted an all-encompassing science of government, one closely associated with civic republican ideas about the subordination of private interests to the common good. State courts in the antebellum era had drawn upon this communitarian understanding of "state police power" in sanctioning a wide range of regulations of individual and business conduct in the name of public health, safety, and morals.[28] Postbellum jurists, largely led by Cooley, elaborated the theory of police power into an expansive new basis for the regulatory state in the age of corporate capital.[29] "The police of a State," he wrote in *Constitutional Limitations*, referred to the "system of internal regulation" designed to enforce "rules of good manners and good neighborhood" as well as more limited rules of public order, including "extensive and varied regulations as to the time, mode, and circumstances in and under which parties shall assert, enjoy, or exercise their rights." "Perhaps the most striking illustration" of the police power, according to Cooley, could be found in the expanding authority of state legislatures to restrict the property rights of corporations in the interests of "public protection, health, and safety."[30] Indeed the main purpose of the police power, as he saw it, was to bring corporate power under public control while fending off a popular assault upon corporate property itself.

The jurisprudence of taxation and eminent domain, as Cooley understood it, was informed by the liberal political model of the social contract from which the state derived its authority. Governmental power was balanced by individual right: the right to "just compensation" for the individual's property in the

case of eminent domain and the right to "protection" for the individual's property in the case of taxation.[31] But such a contractual basis for public regulation
of corporations was critically weakened by the decline of the theory of corporate charters as special privileges granted by government.[32] So Cooley rested
the rationale for the police power upon different ground.

"Whence did the State derive the power to intervene?" he wrote of the
Supreme Court's decision upholding the regulation of rates for the storage of
grain in *Munn v. Illinois* (1876),[33] which provided the precedent for similar rulings on the regulation of railroad rates. "The case was new and without precedent; and if the Constitution of the State did not determine the limit of State
power, it must be sought for in such principles of government as were embodied in the common law, and as have been adopted by the people as part of their
heritage of freedom."[34] Chief Justice Morrison B. Waite indeed relied upon
common law to justify the Court's broad interpretation of the "public interest"
in *Munn*, citing for support a well-known seventeenth-century legal tract by
Sir Matthew Hale, one of the foremost scholars of the history of the common
law.[35] Along with his elder contemporary, Sir Edward Coke, Hale had propounded the theory of the common law as the product of immemorial custom,
embodying the unwritten, bedrock values of Anglo-Saxon culture as they had
evolved over countless centuries. The common law was not, in other words, the
expression of the sovereign authority of either the king (as in Hobbes) or the
people (as in Locke), but rather reflected the timeless, yet ever-evolving wisdom of society itself as interpreted by common-law judges. It was to this profoundly conservative, yet paradoxically progressive common-law tradition,
which (like the eighteenth-century idea of "police") had formed a persistent
undercurrent within the mainstream of liberal political theory in the early American republic, that Cooley appealed in support of the modern regulatory state.[36]

Like his contemporary in legal theory, Francis Lieber, upon whom he drew,
Cooley gravitated in the postbellum period toward an organic conception of a
society founded upon racial values, habits, and common customs, rather than
upon independent proprietorship and republican government. He invoked the
tradition of Edmund Burke in rejecting the liberal ideals of natural right and
social contract, and in finding within the common law what Burke called "one
great, immutable, pre-existent law, prior to all our devices, and prior to all our
contrivances, paramount to all our ideas and all our sensations, antecedent to
our very existence, by which we are knit and connected in the eternal frame of
the universe, out of which we cannot stir."[37] In an 1871 state supreme court decision, he likewise found the "living spirit" of the law in "the usages, the customs, the maxims, that have sprung from the habits of life" and the "modes of

thought" of the people of Michigan.[38] "Legal rules long observed create a reason for themselves, and the citizen conforms to them without question as he
does to the laws of nature whose operations he perceives about him," Cooley
wrote in 1888. "He yields as by a sort of instinct to what the law, expressing the
common opinion, has settled upon as right, and the law is a master which he
follows without seeing, and obeys without waiting for a command."[39]

But Cooley invoked this traditionally conservative vision in a new way, as a
license for the police power and an alternative to "class legislation." Like Hale
before him, Cooley emphasized the common law's capacity for effortless adaptation to societal change, and he brought that power to bear upon the emerging corporate-industrial order.[40] The evolution of industrial and commercial
practices, he contended in "Labor and Capital Before the Law," called forth a
corresponding evolution of the common law and expansion of the scope of
regulatory authority. The "wonderful activity of invention and production,"
along with "the marvelous expansion of business," created "new conditions to
which the law must be conformed." When "new statutes" did not keep abreast
of "the new ways, new things, and new conditions," he wrote, "the legislation of
usage must supply the defects." Since "some kinds of business are so entirely
new in some of their features that precedents are nearly worthless," as was the
case with the railroads, Cooley advised judges to consult the "store of wisdom
[that] has been accumulated by various classes and various interests" in establishing new rules in accord with the common law. In this way, he described an
evolutionary, common-law basis for the regulatory state. "[M]uch direct legislation of a very effective and important nature is constantly going on, at the
time attracting little or no attention," he wrote. "This is the steady modification
of the common law by public sentiment, noticeable only when it has crystal-
lized in general custom. The best of all laws for all countries are made in this
way."[41]

In arguing for custom and convention as the newly sociological rather than
political-economic bases of popular sovereignty, Cooley signaled a pronounced
shift away from the Jacksonian vision of a republic of freeholders with which
he had begun his career. So too, his defense of property rights carried him from
the proprietary individualism of the antebellum era into the new logic of a corporate economy in which the autonomous household had no place. In his conception of the police power, as in his theories of "public purpose" and "substantive due process," he moved from the agrarian understanding of market
society inherent in classical political economy toward a still-undefined social-
scientific understanding that was consonant, as the earlier view was not, with

both the economic supremacy of corporate capital and the political authority of the regulatory state.

That ideological movement, which was characteristic of the academy and the professions in the late nineteenth and early twentieth centuries, informed Cooley's leadership of the first, precedent-setting federal regulatory agency, the Interstate Commerce Commission, from 1887 to 1890. In an 1886 address, Cooley explained the specific relevance of the common-law tradition to the regulation of interstate commerce. "[A]s year by year new inventions keep coming to modify and quicken industrial and social life, this power of regulation naturally ... takes them under its protection; so that the statesman who contemplates the power enlightened by the wonderful contrivances whereby commerce is now enabled to accomplish such marvels, seems to see new meaning in the grant and sees it grow before his eyes ... ," he said. "So day by day the Government control of Inter-State commerce takes upon itself importance and enlists more and more the interest of all the people."[42] His policy while on the ICC anticipated the dominant administrative approach to corporate power in the Progressive Era: sanctioning corporate consolidation while demanding "reasonable" rates and prohibiting discriminatory practices; endorsing regulation rather than state ownership of major industries; and favoring moral suasion over punitive action as the main means of regulation.[43] While his *Constitutional Limitations* was no simple defense of "laissez faire capitalism" in response to *Das Kapital,* as Benjamin Twiss long ago supposed, Cooley's theory and practice of corporate regulation laid the foundation for a social-scientific, evolutionary alternative to revolutionary socialism.

Charles H. Cooley and the Social Self

Thomas Cooley's tenure on the ICC marked the endpoint of his career and the beginning of his son's. Charles Cooley's work at the ICC, studying railway accidents, provided the material for his doctoral dissertation in political economy at the University of Michigan, which he completed in 1894, two years after he had begun teaching there. Entitled "The Theory of Transportation," his thesis addressed what he called "the present railroad problem," meaning the need of a new rationale for regulation in the face of the unprecedented power of the railroads over the emerging national market.[44] Thomas Cooley had offered his own tentative answer to that problem in his theory of "police power" based upon a sociological reconstruction of the common law tradition. But the father's theory betrayed a fundamental tension between the limits of governmental authority dictated by the doctrine of "public purpose" and the expansive implications of regrounding government in "public sentiment." The younger Cooley resolved that tension by setting the railroad problem within a new theoretical framework suggested to him by his minor field in sociology, and particularly by the work of Franklin Giddings. His aim, he wrote, was to formulate "a theory of transportation from a sociological standpoint."[45]

As Charles Cooley conceived it, the railroad problem was rooted in the outdated notion that transportation was "an industry essentially like other industries," when in truth "such an assumption implies a failure to get to the social point of view." From this new vantage point, transportation appeared as the very basis of modern society itself, "an agency by which every part of society is brought into relation with every other, and interdependence, specialization, in a word, organization made possible." It was, he wrote, "a highly organic activity, requiring to be conducted according to a comprehensive plan and methods." Because it related to "society as a whole rather than to any particular part of it," the transportation industry naturally required both corporate consolidation and a merger of public and private governance. Like his father, Cooley favored public regulation of private railroads over public ownership. "Rightly understood the case is not so much that of the public *versus* the railroads, as that of the public and the railroads *versus* disorganizing private interests," he wrote, calling for a prototypically Progressive partnership of government and big business in regulating the market.[46]

In describing the "social point of view" from which transportation appeared unlike other industries, Cooley subtly shifted the focus of political economy from the sphere of production—that is, of labor and industrial capital—to the sphere of distribution or exchange. It was the "distinct social function" of the railroads to serve as a main means of exchanging goods, not of producing them. "As the efficiency of productive processes is multiplied by the division of labor," he contended, " ... [a] greater share of the whole product must be conveyed from one place to another.... Conveyance, then, is an industry that must ever grow much more rapidly than industries in general."[47] Like contemporary economists such as Simon Patten, Cooley appeared to suggest that with the development of new technologies of mass production, the problem of maximizing production, which had been the central concern of classical political economy, was gradually yielding center stage to the problem of distributing what was being ever more rapidly produced. Transportation, as the means of exchange, therefore increasingly became the primary resource that determined the division of wealth by controlling the process of distribution. Echoing contemporary Populist claims upon the system of transportation and distribution (as well as upon the currency system, the other essential means of exchange), Cooley argued that the crux of the railroad problem in material terms was the determination of freight rates. Completed in the year of the great Pullman railroad strike, his thesis nevertheless had nothing to say, by contrast, about the determination of wages and profits.[48]

From his "sociological standpoint," Cooley turned away from political economy's traditional concern with the factors of production toward a new focus upon the factors of exchange. But his thesis marked the beginning of another, equally profound shift in his main subject of study: from the exchange of goods to the exchange of ideas or, in his terms, from "material transportation" to "the communication of thought." While transportation made possible the "physical organization of society," he wrote, communication was the basis of its "psychical organization." "If one rightly considers the enormous intricacy and importance of these psychical processes of society, this social thinking, perceiving, feeling and deciding in all its unspeakable multiplicity, he may well conclude that its adequate analysis and interpretation is the most complex and difficult problem ever offered to science," Cooley wrote. Though transportation could still be understood in the terms of political economy, communication, he argued, "belongs to a distinctive branch of study of immeasurable importance and complexity, namely social psychology."[49] In the parallel between transportation and communication, his first work bore the seed of those to come. What he famously called, years later, "the stream of communication" was both a sociological version of William James's "stream of consciousness" and a psychological version of the sociology of transportation.[50]

In an 1899 article entitled "Personal Competition" and published in *Economic Studies*, Cooley elaborated upon the vital connection between economic relations and psychological relations that he had drawn in his thesis. Much as he had earlier endorsed corporate consolidation and public regulation in the railroad industry, he now more broadly supported the massive transformation of the American economy that reached its apotheosis in the great merger movement of the turn of the century. Yet, he lamented, as he had in his earlier work, that the great corporations remained beholden to an older ethic of adversarial competition, and he called for the regulatory state to coordinate industrial affairs in the spirit of cooperation and harmony.[51]

Similarly, Cooley maintained that individuals' "struggle for existence," to fulfill their basic needs of food and shelter, had largely given way in modern society to a new kind of competition: "the struggle to maintain what is called a standard of living; and this is altogether a social or psychological phenomenon. Our standard of living is fixed by what others think, by what those whose respect we wish to retain regard as decent and necessary." Like Patten, but also like Thorstein Veblen, whose *Theory of the Leisure Class* was published the same year, he argued that success was increasingly defined not by the production of wealth, but by "the production of some effect upon the minds of others, the achievement of respect, honor, power, love, or beneficence." But just as the leaders of the great corporations continued to operate according to the anachronistic principles of the competitive market, so many individuals still labored under the selfish standards of success appropriate to an earlier age, according to Cooley. Fortunately, he concluded, such standards were set not by human nature, but by society itself. In the same way that the rise of corporate capitalism called, in his view, for a new model of a planned economy, one organized according to cooperative rather than competitive dictates, so the rising standard of living made possible "a larger, richer personality" attuned to new cultural norms.[52] The emerging corporate order provided the incubator for a newly socialized self.

The embryo of the social or "looking-glass" self that formed the subject of all his subsequent work lay in Cooley's conception of the "standard of living" as a measure of what people imagined others thought of them. His theory of selfhood also drew upon the romantic psychology of Goethe, Emerson, and James as well as upon a wide range of contemporary social scientists. But his most important model for the social self was avowedly himself. So it is more than a personal curiosity that the great analyst of social selfhood was a lifelong near-recluse, that the author of "The Theory of Transportation" seldom ventured beyond his hometown of Ann Arbor, and that the foremost theorist of the "stream of communication" struggled for much of his life with a voice so feeble that he could barely make himself heard as a child, though he fancied himself even then a famous orator. Even written communication was for the young Cooley a breathtaking chore.[53]

Yet in his mind, Cooley traveled widely and held endless conversations with imaginary peers. These mental adventures, painstakingly recorded in his journal, formed the raw material from which he made up the social self. Introducing this ultimate figment of his imagination in his first book, *Human Nature and the Social Order* (1902), he wrote, "[T]here is no separation between real and imaginary persons; indeed, to be imagined is to become real, in a social sense." The "imaginative sociability" that Cooley knew from firsthand experience was to him no different, "in a social sense," from the actual interaction of real people. "[W]e are accustomed to talk and think . . . as if a person were a material rather than a psychical fact," he acknowledged, but such pretensions were as illusory as imaginary persons were real. "I conclude, therefore, that the imaginations which people have of one another are the *solid facts* of society, and that to observe and interpret these must be a chief aim of sociology," he wrote.[54]

Cooley articulated a distinctly modern—or rather, postmodern—view of social relations as essentially psychological constructs. "Society, then, in its immediate aspect, *is a relation among personal ideas.* In order to have society it is evidently necessary that persons should get together somewhere; and they get together only as personal ideas in the mind," he wrote. " ... Society exists in my mind as the contact and reciprocal influence of certain ideas named 'I,' Thomas, Henry, Susan, Bridget, and so on. It exists in your mind as a similar group, and so in every mind."[55] Conversely, he conceived the human psyche as a thoroughly social construct, comprising feelings and ideas conveyed from person to person and from generation to generation by the stream of psychic communication.[56] The fundamental dichotomy of individual and society, which underlay the classical political-economic precepts of natural right and social contract, of self-interest as well as sovereignty, dissolved in Cooley's mental mainstream. "Mind is an organic whole made up of coöperating individualities," he wrote in his second book, *Social Organization: A Study of the Larger Mind* (1909). " ... Self and society are twin-born."[57]

Cooley's conception of social selfhood was shaped by the complex connection he continued to elaborate between psychological exchange and economic exchange, or communication and transportation. Much as his theory of transportation emphasized the primacy of relations of exchange rather than relations of production in economic affairs, so his theory of communication highlighted the formative role of social exchange in human psychology. "A mind without words would make only such feeble and uncertain progress as a traveler set down in the midst of a wilderness where there were no paths or conveyances and without even a compass," he wrote. "A mind with them is like the same traveller in the midst of civilization, with beaten roads and rapid vehicles ready to take him in any direction where men have been before."[58] Seen in this way, the development of new communications technology such as the telephone, the telegraph, low-cost printing, and the modern postal service appeared to usher in a new age of mental commerce just as the railroad seemingly raised market relations to a loftier level, freed from parochial bonds. If the railroad transported Americans into an economy of abundance and interdependence, the communications revolution of the nineteenth century promised no less than "the expansion of human nature" itself, according to Cooley. It meant "freedom, outlook, indefinite possibility. The public consciousness, instead of being confined as regards its more active phases to local groups, extends by even steps with that give-and-take of suggestions that the new intercourse makes possible, until wide nations, and finally the world itself, may be included in one lively mental whole."[59]

Cooley did not imagine that the emerging "social organization" had already delivered on its full utopian promise. Progress in industrial and commercial organization had outpaced the psychological socialization it made possible, he argued, along with many Progressive thinkers. Wage workers, no less than capitalists and many in the new "professional classes," continued to pursue the phantom of purely pecuniary success.[60] The central social problem of the age of capital, as he saw it, was not that economic self-reliance was increasingly unattainable for a growing majority of Americans, but that they nevertheless clung to that reactionary ideal in the absence of any clearly conceived alternative. The mission of modern American social science was to provide such a new understanding of freedom and equality, much as political economy had done a century earlier.

Politically, his conception of society as the common stream of consciousness meant redefining democracy in terms of the organization of "public opinion" rather than of popular sovereignty. "Public opinion is no mere aggregate of separate individual judgments," he explained, "but an organization, a coöperative product of communication and reciprocal influence." Further, it was less a matter of collective judgment than of common "sentiment," arising less from willful deliberation than from the kind of instinctive, unquestioned beliefs and values that his father had found in the common law.[61] Economically, Cooley similarly reconceived the market in terms of the organization of consumer demand rather than of productive labor, and he described demand itself as a function of social norms and desires instead of self-interested calculation. In a 1910 paper entitled "Political Economy and Social Process," he joined the chorus of social scientists (as well as merchants and advertisers) calling for greater understanding of how the market created new wants instead of simply administering preexisting ones. Like many of his contemporaries, he bemoaned the market's nurture of self-destructive or dangerous desires as well as of "pecuniary values." Unlike many, he also sharply criticized the dollar democracy that allowed those with the highest disposable income to determine the shape of the consumer market as a whole. As important as his critique of the consumer market, however, was Cooley's identification of consumption and the social psychology upon which it was based, rather than property in productive resources, as the proper objects of social reform.[62]

Convinced that industrial exploitation and inequality were rooted in the

materialistic, individualistic values of an older America, he was infinitely op-
timistic about the potential of the new corporate order to foster new values
that transcended the competitive pursuit of self-interest and that would "humanize" the corporate order in turn. A fully social self, as he envisioned it, held
the keys to a truly social order. Like Edward Bellamy and the utopian novelist's
brilliant admirer, Veblen, Cooley contended that people's most basic need for
social esteem, the basis of selfhood itself, could be channeled in the direction of
public service rather than private gain. "What the individual demands with reference to this reorganizing process is opportunity; that is, such freedom of
conditions that he may find his natural place, that he may serve society in the
way for which his native capacity and inclination . . . will fit him," Cooley wrote
in his third major work, *Social Process* (1918). "In so far as he can have this he
can realize himself best, and do most for the general good."[63] Even as he deplored the values of the profit system, Cooley offered an alternative ideal to
which a nation of wage earners might safely aspire within the bounds of the
emerging corporate order. "The feeling between classes will not be very bitter
so long as the ideal of service is present in all and mutually recognized," he
noted.[64]

Service, as he conceived it, did not mean sacrificing one's own needs or desires for the good of society, much less for that of corporate stockholders. For
Cooley, as for Dewey, the essential counterpart of social service was "self-
expression," the realization of one's full personality or social self through active,
ennobling participation in society as a whole. Such self-fulfillment could not
be attained so long as labor was treated as a means of income rather than an
end in itself. But Cooley's social ideal did not necessarily require collective control over productive resources. Indeed, he explicitly described self-expression
as a goal that transcended rather than transformed material self-interest in traditional terms. "The main need of men is life, self-expression," he wrote, " . . . and
if self-expression can be made general[,] material inequalities alone will excite
but little resentment." A "democracy of sentiment," he explained, "might make
life beautiful and hopeful for those who have little money," but it would do so by
means of a redirection of social esteem, not a redistribution of property.[65]

Ultimately, Cooley offered a new answer to the profound problem that his
father had also faced, the challenge of ameliorating the class conflict resulting
from capital accumulation without threatening private ownership of productive resources. The younger Cooley's enormously influential answer was to socialize the psyche rather than property. "We do not want uniformity in earning
and spending, . . . only unity of spirit," he wrote in *Social Organization*. For, as

he noted, "[a]ll solid betterment of the workers must be based on and get its nourishment from the existing system of production."[66] A decade later in *Social Process*, he further explained the nature of the "self-expressive social order" he envisioned: "There is such a thing as a human equality—as distinguished from one that is mechanical—which would consist in everyone having, in one way or another, a suitable field of self-expression and growth. This would be reconcilable with great differences of environment and wealth, but not with ignorance or extreme poverty." He concluded by calling for a spiritual regeneration and elevation of market society. "Our line of progress lies, in part at least, not over commercialism but through it," he wrote. "The dollar is to be reformed rather than repressed."[67]

Conclusion

The combined work of Thomas and Charles Cooley illustrates the filial relationship between corporate property and social selfhood in American thought. Thomas Cooley's antebellum allegiance to individual property rights and the neutral state led him to defend corporate property against public appropriation in the postbellum era. But his Jacksonian belief in economic equality made him profoundly uneasy about the monopoly power of corporate capital and the resultant rise of class politics. In response, he fashioned a theory of the regulatory state that was premised not upon a social contract among independent proprietors, but rather upon an organicist understanding of the common law as the embodiment of the unwritten values and ideals of the American people, gradually evolving in accord with the changing demands of industrial life. His sociological reconception of sovereignty as well as property represented a momentous shift away from the liberal-republican ideology of the early market republic and toward the corporate-regulatory ideology of the Progressive Era.

It was left for his son to complete that ideological movement by repudiating the social-scientific model of selfhood and society that had framed political debate in the United States since the Revolution, and by constructing a new model of social selfhood in its place. Charles Cooley located the new source of social power not in the independent ownership of productive resources, but in the interdependent exchange of thoughts as well as things. From the standpoint of his social psychology, the new corporate order appeared less as an autocracy of property than as a dawning democracy of the psyche, in which increasing economic as well as psychological interaction made possible a collective transcendence of competition and social strife. Identifying the cause of class conflict in the self-destructive pursuit of self-interest, he envisioned a newly socialized consciousness that would find in social service the true means of individual as well as collective self-expression. Yet while he condemned what Max Weber called the "spirit of capitalism," he evoked instead a socialist spirit that was oddly at home in the new world of wage labor and corporate capital.

Conclusion

I f there is any period one would desire to be born in," wrote
Emerson, "is it not the age of Revolution . . . when the historic
glories of the old can be compensated by the rich possibilities
of the new era?" In his famed 1837 address, "The American
Scholar," Emerson had in mind a cultural and intellectual revolution, "a revolution in the leading idea." The leading idea of his time, he told the Cambridge
society of Phi Beta Kappa, was "Introversion," the search for universal principles within the individual psyche or soul. Such "self-trust," as he described it,
did not mean a retreat from the mundane world of milk and meal, newspaper
and ballad, into an otherworldly realm of timeless truth. For truth was to be
found only in everyday life itself; each individual must derive it anew from his
or her own experience. The challenge was to discover the profound reality concealed within the commonplace, to discern the sublime landscape in land, the
heroic struggle in labor, the universal Man in men.[1]

This was the calling with which Emerson charged the American Scholar: to
be "the world's eye," seeing through the veil of ordinary appearances to the
deeper significance they contained. In revealing the enduring values beneath
the ephemeral surface of things, the scholars of the new era would do more
than cast society and history in an ennobling light. They would bring about the
final realization of the ideals they distilled from the mass of mental and material phenomena, the fulfillment of modern America's implicit promise. Like
scholars of an earlier age, they would turn business into poetry in the ultimate

triumph of mind over matter. To cultivate in this way the embryonic truth and beauty in contemporary life was for Emerson the most revolutionary of acts, lending new meaning and mission to the idea of "culture" itself.[2]

For aspiring American scholars like G. Stanley Hall, who heard him speak while in college, Emerson appeared as a prophet, divining a glorious destiny for them and the rising nation they must lead.[3] Emerson's empowering vision of scholarship encapsulated an understanding of the dialectical relationship between culture and society that guided many of Hall's peers in founding the modern American university. According to this widely shared view, the advent of a new social order gave rise to new insight and knowledge, which inevitably inspired new social arrangements and institutions in turn. This image of perpetual revolution especially animated social science, which aimed to uncover the essential logic of societal development in order to steer public policy as well as private initiative in a progressive direction, to realize in more ways than one the nascent ideals arising from modern society itself.

From their intellectual origins in seventeenth-century court society to their professional establishment in the nineteenth-century university, the social sciences did not simply purport to hold up a mirror to the sweeping changes underway, reflecting the tumult and confusion of the long transition from feudalism to capitalism. Rather, writers on mental and moral philosophy, politics, economics, and law deliberately disregarded what they deemed the incidental or inessential features of contemporary affairs in order to disclose the underlying nature of the new society being born. Their object was not merely description, but prescription. For in so articulating the fundamental principles of what Adam Smith called "commercial society," social scientists found in it the crucible of a more prosperous and powerful, more civil and social order still being forged. Much like Emerson, they sought to liberate the transcendent spirit borne by Euro-American civilization like a genie in a bottle. Such a quintessentially progressive conception of the scholar's mission underpinned the radical dimension of the social-scientific project, highlighting the gap between the current limits of modern society and the limitless potential to be unlocked by enlightened reform. In this sense, Emerson inherited the revolutionary tradition of Jefferson, Paine, and Smith at the end of the eighteenth century, and he bequeathed it to writers like Henry George, John Dewey, and Charles Horton Cooley at the end of the nineteenth.

At the same time, social scientists' trust in the capacity of their ceaselessly changing society to transcend its own limits ironically called into question the need for any basic reconstruction of the social order. Or rather, in attributing the potential for such structural change to the uniquely supple structure of modern society itself, they tended to regard any fundamental attack upon the existing social system as, paradoxically, a counterrevolutionary threat to the very basis of societal reformation. In fact, many writers came to conclude that the genie of the future society they envisioned was already out of the bottle, or at least well on its way. Prescription shaded into description as social scientists blurred the boundary between current practice and progressive ideals, looking forward to an increasingly steady growth of new social relations out of old institutions rather than a decisive departure in the manner of revolutions past. Utopian anticipation of what could be merged with ideological justification of what already was, as Karl Mannheim and others have observed in related contexts.[4]

In this regard as well, the Gilded Age founders of professional, academic social science followed the example of their Revolutionary Era forebears. Informed by British and French political economy, early American writers abstracted from the welter of social relations in their agrarian republic the cardinal principles of propertied independence and social compact. These ideals they held to inhere in a society of freehold farms and workshops, in which household control of the means of subsistence formed the basis of political as well as economic rights. Freed from feudal or monarchical fetters, such a social order seemed destined to develop in the direction of increasing self-determination, for individuals as for the society they together formed.

That belief in the natural progress of free society inspired the American Revolution as well as subsequent campaigns to extend the rights of self-rule to debtors and tenants, wives and slaves, yeomen fighting for their farms and journeymen fighting for their crafts. So too, the model of harmonious competition and free enterprise common to the Physiocrats and Adam Smith informed eighteenth-century Americans' critique of British mercantilism as well as nineteenth-century crusades against "special privilege" and the "money power." Yet, in defining the autonomous household as the elemental unit of political and economic life, political economy entailed a tacit defense of racial and sexual hierarchy within the household itself. In likewise naturalizing competition between individual businesses, the Smithian science also rationalized capital accumulation within them, making class inequality along with caste hierarchy the twin engines of economic growth.

The slow eclipse of the household economy in the nineteenth century rendered the proprietary autonomy prized by early Americans an ever more embattled ideal. As the dream of self-employment grew increasingly remote from the realities of the burgeoning labor market, political economy appeared at once more fancifully utopian and more baldly ideological, the meeting-ground of starry-eyed radicals demanding a thorough reorganization of property and power, on the one hand, and of unabashed apologists for plutocracy and plunder, on the other. Shorn of their social basis in what C. B. Macpherson has called "simple market society," the agrarian premises of eighteenth-century social science gradually ceased to afford a reliable basis for either progressive reform or conservative reaction.[5] So it seemed, at least, to the handful of antebellum social theorists and the larger number of postbellum social scientists who highlighted the inadequacies of political economy and fashioned a new science of American society in its stead.

For the philosophical founders of modern American social science, the classical model of a social contract among independent individuals no longer embodied the promise of endlessly expanding freedom and democracy. Instead, the myth of "economic man" represented to them the main obstacle to the realization of those lasting ideals. The self-maximizing sovereign of political economy, they believed, stood behind the consuming race for riches that impoverished rather than enriched modern society, fueling the self-destructive spiral of competition and class conflict they came to abhor. Many remained committed to the primacy that political economy placed upon self-determination. But nearly all agreed that individual liberty as well as collective self-government depended upon a progressive emancipation from the narrow pursuit of self-interest that they ascribed to the aging science of wealth. They valorized instead an ever-widening identification of self and world, individual and society, conceived not as a federation of autonomous agents, but as an indivisible union of interdependent parts. The organic "association" envisioned by European socialists such as Charles Fourier, Henri de Saint-Simon, and Robert Owen supplanted the voluntary compact of classical theory at the heart of American social science and social thought.

At its most romantic, the social spirit exalted by Emerson or Cooley appeared far removed from the hurly-burly of work and wealth described in political economy. Like their social-scientific predecessors, however, the pioneering theorists of modern psychology, sociology, and social economy tended to see the ideal society they imagined embedded within the actual society they inhabited, rather than outside it. Much as writers in the tradition of political economy drew the kernel of agrarian independence from the husk of the household economy, so the leading critics of that tradition found the seed of what Durkheim called "organic solidarity" already implanted within the emerging industrial order. The latent logic of market relations seemed to these revisionists, in sharp contrast to their forebears, to lead away from an atomistic individualism rooted in innate human interests and needs, toward a holistic communitarianism founded upon socially created norms and desires. In the absence of friction or obstruction, the socializing force of free exchange would naturally bring an end to the selfish struggle over scarce resources, ushering in a cooperative commonwealth and boundless abundance.

Such confidence that history was on their side could bolster the kind of conservative resistance to social reform associated with laissez-faire polemicists such as the young William Graham Sumner. Yet the revolt against political economy was predominantly a progressive movement, lending theoretical support for a wide spectrum of reform causes—from tariff protection, civil service, and scientific charity to cheap currency, railroad regulation, Henry George's "single tax," and even Margaret Fuller's late embrace of proletarian revolution. Indeed, the rival social-scientific tradition of Marxist historical materialism depended upon a similar expectation that socialism would gestate within the womb of market society as improvements in productivity outgrew the class structure upon which they were based.[6] The stark opposition between capitalist and communist social science, long maintained by both sides, overlooked the deep affinities between the two main successors to political economy.[7]

The pivotal figures in the transformation of American social science, however, generally rejected the notion that the groundwork was being laid for the overthrow of bourgeois rule by an ascendant working class. For them the concept of class struggle, implicit in the *Wealth of Nations* and explicit in the *Communist Manifesto*, grievously mistook the nature of both capitalist development and socialist revolution. The fatal error lay in the assumption that social relations were anchored in ownership of land, labor, and capital: in the competing interests arising from private property in productive resources, and in the common interest that only common property could secure. From the reformers' standpoint, it was just this contractual conception of society that rendered market relations adversarial, rather than the class structure itself. As Marx wrote of Henry Carey, these writers held "that the theorems of Ricardo and others, in which existing social antagonisms and contradictions are formulated, are not the ideal product of the real economic movement, but on the contrary, that the real antagonisms of capitalist production in England and elsewhere are the result of the theories of Ricardo and others!"[8]

More precisely, Carey and his successors found the real basis of market society in the web of cultural conventions, standards, and values that emerged through the process of exchange itself. Market transactions were not governed by class interests, which were not predetermined by property rights. On the contrary, property rights and class interests themselves arose from commerce in goods and services, which was rooted in turn in the interchange of wants and needs, habits and norms, that Dewey called "social consciousness." Only by so reconceiving the platonic essence of market relations to begin with could avant-garde writers regard the yawning class divide as an anomaly or anachronism, a relic of outdated patterns of thought and behavior rather than an intrinsic attribute of the emerging market society. What Simon Patten called "evolutionary socialism," in other words, rested upon the new view of human nature and social order that took shape in modern American psychology and sociology. Such a progressive politics depended upon the redefinition of personal autonomy in terms of self-expression rather than self-employment, or in terms of the willful exercise of "interest" in the psychological rather than the political or economic sense. It depended as well upon the reconception of popular sovereignty in terms of common sentiment and sensibility instead of deliberate consent, or as a matter of cultural kinship instead of voluntary compact.

In the glaring disparity between the social strife of the Gilded Age and the solidarity inherent in market relations, social scientists found a broad warrant for political and economic reform. At the same time, the displacement of political economy by social psychology enabled them to foresee the cooperative commonwealth they desired naturally evolving out of the increasing universality of market relations, rather than requiring a democratic redistribution of the means of production. The system of wage labor and capital accumulation no longer appeared to be predicated upon competing individual and class interests, but instead seemed rooted in the organic association from which such interests derived. It was not that the commodification of labor and the engrossment of land and capital gave rise to class conflict and secular crisis that would split capitalism asunder, as radical Ricardians claimed. Progressive social scientists rather maintained that the tendency of capitalist development was toward the erosion of class boundaries and separate interests by the rising tide of material and mental commerce. The psychosocial union they envisioned would come about not through a new American Revolution or second Civil War, but through the kind of collective coming-of-age prefigured in G. Stanley Hall's developmental psychology.

Subsequent history has tended to temper the millennial faith that radical critics of capitalism once vested in class struggle. For those still inspired to greater or lesser extent by socialist ideals, the alternative of "revolutionary evolution" espoused by leading American social theorists (among others) a hundred years ago might seem to hold out greater promise. But has the past century borne out their belief in a smoother, more peaceful passage beyond the capitalist frontier? While the answer to that question cannot illuminate what modern American social science meant to its forward-looking founders, it must inevitably color what their creation means to historians today.[9]

From the Progressive Era through the New Deal to the New Left, the vision of a gradual metamorphosis of market society into something like socialism has inspired successive waves of radicalism and reform. In the 1930s, Adolf A. Berle and Gardiner C. Means drew upon Thorstein Veblen in their influential analysis of the modern business corporation as the deathbed of private property, severing ownership from management as ownership had earlier been severed from labor, paving the way for a "neutral technocracy" to administer economic affairs "on the basis of public policy rather than private cupidity."[10] As Howard Brick has shown, the rising stature of "the 'new social sciences' of sociology, anthropology, and psychology" bolstered the vogue of "postcapitalist" and then "postindustrial" readings of American society in the 1950s and 1960s. Liberals and leftists hailed the incipient demise of property and profit, welcoming the widening scope of social regulation and social provision as signs that capitalism itself was on the wane.[11] John Kenneth Galbraith brought a broader readership to such revolutionary expectations in his landmark works, *The Affluent Society* (1958) and *The New Industrial State* (1967). As land had once given way to capital as the locus of social power, he argued, capital was rapidly yielding to "organized intelligence," and the profit motive to "identification and adaptation" as the rules of economic life.[12] More recently, many observers have greeted the growth of participatory programs of labor relations, along with pension and mutual fund investment in corporate stock, as evidence of a general fading of class lines.[13] Similar excitement surrounds the notion of an "information age" or "new economy," in which the advent of "high tech" and "lean production" are ostensibly rendering the exploitation of labor, if not work itself, increasingly obsolete.[14]

To be sure, the rise of mass production and mass consumption entailed a more general socialization of many aspects of life in the twentieth century, as the founders of modern American social science foresaw. The qualitative enlargement of the role of government in economic planning, the establishment of collective bargaining in core industries, and the massive expansion of public education, arriving together in the middle third of the century, laid the foundation for a developing welfare state, if hardly creeping communism. But the landslide rightward retrenchment of the 1970s and 1980s in all these areas, entailing a resumption of class warfare on the part of central bankers and major employers, should have dispelled any illusion that the reign of capital had yielded to a new industrial democracy or liberal consensus.[15] Indeed, the flourishing of Deweyan ideals in management circles—"quality of work life," "teamwork," "reengineering," and the like—went along with a wave of downsizing, outsourcing, union-busting, and speed-up techniques that left no doubt as to who was boss.[16] Paeans to "pension socialism" and "investor democracy" accompanied a radical upward redistribution of wealth and income, seen in stagnating wages, advancing profits, and skyrocketing executive salaries, in the mounting consumer debt of a growing majority and the soaring financial assets of a relative few.[17] Even as writers across the political spectrum heralded the dawning technological transcendence of human labor, most Americans juggled more (largely low-skill, low-wage) jobs, worked harder and longer hours, and reaped a diminishing share of the rewards of rising productivity in their paychecks.[18] It should be no surprise that at the very moment, in the aftermath of the Cold War, when the American working class was widely presumed dead, rank-and-file resistance to global capital showed renewed vigor in the United States as well as abroad.[19]

If twentieth-century progress fell far short of nineteenth-century expectations, the reason lies as much in the powerful forces that opposed progressive reform as in the social science that supported it. But the progenitors of modern sociology, psychology, and social economy identified those conservative forces holding back or perverting the natural course of social development with the freehold individualism of political economy. It is a lesson the American left may have learned all too well. For in conflating capitalist exploitation and class rule with the waning science of wealth, the new social psychology obscured the enduring basis of such inequality in the system of wage labor. In disavowing the fictions of propertied independence and social contract, the transformation of social science also discredited the class analysis essential to any fundamental transformation of the social order, then and since. Finally, in revealing the ideological limits of political economy, the new science of market society concealed its own. It mystified the ways in which the principles of interdependence and social selfhood would help to sustain, on a new basis, the very pursuit of private profit at the expense of social welfare they were meant to transcend.

NOTES

Introduction

1. See Kim Moody, *Workers in a Lean World: Unions in the International Economy* (New York: Verso, 1997); Harry Magdoff, Ellen Meiksins Wood, and David McNally, eds., "Capitalism at the End of the Millennium: A Global Survey," *Monthly Review* 51, no. 3 (July/Aug. 1999); Doug Henwood, "Wealth News," *Left Business Observer* 94 (5 May 2000): 3, 5; Patrick Morgan, "'New Economy' High-Tech Jobs Look Much Like Old Economy Low-Wage Work," *Labor Notes* 266 (May 2001): 7, 14.

2. On the fate of European social democracy, see Daniel Singer, *Whose Millennium? Theirs or Ours?* (New York: Monthly Review Press, 1999). On the decline of New Deal liberalism, see Steve Fraser and Gary Gerstle, eds., *The Rise and Fall of the New Deal Order, 1930–1980* (Princeton, N.J.: Princeton University Press, 1989); and Alan Brinkley, *Liberalism and Its Discontents* (Cambridge, Mass.: Harvard University Press, 1998). On the economics of neoliberalism in the United States, see Robert Pollin, "Anatomy of Clintonomics," *New Left Review* 2, no. 3 (May/June 2000): 17–46. For a sobering assessment of the current conditions of leftist thought and politics, see Perry Anderson, "Renewals," *New Left Review* 1, no. 1 (Jan./Feb. 2000): 5–24. On the politics of recognition and redistribution, see Nancy Fraser, "Rethinking Recognition," *New Left Review* 2, no. 3 (May/June 2000): 107–20. For a sharp critique of capitalist "cosmopolitanism" on the academic left, see William Leach, *Country of Exiles: The Destruction of Place in American Life* (New York: Pantheon, 1999), 150–77. For a critical genealogy of the concept of "postindustrial society," see Howard Brick, "Optimism of the Mind: Imagining Postindustrial Society in the 1960s and 1970s," *American Quarterly* 44, no. 3 (Sept. 1992): 348–80. On capitalist development and postmodernist thought, see David Harvey, *The Condition of Postmodernity: An Enquiry into the Origins of Cultural Change* (Cambridge, Mass.: Blackwell, 1990); David McNally, "Marxism in the Age of Information," *New Politics* 6, no. 4 (Winter 1998): 99–106; Ellen Meiksins Wood, "What Is the 'Postmodern' Agenda?" in *In Defense of History: Marxism and the Postmodern Agenda*, ed. Ellen Meiksins Wood and John Bellamy Foster (New York: Monthly Review Press, 1997), 1–16.

3. Two definitive studies of the advent of corporate capitalism are: Martin J. Sklar, *The*

Corporate Reconstruction of American Capitalism, 1890–1916: The Market, the Law, and Politics (New York: Cambridge University Press, 1988); and David Montgomery, *The Fall of the House of Labor: The Workplace, the State, and American Labor Activism, 1865–1925* (New York: Cambridge University Press, 1987). For an incisive synthesis of this social and economic history, including a discussion of growing economic inequality, see Walter Licht, *Industrializing America: The Nineteenth Century* (Baltimore, Md.: Johns Hopkins University Press, 1995), 133–96. On the resemblance of late-nineteenth-century and late-twentieth-century capitalist development, see Samir Amin, "The Political Economy of the Twentieth Century," *Monthly Review* 52, no. 2 (June 2000): 1–17; Moody, *Lean World*, 295–96.

4. For a useful overview of changing ideas about the distribution of wealth, see James L. Huston, *Securing the Fruits of Labor: The American Concept of Wealth Distribution, 1765–1900* (Baton Rouge: Louisiana State University Press, 1998).

5. On the dual development of revisionist social democracy and Progressivism, see James T. Kloppenberg, *Uncertain Victory: Social Democracy and Progressivism in European and American Thought, 1870–1920* (New York: Oxford University Press, 1986). On the shifting position of much of organized labor regarding the wage system, see Lawrence B. Glickman, *A Living Wage: American Workers and the Making of Consumer Society* (Ithaca, N.Y.: Cornell University Press, 1997); Rosanne Nellie Currarino, "Labor Intellectuals and the Labor Question: Wage Work and the Making of Consumer Society in America, 1873–1905," Ph.D. diss., Rutgers University, 1999.

6. On the rise of professional social science in the United States, the authoritative overview is Dorothy Ross, *The Origins of American Social Science* (New York: Cambridge University Press, 1991). See also Thomas L. Haskell, *The Emergence of Professional Social Science: The American Social Science Association and the Nineteenth-Century Crisis of Authority* (Chicago: University of Illinois Press, 1977); Mary O. Furner, *Advocacy and Objectivity: A Crisis in the Professionalization of American Social Science, 1865–1905* (Lexington: University Press of Kentucky, 1975). On the origins of the "social self," see Marshall Cohen, *Charles Horton Cooley and the Social Self in American Thought* (New York: Garland, 1982); Wilfred M. McClay, *The Masterless: Self and Society in America* (Chapel Hill: University of North Carolina Press, 1994).

7. On the ideal of "interdependence," see the contrasting interpretations in Haskell, *Social Science*, 12–16; and William Leach, *Land of Desire: Merchants, Power, and the Rise of a New American Culture* (New York: Vintage, 1993), 424–25, n. 13.

8. For examples of the "corporate liberal" thesis, see James Weinstein, *The Corporate Ideal in the Liberal State, 1900–1918* (Boston: Beacon, 1968); William Appleman Williams, *The Contours of American History* (New York: W. W. Norton, 1968), 343–478; R. Jeffrey Lustig, *Corporate Liberalism: The Origins of Modern American Political Theory, 1890–1920* (Berkeley: University of California Press, 1982).

9. See, for example, Gerald Berk, *Alternative Tracks: The Constitution of American Industrial Order, 1865–1917* (Baltimore, Md.: Johns Hopkins University Press, 1994); Mary O. Furner, "The Republican Tradition and the New Liberalism: Social Investigation, State Building, and Social Learning in the Gilded Age," in Michael J. Lacey and Mary O. Furner, eds., *The State and Social Investigation in Britain and the United States* (New York: Cambridge University Press and Woodrow Wilson Center Press, 1993), 171–241; Daniel T. Rodgers, *Atlantic Crossings: Social Politics in a Progressive Age* (Cambridge, Mass.: Belknap

Press of Harvard University Press, 1998); Alan Brinkley, *The End of Reform: New Deal Liberalism in Recession and War* (New York: Vintage, 1995); Howard Brick, "The Reformist Dimension of Talcott Parsons's Early Social Theory," in *The Culture of the Market: Historical Essays*, ed. Thomas L. Haskell and Richard F. Teichgraeber III (New York: Cambridge University Press, 1996): 357–96.

10. See, for example, Robert B. Westbrook, *John Dewey and American Democracy* (Ithaca, N.Y.: Cornell University Press, 1991); Eldon J. Eisenach, *The Lost Promise of Progressivism* (Lawrence: University Press of Kansas, 1994); Kloppenberg, *Uncertain Victory*; James Livingston, *Pragmatism and the Political Economy of Cultural Revolution, 1850–1940* (Chapel Hill: University of North Carolina Press, 1994). For a Leninist critique of the American left in the Progressive Era and its current academic admirers, see Brian Lloyd, *Left Out: Pragmatism, Exceptionalism, and the Poverty of American Marxism* (Baltimore, Md.: Johns Hopkins University Press, 1997).

11. The most rigorous theoretical exponents of this position among U.S. historians are Thomas L. Haskell and James Livingston. See Haskell, "Capitalism and the Origins of the Humanitarian Sensibility," *American Historical Review* 90 (1985): 339–61, 547–66; Haskell, "Convention and Hegemonic Interest in the Debate over Antislavery: A Reply to Davis and Ashworth," *American Historical Review* 92 (1987): 829–78; Haskell, *Social Science*; Livingston, *Cultural Revolution*; Livingston, "The Politics of Pragmatism," *Social Text* 49 (Winter 1996): 149–72; Livingston, "Modern Subjectivity and Consumer Culture," in *Getting and Spending: European and American Consumer Societies in the Twentieth Century* (New York: Cambridge University Press, 1998); Livingston, "The Strange Career of the 'Social Self,'" *Radical History Review* 76 (Winter 2000): 53–79. See also Glickman, *Living Wage*; Linda J. Nicholson, *Gender and History: The Limits of Social Theory in the Age of the Family* (New York: Columbia University Press, 1986), 3–4, 49–65; Mary Britton King, "Make Love, Not Work: New Management Theory and the Social Self," *Radical History Review* 76 (Winter 2000): 15–24; Barry Shank, "Subject, Commodity, Marketplace: The American Artists Group and the Mass Production of Distinction," *Radical History Review* 76 (Winter 2000): 25–52. Leading champions of the Populist tradition in recent years have cemented the association of the critique of industrialization with a lament over the decline of petty proprietorship. See especially Christopher Lasch, *The True and Only Heaven: Progress and Its Critics* (New York: W. W. Norton, 1991).

12. For a useful riposte to such free-market faith on the left, see Thomas Frank, "The Rise of Market Populism: America's New Secular Religion," *The Nation* 271, no. 13 (2000): 13. For a suggestive exploration of the ways in which subversion and legitimation, "dissent" and "assent," go hand in hand in American thought and culture, see Sacvan Bercovitch, *The Rites of Assent: Transformations in the Symbolic Construction of America* (New York: Routledge, 1993).

13. Recent scholarship, by contrast, has tended to move away from an earlier emphasis upon the ideological limits of Gilded Age culture and to highlight instead its multiple meanings and radical potential. See Richard F. Teichgraeber III, "'Culture' in Industrializing America," *Intellectual History Newsletter* 21 (1999): 11–23. For a related reflection on recent trends in the history of consumer culture, see Jean-Christophe Agnew, "Coming Up for Air: Consumer Culture in Historical Perspective," in *Consumption and the World of Goods*, ed. John Brewer and Roy Porter (New York: Routledge, 1993), 19–39.

14. C. B. Macpherson, *The Political Theory of Possessive Individualism: Hobbes to Locke* (New York: Oxford University Press, 1962). For a discussion of Macpherson's work in relation to subsequent historiography, see Chapter 1, note 40.

15. For recent arguments along these lines, see Martin J. Sklar, *The United States as a Developing Country: Studies in U.S. History in the Progressive Era and the 1920s* (New York: Cambridge University Press, 1992), 20–36, 143–96; Livingston, *Cultural Revolution*, 85–112. See also Adolf A. Berle and Gardiner C. Means, *The Modern Corporation and Private Property*, rev. ed. (New York: Harcourt, Brace & World, 1968); John Kenneth Galbraith, *The New Industrial State*, 4th ed. (Boston: Houghton Mifflin, 1985); Joseph Schumpeter, *Capitalism, Socialism, and Democracy*, 3d ed. (New York: Harper & Bros., 1950).

16. Peter Kolchin offers a succinct statement of the "labor question": "who should work for whom, under what terms should work be performed, and how should it be compelled or rewarded?" Kolchin, "The Big Picture: A Comment on David Brion Davis's 'Looking at Slavery from Broader Perspectives,'" *American Historical Review* 105, no. 2 (Apr. 2000): 467–71; quoted passage at 468. On the "labor question" in the Gilded Age, see Currarino, "Labor Intellectuals." For a discussion of the "labor question" in the 1930s and after, see Steve Fraser, "The 'Labor Question,'" in Fraser and Gerstle, *New Deal Order*, 55–84.

Chapter One

1. "A Modest Inquiry into the Nature and Necessity of a Paper-Currency," in *Benjamin Franklin: Writings*, ed. J. A. Leo Lemay (New York: Literary Classics of the United States, 1987), 119.

2. On the social and intellectual roots of European social science, see Richard Olson, *The Emergence of the Social Sciences, 1642–1792* (New York: Twayne, 1993), 6–26.

3. Adam Smith, *An Inquiry into the Nature and Causes of the Wealth of Nations*, 2 vols., eds. R. H. Campbell and A. S. Skinner (Indianapolis: Liberty Classics, 1981); Olson, *Social Sciences*, 162–89; Daniel Walker Howe, *Making the American Self: Jonathan Edwards to Abraham Lincoln* (Cambridge, Mass.: Harvard University Press, 1997), 52.

4. Howe, *American Self*, 57. On the close but complex connection between the *Wealth of Nations* and the American Revolution, see Donald Winch, *Riches and Poverty: An Intellectual History of Political Economy in Britain, 1750–1834* (New York: Cambridge University Press, 1996), 3; Peter McNamara, *Political Economy and Statesmanship: Smith, Hamilton, and the Foundation of the Commercial Republic* (Dekalb: Northern Illinois University Press, 1998), 92–93; Michael Merrill, "The Anticapitalist Origins of the United States," *Review: A Journal of the Ferdinand Braudel Center* 13 (Fall 1990): 465–97; Paul K. Conkin, *Prophets of Prosperity: America's First Political Economists* (Bloomington: Indiana University Press, 1980), 18.

5. According to J. G. A. Pocock, "The rapidly developing style of political economy, which is the dominant mode of Augustan political thought, took shape around the various relations which publicists were prepared to allow between land, trade, and credit as sources not merely of public wealth, but of political stability and virtue." Pocock, *The Machiavellian Moment: Florentine Political Thought and the Atlantic Republican Tradition* (Princeton, N.J.: Princeton University Press, 1975), 426. Whether finding the roots of Enlightenment social science in natural jurisprudence, Calvinist theology, Hobbesian materialism, or Pocock's classical republicanism, scholars directly or indirectly inspired by his work have recon-

structed the broad-based intellectual framework of eighteenth-century political economy, reaching far beyond the restricted realm of neoclassical economics. See Istvan Hont and Michael Ignatieff, eds., *Wealth and Virtue: The Shaping of Political Economy in the Scottish Enlightenment* (New York: Cambridge University Press, 1983); R. H. Campbell and A. S. Skinner, "General Introduction," in Smith, *Wealth of Nations,* 1:1–60; Winch, *Riches and Poverty,* 17–22. On the broad construction of political economy in America, see John R. Nelson Jr., *Liberty and Property: Political Economy and Policymaking in the New Nation, 1789–1812* (Baltimore, Md.: Johns Hopkins University Press, 1987), xi–xiii; Conkin, *Prophets of Prosperity,* ix. See also Drew McCoy, *The Elusive Republic: Political Economy in Jeffersonian America* (New York: W. W. Norton, 1980). "It is not only the most important, but the most comprehensive science," wrote Daniel Raymond in his pioneering American treatise on political economy. "It not only comprehends a knowledge of the influence of agriculture, commerce, and manufactures, on public wealth; but the administration of justice, civil liberty, public morals, and even the arts and sciences themselves are but branches of this science, in as much as they all have their influence in promoting national wealth." Raymond, *The Elements of Political Economy,* 2d ed., 2 vols. (1823; reprint, New York: Augustus M. Kelley, 1964), 1:10.

6. Raymond, *Political Economy,* 2:395.

7. On Edwards's debt to Locke, see Sydney E. Ahlstrom, *A Religious History of the American People* (New Haven, Conn.: Yale University Press, 1972), 298–99, 351. On Locke's appropriation of Puritan ideas about labor and property, see John Dunn, *The Political Thought of John Locke: An Historical Account of the Argument of the 'Two Treatises of Government'* (New York: Cambridge University Press, 1969), 218–19; Richard Ashcraft, *Revolutionary Politics and Locke's Two Treatises of Government* (Princeton, N.J.: Princeton University Press, 1986), 258–62.

8. Barry Alan Shain has argued that eighteenth-century Americans' often unrecorded conceptions of "the political good" were rooted in Protestant communalism, while their voluminously documented ideas about "the shape of regimes, their goals, and the political institutions necessary for achieving the desired ends" constituted a "political science" more familiar to students of the Revolutionary Era. Shain, *The Myth of American Individualism: The Protestant Origins of American Political Thought* (Princeton, N.J.: Princeton University Press, 1994), 14–15. Though Shain may underestimate the moral and spiritual content of political economy as well as the political-economic character of much religious writing, he rightly highlights the tensions between religious and scientific depictions of human nature and society.

9. On the construction of "political economy" in contrast to "domestic economy," see Conkin, *Prophets of Prosperity,* ix.

10. On the depoliticization of the family in Western political thought, see Jean Bethke Elshtain, *Public Man, Private Woman: Women in Social and Political Thought* (Princeton, N.J.: Princeton University Press, 1981); Linda J. Nicholson, *Gender and History: The Limits of Social Theory in the Age of the Family* (New York: Columbia University Press, 1986).

11. On the distinction between familial and nonfamilial relations in Anglo-American common law, see Norma Basch, *In the Eyes of the Law: Women, Marriage, and Property in Nineteenth-Century New York* (Ithaca, N.Y.: Cornell University Press, 1982), 47–48.

12. On the exclusion of women from "the political" in Western political theory, see Wendy Brown, *Manhood and Politics: A Feminist Reading in Political Theory* (Totowa, N.J.: Rowman

& Littlefield, 1988); Christine Di Stefano, *Configurations of Masculinity: A Feminist Perspective on Modern Political Theory* (Ithaca, N.Y.: Cornell University Press, 1991); Susan Moller Okin, *Women in Western Political Thought* (Princeton, N.J.: Princeton University Press, 1979); Carole Pateman, *The Disorder of Women: Democracy, Feminism, and Political Theory* (Stanford, Calif.: Stanford University Press, 1989); Hanna Fenichel Pitkin, *Fortune Is a Woman: Gender and Politics in the Thought of Niccolò Machiavelli* (Berkeley: University of California Press, 1984); Elshtain, *Public Man*; Nicholson, *Gender and History*.

13. Jay Fliegelman, *Prodigals and Pilgrims: The American Revolution Against Patriarchal Authority, 1750–1800* (New York: Cambridge University Press, 1982); see also, on the transformation of family relations, Michael Grossberg, *Governing the Hearth: Law and the Family in Nineteenth-Century America* (Chapel Hill: University of North Carolina Press, 1985), 3–8. "[A]lthough the ideal of equality espoused in the Declaration of Independence did not work immediately to allow women greater autonomy, it represented a powerful weapon for future use." Marylynn Salmon, *Women and the Law of Property in Early America* (Chapel Hill: University of North Carolina Press, 1986), xvii.

14. On the burgeoning popular readership for Enlightenment writings, see David Jaffee, "The Village Enlightenment in New England, 1760–1820," *William and Mary Quarterly*, 3d ser., 47, no. 3 (July 1990): 327–46. For an example of the way upcountry farmers took part in the rhetoric of the Revolution, see Richard L. Bushman, "Massachusetts Farmers and the Revolution," in Richard M. Jellison, ed., *Society, Freedom, and Conscience: The American Revolution in Virginia, Massachusetts, and New York* (New York: W. W. Norton, 1976), 77–124. On the contrast between the politics of laboring Americans in the Revolutionary Era and that of the eighteenth-century "English crowd" famously described by E. P. Thompson, see Ruth Bogin, "Petitioning and the New Moral Economy of Post-Revolutionary America," *William and Mary Quarterly*, 3d ser., 45, no. 3 (July 1988): 391–425; cf., E. P. Thompson, "The Moral Economy of the English Crowd in the Eighteenth Century," in Thompson, *Customs in Common* (New York: New Press, 1991), 185–258. On the appropriation of the elite ideal of propertied independence on behalf of the poor and propertyless as well as women and slaves, see Allan Kulikoff, *The Agrarian Origins of American Capitalism* (Charlottesville: University of Virginia Press, 1992), 115–19. On the Enlightenment in America more generally, see Robert A. Ferguson, *The American Enlightenment, 1750–1820* (Cambridge, Mass.: Harvard University Press, 1997); Henry F. May, *The Enlightenment in America* (New York: Oxford University Press, 1976).

15. Thomas Paine, *Collected Writings*, ed. Eric Foner (New York: Literary Classics of the United States, 1995), 536.

16. "In the relationship with God, there was given to every man an Archimedian point outside the realm of human contingency from which the rational individual could judge the world and act upon it." Dunn, *John Locke*, 261.

17. Olson, *Social Sciences*, 55, 143.

18. Ibid., 103–15; Benjamin Rush, "On Securities for Liberty," in *The Selected Writings of Benjamin Rush*, ed. Dagobert D. Runes (New York: The Philosophical Library, 1947), 34.

19. See Howe, *American Self*.

20. "On the Different Species of Mania," n.d., in Rush, *Selected Writings*, 219.

21. Nathaniel Niles, *Two Discourses on Liberty* (Newbury-Port, Mass.: I. Thomas and H. W. Tinges, 1774), 60.

22. Adam Smith, *The Theory of Moral Sentiments* (Indianapolis: Liberty Classics, 1969), 392.

23. "Federalist No. 49," in *The Federalist*, ed. Jacob E. Cooke (Middletown, Conn.: Wesleyan University Press, 1961), 343. On "self-government" as both a psychological and political ideal, see Louis P. Masur, "'Age of the First Person Singular': The Vocabulary of the Self in New England, 1780–1850," *Journal of American Studies* 25, no. 2 (Aug. 1991): 189–211.

24. Ashcraft, *Revolutionary Politics*, 51–54; Rush, "The Influence of Physical Causes Upon the Moral Faculty," 1786, in Rush, *Selected Writings*, 181.

25. Joyce Oldham Appleby, *Economic Thought and Ideology in Seventeenth-Century England* (Princeton, N.J.: Princeton University Press, 1978), 247–48; Olson, *Social Sciences*, 66–67.

26. Franklin, "Paper-Currency," 124.

27. John Adams, *Defence of the Constitutions of the Government of the United States of America* (1786–1787), in *The Political Writings of John Adams: Representative Selections*, ed. George A. Peek, Jr. (New York: Bobbs-Merrill, 1954), 150.

28. William Manning, *The Key of Liberty: The Life and Democratic Writings of William Manning, 'A Laborer,' 1747–1814*, ed. Michael Merrill and Sean Wilentz (Cambridge, Mass.: Harvard University Press, 1993), 129.

29. Albert O. Hirschman, *The Passions and the Interests: Political Arguments for Capitalism Before Its Triumph* (Princeton, N.J.: Princeton University Press, 1977), 32, 107–10; Smith, *Moral Sentiments*, 112–13.

30. Howe, *American Self*, 11–28; Jerry Z. Muller, *Adam Smith in His Time and Ours: Designing the Decent Society* (New York: Free Press, 1993), 6.

31. Joyce Appleby, *Capitalism and a New Social Order: The Republican Vision of the 1790s* (New York: New York University Press, 1984), 94; Gordon Wood, *The Radicalism of the American Revolution* (New York: Alfred A. Knopf, 1992), 245–47; Campbell and Skinner, "General Introduction," 18; Smith, *Wealth of Nations*, 1:338, 340. See also Hirschman, *Passions and Interests*, 41, 58; Istvan Hont and Michael Ignatieff, "Needs and Justice in the *Wealth of Nations*: An Introductory Essay," in Hont and Ignatieff, *Wealth and Virtue*, 1–44.

32. "Federalist No. 10," in *The Federalist*, 58, 60.

33. On the eclipse of the ideal of "disinterestedness," see Wood, *Radicalism of the Revolution*, 247. On the valorization of labor as opposed to leisure, see Isaac Kramnick, *Republicanism and Bourgeois Radicalism: Political Ideology in Late Eighteenth-Century England and America* (Ithaca, N.Y.: Cornell University Press, 1990), 1–2, 8.

34. See Mark Blaug, *Economic Theory in Retrospect*, 3d ed. (New York: Cambridge University Press, 1978), 10–11; Smith, *Wealth of Nations*, 1:438–50. On the origins of classical economic theory generally, see David McNally, *Political Economy and the Rise of Capitalism: A Reinterpretation* (Berkeley: University of California Press, 1988); Terence Hutchinson, *Before Adam Smith: The Emergence of Political Economy, 1662–1776* (Cambridge, Mass.: Basil Blackwell, 1988).

35. Smith, *Wealth of Nations*, 1:10, 25, 22.

36. Franklin, "Paper-Currency," 128.

37. See Ronald L. Meek, *Studies in the Labor Theory of Value*, 2d ed. (New York: Monthly Review Press, 1976), 22–80; Maurice Dobb, *Political Economy and Capitalism: Some Essays in Economic Tradition* (1945; reprint, Westport, Conn.: Greenwood, 1972), 19–30; A. K. Dasgupta, *Epochs of Economic Theory* (New York: Basil Blackwell, 1985), 13–14; Phyllis Deane,

The Evolution of Economic Ideas (New York: Cambridge University Press, 1978), 22–26; Blaug, *Economic Theory*, 37–52.

38. Adams, *Political Writings*, 192.

39. Smith, *Wealth of Nations*, 1:330–31.

40. John Locke, *Second Treatise of Government*, ed. Richard H. Cox (Arlington Heights, Ill.: Harlan Davidson, 1982), 18. On the significance of Locke's theory of labor for Anglo-American ideas about private property, see C. B. Macpherson, *The Political Theory of Possessive Individualism: Hobbes to Locke* (New York: Oxford University Press, 1962), 194–262. Macpherson has been justly criticized for conflating to some extent seventeenth-century "possessive individualism" with later apologies for industrial capitalism and for slighting in certain respects the intellectual context of Calvinism, political radicalism, and classical republicanism in which Lockean liberalism arose. Cf. Dunn, *John Locke*, esp. 214–41; Ashcraft, *Revolutionary Politics*, 150–60. As the present chapter suggests, early political-economic ideas about private property and social contract lent themselves as much to the critique of emergent capitalism as to its defense. Yet Macpherson's explication of the origins of modern property theory remains indispensable. See also Macpherson, ed., *Property: Mainstream and Critical Positions* (Toronto: University of Toronto Press, 1978).

41. See James L. Huston, *Securing the Fruits of Labor: The American Concept of Wealth Distribution, 1765–1900* (Baton Rouge: Louisiana State University Press, 1998), 8.

42. John Dickinson, "A Song for American Freedom," July 1768, in *The Writings of John Dickinson*, vol. 1, *Political Writings, 1764–1774*, ed. Paul Leicester Ford (Philadelphia: Historical Society of Pennsylvania, 1895), 431.

43. Thomas Paine, "Common Sense, on the King of England's Speech," 19 and 28 Feb. 1782, in Paine, *Collected Writings*, 290.

44. George Logan, *Five Letters Addressed to the Yeomanry* (Philadelphia: Oswald, 1792), 10. Cf. Smith, *Wealth of Nations*, 1:138: "The right which every man has in his own labour, as it is the original foundation of all other property, so it is the most sacred and inviolable."

45. Manning, *Key of Liberty*, 136.

46. Howe, *American Self*, 5.

47. Moses Mather (assumed author), *America's Appeal to the Impartial World* (Hartford, Conn.: Ebenezer Watson, 1775), 5.

48. Olson, *Social Sciences*, 71–77.

49. Ronald L. Meek, *Social Science and the Ignoble Savage* (New York: Cambridge University Press, 1976), 22, 37–67.

50. See generally Audrey Smedley, *Race in North America: Origin and Evolution of a Worldview* (Boulder, Colo.: Westview, 1993). On early Anglo-American perceptions of American Indians, see Karen Ordahl Kupperman, *Settling with the Indians: The Meeting of English and American Cultures in America, 1580–1640* (Totowa, N.J.: Rowman and Littlefield, 1980). On the dual development of racism and slavery, see Edmund Morgan, *American Slavery, American Freedom: The Ordeal of Colonial Virginia* (New York: W. W. Norton, 1975).

51. Thomas Jefferson, *Thomas Jefferson: Writings*, ed. Merrill D. Peterson (New York: Literary Classics of the United States, 1984), 187, 270.

52. Denise Riley, *"Am I That Name?": Feminism and the Category of "Women" in History* (Minneapolis: University of Minnesota Press, 1988), 31–43. See also, Nancy Leys Stepan, "Race and Sex: The Role of Analogy in Science," *Isis* 77 (1986): 261–79.

53. On the economic value attributed to women's work in early America, see Jeanne Boydston, *Home and Work: Housework, Wages, and the Ideology of Labor in the Early Republic* (New York: Oxford University Press, 1990), 1–29; Laurel Thatcher Ulrich, *Good Wives: Image and Reality in the Lives of Women in Northern New England, 1650–1750* (New York: Alfred A. Knopf, 1982).

54. Elshtain, *Public Man*, 117–19; Ruth Bloch, "The Gendered Meanings of Virtue in Revolutionary America," *Signs: Journal of Women in Culture and Society* 13, no. 1 (Autumn 1987): 37–58; Linda K. Kerber, *Toward an Intellectual History of Women* (Chapel Hill: University of North Carolina Press, 1997), 52, 105–7, 202.

55. On European feminism and Enlightenment psychology, see Olson, *Social Sciences*, 112–14. On Murray as the leading feminist writer of the early republic, see Mary Beth Norton, *Liberty's Daughters: The Revolutionary Experience of American Women, 1750–1800* (Boston: Little, Brown, 1980), 238–47; Kerber, *Intellectual History*, 115–21.

56. Judith Sargent Murray, *The Gleaner* (Schenectady, N.Y.: Union College Press, 1992), 214–18, 710, 705.

57. Smith, *Wealth of Nations*, 1:65; Meek, *Ignoble Savage*, 21; Campbell and Skinner, "General Introduction," 11–15.

58. See Morgan, *American Slavery*, 316–37.

59. See Elizabeth Blackmar, *Manhattan for Rent, 1785–1850* (Ithaca, N.Y.: Cornell University Press, 1989), 125–26.

60. Widows, however, held a life interest in a share of their husbands' real estate under the common law, and equity law—in those colonies that recognized it—enabled married women to retain separate title to property set aside in prenuptial settlements. See Peggy A. Rabkin, *Fathers to Daughters: The Legal Foundations of Female Emancipation* (Westport, Conn.: Greenwood, 1980), 19–21; Elizabeth Bowles Warbasse, *The Changing Legal Rights of Married Women, 1800–1861* (New York: Garland, 1987; originally Ph.D. diss., Radcliffe College, 1960), 7–9, 31–34; Salmon, *Women and Property*, xv–xvi, 11–16, 81, 143; Basch, *Eyes of Law*, 17–20, 73–74.

61. Nelson, *Liberty and Property*, 9.

62. Adams, *Defence of Constitutions*, 148.

63. Christopher Clark, *The Roots of Rural Capitalism: Western Massachusetts, 1780–1860* (Ithaca, N.Y.: Cornell University Press, 1990), 22–23; Kulikoff, *Agrarian Origins*, 35; Wood, *Radicalism of Revolution*, 56, 123.

64. On the significance of the freehold in early American thought, see Daniel Vickers, "Competency and Competition: Economic Culture in Early America," *William and Mary Quarterly*, 3d ser., 47, no. 1 (Jan. 1990): 3–29; Gregory S. Alexander, *Commodity and Propriety: Competing Visions of Property in American Legal Thought, 1776–1970* (Chicago: University of Chicago Press, 1997), 50. On the Revolution as a revolt against "lordship" on behalf of the freehold, see Merrill, "Anticapitalist Origins"; Wood, *Radicalism of Revolution*; Bushman, "Massachusetts Farmers."

65. Clark, *Rural Capitalism*, 24–27. On women's dependence as the basis of men's "independence," see Nancy Fraser and Linda Gordon, "A Genealogy of *Dependency*: Tracing a Keyword of the U.S. Welfare State," *Signs* 19, no. 2 (Winter 1994): 309–36. For a related discussion of the sexual subordination underlying the yeoman ideal in the antebellum South, see Stephanie McCurry, "The Politics of Yeoman Households in South Carolina," in *Divided*

Houses: Gender and the Civil War, ed. Catherine Clinton and Nina Silber (New York: Oxford University Press, 1992), 22–38.

66. Benjamin Franklin, "Advice to a Young Tradesman, Written by an Old One," 1748, in Franklin, *Writings,* 320–21.

67. Vickers, "Competency and Competition"; Christopher Clark, "Introduction," in Clark, ed., "The Transition to Capitalism in America: A Panel Discussion," *History Teacher* 27, no. 3 (May 1994), 264–67; Merrill, "Anticapitalist Origins"; Kulikoff, *Agrarian Origins,* 20–22; James Henretta, *The Origins of American Capitalism: Collected Essays* (Boston: Northeastern University Press, 1991), xxiii–xxiv. See also the discussion of "property as propriety" as opposed to "property as commodity" in Alexander, *Commodity and Propriety;* Carol Rose, *Property and Persuasion: Essays on the History, Theory, and Rhetoric of Ownership* (Boulder, Colo.: Westview, 1994), 1–5. On the gendered identification of competency with manhood, see Anne S. Lombard, "Playing the Man: Conceptions of Manliness in Early Anglo-American New England, 1675 to 1765," Ph.D. diss., University of California, Los Angeles, 1998, 4–8.

68. "Letters from a Farmer in Pennsylvania, to the Inhabitants of the British Colonies," 1768, in Dickinson, *Writings,* 1:307.

69. See the useful distinction between "autonomy" and "freedom" in James T. Kloppenberg, "The Virtues of Liberalism: Christianity, Republicanism, and Ethics in Early American Political Discourse," *Journal of American History* 74, no. 1 (June 1987): 9–33, esp. 23. See also Rose, *Property and Persuasion,* 51–62; Alexander, *Commodity and Propriety,* 8–10, 29–31.

70. Letter to James Madison, 6 Sept. 1789, in Jefferson, *Writings,* 960.

71. C. E. Merriam Jr., *History of the Theory of Sovereignty Since Rousseau* (New York: Columbia University Press, 1900), 36–37.

72. Paine, *Rights of Man,* in Paine, *Collected Writings,* 465, 467 (emphasis in original).

73. Logan, *Five Letters,* 7. See Yehoshua Arieli, *Individualism and Nationalism in American Ideology* (Cambridge, Mass.: Harvard University Press, 1964), 39–42.

74. [Theophilus Parsons], *The Essex Result,* 1778, in *American Political Writing during the Founding Era, 1760–1805,* vol. 1, ed. Charles S. Hyneman and Donald S. Lutz (Indianapolis: Liberty Press, 1983), 487.

75. Edmund S. Morgan, *Inventing the People: The Rise of Popular Sovereignty in England and America* (New York: W. W. Norton, 1988), 239–40; Thomas P. Slaughter, *The Whiskey Rebellion: Frontier Epilogue to the American Revolution* (New York: Oxford University Press, 1986), 15–19; Richard L. Bushman, *King and People in Provincial Massachusetts* (Chapel Hill: University of North Carolina Press, 1985), 176–210; Julian H. Franklin, *John Locke and the Theory of Sovereignty: Mixed Monarchy and the Right of Resistance in the Political Thought of the English Revolution* (New York: Cambridge University Press, 1978).

76. A Son of Liberty [Silas Downer], "A Discourse at the Dedication of the Tree of Liberty," 1768, in Hyneman and Lutz, *American Political Writing,* 1:104 (emphasis in original).

77. John Taylor, *An Inquiry into the Principles and Policy of the Government of the United States* (1814; reprint, New Haven: Yale University Press, 1950), 365. On popular sovereignty in the early republic in general, see Michael Kammen, *Sovereignty and Liberty: Constitutional Discourse in American Culture* (Madison: University of Wisconsin Press, 1988). See also, on the concept of "the People," Daniel T. Rodgers, *Contested Truths: Keywords in American Politics Since Independence* (New York: Basic, 1987), 80–111.

78. Charles A. Beard, *An Economic Interpretation of the Constitution of the United States* (1913; reprint, New York: Macmillan, 1961).

79. Adams, *Defence of Constitutions*, 158; Manning, *Key of Liberty*, 137.

80. Letter No. VII, 31 Dec. 1787, "An Additional Number of Letters from the Federal Farmer to the Republican Leading to a Fair Examination of the System of Government Proposed by the Late Convention; to Several Essential and Necessary Alterations in it; and Calculated to Illustrate and Support the Principles and Positions Laid Down in the Preceding Letters," in Herbert J. Storing, ed., *The Complete Anti-Federalist*, vol. 2 (Chicago: University of Chicago Press, 1981), 268.

81. *The Federalist*, 59.

82. See generally, Shain, *Myth of Individualism*.

83. Niles, *Two Discourses*, 9, 13, 15–16, 22, 23, 24. On Niles and his *Two Discourses* as representative expressions of "Revolutionary Calvinism," see Alan Heimert, *Religion and the American Mind: From the Great Awakening to the Revolution* (Cambridge, Mass.: Harvard University Press, 1966), 454–57, 514–18. On the revolutionary implications of the belief that the king had broken his contract with the people, see Bushman, *King and People*.

84. On Barlow and the Connecticut Wits, see Vernon Louis Parrington, *The Colonial Mind: 1620–1800*, vol. 1 of *Main Currents in American Thought* (New York: Harcourt, Brace, 1927), 364–73, 387–95; Robert E. Shalhope, *The Roots of Democracy: American Thought and Culture, 1760–1800* (Boston: Twayne, 1990), 68–71; May, *Enlightenment in America*, 185–93.

85. Joel Barlow, *Advice to the Privileged Orders in the Several States of Europe, Resulting from the Necessity and Propriety of a General Revolution in the Principles of Government*, in *The Political Writings of Joel Barlow* (New York: Mott & Lyon, 1796), 24; Joel Barlow, *A Letter to the National Convention of France, on the Defects in the Constitution of 1791, and the Extent of the Amendments Which Ought to be Applied*, in *Political Writings*, 170.

86. Barlow, *Letter to Convention*, 176, 177–78.

87. Barlow, *Advice to the Privileged Orders*, 81, 110.

88. On public policy and economic development in Revolutionary America, see generally Cathy D. Matson and Peter S. Onuf, *A Union of Interests: Political and Economic Thought in Revolutionary America* (Lawrence: University Press of Kansas, 1990).

89. Campbell and Skinner, "General Introduction," 12.

90. Hont and Ignatieff, "Needs and Justice," 2, 23–24.

91. Adams, *Defence of Constitutions*, 156.

92. *The Federalist*, 56–65.

93. Bogin, "New Moral Economy," 403.

94. Olson, *Social Sciences*, 82.

95. Letter No. 1, "Letters of Centinel," Oct. 1787–Apr. 1788, in Storing, *Complete Anti-Federalist*, 139.

96. Logan, *Five Letters*, 11.

97. Henretta, *American Capitalism*, 203–55; Kulikoff, *Agrarian Origins*, 34–59, 99–126; Clark, *Rural Capitalism*, 21–58; Huston, *Fruits of Labor*, xv; David P. Szatmary, *Shays' Rebellion: The Making of an Agrarian Insurrection* (Amherst: University of Massachusetts Press, 1980), 1–18. On economic development in Revolutionary America in general, see Ronald Hoffman, John J. McCusker, Russell R. Menard, and Peter J. Albert, eds., *The Economy of Early America: The Revolutionary Period, 1763–1790* (Charlottesville: University Press of Virginia, 1988); John J. McCusker and Russell R. Menard, *The Economy of British America, 1607–1789* (1985; reprint, with a supplementary bibliography, Chapel Hill: University of North Carolina Press, 1991). For a related case against conflating the end of feudalism—or the ex-

pansion of commerce, or the rise of petty proprietorship—with the emergence of capitalism, see Ellen Meiksins Wood, *The Origin of Capitalism* (New York: Monthly Review Press, 1999).

98. Jefferson, *Notes on the State of Virginia* (1787), in Jefferson, *Writings*, 290.

99. Slaughter, *Whiskey Rebellion*, 61–74.

100. Bogin, "New Moral Economy," 405–8; Alexander, *Commodity and Propriety*, 70; Szatmary, *Shays' Rebellion*, 19–36; Merrill Jensen, *The New Nation: A History of the United States During the Confederation, 1781–1789* (New York: Alfred A. Knopf, 1950).

101. See Nelson, *Liberty and Property*; Henretta, *American Capitalism*, 293–94; Merrill, "Anticapitalist Origins"; Appleby, *New Social Order*; McCoy, *Elusive Republic*; Michael Durey, *Transatlantic Radicals and the Early American Republic* (Lawrence: University Press of Kansas, 1997), 221–57.

102. Merrill, "Anticapitalist Origins," 469–77.

103. On the roots of agrarian radicalism in Anglo-American political economy, see Conkin, *Prophets of Prosperity*, 222–30.

104. Letter, 28 Oct. 1785, in Jefferson, *Writings*, 840.

105. On Anglo-American plebeian radicalism in general in the late eighteenth century, see Durey, *Transatlantic Radicals*; Richard J. Twomey, *Jacobins and Jeffersonians: Anglo-American Radicalism in the United States, 1790–1820* (New York: Garland, 1989); Kramnick, *Bourgeois Radicalism*; Seth Aaron Cotlar, "In Paine's Absence: The Trans-Atlantic Dynamics of American Popular Political Thought, 1789–1804," Ph.D. diss., Northwestern University, 2000.

106. Barlow, *Advice to the Privileged Orders*, 76.

107. Paine, *Agrarian Justice*, in Paine, *Collected Writings*, 396–413.

Chapter Two

1. Peter Temin, *The Jacksonian Economy* (New York: W. W. Norton, 1969), 113–47; Douglass C. North, *The Economic Growth of the United States, 1790–1860* (Englewood Cliffs, N.J.: Prentice-Hall, 1961), 200–202.

2. Barbara J. Packer, "The Transcendentalists," in *The Cambridge History of American Literature*, vol. 2 (New York: Cambridge University Press, 1995), 395.

3. Horace Bushnell, "The True Wealth or Weal of Nations," in Bushnell, *Work and Play, or, Literary Varieties* (New York: Charles Scribner, 1864), 48–49, 51–52 (emphasis in original), 44–45.

4. North, *Economic Growth*, 61; David M. Gordon, Richard Edwards, and Michael Reich, *Segmented Work, Divided Workers: The Historical Transformation of Labor in the United States* (New York: Cambridge University Press, 1982), 54–56; Gregory S. Alexander, *Commodity and Propriety: Competing Visions of Property in American Legal Thought, 1776–1970* (Chicago: University of Chicago Press, 1997), 70; Paul K. Conkin, *Prophets of Prosperity: America's First Political Economists* (Bloomington: Indiana University Press, 1980), 5.

5. Gordon, Edwards, and Reich, *Segmented Work*, 56–80; North, *Economic Growth*, 61–71, 156–70; Stuart Bruchey, *The Roots of American Economic Growth, 1607–1861: An Essay in Social Causation* (New York: Harper & Row, 1965), 85–150; Peter Dobkin Hall, *The Organization of American Culture, 1700–1900: Private Institutions, Elites, and the Origins of American Nationality* (New York: New York University Press, 1982), 122–23; Thomas Dublin, *Women*

and Work: The Transformation of Work and Community in Lowell, Massachusetts, 1826–1860 (New York: Columbia University Press, 1979); Alan Dawley, *Class and Community: The Industrial Revolution in Lynn* (Cambridge, Mass.: Harvard University Press, 1976). For a general social history of these changes, see Charles Sellers, *The Market Revolution: Jacksonian America, 1815–1846* (New York: Oxford University Press, 1991).

6. Bruce Levine et al., *Who Built America?: Working People and the Nation's Economy,Politics, Culture, and Society*, vol. 1 (New York: Pantheon, 1989), 319–63; Sean Wilentz, *Chants Democratic: New York City and the Rise of the American Working Class, 1788–1850* (New York: Oxford University Press, 1984), 145–296; Conkin, *Prophets of Prosperity*, 222–43; David Montgomery, *Citizen Worker: The Experience of Workers in the United States with Democracy and the Free Market During the Nineteenth Century* (New York: Cambridge University Press, 1993), 17–20; Harry L. Watson, *Liberty and Power: The Politics of Jacksonian America* (New York: Hill and Wang, 1990), 143–48.

7. See generally Vernon Louis Parrington, *The Romantic Revolution in America, 1800–1860*, vol. 2 of *Main Currents in American Thought* (New York: Harcourt, Brace, 1927); Sydney E. Ahlstrom, *A Religious History of the American People* (New Haven, Conn.: Yale University Press, 1972), 583–614.

8. S. T. Coleridge, *Aids to Reflection in the Formation of a Manly Character on the Several Grounds of Prudence, Morality, and Religion* (London: Taylor and Hessey, 1825), 208–29; Packer, "Transcendentalists," 353–57; Daniel Walker Howe, *Making the American Self: Jonathan Edwards to Abraham Lincoln* (Cambridge, Mass.: Harvard University Press, 1997), 190–211.

9. F. O. Matthiessen makes this point in *American Renaissance: Art and Expression in the Age of Emerson and Whitman* (New York: Oxford University Press, 1941), and it is reiterated in Jeffrey Steele, *The Representation of Self in the American Renaissance* (Chapel Hill: University of North Carolina Press, 1987), 1. Of the word "psychological," Coleridge wrote, "It is one of which our language stands in great need. We have no single term to express the Philosophy of the Human Mind." Raymond Williams, *Keywords: A Vocabulary of Culture and Society*, rev. ed. (New York: Oxford University Press, 1983), 246.

10. Henry David Thoreau, *Walden, and Other Writings*, ed. Joseph Wood Krutch (New York: Bantam, 1962), 108–9.

11. Ralph Waldo Emerson, "Self Reliance," in *Essays: First Series*, vol. 2 of *The Collected Works of Ralph Waldo Emerson* (Cambridge, Mass.: Harvard University Press, 1979), 35. "To confront American culture is to feel oneself encircled by a thin but strong presence: a mist, a cloud, a climate. I call it Emersonian. . . . How grasp the very air we breathe?" Irving Howe, *The American Newness: Culture and Politics in the Age of Emerson* (Cambridge, Mass.: Harvard University Press, 1986), n.p.

12. Alexis de Tocqueville, *Democracy in America*, vol. 2 (New York: Random House, 1945), 104–6; Yehoshua Arieli, *Individualism and Nationalism in American Ideology* (Cambridge, Mass.: Harvard University Press, 1964), 183–211. On Tocqueville's seminal role in the origins of sociology, see Robert A. Nisbet, *The Sociological Tradition* (New York: Basic, 1966). On Tocqueville's counterrevolutionary role in French political discourse, see Jacques Donzelot, *L'Invention du Social: Essai sur le Déclin des Passions Politiques* (Paris: Librairie Arthème Fayard, 1984), 42–44.

13. Mary Kupiec Cayton, *Emerson's Emergence: Self and Society in the Transformation of*

New England, 1800–1845 (Chapel Hill: University of North Carolina Press, 1989), 6–9, 33–40, 48–49.

14. "Emerson taught a generation of Americans how to read themselves." Steele, *Representation of Self*, 14.

15. See, for example, Stephen E. Whicher, *Freedom and Fate: An Inner Life of Ralph Waldo Emerson* (Philadelphia: University of Pennsylvania Press, 1953), 14, 28–49, 69; R. W. B. Lewis, *The American Adam: Innocence, Tragedy, and Tradition in the Nineteenth Century* (Chicago: University of Chicago Press, 1955); Matthiessen, *American Renaissance*. On the related revival of Tocqueville in the postwar era, see Wilfred M. McClay, *The Masterless: Self and Society in America* (Chapel Hill: University of North Carolina Press, 1994), 235; and see, for example, Louis Hartz's classic, *The Liberal Tradition in America: An Interpretation of American Political Thought Since the Revolution* (1955; reprint, New York: Harcourt Brace Jovanovich, 1991), 31.

16. See, for example, Quentin Anderson, *The Imperial Self: An Essay in American Literary and Cultural History* (New York: Alfred A. Knopf, 1971), viii–x, 14, 31–57, 237–41; R. Jackson Wilson, *In Quest of Community: Social Philosophy in the United States, 1860–1920* (New York: John Wiley and Sons, 1968), 1–31.

17. Lawrence Buell first observed what he called the "de-Transcendentalization" of Emerson in "The Emerson Industry in the 1980s: A Survey of Trends and Achievements," *ESQ: A Journal of the American Renaissance* 30, no. 2 (2d qtr. 1984): 117–36. The revisionist scholarship is now too vast to be adequately surveyed here. But among the works situating Emerson within an ongoing "pragmatist tradition" philosophically engaged with contemporary social issues, see, for example, Cornel West, *The American Evasion of Philosophy: A Genealogy of Pragmatism* (Madison: University of Wisconsin Press, 1989), 9–41; David M. Robinson, *Emerson and the Conduct of Life: Pragmatism and Ethical Purpose in the Later Work* (New York: Cambridge University Press, 1993). On Emerson as a philosopher of power closely akin to Nietzsche, see, for example, Michael Lopez, *Emerson and Power: Creative Antagonism in the Nineteenth Century* (Dekalb: Northern Illinois University Press, 1996). On Emerson's response to the market revolution and the advent of industrial capitalism, see, for example, Michael T. Gilmore, *American Romanticism and the Marketplace* (Chicago: University of Chicago Press, 1985), 18–34; Richard F. Teichgraeber III, *Sublime Thoughts/Penny Wisdom: Situating Emerson and Thoreau in the American Market* (Baltimore, Md.: Johns Hopkins University Press, 1995), 3–43; Carolyn Porter, *Seeing and Being: The Plight of the Participant Observer in Emerson, James, Adams, and Faulkner* (Middletown, Conn.: Wesleyan University Press, 1981), 55–118; Christopher Newfield, *The Emerson Effect: Individualism and Submission in America* (Chicago: University of Chicago Press, 1996); R. Jackson Wilson, *Figures of Speech: American Writers and the Literary Marketplace, from Benjamin Franklin to Emily Dickinson* (New York: Alfred A. Knopf, 1989), 161–218; Carey Wolfe, *The Limits of American Literary Ideology in Pound and Emerson* (New York: Cambridge University Press, 1993); Maurice Gonnaud, *An Uneasy Solitude: Individual and Society in the Work of Ralph Waldo Emerson*, trans. Lawrence Rosenwald (Princeton, N.J.: Princeton University Press, 1987); Cayton, *Emerson's Emergence*. On Emerson's seminal importance in the development of nineteenth-century American economic theory, see John Eric Wenzler, "Transcendental Economics: The Quest to Harmonize Economic and Moral Law in Nineteenth-Century American Social Thought," Ph.D. diss., University of Rochester, 1998.

18. For a recent review of the voluminous literature on Transcendentalism, see Charles

Capper, "'A Little Beyond': The Problem of the Transcendentalist Movement in American History," *Journal of American History* 85, no. 2 (1998): 502–39.

19. "On the one hand, Emerson—especially during his early and most fecund period—puts forward powerful moral critiques of market culture. . . . On the other hand, Emerson projects a conception of the self that can be easily appropriated by market culture for its own perpetuation and reproduction." West, *Evasion of Philosophy*, 26–27. West rightly compares Emerson with his younger contemporary, Marx, who constructed a radically different response to capitalist development, predicated upon an immanent critique of political economy rather than a transcendent rejection of the science of wealth itself. Ibid., 9–10. Similarly, Sacvan Bercovitch argues that Emerson's confrontation with socialist theory and practice led him increasingly to identify his utopian vision of "individuality" with the liberal democracy and possessive individualism of the northern United States in the antebellum era. In so doing, Emerson exemplified what Bercovitch sees as a distinctively American brand of liberal dissent, which at once "absorb[s] the radical communitarian vision it renounces" and is "nourished by the liberal structures it resists." Bercovitch, *The Rites of Assent: Transformations in the Symbolic Construction of America* (New York: Routledge, 1993), 307–52; quoted passage at 348.

20. Porter, *Seeing and Being*, 57–58.

21. Ahlstrom, *Religious History*, 398.

22. Ibid., 388–402; Parrington, *Romantic Revolution*, 313–30; Packer, "Transcendentalists," 332–49; Hall, *American Culture*, 72, 108; Howe, *American Self*, 130–35.

23. Cayton, *Emerson's Emergence*, 15–16.

24. Whicher, *Freedom and Fate*, 3–4.

25. Robert D. Richardson Jr., *Emerson: The Mind on Fire* (Berkeley: University of California Press, 1995), 20–27; Phyllis Cole, *Mary Moody Emerson and the Origins of Transcendentalism: A Family History* (New York: Oxford University Press, 1998).

26. Packer, "Transcendentalists," 350–57; Cayton, *Emerson's Emergence*, 25–29.

27. Richardson, *Emerson*, 108–18; quoted passage at 118.

28. Ibid., 175; Whicher, *Freedom and Fate*, 27; Cayton, *Emerson's Emergence*, 149–50; Packer, "Transcendentalists," 393–94.

29. On Unitarian "self-culture" and Emersonian individualism, see David Robinson, *Apostle of Culture: Emerson as Preacher and Lecturer* (Philadelphia: University of Pennsylvania Press, 1982).

30. Emerson, *Nature* (1836), in *The Works of Ralph Waldo Emerson*, 5 vols. (New York: Bigelow, Brown and Co., Inc., n.d.), 4:1.

31. On Emerson and the problem of alienation in market society, see also Porter, *Seeing and Being*, 55–118.

32. Emerson, *Nature*, 52.

33. For a recent critique of the enduring Romantic view of humans' relationship with the natural world, see William Cronon, "The Trouble with Wilderness; Or, Getting Back to the Wrong Nature," in Cronon, ed., *Uncommon Ground: Toward Reinventing Nature* (New York: W. W. Norton, 1995), 69–90.

34. Emerson, *Nature*, 14.

35. Ibid., 6.

36. Ibid., 53.

37. Ibid., 55.

38. Cf. George Kateb's conception of "democratic individuality" as exemplified by Emerson. Kateb, *Emerson and Self-Reliance* (Thousand Oaks, Calif.: Sage, 1995).

39. Emerson, "The American Scholar," address to Phi Beta Kappa Society, 31 Aug. 1837, in *Works of Emerson*, 4:60–61.

40. See the distinction between "the division of labour in manufacture" and "the division of labour in society" in Karl Marx, *Capital*, vol. 1, trans. Ben Fowkes (New York: Penguin, 1990), 470–80.

41. Emerson, "American Scholar," 4:60.

42. Ibid., 4:77.

43. Emerson, "Self-Reliance," 37.

44. Ibid., 37–38.

45. Ibid., 30, 33, 50.

46. Ibid., 29.

47. Emerson, "Over-Soul," in *Collected Works*, 2:161.

48. Emerson, "History," in *Collected Works*, 2:3.

49. Emerson, "Spiritual Laws," in *Collected Works*, 2:81.

50. Emerson, "Man the Reformer," lecture to the Mechanics' Apprentices' Library Association in Boston, 25 Jan. 1841, in *Works of Emerson*, 4:206.

51. Ibid., 4:208.

52. Emerson, "New England Reformers," in *Works of Emerson*, 1:413.

53. Ibid., 1:417.

54. Emerson, "Man the Reformer," 4:213.

55. Ibid., 4:211.

56. Ibid., 4:211, 213.

57. Ibid., 4:221–22.

58. Emerson, "Introductory Lecture," 2 Dec. 1841, in *Works of Emerson*, 4:263.

59. Ibid. On Emerson's response to associationism and socialism more broadly, see Bercovitch, *Rites of Assent*, 307–52.

60. Emerson, "New England Reformers," 1:417–18.

61. Emerson, "The Young American," 7 Feb. 1844, in *Works of Emerson*, 4:482.

62. Ibid., 4:472, 475.

63. Carey Wolfe notes that this transposition of the categories of the market into those of the mind, and vice versa, runs throughout Emerson's work, as well as that of later U.S. writers. "[There is] a tendency, in Emerson, [Ezra] Pound, William James, and many another, to figure the self in terms that reproduce the language, structure, and contradictions of private property." Wolfe, *Literary Ideology*, 10.

64. Emerson, "Young American," 4:471.

65. Ibid., 4:476.

66. Ibid., 4:479.

67. Ibid.

68. Robinson, *Conduct of Life*, 134–80.

69. Emerson, "Wealth," in *The Complete Works of Ralph Waldo Emerson*, vol. 6: *The Conduct of Life* (New York: Sully and Kleinteich, 1860), 85–123.

70. Ibid., 121–22, 100.

71. Emerson, *The Complete Works of Ralph Waldo Emerson*, vol. 7: *Society and Solitude* (New York: Sully and Kleinteich, 1870), 273, 290.

72. Emerson, "Wealth," 104.

73. Barbara M. Cross, *Horace Bushnell: Minister to a Changing America* (Chicago: University of Chicago Press, 1958), 31–34, 45–48; Horace Bushnell, "Prosperity Our Duty" (1847), in Bushnell, *The Spirit in Man: Sermons and Selections* (New York: Charles Scribner's Sons, 1903), 135–58; Horace Bushnell, "A Week-Day Sermon to the Business Men of Hartford" (1857), in Bushnell, *Spirit in Man*, 120–34.

74. On Bushnell's significance in American religious history, see Robert L. Edwards, *Of Singular Genius, Of Singular Grace: A Biography of Horace Bushnell* (Cleveland, Ohio: Pilgrim, 1992), 2; David L. Smith, "Introduction," in Horace Bushnell, *Selected Writings on Language, Religion, and American Culture*, ed. David L. Smith (Chico, Calif.: Scholars Press, 1984), 2–4.

75. Horace Bushnell, "The Age of Homespun" (1851), in Mary Bushnell Cheney, ed., *Life and Letters of Horace Bushnell* (New York: Harper & Bros., 1880), 13.

76. Cross, *Horace Bushnell*, 1–21; Edwards, *Singular Genius*, 10–38; Cheney, *Life and Letters*, 16–17, 32; Smith, "Introduction," 5–7; Howard A. Barnes, *Horace Bushnell and the Virtuous Republic* (Metuchen, N.J.: American Theological Association and the Scarecrow Press, 1991), 63–67.

77. Horace Bushnell, *God in Christ; Three Discourses, Delivered at New Haven, Cambridge, and Andover, with a Preliminary Dissertation on Language* (Hartford, Conn.: Brown and Parsons, 1849). See also Bushnell, "The Christian Trinity a Practical Truth," *New Englander* 12 (Nov. 1854), in Bushnell, *Building Eras in Religion* (New York: Charles Scribner's Sons, 1903), 106–49; David L. Smith, *Symbolism and Growth: The Religious Thought of Horace Bushnell* (Chico, Calif.: Scholars Press, 1981), x–xi.

78. Horace Bushnell, *Christ in Theology; Being the Answer of the Author, Before the Hartford Central Association of Ministers, October, 1849, For the Doctrines of the Book Entitled "God in Christ"* (Hartford, Conn.: Brown and Parsons, 1851), 17.

79. Bushnell, *God in Christ*, 72.

80. Coleridge, *Aids to Reflection*, 6; Bushnell, "Christian Trinity," 113–15.

81. Smith, "Introduction," 8–10.

82. Bushnell, *God in Christ*, 28, 30.

83. Smith, *Symbolism and Growth*, x.

84. Horace Bushnell, *Views of Christian Nurture and of Subjects Adjacent Thereto* (1847; reprint, Delmar, N.Y.: Scholars' Facsimiles & Reprints, 1975); Edwards, *Singular Genius*, 92.

85. Cross, *Horace Bushnell*, 54–60.

86. Peter Gregg Slater, *Children in the New England Mind: In Death and In Life* (Hamden, Conn.: Archon, 1977), esp. 152–56; Cross, *Horace Bushnell*, 61–67. On the Enlightenment revolution in parenting, see Jay Fliegelman, *Prodigals and Pilgrims: The American Revolution Against Patriarchal Authority, 1750–1800* (New York: Cambridge University Press, 1982).

87. Bushnell, *Christian Nurture*, 6.

88. Ibid., 15, 13, 14, 107, 105.

89. Ibid., 22.

90. Horace Bushnell, "Unconscious Influence" (1846), in Bushnell, *Sermons for the New Life*, rev. ed. (New York: Charles Scribner's Sons, 1886), 186–205.

91. Ibid., 192–93.

92. Ibid., 186, 194.

93. Bushnell, *Christian Nurture*, 18, 186, 194.

94. Horace Bushnell, "Popular Government by Divine Right" (1864), in Bushnell, *Building Eras*, 297, 295, 296.

95. See generally Arieli, *Individualism and Nationalism*.

96. Bushnell, *Christian Nurture*, 18.

97. On the classically liberal model of a "one-class society" of independent proprietors, see C. B. Macpherson, *The Life and Times of Liberal Democracy* (New York: Oxford University Press, 1977), 18–19.

98. Ibid., 148, 150.

99. On the racial essentialism entailed in the widespread conception of society as a family in the early twentieth century, see Walter Benn Michaels, *Our America: Nativism, Modernism, and Pluralism* (Durham, N.C.: Duke University Press, 1995).

100. Bushnell, "Popular Government," 308.

101. Cheney, *Life and Letters*, 111.

102. See Ann Douglas, *The Feminization of American Culture* (New York: Alfred A. Knopf, 1977); Nancy F. Cott, *The Bonds of Womanhood: 'Woman's Sphere' in New England, 1780–1835* (New Haven, Conn.: Yale University Press, 1977); Barbara Leslie Epstein, *The Politics of Domesticity: Women, Evangelism, and Temperance in Nineteenth-Century America* (Middletown, Conn.: Wesleyan University Press, 1981); Paula Baker, "The Domestication of Politics: Women and American Political Society, 1780–1920," *American Historical Review* 89 (June 1984): 620–47; Mary Ryan, *Cradle of the Middle Class: The Family in Oneida County, New York, 1790–1865* (New York: Cambridge University Press, 1981); Kathryn Kish Sklar, *Catharine Beecher: A Study in Domesticity* (New Haven, Conn.: Yale University Press, 1973).

103. Douglas, *Feminization of Culture*.

104. On the close relationship between the construction of "the social" and nineteenth-century feminism generally, see Denise Riley, *"Am I That Name?": Feminism and the Category of "Women" in History* (Minneapolis: University of Minnesota Press, 1988).

105. See Parrington, *Romantic Revolution*, 418–26; Perry Miller, "Foreword," in *Margaret Fuller: American Romantic; A Selection From Her Writings and Correspondence* (New York: Anchor, 1963), ix–xxviii.

106. On *Woman in the Nineteenth Century* as the transition point between the Transcendentalist and journalistic phases of Fuller's career, see the alternative interpretations of David M. Robinson, who views the work and the move toward political and social activism that it signaled as outgrowths of Fuller's Transcendentalism, and Bell Gale Chevigny, who sees Fuller's feminism and politicization as sharp departures from her early idealism. Robinson, "Margaret Fuller and the Transcendental Ethos: *Woman in the Nineteenth Century*," in Fuller, *Woman in the Nineteenth Century*, ed. Larry J. Reynolds (New York: W. W. Norton, 1998), 243–57; Chevigny, "To the Edges of Ideology: Margaret Fuller's Centrifugal Evolution," in Fuller, *Woman in the Nineteenth Century*, 257–64.

107. Margaret Fuller Ossoli, *Woman in the Nineteenth Century, and Kindred Papers, Relating to the Sphere, Condition and Duties of Woman*, ed. Arthur B. Fuller (Boston: John Jewett & Co., 1855), 115–16. See also Howe, *American Self*, 213–14, 228–29.

108. Howe, *American Self*, 169.

109. On the ideal of sexual "balance" in nineteenth-century American feminism, see William Leach, *True Love and Perfect Union: The Feminist Reform of Sex and Society* (New York: Basic, 1980).

110. Many scholars have emphasized the tension between "masculine" and "feminine" allegiances in Fuller's thought. See, for example, Douglas, *Feminization of Culture*, 313–48; Joan von Mehren, *Minerva and the Muse: A Life of Margaret Fuller* (Amherst: University of Massachusetts Press, 1994). On the tension between Fuller's early embrace of Transcendentalism and her later revolutionary politics, see especially Bell Gale Chevigny, *The Woman and the Myth: Margaret Fuller's Life and Writings* (New York: Feminist Press, 1976).

111. On 1848 as the culmination of the "Age of Revolution" and the beginning of the "Age of Capital," see Eric Hobsbawm, *The Age of Capital, 1848–1875* (New York: Vintage, 1975), 9–26. See also Donzelot, *L'Invention du Social*, 18–67. On the significance of 1848 for Fuller and her American literary contemporaries, see Larry J. Reynolds, *European Revolutions and the American Literary Renaissance* (New Haven, Conn.: Yale University Press, 1988), esp. 54–78.

112. On the relationship between the breakdown of the household economy and the rise of nineteenth-century feminism generally, see Linda J. Nicholson, *Gender and History: The Limits of Social Theory in the Age of the Family* (New York: Columbia University Press, 1986), 4, 49–65.

113. See Peggy A. Rabkin, *Fathers to Daughters: The Legal Foundations of Female Emancipation* (Westport, Conn.: Greenwood, 1980); Marylynn Salmon, *Women and the Law of Property in Early America* (Chapel Hill: University of North Carolina Press, 1986); Elizabeth Bowles Warbasse, *The Changing Legal Rights of Married Women, 1800–1861* (New York: Garland, 1987); Norma Basch, *In the Eyes of the Law: Women, Marriage, and Property in Nineteenth-Century New York* (Ithaca, N.Y.: Cornell University Press, 1982); Richard H. Chused, "Married Women's Property Law: 1800–1850," *Georgetown Law Journal* 71 (1982–83): 1359–1425; Gregory S. Alexander, *Commodity and Propriety: Competing Visions of Property in American Legal Thought, 1776–1970* (Chicago: University of Chicago Press, 1997), 158–84.

114. Nicholson, *Gender and History*, 49 (emphasis added).

115. Jeanne Boydston, *Home and Work: Housework, Wages, and the Ideology of Labor in the Early Republic* (New York: Oxford University Press, 1990), 159. See also Elizabeth Blackmar, *Manhattan for Rent, 1785–1850* (Ithaca, N.Y.: Cornell University Press, 1989), 120–26; Nancy Folbre, "The Unproductive Housewife: Her Evolution in Nineteenth-Century Economic Thought," *Signs: Journal of Women in Culture and Society* 16, no. 3 (Spring 1991): 463–84; Christine Stansell, *City of Women: Sex and Class in New York, 1789–1860* (Chicago: University of Illinois Press, 1987), 105–29.

116. Reva B. Siegel, "Home as Work: The First Woman's Rights Claims Concerning Wives' Household Labor, 1850–1880," *Yale Law Journal* 103 (Mar. 1994): 1112–46. On the ways in which legislative and judicial interpretations of the "earning statutes" of the mid-nineteenth century, which granted married women property in their "separate" earnings from paid labor, rejected feminists' claims upon women's unpaid housework, see Reva B. Siegel, "The Modernization of Marital Status Law: Adjudicating Wives' Rights to Earnings, 1860–1930," *Georgetown Law Journal* 82 (1993–94): 2127–2211; Amy Dru Stanley, "Conjugal Bonds and Wage Labor: Rights of Contract in the Age of Emancipation," *Journal of American History* 75, no. 2 (Sept. 1988): 471–500.

117. "Fuller's life can be viewed as an effort to find what she called her 'sovereign self' by disavowing fiction for history, the realm of 'feminine' fantasy for the realm of 'masculine' reality." Douglas, *Feminization of Culture*, 317. My analysis here is particularly indebted to Douglas.

118. Ossoli, *Memoirs of Margaret Fuller Ossoli*, ed. R. F. Fuller, vol. 1 (Boston: Phillips, Sampson and Co., 1851), 19; Douglas, *Feminization of Culture*, 320–21; Charles Capper, *Margaret Fuller: An American Romantic Life* (New York: Oxford University Press, 1992), 10–13, 29–30, 133–34; Howe, *American Self*, 214; Chevigny, *Woman and Myth*, 282; Thomas Wentworth Higginson, *Margaret Fuller Ossoli* (Boston: Houghton, Mifflin, 1890), 21–22.

119. Douglas, *Feminization of Culture*, 321; Higginson, *Fuller Ossoli*, 54; Capper, *Margaret Fuller*, 11–13, 160–62; Howe, *American Self*, 212, 216.

120. Ossoli, *Memoirs*, 1:12, 14–16, 23. See also her fictionalized account of her girlhood experience at Miss Susan Prescott's Young Ladies' Seminary: the story of "Mariana," whose "ardent and too early stimulated nature was constantly increased by the restraints and narrow routine of the boarding school," in Margaret Fuller, *Summer on the Lakes, in 1843* (1844; reprint, Urbana: University of Illinois Press, 1991), 51–64; quoted passage at 52.

121. Ossoli, *Memoirs*, 1:22; Capper, *Margaret Fuller*, 252–306.

122. Ossoli, *Nineteenth Century*, xiii.

123. Ibid., 172.

124. See Howe, *American Self*, 229–30.

125. Ossoli, *Nineteenth Century*, 169, 115, 103, 38, 63.

126. Cf. Catharine E. Beecher, *A Treatise on Domestic Economy, For the Use of Young Ladies at Home, and at School* (Boston: Marsh, Capen, Lyon, & Webb, 1841).

127. Ibid., 116, 115.

128. The book's "pantheon of representative women—historical personages, famous writers, literary characters, and goddesses—defined a wide repertoire of subject-positions, each one articulating a different model of female power." Jeffrey Steele, "Margaret Fuller's Rhetoric of Transformation," in Fuller, *Nineteenth Century*, 286. Steele, however, contrasts the multiple identities in Fuller's work with the "single male persona" he finds in Emerson and Whitman.

129. Ossoli, *Nineteenth Century*, 170, 118.

130. Ibid., 30–32, 34–35, 219–20.

131. Ibid., 21, 174.

132. Ibid., 36, 37 (emphasis on "and outward" added to second quote).

133. Ibid., 119, 176.

134. On the relationship between Fuller's work and Beecher's, see also Nicole Tonkovich, *Domesticity with a Difference: The Nonfiction of Catharine Beecher, Sarah J. Hale, Fanny Fern, and Margaret Fuller* (Jackson: University Press of Mississippi, 1997).

135. Catharine Esther Beecher, *The Elements of Mental and Moral Philosophy, Founded Upon Experience, Reason, and the Bible* (Hartford, Conn.: n.p., 1831), iii–v, 244, 255, 261–67.

136. See also Beecher's renowned criticism of the equalitarian radicalism of the abolitionist-feminist sisters, Angelina and Sarah Grimké. Catharine E. Beecher, *An Essay on Slavery and Abolitionism, with Reference to the Duty of American Females* (Philadelphia: Henry Perkins, 1837).

137. Beecher, *Domestic Economy*, 2, 3, 13–14.

138. [Catharine Beecher], *The Duty of American Women to Their Country* (New York: Harper & Bros., 1845), 12, 64 (emphasis in original).

139. Margaret Fuller, "The Poor Man—An Ideal Sketch" (25 Mar. 1846), in *Margaret Fuller's New York Journalism: A Biographical Essay and Key Writings*, ed. Catharine C. Mitchell (Knoxville: University of Tennessee Press, 1995), 71; Fuller, "The Rich Man—An Ideal Sketch" (6 Feb. 1846), in *New York Journalism*, 55. See also the discussions of Indians and frontier women in Fuller's *Summer on the Lakes*, based upon her travels on the Great Lakes and in the Wisconsin Territory in the summer of 1843.

140. The standard biographical account of Fuller's final years is Joseph Jay Deiss, *The Roman Years of Margaret Fuller* (New York: Thomas Y. Crowell, 1969).

141. Margaret Fuller, *"These Sad But Glorious Days": Dispatches From Europe, 1846–1850*, ed. Larry J. Reynolds and Susan Belasco Smith (New Haven, Conn.: Yale University Press, 1991), 88, 57, 88.

142. Larry J. Reynolds and Susan Belasco Smith, "Introduction," in Fuller, *Glorious Days*, 13–17; Chevigny, *Woman and Myth*, 298–301.

143. Fuller, *Glorious Days*, 120, 156.

144. Ibid., 129.

145. Ibid., 164–65.

146. Ibid., 211.

147. Ibid., 225; Chevigny, *Woman and Myth*, 369–70. On Mazzini's and other radicals' opposition to the social revolution embraced by Europe's laboring classes in 1848, see Hobsbawm, *Age of Capital*, 18.

148. On Fuller and Emerson's divergent reactions to revolutionary Europe, see Reynolds, *European Revolutions*, 54–78. For a contrasting interpretation that emphasizes the importance of Emerson's European tour in his own pragmatic politicization, see Robinson, *Conduct of Life*, 6.

149. Fuller, *Glorious Days*, 304, 322.

Chapter Three

1. Alexis de Tocqueville, *Democracy in America*, vol. 1 (New York: Vintage, 1945), 14, 8, 7.

2. Robert A. Nisbet, *The Sociological Tradition* (New York: Basic, 1966). On French sociology as an outgrowth of Tocqueville and Comte's response to the Revolutionary heritage of contemporary working-class politics, see Jacques Donzelot, *L'Invention du Social: Essai sur le Déclin des Passions Politiques* (Paris: Librairie Arthème Fayard, 1984), esp. 18–66; Göran Therborn, *Science, Class, and Society: On the Formation of Sociology and Historical Materialism* (London: NLB, 1976), 145–54, 170–72. On sociology as an ideological alternative to Marxist social science generally, see also Alvin W. Gouldner, *The Coming Crisis of Western Sociology* (New York: Basic, 1970); Irving M. Zeitlin, *Ideology and the Development of Sociological Theory* (Englewood Cliffs, N.J.: Prentice Hall, 1994); Gertrude Lenzer, "Introduction," in Comte, *Auguste Comte and Positivism: The Essential Writings*, ed. Gertrude Lenzer (Chicago: University of Chicago Press, 1975); Antonio Gramsci, *Selections from the Prison Notebooks of Antonio Gramsci*, ed. and trans. Quintin Hoare and Geoffrey Nowell Smith (New York: International, 1971), 243–45, 425–30. But see Therborn's instructive critique of Nisbet and others' argument that Comtean sociology represented a conservative rejection of Enlighten-

ment individualism in favor of social order. Therborn rightly notes that Enlightenment thinkers were also profoundly wedded to certain traditional ideas about social order, that nineteenth-century sociologists such as Herbert Spencer were strongly individualistic in important respects, and, most importantly, that the "sociological tradition" itself shared many of its founding premises with the tradition of historical materialism. Therborn, *Science, Class, and Society*, esp. 119–24.

3. Richmond Laurin Hawkins, *Auguste Comte and the United States (1816–1853)* (Cambridge, Mass.: Harvard University Press, 1936), 4–9.

4. Therborn, *Science, Class, and Society*, 156–61; Stanislav Andreski, "Introduction," in *The Essential Comte*, ed. Stanislav Andreski, trans. Margaret Clarke (London: Croom Helm, 1974), 17–18.

5. Hawkins, *Auguste Comte*, 10–13.

6. Comte, *Comte and Positivism*, 10–15, 27, 203, 214–15.

7. Ibid., 25–26; Andreski, "Introduction," 9, 18.

8. Therborn, *Science, Class, and Society*, 224.

9. Hawkins, *Auguste Comte*, 14–16.

10. Henry Hughes, *Treatise on Sociology, Theoretical and Practical* (1854; reprint, New York: Negro Universities Press, 1968); George Fitzhugh, *Sociology for the South, or the Failure of Free Society* (Richmond, Va.: A. Morris, 1854); Henry Hughes, *Selected Writings of Henry Hughes: Antebellum Southerner, Slavocrat, Sociologist*, ed. Stanford M. Lyman (Jackson, Miss.: University Press of Mississippi, 1985), 1–17; Louis Hartz, *The Liberal Tradition in America: An Interpretation of American Political Thought Since the Revolution* (1955; reprint, New York: Harcourt Brace Jovanovich, 1991), 184–89. Comte himself, however, deemed American slavery a "social monstrosity." Hawkins, *Auguste Comte*, 12.

11. Henry C. Carey, *Principles of Social Science*, 3 vols. (1858–1859; reprint, New York: Augustus M. Kelley, 1963).

12. David Brion Davis, "Reflections on Abolitionism and Ideological Hegemony," *American Historical Review* 92 (1987): 797–812; Eric Foner, *Politics and Ideology in the Age of the Civil War* (New York: Oxford University Press, 1980), 57–76. See also John Ashworth, "The Relationship Between Capitalism and Humanitarianism," *American Historical Review* 92 (1987): 813–28.

13. Quoted in Foner, *Politics and Ideology*, 63.

14. John Ashworth, *Slavery, Capitalism, and Politics in the Antebellum Republic*, vol. 1: *Commerce and Compromise, 1820–1850* (New York: Cambridge University Press, 1995), 192–285.

15. Elizabeth Fox-Genovese and Eugene D. Genovese usefully frame the essential problem of antebellum political economy this way: "In the United States, the class issue remained confused by the marked regional divisions that nonetheless rested upon competing systems of class relations. Industrialization and economic development, as distinct from simple economic growth, forced both Northerners and Southerners to confront the implications of the transfer of labor from the domestic to the public spheres." Fox-Genovese and Genovese, "Foreword," in Allen Kaufman, *Capitalism, Slavery, and Republican Values: Antebellum Political Economists, 1819–1848* (Austin: University of Texas Press, 1982), xv.

16. "Wages, profit, and rent, are the three original sources of all revenue as well as of all exchangeable value. All other revenue is ultimately derived from some one or other of these." Adam Smith, *An Inquiry into the Nature and Causes of the Wealth of Nations*, ed. R. H.

Campbell and A. S. Skinner, vol. 1 (Indianapolis: Liberty Classics, 1981), 69. On antebellum American political economy, see Paul K. Conkin, *Prophets of Prosperity: America's First Political Economists* (Bloomington: Indiana University Press, 1980); James L. Huston, *Securing the Fruits of Labor: The American Concept of Wealth Distribution, 1765–1900* (Baton Rouge: Louisiana State University Press, 1998), 152–83; Herbert Hovenkamp, "The Political Economy of Substantive Due Process," *Stanford Law Review* 40 (1988): 379–447; Tony A. Freyer, *Producers Versus Capitalists: Constitutional Conflict in Antebellum America* (Charlottesville: University Press of Virginia, 1994); Ernest Teilhac, *Pioneers of American Economic Thought in the Nineteenth Century*, trans. E. A. J. Johnson (1936; reprint, New York: Russell & Russell, 1967), 1–113; Kaufman, *Capitalism, Slavery, and Republican Values*; John Roscoe Turner, *The Ricardian Rent Theory in Early American Economics* (New York: New York University Press, 1921). On classical political economy in general and Ricardian economics in particular, see Phyllis Deane, *The Evolution of Economic Ideas* (New York: Cambridge University Press, 1978), 1–92; A. K. Dasgupta, *Epochs of Economic Theory* (New York: Basil Blackwell, 1975), 1–70; Mark Blaug, *Economic Theory in Retrospect*, 3d ed. (New York: Cambridge University Press, 1978), 10–235; David McNally, *Political Economy and the Rise of Capitalism: A Reinterpretation* (Berkeley: University of California Press, 1988); Ronald L. Meek, *Studies in the Labor Theory of Value*, 2d ed. (New York: Monthly Review Press, 1976), 12–120; Maurice Dobb, *Political Economy and Capitalism: Some Essays in Economic Tradition* (1945; reprint, Westport, Conn.: Greenwood, 1972); Maurice Dobb, *Theories of Value and Distribution Since Adam Smith: Ideology and Economic Theory* (New York: Cambridge University Press, 1973), 1–136.

17. Smith, *Wealth of Nations*, vol. 1, 66–69, 82–85, 105, 109; quoted passage at 109; Dasgupta, *Economic Theory*, 63–64.

18. David Ricardo, *The Works and Correspondence of David Ricardo*, ed. Piero Sraffa, with the collaboration of M. H. Dobb, vol. 1: *On the Principles of Political Economy and Taxation* (New York: Cambridge University Press, 1951), 5; Meek, *Labor Theory*, 84.

19. Ricardo, *Works and Correspondence*, vol. 1, 27, 93–94, 121; Blaug, *Economic Theory*, 69–82, 91–99; Deane, *Economic Ideas*, 38.

20. Huston, *Fruits of Labor*, 159.

21. Meek, *Labor Theory*, 121–25; Dobb, *Theories of Value*, 103. "It is surely not merely fanciful to see much of this reaction against Ricardo as a reflection of the general shift by the British bourgeoisie at about this time from an offensive position as against the landlords to a defensive position as against the rising working-class movement." Meek, *Labor Theory*, 125. For an alternative view of Ricardo, emphasizing his reservations regarding the role of labor cost in determining exchange value, see Blaug, *Economic Theory*, 95. Yet regardless of how Ricardo ought to be or intended to be read, contemporary working-class advocates drew inspiration and support from his work. Similarly, Joseph Schumpeter has contended that "the class connotations of Ricardo's categories are in fact no more than survivals and nonessential to his system," "the inevitable result of a defective analytic apparatus [rather] than of any intention to emphasize class aspects." Schumpeter, *History of Economic Analysis*, ed. Elizabeth Boody Schumpeter (New York: Oxford University Press, 1954), 554, 553. Aside from the tendentiousness of Schumpeter's judgment, the essential historical point here is that, as Schumpeter acknowledges, Carey and like-minded writers, "believing that the Ricardian tendencies in distributive shares spelled social warfare, . . . set about disproving them." Ibid., 554.

22. Conkin, *Prophets of Prosperity*, 222–58, 111–23; Huston, *Fruits of Labor*, 152–53, 161; Martin Joseph Burke, "The Conundrum of Class: Public Discourse on the Social Order in America," Ph.D. diss., University of Michigan, 1987, 117–213. See, for example, Francis Wayland, *The Elements of Political Economy*, 2d ed. (New York: Robinson & Franklin, 1838); J. R. McCulloch, *A Treatise on the Circumstances Which Determine the Rate of Wages and the Condition of the Labouring Classes*, 2d ed. (1854; reprint, New York: Augustus M. Kelley, 1963 [1st. ed. 1826]).

23. On Carey and the French economist Frédéric Bastiat, whose ideas closely paralleled his, as preeminent theorists of class harmony in reaction to the Ricardian analysis of competing class interests, see Karl Marx, *Grundrisse: Foundations of the Critique of Political Economy*, trans. Martin Nicolaus (New York: Vintage, 1973), 883–93. On Carey's economic theory, see also A. D. H. Kaplan, *Henry Charles Carey: A Study in American Economic Thought* (Baltimore, Md.: Johns Hopkins University Press, 1931); Rodney J. Morrison, *Henry C. Carey and American Economic Development* (Philadelphia: American Philosophical Society, 1986); Joseph Dorfman, *The Economic Mind in American Civilization, 1606–1865*, vol. 2 (New York: Viking, 1946), 789–804; Turner, *Ricardian Rent Theory*, 110–42; Teilhac, *Economic Thought*, 53–113; Schumpeter, *Economic Analysis*, 515–18; Conkin, *Prophets of Prosperity*, 261–312. On Carey as a progenitor of modern sociology, see Arnold W. Green, *Henry Charles Carey: Nineteenth-Century Sociologist* (Philadelphia: University of Pennsylvania Press, 1951); L. L. Bernard and Jessie Bernard, *Origins of American Sociology: The Social Science Movement in the United States* (1943; reprint, New York: Russell & Russell, 1965), 398–457. Teilhac notes that "Carey abandons the old form of political economy and attempts to supplant it by a rather vague sociology in which economic phenomena are treated as social phenomena." Teilhac, *Economic Thought*, 60. On Carey's personal and intellectual ties to Emerson, see John Wenzler, "Transcendental Economics," *Intellectual History Newsletter* 21 (1999): 1–10.

24. See George Winston Smith, *Henry C. Carey and American Sectional Conflict* (Albuquerque: University of New Mexico Press, 1951).

25. Green, *Henry Charles Carey*, 1–25; G. W. Smith, *Sectional Conflict*, 7–14. See especially, Henry C. Carey, *The Harmony of Interests: Agricultural, Manufacturing, and Commercial* (1851; reprint, New York: Augustus M. Kelley, 1967); Henry C. Carey, *The Slave Trade, Domestic and Foreign: Why It Exists and How It May Be Extinguished* (1853; reprint, New York: Augustus M. Kelley, 1967).

26. See Freyer, *Producers Versus Capitalists*, 3–8, 45–50.

27. Daniel Walker Howe, *The Political Culture of the American Whigs* (Chicago: University of Chicago Press, 1979), 108–22; quoted passage at 115. See also Eric Foner, *Free Soil, Free Labor, Free Men: The Ideology of the Republican Party Before the Civil War* (New York: Oxford University Press, 1970), 36–37.

28. H. C. Carey, *Essay on the Rate of Wages: With an Examination of the Causes of the Differences in the Condition of the Labouring Population Throughout the World* (Philadelphia: Carey, Lea, & Blanchard, 1835), 8, 15–17, 22, 28; quoted passage at 15.

29. See, for example, Carey, *Slave Trade*, 281; Carey, *Social Science*, 3:154.

30. Ricardo, *Works and Correspondence*, 93.

31. McCulloch, *Treatise on Wages*, 28.

32. Smith, *Wealth of Nations*, 1:85–91.

33. Ricardo acknowledged, however, that "subsistence" itself was defined by social norms

as well as biological needs. The natural price of labor, he wrote, "depends on the habits and customs of the people." Ricardo, *Works and Correspondence,* 97.

34. Henry C. Carey, *The Past, the Present, and the Future* (Philadelphia: Henry Carey Baird, 1847), 9–93; quoted passage at 74. On related challenges to the premise of naturally declining fertility, see John Bellamy Foster and Fred Magdoff, "Liebig, Marx, and the Depletion of Soil Fertility: Relevance for Today's Agriculture," *Monthly Review* 50, no. 3 (1998): 32–45.

35. Smith, *Wealth of Nations,* 1:65, 47.

36. Ricardo, *Works and Correspondence,* 11, 24–25, 74–77. However, Ricardo recognized an exception to this rule in the case of scarce, irreplaceable items like artworks or fine wines. Ibid., 12. He also contended that the relative values of different commodities were affected by differing compositions of fixed and circulating capital, or differing durabilities of fixed capital, expended in their production. Ibid., 30–43.

37. Carey himself regarded the cost-of-reproduction theory of value as the foundation of his entire understanding of distribution, i.e., of the harmony of interests. See Carey, *Social Science,* 1:iii–iv. See also Kaplan, *Henry Charles Carey,* 39–46.

38. Carey, *Principles of Political Economy,* vol. 1 (Philadelphia: Carey, Lea & Blanchard, 1837), 7–143, 337–41; Carey, *Social Science,* 1:149–53, 111–13.

39. Carey, *Political Economy,* 1:339.

40. Carey, *Social Science,* 3:113.

41. Henry C. Carey, *The Past, the Present, and the Future* (Philadelphia: Henry Carey Baird, 1847), 95–99; quoted passage at 95. See also Turner, *Ricardian Rent Theory,* 118; Kaplan, *Henry Charles Carey,* 36.

42. On Carey as a progenitor of the modern concept of "human capital," see Huston, *Fruits of Labor,* 179–80.

43. Carey, *Social Science,* 3:234.

44. See Marx, *Grundrisse,* 579–80. "In short, [Carey] regards the working days as working days belonging to the worker, and *instead of concluding that he has to produce more capital in order to be employed for the same labour time, he concludes that he has to work less in order to buy the capital* (to appropriate the conditions of production for himself)." Ibid., 579 (emphasis in original).

45. Carey, *Political Economy,* 3:200–201.

46. Carey, *Slave Trade,* 89 (emphasis in original).

47. Carey, *Political Economy,* 3:207 (emphasis in original).

48. For the fullest exposition of his argument regarding slavery and wage labor, see Carey, *Slave Trade.*

49. Carey, *Social Science,* 3:368–69; quoted passage at 369. See also Carey, *Past, Present, Future,* 262–73.

50. See his critique of the idea "that all the poverty and wretchedness that exist, arise out of the erroneous arrangements of the Deity," in Carey, *Rate of Wages,* 232–45; quoted passage at 232.

51. My formulation of the issue here is indebted to Robert Brenner's critique of historical interpretations of the transition from feudalism to capitalism as the result of "what might loosely be called 'objective' economic forces—in particular, demographic fluctuations and the growth of trade and markets." Brenner, "Agrarian Class Structure and Economic Devel-

opment in Pre-Industrial Europe," in *The Brenner Debate: Agrarian Class Structure and Economic Development in Pre-Industrial Europe*, ed. T. H. Aston and C. H. E. Philpin (New York: Cambridge University Press, 1985), 10–63; quoted passage at 10. For a related debate on this question, see Rodney Hilton, ed., *The Transition from Feudalism to Capitalism* (London: NLB, 1976).

52. Carey, *Social Science*, 3:462.

53. For his most thorough case for protectionism as a social panacea, see Carey, *Harmony of Interests*.

54. Carey, *Social Science*, 1:210–13; quoted passage at 210.

55. Carey, *Past, Present, Future*, 289. Carey also advanced an innovative ecological argument that increasing direct exchange between the producers and consumers of farm goods heightened the returns from agriculture. The more immediate the ties between town and country or industry and agriculture, he contended, the more swiftly and completely the waste from consumption of farm goods returned as manure to fertilize the soil. For a related discussion of this issue, see Foster and Magdoff, "Soil Fertility."

56. Carey, *Social Science*, 1:212, 213.

57. Gerald Berk, *Alternative Tracks: The Constitution of American Industrial Order, 1865–1917* (Baltimore, Md.: Johns Hopkins University Press, 1994).

58. Carey, *Harmony of Interests*, 228–29.

59. Carey, *Social Science*, 3:95–96, 229.

60. See Marx, *Grundrisse*, 885–87.

61. See the discussion of the centrality to classical political economy of the category of "profit on capital" as opposed to that of "profit upon alienation" in Meek, *Labor Theory*, 24–27. ,

62. Carey, *Social Science*, 1:198. On the meaning of "association" in Carey's work, see G. W. Smith, *Sectional Conflict*, 18–20; Green, *Henry Charles Carey*, 105–10, 151–53.

63. Carey, *Social Science*, 3:422.

64. Carey, *Rate of Wages*, 249–55.

65. Carey, *Social Science*, 1:28–31; quoted passage at 31.

66. Ibid., 1:41, 52.

67. Ibid., 3:456–57.

68. Ibid., 1:63 (emphasis in original).

69. On Carey's anticipation of Durkheim, see Green, *Henry Charles Carey*, 88–89.

70. Carey, *Social Science*, 3:415–20; quoted passage at 420. See also Carey, *Political Economy*, 2:248–50. "No one else in pre–Civil War America enveloped early forms of economic collectivism in such a moral glow." Conkin, *Prophets of Prosperity*, 276.

71. Carey, *Political Economy*, 2:234–35, 264; Carey, *Social Science*, 2:298–301, 327, 333, 343, 446–80.

72. For influential contemporary expositions of greenback theory that bear a similarly revisionist relation to classical political economy, see Edward Kellogg, *Labor and Other Capital: The Rights of Each Secured and the Wrongs of Both Eradicated. Or, An Exposition of the Cause Why Few Are Wealthy and Many Poor, and the Delineation of a System, Which, Without Infringing the Rights of Property, Will Give to Labor Its Just Reward* (New York: Edward Kellogg, 1849); Alexander Campbell, *The True American System of Finance; The Rights of Labor and Capital, and the Common Sense Way of Doing Justice to the Soldiers and their Fam-*

ilies. No Banks: Greenbacks the Exclusive Currency (Chicago: Evening Journal Book and Job Print, 1864). See also the major popular theorist of the "free silver" movement of the 1890s: William H. Harvey, *Coin's Financial School*, ed. Richard Hofstadter (1894; reprint, Cambridge, Mass.: Belknap Press of Harvard University Press, 1963). On the importance of Carey's ideal of "association" in the greenback movement, see Walter T. K. Nugent, *Money and American Society, 1865–1880* (New York: Free Press, 1968), 24, 29–31, 39–41. See also the discussion of greenback theory in Chapter 4 below.

73. Drew Gilpin Faust, "Introduction," in *The Ideology of Slavery: Proslavery Thought in the Antebellum South, 1830–1860*, ed. Drew Gilpin Faust (Baton Rouge: Louisiana State University Press, 1981), 2–10.

74. The leading exponent of the "paternalist" interpretation of slaveholder ideology is Eugene D. Genovese. Genovese, *The Political Economy of Slavery*, 2d ed. (1961; reprint, Middletown, Conn.: Wesleyan University Press, 1989), 15–17, 28; Genovese, *The World the Slaveholders Made: Two Essays in Interpretation* (New York: Pantheon, 1969), 118–25; Genovese, *Roll, Jordan, Roll: The World the Slaves Made* (New York: Vintage, 1972), 3–7. See also Manisha Sinha, "The Counter-Revolution of Slavery: Class, Politics and Ideology in Antebellum South Carolina," Ph.D. diss., Columbia University, 1994; Faust, "Introduction," 10–13. For related views of southern gender ideology and southern law, respectively, see Stephanie McCurry, "The Two Faces of Republicanism: Gender and Proslavery Politics in Antebellum South Carolina," *Journal of American History* 78 (Mar. 1992): 1245–64; Mark V. Tushnet, *The American Law of Slavery, 1810–1860: Considerations of Humanity and Interest* (Princeton, N.J.: Princeton University Press, 1981). For the "liberal democratic" interpretation of slaveholder ideology, emphasizing the basis of that ideology in capitalism, see James Oakes, *The Ruling Race: A History of American Slaveholders* (New York: Alfred A. Knopf, 1982), 127–39; Oakes, *Slavery and Freedom: An Interpretation of the Old South* (New York: Alfred A. Knopf, 1990), 40–79; and, emphasizing the basis of that ideology in racism, George M. Fredrickson, *The Black Image in the White Mind: The Debate on Afro-American Character and Destiny, 1817–1914* (New York: Harper & Row, 1971), 43–70.

75. Oakes, *Ruling Race*, 196. See also Louis Hartz's analysis of the "feudal dream of the South," which he likewise describes as an ideological cul-de-sac with no lasting legacy. Hartz, *Liberal Tradition*, 143–200, esp. 171.

76. Drew Gilpin Faust notes that the social organicism of proslavery paternalists echoed that of leading evangelical and Unitarian thinkers in the North and in England. Faust, *A Sacred Circle: The Dilemma of the Intellectual in the Old South, 1840–1860* (Baltimore, Md.: Johns Hopkins University Press, 1977), 130.

77. See the analysis of the plantation romance in William R. Taylor, *Cavalier and Yankee: The Old South and American National Character* (1957; reprint, New York: Oxford University Press, 1993).

78. Douglas Ambrose, *Henry Hughes and Proslavery Thought in the Old South* (Baton Rouge: Louisiana State University Press, 1996), 6; Stanford M. Lyman, "Henry Hughes and the Southern Foundations of American Sociology," in Hughes, *Selected Writings*, 1–2; Faust, "Introduction," 11.

79. See Genovese, *World the Slaveholders Made*, 115–244; Hartz, *Liberal Tradition*, 171; Oakes, *Ruling Race*, 211–16; Richard Hofstadter, *The American Political Tradition: And the Men Who Made It* (New York: Alfred A. Knopf, 1948), 89, 117.

80. Harvey Wish, *George Fitzhugh: Propagandist of the Old South* (1943; reprint, Glouces-ter, Mass.: Peter Smith, 1962), 3–4, 44, 7, 10–11, 91. For a recent appreciation of Fitzhugh's vi-sion of economic development as a precursor of twentieth-century dependency theory, see Joseph Persky, "Unequal Exchange and Dependency Theory in George Fitzhugh," *History of Political Economy* 24, no. 1 (Spring 1992): 117–28.

81. C. Van Woodward, "George Fitzhugh, *Sui Generis*," in George Fitzhugh, *Cannibals All! or, Slaves Without Masters*, ed. C. Vann Woodward (Cambridge, Mass.: Harvard University Press, 1960), xxxi–xxxii.

82. Lyman, "Henry Hughes," 28–35, 58–59; Ambrose, *Henry Hughes*, 2–13, 54–68, 71; Ronald Takaki, *Iron Cages: Race and Culture in Nineteenth-Century America* (New York: Ox-ford University Press, 1990), 130.

83. Stanford M. Lyman, "Preface," in Hughes, *Selected Writings*, ix. Fitzhugh's work receives but brief mention in Dorothy Ross, *The Origins of American Social Science* (New York: Cam-bridge University Press, 1991), 32; Hughes is absent. Similarly, Fitzhugh and Hughes are ref-erenced only in passing in Bernard and Bernard, *American Sociology*, 7.

84. Fitzhugh, *Sociology for the South*, 90.

85. Wish, *George Fitzhugh*, 43, 94–96.

86. Fitzhugh, *Sociology for the South*, 177–79.

87. Hughes, *Treatise on Sociology*, 176.

88. Fitzhugh, *Sociology for the South*, 25.

89. Genovese, *Political Economy of Slavery*, 23; Tushnet, *Law of Slavery*, 231.

90. Fitzhugh, *Sociology for the South*, 28.

91. Ibid., 29.

92. Hughes, *Treatise on Sociology*, 170.

93. On the contemporary scientific debate over whether black people constituted a dif-ferent species from white people, see Fredrickson, *Black Image*, 71–95.

94. Fitzhugh, *Sociology for the South*, 248; Fitzhugh, *Cannibals All*, 53.

95. Hughes, *Treatise on Sociology*, 186.

96. Ibid., 55.

97. Fitzhugh, *Sociology for the South*, 69 (emphasis in original).

98. Hughes, *Treatise on Sociology*, 167.

99. Douglas Ambrose describes the combination of utopian critique and ideological ra-tionale in Hughes's work this way: "At times the *Treatise* seems to describe an artificial model of a proposed society; other times it appears to describe the contemporary South. This ten-dency reveals Hughes's dual purpose: to defend the basic principles of the southern social order while simultaneously advocating major reforms that would place it on a firmer, more theoretically sound foundation." Ambrose, *Henry Hughes*, 81. Karl Mannheim, noting that "liberal utopias" are typically characterized by a "relative approximation" between the ideal and the actually existing social order, has commented: "In conservatism, we find the process of approximation to the 'here and now' completed. The utopia in this case is, from the very beginning, embedded in existing reality. . . . [T]he 'here and now,' is no longer experienced as an 'evil' reality but as the embodiment of the highest values and meanings." Karl Mannheim, *Ideology and Utopia: An Introduction to the Sociology of Knowledge*, trans. Louis Wirth and Edward Shils (New York: Harcourt, Brace and World, 1936), 233.

100. Hughes, *Treatise on Sociology*, 167.

101. Fitzhugh, *Sociology for the South*, 67–68, 300, 297–98.

102. Hughes, *Treatise on Sociology*, 230.

103. Fitzhugh, *Sociology for the South*, 83.

104. Woodward, "George Fitzhugh," xxxv–xxxviii.

105. See Hughes, "Woman in Sociology," in Hughes, *Selected Writings*, 186–88.

106. See Oakes, *Ruling Race*, 153–91; Elizabeth Fox-Genovese, *Within the Plantation Household: Black and White Women of the Old South* (Chapel Hill: University of North Carolina Press, 1988).

107. Hughes, *Treatise on Sociology*, 231.

108. Fitzhugh, *Sociology for the South*, 189, 191, 193.

109. Ibid., 296–97, 5.

110. Ibid., 27–28, 248.

111. Ambrose, *Henry Hughes*, 181–82, 183–86.

112. Wish, *George Fitzhugh*, 336; Jonathan M. Wiener, "Coming to Terms with Capitalism: The Postwar Thought of George Fitzhugh," *The Virginia Magazine of History and Biography* 87, no. 4 (Oct. 1979): 438–47.

113. Wiener, "Coming to Terms," 438; Hartz, *Liberal Tradition*, 172.

114. "Possibly, Fitzhugh now recognized heroic virtues in the feudal ideals of monopoly capitalism." Wish, *George Fitzhugh*, 336.

Chapter Four

1. "Sketch of William Graham Sumner," *Popular Science Monthly* 35 (June 1889): 261–68, reprinted in W. G. Sumner, *The Challenge of Facts and Other Essays*, ed. Albert Galloway Keller (New Haven, Conn.: Yale University Press, 1914), 5–6.

2. Henry George, *Social Problems* (New York: Robert Schalkenbach Foundation, 1934; originally serialized in *Frank Leslie's Illustrated Newspaper*, 1883), 165; Henry George, *Progress and Poverty: An Inquiry Into the Cause of Industrial Depressions and of Increase of Want with Increase of Wealth . . . The Remedy* (1879; New York: Robert Schalkenbach Foundation, 1962), 357; Charles Albro Barker, *Henry George* (New York: Oxford University Press, 1955), 6–10; Edward Thomas O'Donnell, "Henry George and the 'New Political Forces': Ethnic Nationalism, Labor Radicalism and Politics in Gilded Age New York City," Ph.D. diss., Columbia University, 1995, 13; John L. Thomas, *Alternative America: Henry George, Edward Bellamy, Henry Demarest Lloyd, and the Adversary Tradition* (Cambridge, Mass.: Harvard University Press, 1983), 7–12.

3. Walter Licht, *Industrializing America: The Nineteenth Century* (Baltimore, Md.: Johns Hopkins University Press, 1995), 97. On the limits to the widely heralded political and economic transformation brought by the war, see Morton Keller, *Affairs of State: Public Life in Late Nineteenth Century America* (Cambridge, Mass.: Harvard University Press, 1977).

4. Robert McCloskey, *American Conservatism in the Age of Enterprise: A Study of William Graham Sumner, Stephen J. Field, and Andrew Carnegie* (Cambridge, Mass.: Harvard University Press, 1951), 42.

5. On the currency crusades of the late nineteenth century, see James Livingston, *Pragmatism and the Political Economy of Cultural Revolution, 1850–1940* (Chapel Hill: University of North Carolina Press, 1994), 146–49; Walter T. K. Nugent, *Money and American Society,*

1865–1880 (New York: Free Press, 1968); Irwin Unger, *The Greenback Era: A Social and Political History of American Finance, 1865–1879* (Princeton, N.J.: Princeton University Press, 1964); Gretchen Ritter, *Goldbugs and Greenbacks: The Antimonopoly Tradition and the Politics of Finance in America* (New York: Cambridge University Press, 1997); David Montgomery, *Beyond Equality: Labor and the Radical Republicans, 1862–1872* (1967; Chicago: University of Illinois Press, 1981), 425–47; Lawrence Goodwyn, *The Populist Moment: A Short History of the Agrarian Revolt in America* (New York: Oxford University Press, 1978), 3–19. On the rise of investment banking and the securities market, see William G. Roy, *Socializing Capital: The Rise of the Large Industrial Corporation In America* (Princeton, N.J.: Princeton University Press, 1997), 115–43. On public finance in the Civil War era, see Bray Hammond, *Sovereignty and an Empty Purse: Banks and Politics in the Civil War* (Princeton, N.J.: Princeton University Press, 1970), 37–260; Margaret G. Myers, *A Financial History of the United States* (New York: Columbia University Press, 1970), 148–222; C. K. Yearley, *The Money Machines: The Breakdown and Reform of Governmental and Party Finance in the North, 1860–1920* (Albany, N.Y.: State University of New York Press, 1970).

6. Hans L. Trefousse, *Ben Butler: The South Called Him BEAST!* (New York: Twayne, 1957), 218. John G. Sproat calls Butler "the outstanding political rebel of his day." Sproat, *"The Best Men": Liberal Reformers in the Gilded Age* (1968; Chicago: University of Chicago Press, 1982), 276. See also Montgomery, *Beyond Equality*, 75, 117–18, 360–68.

7. *Biographical Directory of the American Congress, 1774–1971* (Washington, D.C.: U.S. Government Printing Office, 1971), 696–97; Unger, *Greenback Era*, 97–99; Montgomery, *Beyond Equality*, 426–33.

8. Alexander Campbell, *The True American System of Finance; The Rights of Labor and Capital, and the Common Sense Way of Doing Justice to the Soldiers and their Families. No Banks: Greenbacks the Exclusive Currency* (Chicago: Evening Journal Book and Job Print, 1864), 3, 47.

9. Cf. Edward Kellogg, *Labor and Other Capital: The Rights of Each Secured and the Wrongs of Both Eradicated. Or, An Exposition of the Cause Why Few Are Wealthy and Many Poor, and the Delineation of a System, Which, Without Infringing the Rights of Property, Will Give to Labor Its Just Reward* (New York: Edward Kellogg, 1849). On Kellogg's book, which closely resembles Campbell's later work in argument and analysis, see Chester McArthur Destler, *American Radicalism, 1865–1901: Essays and Documents* (New London, Conn.: Connecticut College, 1946), 51–74; Joseph Dorfman, *The Economic Mind in American Civilization, 1606–1865*, vol. 2 (New York: Viking, 1946), 678–80.

10. Campbell, *American System*, 4. My analysis of Campbell's value theory is especially indebted to Montgomery, *Beyond Equality*, 426–33.

11. Ritter, *Goldbugs and Greenbacks*, 95–98.

12. Cf. William H. Harvey, *Coin's Financial School*, ed. Richard Hofstadter (Cambridge, Mass.: Belknap Press of Harvard University Press, 1963). On the political and philosophical divide between greenbackism and free silver, see Walter T. K. Nugent, *The Money Question During Reconstruction* (New York: W. W. Norton, 1967), 58–64; Goodwyn, *Populist Moment*, 216–322. On their underlying commonalities, see James Livingston, *Origins of the Federal Reserve System: Money, Class, and Corporate Capitalism, 1890–1913* (Ithaca, N.Y.: Cornell University Press, 1986), 90–94. For a provocative exploration of the intellectual affinities of goldbugs and silverites in developing the "logic of naturalism," see Walter Benn Michaels, *The Gold Standard and the Logic of Naturalism: American Literature at the Turn of the Century* (Berkeley: University of California Press, 1987), 137–80.

13. On the American Social Science Association, see Thomas L. Haskell, *The Emergence of Professional Social Science: The American Social Science Association and the Nineteenth-Century Crisis of Authority* (Chicago: University of Illinois Press, 1977); William Leach, *True Love and Perfect Union: The Feminist Reform of Sex and Society* (New York: Basic, 1980), 297–300, 323–46; L. L. Bernard and Jessie Bernard, *Origins of American Sociology: The Social Science Movement in the United States* (New York: Russell and Russell, 1965), 527–607; Thomas Bender, *Intellect and Public Life: Essays on the Social History of Academic Intellectuals in the United States* (Baltimore, Md.: Johns Hopkins University Press, 1993), 42–46.

14. On the long boom of the 1840s to the 1870s, see David M. Gordon, Richard Edwards, and Michael Reich, *Segmented Work, Divided Workers: The Historical Transformation of Labor in the United States* (New York: Cambridge University Press, 1982), 79–94.

15. On the development of "scientific charity," see Michael B. Katz, *In the Shadow of the Poorhouse: A Social History of Welfare in America* (New York: Basic, 1986), 58–84.

16. Quoted in Bernard and Bernard, *American Sociology*, 540–41.

17. Ibid., 546.

18. Haskell, *Social Science*, 56; Ralph Waldo Emerson, "The American Scholar," in Emerson, *Selected Essays*, ed. Larzer Ziff (New York: Penguin, 1982), 103.

19. Leach, *True Love*, 326, 424–25 n. 13. For a contrary interpretation, see Haskell, *Social Science*, 14–16, which argues that "interdependence" represented "an intellectualization of the *direction* in which objective conditions were changing" (16), as the United States became increasingly interdependent in fact as well as in theory.

20. "Introductory Note," *Journal of Social Science* 1 (June 1869): 1–4; quoted passage at 2.

21. On the International Workingmen's Association in the United States, see Timothy Messer-Kruse, *The Yankee International: Marxism and the American Reform Tradition, 1848–1876* (Chapel Hill: University of North Carolina Press, 1998).

22. Mary O. Furner, *Advocacy and Objectivity: A Crisis in the Professionalization of American Social Science, 1865–1905* (Lexington: University Press of Kentucky, 1975), 4–5; Bender, *Public Life*, 42–43; Haskell, *Social Science*, 144–66, 234.

23. Bernard and Bernard, *American Sociology*, 546; Haskell, *Social Science*, 86.

24. For alternative interpretations of the rise of academic professions, see Burton J. Bledstein, *The Culture of Professionalism: The Middle Class and the Development of Higher Education in America* (1976; New York: W. W. Norton, 1978); Thomas Bender, "The Cultures of Intellectual Life: The City and the Professions," in *New Directions in American Intellectual History*, ed. John Higham and Paul Conkin (Baltimore, Md.: Johns Hopkins University Press, 1979), 181–95; Bender, *Public Life*, 127–39; John Higham, "The Matrix of Specialization," in *The Organization of Knowledge in Modern America, 1860–1920*, ed. Alexandra Oleson and John Voss (Baltimore, Md.: Johns Hopkins University Press, 1979), 3–18; Furner, *Advocacy and Objectivity*. For a useful critique of the literature on "professionalization" in general, see Andrew Abbott, *The System of Professions: An Essay on the Division of Expert Labor* (Chicago: University of Chicago Press, 1988).

25. On the rise of the modern research university in the United States, see Lawrence R. Vesey, *The Emergence of the American University* (Chicago: University of Chicago Press, 1965); Edward Shils, "The Order of Learning in the United States: The Ascendancy of the University," in Oleson and Voss, *Organization of Knowledge*, 19–47. On the dual commitment to specialized research and "liberal culture," see Caroline Winterer, "The Classics and Culture in the Transformation of American Higher Education, 1830–1930," Ph.D. diss., Uni-

versity of Michigan, 1996; Louise L. Stevenson, *Scholarly Means to Evangelical Ends: The New Haven Scholars and the Transformation of Higher Learning in America, 1830–1930* (Baltimore, Md.: Johns Hopkins University Press, 1986). See also, for further elaboration of the themes broached in this paragraph, Jeffrey Sklansky, "Socializing the Psyche: The Fall of Political Economy and the Rise of Social Psychology in the United States, 1830–1930," Ph.D. diss., Columbia University, 1996, 241–52.

26. Gordon, Edwards, and Reich, *Segmented Work*, 95–98; Eric Hobsbawm, *The Age of Capital, 1848–1875* (New York: Vintage, 1975), 46; Licht, *Industrializing America*, 130; James Livingston, "The Social Analysis of Economic History and Theory: Conjectures on the Late Nineteenth-Century American Development," *American Historical Review* 92, no. 1 (Feb. 1987): 69–95.

27. Nugent, *Money and Society*, 205.

28. See Jeff Sklansky, "The War on Pauperism: Responses to Poverty in New York City During the Depression, 1873–1878," M.A. thesis, Columbia University, 1990.

29. William Graham Sumner, "Introductory Lecture to Courses in Political and Social Science," 1873, in Sumner, *The Challenge of Facts and Other Essays*, ed. Albert Galloway Keller (New Haven, Conn.: Yale University Press, 1914), 399.

30. See Bruce Curtis, *William Graham Sumner* (Boston: Twayne, 1981); Robert C. Bannister, *Sociology and Scientism: The American Quest for Objectivity, 1880–1940* (Chapel Hill: University of North Carolina Press, 1987), 87–110; Robert C. Bannister, *Social Darwinism: Science and Myth in Anglo-American Social Thought* (Philadelphia: Temple University Press, 1979), 97–113; Alfred McClung Lee, "The Forgotten Sumner," *Journal of the History of Sociology* 3, no. 1 (1980–81): 87–106; Donald K. Pickens, "William Graham Sumner: Moralist as Social Scientist," *Social Science* 43, no. 4 (Oct. 1968): 202–9; Donald K. Pickens, "Scottish Common Sense Philosophy and *Folkways*," *Journal of Thought* 22, no. 1 (Spring 1987): 39–44; Robert Koegel, "William Graham Sumner: Critical Theorist of Modernity," Ph.D. diss., City University of New York, 1989; Arthur J. Vidich and Stanford M. Lyman, *American Sociology: Worldly Rejections of Religion and Their Directions* (New Haven, Conn.: Yale University Press, 1985), 37–46; Robert Garson and Richard Maidment, "Social Darwinism and the Liberal Tradition: The Case of William Graham Sumner," *South Atlantic Quarterly* 80, no. 1 (Winter 1981): 61–76; Norman E. Smith and Roscoe C. Hinkle, "Sumner versus Keller and the Social Evolutionism of Early American Sociology," *Sociological Inquiry* 49, no. 1 (1979): 41–48; Ronald Fletcher, *The Making of Sociology: A Study of Sociological Theory*, vol. 1: *Beginnings and Foundations* (New York: Charles Scribner's Sons, 1971), 502–37. In my view, the most revealing reinterpretation of Sumner is in R. Jeffrey Lustig, *Corporate Liberalism: The Origins of Modern American Political Theory, 1890–1920* (Berkeley: University of California Press, 1982), 78–90, which argues that Sumner's work was not "simply a reaffirmation of Manchester economics" but rather "presented a new standpoint for liberal theory," for "[b]ehind the individualist tenets of Social Darwinism, Sumner guided a wing of American thought in a corporatist direction" (79). For the earlier view of Sumner as a thoroughgoing Social Darwinist and enthusiast of libertarian laissez-faire, see Richard Hofstadter, *Social Darwinism in American Thought*, rev. ed. (Boston: Beacon, 1955), 51–66; McCloskey, *American Conservatism*, 22–71. The fullest intellectual biography of Sumner remains Harris E. Starr, *William Graham Sumner* (New York: Henry Holt and Co., 1925).

31. See Thomas, *Alternative America*; O'Donnell, "Henry George"; Lustig, *Corporate Liberalism*, 57–77. Two recent studies emphasize the interplay of religious and economic ideas in

George's work: Ronald William Yanosky, "Seeing the Cat: Henry George and the Rise of the Single Tax Movement, 1879–1890," Ph.D. diss., University of California at Berkeley, 1993; and Eileen Williams Lindner, "The Redemptive Politic of Henry George: Legacy to the Social Gospel," Ph.D. diss., Union Theological Seminary, 1985. On George's following within the labor movement, see Steven J. Ross, "The Culture of Political Economy: Henry George and the American Working Class," *Southern California Quarterly* 65, no. 2 (Summer 1983): 145–66; David Scobey, "Boycotting the Politics Factory: Labor Radicalism and the New York City Mayoral Election of 1886," *Radical History Review* 28–30 (1984): 280–325. Charles Albro Barker's still-invaluable biography notes that *Progress and Poverty* comprised "two sequences of thought," an "economic syllogism" and a "moral sequence," and that the entire book was "arranged to accommodate this duality." Barker, *Henry George*, 268–70. Similarly, George Raymond Geiger's pragmatist interpretation of *The Philosophy of Henry George* (New York: The MacMillan Co., 1933) identifies George's main intellectual achievement as his reconciliation of economics and ethics. Among the several Georgist biographies of George, see his son's account, originally published in 1900: Henry George Jr., *The Life of Henry George* (New York: Robert Schalkenbach Foundation, 1960). The *American Journal of Economics and Sociology* consistently publishes scholarship on all aspects of George's life and work, largely by Georgist scholars; a sampling of recent articles may be found in Will Lissner and Dorothy Burnham Lissner, eds., *George and the Scholars: A Century of Scientific Research Reveals the Reformer Was an Original Economist and a World-Class Social Philosopher* (New York: Robert Schalkenbach Foundation, 1991).

32. George, *Progress and Poverty*, 357.

33. William Graham Sumner, *What Social Classes Owe to Each Other* (1883; reprint, Caldwell, Idaho: Caxton Printers, 1961), 15–18, 129.

34. William Graham Sumner, *Folkways: A Study of the Sociological Importance of Usages, Manners, Customs, Mores, and Morals* (1906; reprint, Boston: Ginn and Co., 1940).

35. Barker, *Henry George*, 6–10; O'Donnell, "Henry George," 13; Thomas, *Alternative America*, 7–12.

36. Barker, *Henry George*, 55.

37. Henry George Jr., "Introduction," in George, *Progress and Poverty*, vii.

38. Barker, *Henry George*, 136.

39. H. George Jr., "Introduction," viii, ix.

40. Haskell, *Social Science*, 199; H. George Jr., "Introduction," ix; Paul Conkin, *Prophets of Prosperity: America's First Political Economists* (Bloomington: Indiana University Press, 1980), 311–12; Ross, "Political Economy," 145. On George's seminal influence on Fabian socialism and the British trade union movement, see Geiger, *Henry George*, 227–89. On his similarly powerful influence upon Tolstoy, whose *Confessions* was published the same year as *Progress and Poverty*, and upon Russian agrarian radicals generally, see Kenneth C. Wenzer, "The Influence of Henry George's Philosophy on Lev Nikolaevich Tolstoy: The Period of Developing Economic Thought (1881–1897)," *Pennsylvania History* 63, no. 2 (Spring 1996): 232–52. On Sun Yat-sen's intellectual debt to George, see Geiger, *Henry George*, 461–62. John Kenneth Galbraith has observed that the only two books by nineteenth-century American economists that are still commonly read are *The Theory of the Leisure Class* (1899) by Thorstein Veblen and *Progress and Poverty*. Galbraith, "Introduction," in Veblen, *The Theory of the Leisure Class* (Boston: Houghton Mifflin, 1973), vi.

41. Donald Worster, *Rivers of Empire: Water, Aridity, and the Growth of the American West*

(New York: Pantheon, 1985), 99; George, *Progress and Poverty*, 385–87; Barker, *Henry George*, 84–91.

42. George, *Progress and Poverty*, 357; George, *Social Problems*, 152.

43. George, *Social Problems*, 96, 152.

44. Ibid., 151, 153.

45. George, *Progress and Poverty*, 32–33.

46. Sumner, *Social Classes*, 114.

47. William Lyons Phelps, "Introduction," in Sumner, *Folkways*, xi; Starr, *Sumner*, 129, 154.

48. Phelps, "Introduction," ix–x.

49. Curtis, *William Graham Sumner*, 14–16; Starr, *Sumner*, 1–18.

50. Harriet Martineau, *Illustrations of Political Economy*, 9 vols. (London: Charles Fox, 1834); "Sketch of Sumner," 5.

51. Martineau, *Political Economy*, vol. 3, book 2, 130–32. Martineau also published at the same time *Poor Laws and Paupers Illustrated*, 10 vols. (Boston: Leonard C. Bowles, 1833–34).

52. Sumner, *Social Classes*, 11.

53. Ibid., 18–19.

54. Yearley, *Money Machines*, 3–35. Yearley notes that taxpayers' ability to pass the costs of their rising assessments onto consumers and tenants through higher prices and rents was quite limited amid the long, general deflation of the late nineteenth century. See also, on the Mugwump resistance, Sproat, *"Best Men"*. For a related analysis of the social basis for economists' concerns about a downward redistribution of income in the Gilded Age, see Livingston, "Social Analysis of Economic History."

55. Sumner, "What Makes the Rich Richer and the Poor Poorer?" (1887), in Sumner, *Challenge of Facts*, 75–76; Sumner, "The Conflict of Plutocracy and Democracy" (1889), in Sumner, *Earth-Hunger and Other Essays*, ed. Albert Galloway Keller (New Haven, Conn.: Yale University Press, 1913), 298–300. For Sumner's typically Mugwump opposition to protective tariffs, see Sumner, *Protectionism: The -Ism Which Teaches That Waste Makes Wealth* (New York: Henry Holt and Co., 1885); Sumner, *Lectures on the History of Protection in the United States, Delivered Before the International Free-Trade Alliance* (New York: G. P. Putnam's Sons, 1877). For further insight into Sumner's views of public finance, see Sumner, *The Financier and the Finances of the American Revolution* (New York: Augustus M. Kelley, 1968).

56. See the discussion of the jurisprudence of Thomas Cooley in Chapter 7.

57. Sumner, *Social Classes*, 30, 15 (emphasis in original).

58. Ibid., 129.

59. For George's espousal of free trade, see George, *Protection or Free Trade; An Examination of the Tariff Question, with Especial Regard to the Interests of Labor* (New York: AMS, 1973). For his critique of the fiscal apparatus of public debt and taxes on productive property, see George, *Social Problems*, 164–68; George, *Progress and Poverty*, 408–10, 433–35.

60. George, *Progress and Poverty*, 12, 13.

61. George, *The Science of Political Economy: A Reconstruction of Its Principles in Clear and Systematic Form* (Robert Schalkenbach Foundation, 1981), 163.

62. On the Physiocrats, see Elizabeth Fox-Genovese, *The Origins of Physiocracy: Economic Revolution and Social Order in Eighteenth-Century France* (Ithaca, N.Y.: Cornell University Press, 1976); Ronald L. Meek, *The Economics of Physiocracy: Essays and Translations* (London: Ruskin House, George Allen & Unwin, 1962); Joseph A. Schumpeter, *History of Economic*

Analysis, ed. Elizabeth Moody Schumpeter (New York: Oxford University Press, 1954), 223–43; Karl Marx, *A History of Economic Theories: From the Physiocrats to Adam Smith*, ed. Karl Kautsky, trans. Terence McCarthy (New York: Langland, 1962), 1–94; David McNally *Political Economy and the Rise of Capitalism: A Reinterpretation* (Berkeley: University of California Press, 1988), 85–151. For George's discussion of the Physiocrats, see *Progress and Poverty*, 423–24; *Political Economy*, 159, 162–64.

63. John Stuart Mill, *Principles of Political Economy, with Some of Their Applications to Social Philosophy* (1848; reprint, Toronto: University of Toronto Press, 1965), 188.

64. George, *Progress and Poverty*, 295.

65. Ibid., 389–90. Several writers have noted that George articulated an early version of the Turner thesis. For an interesting discussion, see Barker, *Henry George*, 300–301.

66. George, *Progress and Poverty*, 341, 348.

67. Ibid., 141.

68. Ibid., 227–28.

69. Mill, *Political Economy*, 225–30.

70. See Raymond Williams, *Keywords: A Vocabulary of Culture and Society*, rev. ed. (New York: Oxford University Press, 1983), 166–67.

71. George, *Progress and Poverty*, 234, 241.

72. Ibid., 239–40.

73. Ibid., 240.

74. Ibid., 232.

75. Ibid., 76.

76. Ibid., 28.

77. Along these lines, in his later work, George adopted (without attribution) Carey's theory of exchange value as a measure of the labor that a commodity saved its consumer, rather than of the labor expended in its production, as Ricardian political economy held. George, *Political Economy*, 245–46. On the deep affinities between George's thought and the contemporary "Austrian School" of economics, which formulated the marginal utility theory of value, see Leland B. Yeager, "Henry George and Austrian Economics," in Lissner and Lissner, *George and the Scholars*, 191–202. John Bates Clark, the leading American exemplar of the marginalist school, wrote that his movement into marginalism was prompted by his reading of George. Dorothy Ross, *The Origins of American Social Science* (Cambridge, Mass.: Cambridge University Press, 1991), 177. But see also George's reservations about marginalist economics, in George, *Political Economy*, 217–20.

78. George, *Progress and Poverty*, 37, 48.

79. Sumner, *Social Classes*, 47.

80. Ibid., 129.

81. Curtis notes that when Sumner criticized social reformers, George "was probably most often Sumner's target." Curtis, *William Graham Sumner*, 104.

82. Joshua Freeman et al., *Who Built America?: Working People and the Nation's Economy, Politics, Culture, and Society*, vol. 2 (New York: Pantheon, 1992), 118–28. See also, Leon Fink, *Workingmen's Democracy: The Knights of Labor and American Politics* (Urbana: University of Illinois Press, 1983), 3–37.

83. Frank Luther Mott, *A History of American Magazines*, vol. 2: *1850–1865* (Cambridge, Mass.: Harvard University Press, 1967), 367–79.

84. Sumner, "Who Is Free?: Is It the Savage?" *The Independent*, 18 July 1889, in Sumner, *Earth-Hunger*, 136–40.

85. Sumner, "What Is Civil Liberty?" *Popular Science Monthly*, July 1889, in Sumner, *Earth-Hunger*, 109. On Rodbertus, see George Lichtheim, *A Short History of Socialism* (New York: Praeger, 1970), 90–92.

86. Sumner, "Liberty and Property," *The Independent*, 27 Mar. 1890, in Sumner, *Earth-Hunger*, 171–74. On Laveleye, see *La Grande Encyclopedie, Inventaire Raisonne Des Sciences, Des Lettres et Des Arts, Par une Societe de Savants et de Gens de Lettres*, vol. 21 (Paris: H. Lamirault et Cie., Editeurs, 1885–1901), 1056–57.

87. Sumner, "Liberty and Labor," *The Independent*, 22 May 1890, in Sumner, *Earth-Hunger*, 186–87.

88. Sumner, "Who Is Free?" 140, 139.

89. C. B. Macpherson, *The Political Theory of Possessive Individualism: Hobbes to Locke* (New York: Oxford University Press, 1962).

90. Sumner, "Liberty and Discipline," *The Independent*, 16 Jan. 1890, in Sumner, *Earth-Hunger*, 171. See also Sumner, "Liberty and Responsibility," *The Independent*, 21 Nov. 1889, in Sumner, *Earth-Hunger*, 156–60; and Sumner, "Liberty and Law," *The Independent*, 26 Dec. 1889, in Sumner, *Earth-Hunger*, 162.

91. Sumner, *Social Classes*, 60.

92. Sumner, "Is It the Civilized Man?" 144–45.

93. George, *Progress and Poverty*, xvi.

94. On Proudhon and Lassalle, see Lichtheim, *History of Socialism*, 57–62, 83–84, 90–92.

95. Thomas, *Alternative America*, 230–32; Geiger, *Henry George*, 227–84.

96. Marx noted, however, that "[w]e ourselves . . . adopted this appropriation of ground rent by the state among numerous other *transitional measures*," and he judged *Progress and Poverty* "significant because it is a first, if unsuccessful, attempt at emancipation from the orthodox political economy." Letter, Karl Marx to Friedrich A. Sorge, 30 June 1881, in Barker, *Henry George*, 356 (emphasis in original). For a more extensive Marxist critique of urban reformers who limited their analysis of exploitation to rent, see Frederick Engels, *The Housing Question* (New York: International, 1935). Engels nevertheless supported George's mayoral campaign as a vehicle for working-class politics and a bridge to revolutionary socialism. Michael Harrington, *Socialism* (New York: Bantam, 1973), 146. George made no mention of Marx in *Progress and Poverty*, which was published a decade after the first volume of *Das Kapital* but a decade before the first English translation. George's posthumously published *Science of Political Economy* revealed only a cursory acquaintance with Marx's work, summarizing the central theory of surplus value as the proposition "that through some alchemy of buying and selling the capitalist who hires men to turn material into products gets a larger value than he gives" (97).

97. Laurence Gronlund, *Insufficiency of Henry George's Theory* (New York: New York Labor News Co., 1887), 8–11, 19.

98. George, *Social Problems*, 4.

99. George, *Progress and Poverty*, 515–16; George, *Political Economy*, 399–400 (quoted passages).

100. George, *Progress and Poverty*, 462–63.

101. Ibid., 508, 513.

102. Cf. Yanosky, "Seeing the Cat," 94–95: "George's program was materialist, then, in the sense that it hoped to reform society by changing economic relations. Yet its end was a more spiritual human consciousness able to overcome the 'mechanical' force of self-interest and direct human effort selflessly toward the ideal. In every inspirational impulse, George found a common quality, a native human force that could be liberated and developed universally. . . . This 'force of forces' was the engine George wished to harness in his readers, a consciousness that would be universal in utopia, but that must, for the time being, be the special vision of those who understood the true political economy."

103. George, *Progress and Poverty*, 465, 466.

104. Ibid., 471.

105. Ibid., 456.

106. Several historians have explicitly addressed the relationship between economic, psychological, and sociological ideas in Sumner's work. See Pickens, "William Graham Sumner," 206; Koegel, "William Graham Sumner," 9; Bannister, *Sociology and Scientism*, 99; Fletcher, *Making of Sociology*, 503.

107. "Sketch of Sumner," 9–11; Pierre Saint-Arnaud, *William Graham Sumner et Les Debuts de la Sociologie Americaine* (Quebec: Les Presses de L'Université Laval, 1984), 9. On Sumner's landmark academic freedom case over his teaching of Spencer's work, see Curtis, *William Graham Sumner*, 62–65; Richard Hofstadter and Walter P. Metzger, *The Development of Academic Freedom in the United States* (New York: Columbia University Press, 1995), 335–38.

108. On Spencer's role in the conservative reconstruction of individualism, see M. W. Taylor, *Men Versus the State: Herbert Spencer and Late Victorian Individualism* (Oxford, Eng.: Clarendon, 1992), 49–57. See also Jonathan H. Turner, *Herbert Spencer: A Renewed Appreciation* (Beverly Hills, Calif.: Sage, 1985); Philip Abrams, *The Origins of British Sociology: 1834–1914* (Chicago: University of Chicago Press, 1968), 67–76. Spencer's classic texts on psychology and sociology are *The Principles of Psychology*, 3d ed. (Osnabruck, Ger.: Otto Zeller, 1966); *The Study of Sociology*, 9th ed. (Osnabruck, Ger.: Otto Zeller, 1966). Cf. Henry George, *A Perplexed Philosopher: Being An Examination of Mr. Herbert Spencer's Various Utterances on the Land Question, With Some Incidental Reference to His Synthetic Philosophy* (New York: Charles L. Webster & Co., 1892).

109. Sumner, "Sociology," *Princeton Review*, Nov. 1881, in William Graham Sumner, *War and Other Essays*, ed. Albert Galloway Keller (1911; reprint, Freeport, N.Y.: Books for Libraries Press, 1970), 181.

110. Curtis, *William Graham Sumner*, 56; Phelps, "Introduction," ix; Albert Galloway Keller, "Introduction," in Sumner, *War*, xviii.

111. See Chapter 7 below.

112. Sumner, "The Concentration of Wealth: Its Economic Justification," *The Independent*, Apr.–June 1902, in Sumner, *Challenge of Facts*, 82.

113. Sumner, "War," in Sumner, *War*, 10.

114. On "group theory," see Lustig, *Corporate Liberalism*, 109–49.

115. Sumner, "War," 12.

116. Ibid., 28.

117. Sumner, "The Conquest of the United States By Spain," *Yale Law Journal* 8, no. 4 (1899): 168–93, in Sumner, *War*, 304–5; Sumner, "The Predominant Issue," *The International Monthly* (1900), in Sumner, *War*, 337; Sumner, "War," 35. See also Sumner, "The Proposed

Dual Organization of Mankind," *Appleton's Popular Science Monthly* 49 (1896): 432–39, in Sumner, *War*, 271–81; Sumner, "The Fallacy of Territorial Expansion," *Forum* 21 (1896): 414–19, in Sumner, *War*, 285–93.

118. On the developing discourse of cultural identity, see Walter Benn Michaels, *Our America: Nativism, Modernism, and Pluralism* (Durham, N.C.: Duke University Press, 1995). See in particular Michaels's reading of anti-imperialism in the racist novels of Thomas Nelson Page and Thomas Dixon as well as his challenging analysis of the ways in which cultural pluralism entailed not a rejection but an "intensification" of the racist principle of essential identity. Ibid., 16–23, 64–72. See also Frederick E. Hoxie's related discussion of the movement in American ethnology away from regarding Native Americans as representatives of an earlier stage of social development in favor of viewing them as members of a fundamentally different culture. Hoxie, *The Final Promise: The Campaign to Assimilate the Indians, 1880–1920* (Lincoln: University of Nebraska Press, 1984), 115–45. Finally, see also Sumner's discussion of the "Orient" and the "Occident," which he called "the two great cultural divisions of the human race," in *Folkways*, 6.

119. Sumner, "The First Steps Toward a Millennium," *Cosmopolitan*, Mar. 1888, in Sumner, *Earth-Hunger*, 93–98; Sumner, "The Family Monopoly," *The Independent*, 10 May 1888, in Sumner, *Earth-Hunger*, 255–56. Earlier still, in *What Social Classes Owe to Each Other*, Sumner had indicated a similar sense of the so-called "separate spheres" of family and economy: "At bottom there are two chief things with which government has to deal. They are, the property of men and the honor of women." *Social Classes*, 88.

120. Sumner, *Folkways*, 345–46.

121. See also Sumner, "The Family and Social Change," *The American Journal of Sociology* (1909), in Sumner, *War*, 43–61.

122. Sumner, *Folkways*, 40–43.

123. On the general movement from the science of "natural man" to the science of "normal man" and on the construction of a new sense of "individuality" by reference to a statistical norm, see Ian Hacking, *The Taming of Chance* (Cambridge: Cambridge University Press, 1990); Michel Foucault, *Discipline and Punish: The Birth of the Prison*, trans. Alan Sheridan (New York: Vintage, 1979), 170–94.

124. Sumner, *Folkways*, 50.

125. Ibid., 46.

126. Ibid., 47, 34.

127. Ibid., iv, 4.

128. Ibid., 77.

129. Ibid., 173–74.

Chapter Five

1. Adam Smith, *The Theory of Moral Sentiments* (Indianapolis: Liberty Classics, 1969), 47.

2. Ruth Leys, "Mead's Voices: Imitation as Foundation, or, The Struggle against Mimesis," *Critical Inquiry* 19 (Winter 1993): 277–307, at 277–78. The renewed historical appreciation of the broad dimensions of the "Scottish Enlightenment" in the late twentieth century echoed the rediscovery of the *Theory of Moral Sentiments* a century earlier. See Chapter 1, note 5.

3. Smith, *Moral Sentiments*, 112, 254–57.

4. "The man who feels the most for the joys and sorrows of others, is best fitted for ac-

quiring the most complete control of his own joys and sorrows. The man of the most exquisite humanity is naturally the most capable of acquiring the highest degree of self-command." Smith, *Moral Sentiments*, 255.

5. Though the nature of the mind and of mental experience had been studied in American colleges since the early eighteenth century, the subject was first taught as "psychology" in the early nineteenth century, and it became part of the standard curriculum in the latter half of the century. Rand B. Evans, "The Historical Context," in William James, *The Principles of Psychology*, vol. 1 (Cambridge, Mass.: Harvard University Press, 1981), xliii.

6. On the origins of the intellectual and institutional distinction between psychology and philosophy, see Kurt Danziger, *Constructing the Subject: Historical Origins of Psychological Research* (New York: Cambridge University Press, 1990), 19, 40. "To 'psychologize' is to reflect on ordinary observations and then to offer a plausible interpretation of the relevant experience and behavior. Once expressed, such interpretations are often so plausible that detailed proof would seem irrelevant—or at least too tedious to be worth the effort. . . . Among psychologists, James is the preeminent psychologizer." Ernest R. Hilgard, *Psychology in America: A Historical Survey* (New York: Harcourt Brace Jovanovich, 1987), 50.

7. On the centrality of the problem of the will at the origins of the "new psychology," and on its subsequent transformation or eclipse, see William R. Woodward, "James's Psychology of Will: Its Revolutionary Impact on American Psychology," in Josef Brŏzek, ed., *Explorations in the History of Psychology in the United States* (London: Associated University Presses, 1984), 148–95; Lorraine J. Daston, "The Theory of Will versus the Science of Mind," in William R. Woodward and Mitchell G. Ash, eds., *The Problematic Science: Psychology in Nineteenth-Century Thought* (New York: Praeger, 1982), 88–115, esp. 88–89, 110–11. Professional philosophers in the twentieth century, like their counterparts in psychology and economics, increasingly turned away from the wide-ranging, impressionistic "public philosophy" or "philosophy of life" in which James, Dewey, and Hall engaged, toward more technical, specialized, analytical discursive practices. See Alan Ryan, *John Dewey and the High Tide of American Liberalism* (New York: W. W. Norton, 1995), 22, 350–52; George Cotkin, *William James, Public Philosopher* (Baltimore, Md.: Johns Hopkins University Press, 1990), 13–14; Gerald E. Myers, *William James: His Life and Thought* (New Haven, Conn.: Yale University Press, 1986), 45.

8. On the transatlantic search for what he calls a "*via media*" between the Cartesian poles of subject/object, mind/body, rationalism/empiricism, idealism/materialism, see James T. Kloppenberg, *Uncertain Victory: Social Democracy and Progressivism in European and American Social Thought, 1870–1920* (New York: Oxford University Press, 1986), 46–55.

9. See Richard Olson, *The Emergence of the Social Sciences, 1642–1792* (New York: Twayne, 1993), 96–115.

10. See John M. O'Donnell, *The Origins of Behaviorism: American Psychology, 1870–1920* (New York: New York University Press, 1985); Robert M. Young, *Mind, Brain, and Adaptation in the Nineteenth Century: Cerebral Localization and Its Biological Context from Gall to Ferrier* (1970; New York: Oxford University Press, 1990); Nathan G. Hale Jr., *Freud and the Americans: The Beginnings of Psychoanalysis in the United States, 1876–1917* (New York: Oxford University Press, 1971), 48–92; Gerald N. Grob, *Mental Illness and American Society, 1875–1940* (Princeton, N.J.: Princeton University Press, 1994), 50–62; Daston, "Theory of Will," 97–103; Hilgard, *Psychology in America*, 17–19.

11. See George Dykhuizen, *The Life and Mind of John Dewey* (Carbondale: Southern Illi-

nois University Press, 1973), 15; Ryan, *John Dewey*, 50–51; Daniel W. Bjork, *The Compromised Scientist: William James in the Development of American Psychology* (New York: Columbia University Press, 1983), 6; Hilgard, *Psychology in America*, 56; David E. Leary, "Immanuel Kant and the Development of Modern Psychology," in Woodward and Ash, *Problematic Science*, 17–42. On the increasing conservatism of "common sense" philosophy in Scotland and the United States, see Herbert W. Schneider, *A History of American Philosophy*, 2d ed. (New York: Columbia University Press, 1963), 216–19; Rand B. Evans, "The Origins of American Academic Psychology," in Brožek, *History of Psychology*, 17–60, at 36. On the role of faculty psychology in the political thought of the Founding Era, see Daniel Walker Howe, *Making the American Self: Jonathan Edwards to Abraham Lincoln* (Cambridge, Mass.: Harvard University Press, 1997).

12. See Hale, *Freud and Americans*, 89–138.

13. See Bruce Kuklick, *The Rise of American Philosophy: Cambridge, Massachusetts, 1860–1930* (New Haven, Conn.: Yale University Press, 1977), 19–27, 47–48, 50–54; Edward C. Moore, *American Pragmatism: Peirce, James, and Dewey* (New York: Columbia University Press, 1961). On Bushnell and liberal theology, see Chapter 2.

14. See Lewis Mumford, "The Pragmatic Acquiescence," in Gail Kennedy, ed., *Pragmatism and American Culture* (Boston: D. C. Heath, 1950), 36–49. For a more ambivalent and nuanced critique along these lines, see George Santayana, "William James," in *Santayana on America: Essays, Notes, and Letters on American Life, Literature, and Philosophy* (New York: Harcourt, Brace & World, 1968), 73–88. For a provocative recent polemic in a similarly antimodern spirit, see John Patrick Diggins, *The Promise of Pragmatism: Modernism and the Crisis of Knowledge and Authority* (Chicago: University of Chicago Press, 1994). On antimodernism in fin-de-siècle American culture, see T. J. Jackson Lears, *No Place of Grace: Antimodernism and the Transformation of American Culture, 1880–1920* (1983; Chicago: University of Chicago Press, 1994).

15. On the changing meaning of "interest," see Raymond Williams, *Keywords: A Vocabulary of Culture and Society*, rev. ed. (New York: Oxford University Press, 1983), 171–73.

16. See, for example, Clarence J. Karier, *Scientists of the Mind: Intellectual Founders of Modern Psychology* (Urbana: University of Illinois Press, 1986), 52–53; T. J. Jackson Lears, "From Salvation to Self-Realization: Advertising and the Therapeutic Roots of the Consumer Culture, 1880–1930," in Richard Wightman Fox and T. J. Jackson Lears, eds., *The Culture of Consumption: Critical Essays in American History, 1880–1980* (New York: Pantheon, 1983), 11, 37; Christopher Lasch, *The New Radicalism in America, 1889–1963* (New York: Alfred A. Knopf, 1965), 144–46; Donald Meyer, *The Positive Thinkers: Popular Religious Philosophy from Mary Baker Eddy to Norman Vincent Peale and Ronald Reagan*, rev. ed. (Middletown, Conn.: Wesleyan University Press, 1988).

17. See, for example, Eugene McCarraher, "Heal Me: 'Personality,' Religion, and the Therapeutic Ethic in Modern America," *Intellectual History Newsletter* 21 (1999): 31–40; Beryl Satter, "New Thought and the 1890s 'Era of Woman,'" *Intellectual History Newsletter* 21 (1999): 24–30; James Livingston, "The Strange Career of the 'Social Self,'" *Radical History Review* 76 (Winter 2000): 53–79.

18. Eldon J. Eisenach, *The Lost Promise of Progressivism* (Lawrence: University Press of Kansas, 1994). See also, for example, Louis Menand, *The Metaphysical Club* (New York: Farrar, Straus and Giroux, 2001); Robert B. Westbrook, *John Dewey and American Democracy*

(Ithaca, N.Y.: Cornell University Press, 1991); Ryan, *John Dewey*; Steven C. Rockefeller, *John Dewey: Religious Faith and Democratic Humanism* (New York: Columbia University Press, 1991); Joshua I. Miller, *Democratic Temperament: The Legacy of William James* (Lawrence: University Press of Kansas, 1997); David A. Hollinger, "The Problem of Pragmatism in American History," *Journal of American History* 67 (1980): 88–107; James T. Kloppenberg, "Objectivity and Historicism: A Century of American Historical Writing," *American Historical Review* 94, no. 4 (Oct. 1989): 1011–30; Kloppenberg, *Uncertain Victory*; James Livingston, "The Politics of Pragmatism," *Social Text* 49 (Winter 1996): 149–72; Livingston, *Pragmatism and the Political Economy of Cultural Revolution, 1850–1940* (Chapel Hill: University of North Carolina Press, 1994). For a sympathetic critique of the neopragmatist revival with particular reference to historical writing, see James T. Kloppenberg, "Pragmatism: An Old Name for Some New Ways of Thinking?" *Journal of American History* 83, no. 1 (June 1996): 100–138. For a sampling of neopragmatist work in various fields, see Morris Dickstein, ed., *The Revival of Pragmatism: New Essays on Social Thought, Law, and Culture* (Durham, N.C.: Duke University Press, 1998). For a related discussion of the "new pluralist approach" to the cultural history of the Gilded Age and the Progressive Era, see Richard F. Teichgraeber III, "'Culture' in Industrializing America," *Intellectual History Newsletter* 21 (1999): 11–23. For the older view of Pragmatism as capitalist ideology, see, for example, William Appleman Williams, *The Contours of American History* (Cleveland, Ohio: World, 1961), 341–42, 402–5; Christopher Lasch, *The Agony of the American Left* (New York: Alfred A. Knopf, 1969), 10–11; Harry K. Wells, *Pragmatism: Philosophy of Imperialism* (1954; Freeport, N.Y.: Books for Libraries Press, 1971); George Novack, *Pragmatism versus Marxism: An Appraisal of John Dewey's Philosophy* (New York: Pathfinder, 1975); R. Jeffrey Lustig, *Corporate Liberalism: The Origins of Modern American Political Theory, 1890–1920* (Berkeley: University of California Press, 1982), 150–94; and, more recently, Brian Lloyd, *Left Out: Pragmatism, Exceptionalism, and the Poverty of American Marxism, 1890–1922* (Baltimore, Md.: Johns Hopkins University Press, 1997).

19. See Lasch, *New Radicalism*, 145; Kloppenberg, *Uncertain Victory*, 194. For a searching consideration of this problem, see Cornel West, *The American Evasion of Philosophy: A Genealogy of Pragmatism* (Madison: University of Wisconsin Press, 1989), 69–111.

20. The indispensable starting point for James scholarship is the work of his student, the philosopher Ralph Barton Perry, *The Thought and Character of William James*, 2 vols. (Boston: Little, Brown, 1935). The most important subsequent study of James's life and work is Myers, *William James*; but see also David Hollinger, "William James and the Culture of Inquiry," *Michigan Quarterly Review* 20 (1981): 264–83; Cotkin, *William James*; and Bjork, *Compromised Scientist*. The authoritative biography is Gay Wilson Allen, *William James: A Biography* (New York: Viking, 1967); but see also Howard M. Feinstein, *Becoming William James* (Ithaca, N.Y.: Cornell University Press, 1984); and Linda Simon, *Genuine Reality: A Life of William James* (New York: Harcourt Brace, 1998).

21. Alice James, *The Diary of Alice James*, ed. Leon Edel (New York: Dodd, Mead, 1964), 51.

22. For a historiographical overview along with an argument for viewing the later James as a "communitarian anarchist," see Deborah J. Coon, "'One Moment in the World's Salvation': Anarchism and the Radicalization of William James," *Journal of American History* 83, no. 1 (June 1996): 70–99. On James as a philosophical forerunner of Progressivism, see Kloppenberg, *Uncertain Victory*. On James as an exponent of the socialist promise of corporate

capitalism, see Livingston, *Pragmatism and Revolution*, 158–80. On James as a populistic advocate of petty producerism, see Lloyd, *Left Out*, 24, 39. On James as a theorist of radical participatory democracy, see Miller, *Democratic Temperament*. See also, on James's political and social thought more generally, Clive Bush, *Halfway to Revolution: Investigation and Crisis in the Work of Henry Adams, William James, and Gertrude Stein* (New Haven, Conn.: Yale University Press, 1991); Frank Lentricchia, *Ariel and the Police: Michel Foucault, William James, and Wallace Stevens* (Madison: University of Wisconsin Press, 1988), 104–33; James B. Gilbert, *Work Without Salvation: America's Intellectuals and Industrial Alienation, 1880–1910* (Baltimore, Md.: Johns Hopkins University Press, 1977), 180–211; and Cotkin, *William James*.

23. Cf. Paul F. Boller Jr., "Freedom in the Thought of William James," *American Quarterly* 16, no. 2, part 1 (Summer 1964): 131–52.

24. F. O. Matthiessen, *The James Family, Including Selections from the Writings of Henry James, Senior, William, Henry, and Alice James* (New York: Alfred A. Knopf, 1947), 132. See also R. W. B. Lewis, *The Jameses: A Family Narrative* (New York: Farrar, Straus, and Giroux, 1991); Feinstein, *Becoming William James*.

25. Matthiessen, *James Family*, 8.

26. Feinstein, *Becoming William James*, 90–92; Matthiessen, *James Family*, 49. The quoted passages are from an 1849 lecture on "Socialism and Civilization" that James Sr. delivered to the Town and Country Club of Boston at Emerson's invitation. Though never a faithful follower of Swedenborgian (or any other) teachings, he did attend the Church of the New Jerusalem in New York City. Kenneth T. Jackson, ed., *The Encyclopedia of New York City* (New Haven, Conn.: Yale University Press, 1995), 1144–45.

27. Feinstein, *Becoming William James*, 68.

28. James, *The Varieties of Religious Experience: A Study in Human Nature; Being the Gifford Lectures on Natural Religion Delivered at Edinburgh in 1901–1902* (New York: New American Library, 1958), 135–36. Though attributed to an unnamed French correspondent, the episode has since been identified as James's recollection of his own experience thirty years earlier. Matthiessen, *James Family*, 216–17.

29. Perry, *Thought of James*, 1:654–710.

30. On Renouvier's politics, see John A. Scott, *Republican Ideas and the Liberal Tradition in France, 1870–1914* (New York: Columbia University Press, 1951); cf. William Logue, *Charles Renouvier: Philosopher of Liberty* (Baton Rouge: Louisiana State University Press, 1993). On Renouvier's influence upon Durkheim, see Steven Collins, "Categories, Concepts or Predicaments? Remarks on Mauss's Use of Philosophical Terminology," in Michael Carrithers, Steven Collins, and Steven Lukes, eds., *The Category of the Person: Anthropology, Philosophy, History* (New York: Cambridge University Press, 1985), 46–82.

31. Quoted in Gardner Murphy, "Introduction," in Gardner Murphy and Robert O. Ballou, eds., *William James on Psychical Research* (New York: Viking, 1960), 6. For the relevant discussion of free will in Renouvier's Second Essay, see his *Essais de Critique Générale: Deuxième Essai: Traité de Psychologie Rationnelle D'Après Les Principes du Criticisme*, vol. 1 (1875; Paris: Librairie Armand Colin, 1912), 191–211. This is the revised and augmented second edition of the original *Deuxième Essai: L'Homme. La Raison, La Passion, La Liberté, La Certitude, La Probabilité Morale* (Paris: Librairie Philosophique de Ladrange, 1859), which James was reading when he wrote the entry in his diary.

32. James, *Principles of Psychology*, 1:15–18; James, *Pragmatism: A New Name for Some Old Ways of Thinking* (New York: Longmans, Green, 1907), 12.

33. James, "What the Will Effects," *Scribner's Magazine* 3 (Feb. 1888): 240–50, reprinted in James, *Essays in Psychology* (Cambridge, Mass.: Harvard University Press, 1983), 216–34; quoted passage at 217.

34. James, "The Feeling of Effort," *Anniversary Memoirs of the Boston Society of Natural History* (1880): 3–32, reprinted in James, *Essays in Psychology*, 83–124; quoted passage at 85.

35. James, "What Is An Emotion?" *Mind* 9 (Apr. 1884): 188–205, reprinted in James, *Essays in Psychology*, 168–87; quoted passage at 170.

36. James, "Will Effects," 219–22. For a thorough explication, see Woodward, "James's Psychology," 149–57.

37. James, *Principles of Psychology*, 1:122 (emphasis in original). See also James, *Habit* (New York: Henry Holt and Co., 1890).

38. James, *Principles of Psychology*, 1:121.

39. James, "On Some Omissions in Introspective Psychology," *Mind* 9 (Jan. 1884): 1–26, reprinted in James, *Essays in Psychology*, 142–67; quoted passage at 157. On James's debt to Green, see Kloppenberg, *Uncertain Victory*, 49–50.

40. James, "Brute and Human Intellect," *Journal of Speculative Philosophy* 12 (July 1878), 236–76, reprinted in James, *Essays in Psychology*, 1–37; quoted passage at 19. See also James, "Are We Automata?" *Mind* 4 (Jan. 1879), 1–22, reprinted in James, *Essays in Psychology*, 38–61.

41. James, "Feeling of Effort," 113 (emphasis in original).

42. Ibid., 107. "The action of the will must not be limited to the willing of an act. To exert the will and to make soft muscles hard, are not one thing, but two entirely different things. Extremely frequent association may account for, but not excuse their confusion by the psychologist." Ibid., 115.

43. James, "The Will to Believe," in James, *The Will to Believe and Other Essays* (1896; New York: Dover, 1956); James, *Religious Experience*.

44. James, *Principles of Psychology*, 2:1166.

45. Ibid., 1:296, 319, 307.

46. Ibid., 1:291 (emphasis in original).

47. Ibid., 1:304 (emphasis in original).

48. Charles Taylor, *Sources of the Self: The Making of the Modern Identity* (Cambridge, Mass.: Harvard University Press, 1989), 149, 155.

49. James, *Principles of Psychology*, 1:303. "[A]lthough it is true that a part of our depression at the loss of possessions is due to our feeling that we must now go without certain goods that we expected the possessions to bring in their train, yet in every case there remains, over and above this, a sense of the shrinkage of our personality, a partial conversion of ourselves to nothingness, which is a psychological phenomenon by itself." Ibid., 1:281.

50. Ibid., 1:378.

51. Ibid., 1:324–79; quoted passage at 1:350.

52. Ibid., 1:221 (emphasis in original).

53. Ibid., 1:296–97.

54. Ibid., 2:1056–57.

55. James, "What Makes a Life Significant," in James, *Talks to Teachers on Psychology: And to Students on Some of Life's Ideals* (1899; New York: Henry Holt and Co., 1910), 265–301. His

cursory comment on the Haymarket riot in a letter to his brother, Henry, suggests that James had not thought deeply about the labor question before. "Don't be alarmed about the labor troubles here," he wrote in the letter, dated 9 May 1886. "I am quite sure they are a most healthy phase of evolution, a little costly, but normal, and sure to do lots of good to all hands in the end. I don't speak of the senseless 'anarchist' riot in Chicago, which has nothing to do with 'Knights of Labor,' but is the work of a lot of pathological Germans and Poles." In an uncharacteristically chauvinistic aside relating to his and Henry's Irish ancestry, he added, "All the Irish names are among the killed and wounded policemen. Almost every anarchist name is Continental." James, *The Letters of William James, Edited by His Son, Henry James*, ed. Henry James (Boston: Atlantic Monthly Press, 1920), 252.

56. James, "Life Significant," 269–70, 271–72.

57. Ibid., 274, 275, 288, 290–91.

58. Ibid., 297.

59. Ibid., 294. "Society has, with all this, undoubtedly to pass toward some newer and better equilibrium, and the distribution of wealth has doubtless slowly got to change: such changes have always happened, and will happen to the end of time. But if . . . any of you expect that they will make any *genuine vital difference* on a large scale, to the lives of our descendants, you will have missed the significance of my entire lecture. The solid meaning of life is always the same eternal thing,—the marriage, namely, of some unhabitual ideal, however special, with some fidelity, courage, and endurance; with some man's or woman's pains. And, whatever or wherever life may be, there will always be the chance for that marriage to take place." Ibid., 298–99.

60. See Coon, "One Moment"; Cotkin, *William James*; Miller, *Democratic Temperament*; Perry, *Thought of James*, 2:281–318.

61. Of James's master work, Dewey later wrote, "As far as I can discover one specifiable philosophic factor which entered into my thinking so as to give it a new direction and vitality, it was this one." Dewey, "From Absolutism to Experimentalism," in George P. Adams and William Pepperell Montague, eds., *Contemporary American Philosophy: Personal Statements*, vol. 2 (New York: Macmillan, 1930), 12–27; quoted passage at 23. For a manifesto of functionalist psychology, see James Rowland Angell, "The Relations of Structural and Functional Psychology to Philosophy," in *Investigations Representing the Departments; Decennial Publications*, 1st ser., vol. 3 (Chicago: University of Chicago Press, 1903), 53–74. For representative examples, see Angell, *Psychology: An Introductory Study of the Structure and Function of Human Consciousness* (New York: Henry Holt and Co., 1904); and James Mark Baldwin, *The Individual and Society; or Psychology and Sociology* (Boston: Richard G. Badger, 1911). For Mead's self-styled "social behaviorism," see George Herbert Mead, *Mind, Self and Society, From the Standpoint of a Social Behaviorist* (Chicago: University of Chicago Press, 1934). On the origins of functionalism, see O'Donnell, *Origins of Behaviorism*; Young, *Mind, Brain, and Adaptation*; Hilgard, *Psychology in America*, 79–88; Danziger, *Constructing the Subject*, 25–27.

62. Charles Frankel, "John Dewey's Social Philosophy," in Steven M. Cahn, ed., *New Studies in the Philosophy of John Dewey* (Hanover, N.H.: University Press of New England, 1977), 3–44; relevant passage at 4–5. John J. Stuhr notes that although Dewey's main writings explicitly addressing social and political issues came relatively late in his career, ultimately "all of Dewey's philosophy . . . simply *is* social and political philosophy." Stuhr, "Dewey's Social and Political Philosophy," in Larry A. Hickman, ed., *Reading Dewey: Interpretations for a*

Postmodern Generation (Bloomington: Indiana University Press, 1998), 82–99; quoted passage at 85.

63. "[F]or a man who condemned thinkers who tried to remain above the battle, his own opinions, in their vagueness and generality, often seem disappointingly above the battle." Frankel, "Dewey's Philosophy," 8. See also, on the same point, Ryan, *John Dewey*, 81.

64. Max Eastman, "John Dewey," *Atlantic Monthly* 168, no. 6 (Dec. 1941): 671–85. Dewey's own reflections on the tension between his philosophical emphasis upon practical results and his tendency toward the insubstantial and ideal characteristically framed the problem as a psychological conflict between conscious belief and unconscious impulse: "I imagine that my development has been controlled largely by a struggle between a native inclination toward the schematic and formally logical, and those incidents of personal experience that compelled me to take account of actual material. Probably there is in the consciously articulated ideas of every thinker an over-weighting of just those things that are contrary to his natural tendencies, an emphasis upon those things that are contrary to his intrinsic bent, and which, therefore, he has to struggle to bring to expression, while the native bent, on the other hand, can take care of itself." Dewey, "Absolutism to Experimentalism," 16–17.

65. Eastman, "John Dewey," 672. "The University of Paris, in conferring a degree upon him in 1930, described him as 'the most profound and complete expression of American genius.'" Ibid., 671. Henry Steele Commager's classic study of "the American Mind" dubbed Dewey "the conscience of the American people," noting that "it is scarcely an exaggeration to say that for a generation no major issue was clarified until Dewey had spoken." Commager, *The American Mind: An Interpretation of American Thought and Character Since the 1880s* (New Haven, Conn.: Yale University Press, 1950), 100. For a similarly appreciative appraisal of Pragmatism as "*the* philosophy which best expresses the 'climate of opinion' peculiar to American civilization," enlisting Dewey more explicitly in the Cold War, see Gail Kennedy, "Introduction," in Kennedy, *Pragmatism and American Culture*, v–viii; quoted passage at v. For comparisons to Marx and Marxism, see Eastman, "John Dewey," 682; Frankel, "Dewey's Philosophy," 39–40; and, from a Marxist perspective, Novack, *Pragmatism versus Marxism*. For a more recent reading of Dewey as one of the "most profound expressions" of the "soul of American culture," see Rockefeller, *John Dewey*; quoted passage at 5.

66. On the eclipse of Deweyan Pragmatism by analytical philosophy, see Ryan, *John Dewey*, 350–51. On the decline of Pragmatism along with the "American Mind," see Hollinger, "Problem of Pragmatism," 25–26.

67. On the revival of interest in Dewey, see Ryan, *John Dewey*, 352–61. On the road not taken of "deliberative democracy," see Philip J. Ethington, "The Metropolis and Multicultural Ethics: Direct Democracy versus Deliberative Democracy in the Progressive Era," in Sidney M. Milkis and Jerome M. Mileur, eds., *Progressivism and the New Democracy* (Amherst: University of Massachusetts Press, 1999), 192–225. For important recent historical works reclaiming Dewey as a radical democrat, reformist liberal, and religious humanist, respectively, see Westbrook, *John Dewey*; Ryan, *John Dewey*; and Rockefeller, *John Dewey*. Cf. W. A. Williams, *Contours of History*, 402–5. "[W]hatever Dewey's *personal* history, his philosophy of relativist pragmatism provided in its general impact an encouragement for ameliorative adjustment to things-as-they-are. Extrinsic success was thus strengthened as a standard for judging intrinsic value." Ibid., 405.

68. Steven Rockefeller notes that though Dewey's career is customarily divided into two

periods, before and after his move to Chicago and his avowed break with Hegelian absolutism in 1894, his later work remains deeply informed by his earlier ideas. Rockefeller, *John Dewey*, 19. On Dewey's early career, see Neil Coughlan, *Young John Dewey: An Essay in American Intellectual History* (Chicago: University of Chicago Press, 1975). For a broad survey of his life and work, see Dykhuizen, *Life of Dewey*, along with the recent studies by Westbrook, Ryan, and Rockefeller cited above.

69. John Dewey, "The Significance of the Problem of Knowledge," University of Chicago Contributions to Philosophy, vol. 1, no. 3 (Chicago: University of Chicago Press, 1877), reprinted in Dewey, *The Early Works, 1882–1898*, vol. 5 (Carbondale: Southern Illinois University Press, 1972), 23.

70. "[Dewey's] view of the problem of education and democracy was not an economic, or sociological, or even a political one, except in the broadest sense; it was largely a psychological or sociopsychological one." Richard Hofstadter, "The Child and the World," *Daedalus* 91, no. 3 (Summer 1962): 501–26; quoted passage at 515.

71. Dewey, "Absolutism to Experimentalism," 19.

72. Dykhuizen, *Life of Dewey*, 6–7; Coughlan, *Young Dewey*, 3–5.

73. Ryan, *John Dewey*, 43–44. On the struggle over democratic governance in industrializing Vermont, see Leon Fink, *Workingmen's Democracy: The Knights of Labor and American Politics* (Urbana: University of Illinois Press, 1983), 66–111.

74. *National Cyclopaedia of American Biography*, vol. 13 (New York: James T. White & Co., 1906), 371. See, for example, Davis R. Dewey, "The Relation of Social Reforms," *The Open Court*, 30 June 1892, 3295–98.

75. Ryan, *John Dewey*, 50; Dewey, "Absolutism to Experimentalism," 20.

76. Dewey, "Absolutism to Experimentalism," 13.

77. See James G. Paradis, *T. H. Huxley: Man's Place in Nature* (Lincoln: University of Nebraska Press, 1978), 25–61. For Huxley's refutation of what he called "Rousseauism," see Huxley, "On the Natural Inequality of Men" (1890), reprinted in Huxley, *Method and Results: Essays* (New York: D. Appleton, 1893), 290–335; Huxley, "Natural Rights and Political Rights" (1890), reprinted in Huxley, *Method and Results*, 336–82; and especially Huxley, "Capital—The Mother of Nature. An Economical Problem Discussed From a Physiological Point of View" (1890), reprinted in Huxley, *Evolution and Ethics, and Other Essays* (New York: D. Appleton, 1929), 147–87, in which he likened the relationship of labor and capital to that of animals and plants, or infants and mothers' milk.

78. On the relationship between physiology and experimental psychology, see Danziger, *Constructing the Subject*, 25–27.

79. Dewey, "The New Psychology," *Andover Review* 2 (Sept. 1884): 278–89, reprinted in Dewey, *Early Works*, vol. 1 (Carbondale: Southern Illinois University Press, 1969), 48–60; quoted passage at 51.

80. Ibid., 56, 48–49.

81. Ibid., 56.

82. Morris himself had studied at the University of Berlin with Friedrich Adolf Trendelenburg, and Dewey apparently derived many of his ideas secondhand from that major theorist of the scientific revolution in German philosophy, as Gershon George Rosenstock has demonstrated. See Rosenstock, *F. A. Trendelenburg: Forerunner to John Dewey* (Carbondale: Southern Illinois University Press, 1964). Rosenstock locates the "historical link" between

Trendelenburg and Dewey entirely in Morris's studies with the former and influence upon the latter. Though Rosenstock does not mention it, Trendelenburg's influence on G. Stanley Hall provides another link between Trendelenburg and Dewey, strengthening Rosenstock's argument. On Hall and Trendelenburg, see Hall, *Life and Confessions of a Psychologist* (New York: D. Appleton, 1923), 190–91; Dorothy Ross, *G. Stanley Hall: The Psychologist as Prophet* (Chicago: University of Chicago Press, 1972), 38–39.

83. Leary, "Kant and Psychology," 22–23; Hilgard, *Psychology in America*, 26, 46; Danziger, *Constructing the Subject*, 19–20, 36–37.

84. Dewey, "Absolutism to Experimentalism," 19.

85. See Charles Taylor, *Hegel and Modern Society* (New York: Cambridge University Press, 1979), 1–14, 72–95; Steven B. Smith, *Hegel's Critique of Liberalism: Rights in Context* (Chicago: University of Chicago Press, 1989), 57–131; Herbert Marcuse, *Reason and Revolution: Hegel and the Rise of Social Theory* (New York: Oxford University Press, 1941), 3–16, 169–223; C. E. Merriam Jr., *History of the Theory of Sovereignty Since Rousseau* (New York: Columbia University Press, 1900), 91–94; George Lichtheim, *The Concept of Ideology and Other Essays* (New York: Random House, 1967), 11–17; Leary, "Kant and Psychology," 33–34.

86. Dewey, "The Psychological Standpoint," *Mind* 11 (Jan. 1886): 1–19, reprinted in Dewey, *Early Works*, 1:122–43; quoted passage at 142.

87. Though far less enduring than James's *Principles*, Dewey's *Psychology* was among the first textbooks of modern psychology and a seminal work in its time. It was adopted as a standard text by the University of Michigan, the University of Minnesota, the University of Kansas, the University of Vermont, Brown University, Williams College, Smith College, and Wellesley College, among other schools. Dykhuizen, *Life of Dewey*, 54–55.

88. Dewey, "Knowledge as Idealization," *Mind* 12 (July 1887): 382–96, reprinted in Dewey, *Early Works*, 1:176–93; quoted passage at 178.

89. Dewey, *Psychology*, reprinted in Dewey, *Early Works*, 2:79.

90. See Coughlan, *Young Dewey*, 25–28.

91. Dewey, *Psychology*, 76.

92. Ibid., 185, 192.

93. Ibid., 286.

94. Ibid., 291.

95. Ibid., 254.

96. Dewey, *"Consciousness" and Experience* (Berkeley, Calif.: University Press, 1899), reprinted in Dewey, *The Middle Works*, vol. 1 (Carbondale: Southern Illinois University Press, 1976), 113–30; quoted passages at 113, 128.

97. Dewey, "The Ethics of Democracy," University of Michigan Philosophical Papers, 2d ser., no. 1 (Ann Arbor, Mich.: Andrews & Co., 1888), reprinted in Dewey, *Early Works*, 1:227–49.

98. Sir Henry Sumner Maine, *Popular Government; Four Essays* (New York: Henry Holt and Co., 1886).

99. Dewey, "Ethics of Democracy," 231.

100. Ibid., 237–38.

101. Ibid., 230, 240.

102. Ibid., 244.

103. Ibid., 246–47. On Dewey's debt to Henry Carter Adams, see Coughlan, *Young Dewey*,

90–92. Alan Ryan notes that Dewey always sharply distinguished his economic ideas from both Debsian socialism and Marxism. "What he sought . . . was to democratize work, not to socialize the means of production. Or rather, the sense in which Dewey *did* want to socialize the means of production had nothing to do with expropriating the expropriators in the Marxist sense; owners and workers alike had to gain a sense that work was social service." Ryan, *John Dewey*, 112.

104. Dewey, "Psychology and Social Practice," *Psychological Review* 7 (1900): 105–24, reprinted in Dewey, *Middle Works*, 1:131–50; quoted passage at 1:137.

105. Dewey, *The School and Society* (1899), reprinted in Dewey, *Middle Works*, 1:16.

106. Donald F. Koch, "Editor's Introduction," in John Dewey, *Lectures on Psychological and Political Ethics: 1898*, ed. Koch (New York: Hafner, 1976), xxi.

107. Dewey, *Lectures on Ethics*, 236, 246.

108. Ibid., 221–22.

109. Ibid., 241–43, 249, 409–14, 424, 435.

110. Ibid., 4.

111. Ibid., 389, 397. See also Dewey's comparison of supply and demand with the relationship between the psychological and the social in "Ethical Principles Underlying Education," in *Third Yearbook of the National Herbart Society* (Chicago: National Herbart Society, 1897), 7–33, reprinted in Dewey, *Early Works*, 5:57–60.

112. Dewey, *Lectures on Ethics*, 253.

113. Ibid., 401.

114. Ibid., 400, 403.

115. Ibid., 240–41.

116. Kloppenberg, *Uncertain Victory*, 5–7, 239–47, 281–85.

117. The authoritative intellectual biography is Dorothy Ross, *G. Stanley Hall: The Psychologist as Prophet* (Chicago: University of Chicago Press, 1972). For an early tribute, see Lois N. Wilson, *G. Stanley Hall: A Sketch* (New York: G. E. Stechert and Co., 1914). For an insightful consideration of Hall as a communitarian thinker, see R. Jackson Wilson, *In Quest of Community: Social Philosophy in the United States, 1860–1920* (New York: John Wiley and Sons, 1968), 114–43. On Hall as an ambivalent antimodern who harked back to the "achievement ethos" of the early republic while looking forward to the "therapeutic ethos" of modern consumer culture, see Lears, *No Place of Grace*, 247–51. For a scathing indictment of Hall as a proto-Nazi "prophet of the twentieth-century totalitarian individual," see Karier, *Scientists of Mind*, 159–90. See also Hall's autobiography, *Life and Confessions of a Psychologist* (New York: D. Appleton and Co., 1923).

118. G. Stanley Hall, *Adolescence: Its Psychology and Its Relations to Physiology, Anthropology, Sociology, Sex, Crime, Religion, and Education*, 2 vols. (New York: D. Appleton and Co., 1904).

119. The term "crisis of work" is taken from Gilbert, *Work Without Salvation*, 180.

120. Ross, *G. Stanley Hall*, 6; Wilson, *G. Stanley Hall*, 12–13; Hall, *Life and Confessions*, 22–24.

121. Hall, *Life and Confessions*, 65–67.

122. Hall, *Adolescence*, 1:173.

123. Hall, *Life and Confessions*, 147–50; quoted passage at 149.

124. Ross, *G. Stanley Hall*, 41.

125. On the revealing etymological evolution of the terms "profession" and "expert," see R. Williams, *Keywords*, 129.

126. Hall, *Adolescence*, 1:v–vi.

127. Ibid., 2:59.

128. G. Stanley Hall, "Educational Reforms," *Pedagogical Seminary* 1, no. 1 (Jan. 1891): 1–12; quoted passages at 6–7, 3.

129. G. Stanley Hall, "The New Psychology," *The Andover Review* 3, no. 14 (Feb. 1885): 120–35; 3, no. 15 (Mar. 1885): 239–48; quoted passage at 241.

130. G. Stanley Hall, "Confessions of a Psychologist," *Pedagogical Seminary* 8 (Mar. 1901): 92–143; quoted passages at 119.

131. O'Donnell, *Origins of Behaviorism*, 2, 141. On the dispute between James and Hall over who established the first U.S. laboratory, see Ross, *G. Stanley Hall*, 246–47. "[I]t seems fair to say that Hall's laboratory was the first in this country to function as a university psychological laboratory in the modern sense." Ibid., 247.

132. Hall, *Adolescence*, 1:166–67; see also G. Stanley Hall, "The Education of the Will," *Princeton Review* 10 (Nov. 1882): 306–25, esp. 308; G. Stanley Hall, "Educational Needs," *North American Review* 136 (Mar. 1883): 284–90.

133. Hall, *Adolescence*, 1:233.

134. Ibid., 1:322.

135. See G. Stanley Hall, "The Muscular Perception of Space," *Mind* 3, no. 12 (Oct. 1878): 433–50.

136. Hall, *Life and Confessions*, 162–63, 192–94; Hall, "Educational Reforms," 3–8; G. Stanley Hall, "The Moral and Religious Training of Children," *Princeton Review* 10 (Jan. 1882): 26–48; quoted passage at 29.

137. G. Stanley Hall, "The Education of the Will," *Princeton Review* 10 (Jan. 1882): 306–25; quoted passage at 307.

138. Hall, "Moral and Religious Training," 28; Hall, "Education of the Will," 321.

139. Hall, *Adolescence*, 1:234.

140. Ibid., 2:71.

141. Ibid., 1:xv, xiii–xiv.

142. Ibid., 1:xv.

143. Ibid., 1:xvi–xvii.

144. Ibid., 1:333–34.

145. Ibid., 2:87, 90.

146. Cf. Van Wyck Brooks, *America's Coming-of-Age* (New York: B. W. Huebsch, 1915); George Santayana, "The Genteel Tradition in American Philosophy" (1913), in *Santayana on America*, 36–56.

147. Hall, *Adolescence*, 1:xvi.

148. Ibid., 1:viii.

149. Ibid., 2:281–92, 357, 304. For Hall's debt to Schleiermacher, see ibid., 2:326–27. For further consideration of the "instinct of dependence" as the essence of faith, see G. Stanley Hall, "Laura Bridgman," *Mind* 4, no. 14 (Apr. 1879): 149–72.

150. Hall, *Adolescence*, 2:337. See also G. Stanley Hall, *Jesus, the Christ, in the Light of Psychology* (New York: D. Appleton and Co., 1923).

151. Hall, *Adolescence*, 2:304. On the relation between Quetelet's politics and his contribu-

tion to the history of psychology, see Solomon Diamond, "Introduction," in Lambert A. J. Quetelet, *A Treatise on Man and the Development of His Faculties* (1842; reprint, Gainesville, Fla.: Scholars' Facsimiles & Reprints, 1969). See also Ian Hacking, *The Taming of Chance* (New York: Cambridge University Press, 1990), 105–14.

Chapter Six

1. Albion W. Small, *General Sociology: An Exposition of the Main Development of Sociological Theory From Spencer to Ratzenhofer* (Chicago: University of Chicago Press, 1905), v.

2. Ibid., vii.

3. Albion W. Small, "The Significance of Sociology for Ethics," in *Investigations Representing the Departments: Political Economy, Political Science, History, Sociology, and Anthropology*, Decennial Publications, 1st ser., vol. 4 (Chicago: University of Chicago Press, 1903), 113–49; quoted passage at 118.

4. Small, *General Sociology*, 487–88.

5. Two works by early-twentieth-century American sociologists provide a useful entryway to the large literature on the origins of sociology: Albion W. Small, *Origins of Sociology* (Chicago: University of Chicago, 1924), which emphasizes the influence of German economic theory; and L. L. Bernard and Jessie Bernard, *Origins of American Sociology: The Social Science Movement in the United States* (New York: Russell & Russell, 1943), which focuses on Comtean associationism, the American Social Science Association, and the beginnings of academic social science. See also Howard W. Odum, ed., *American Masters of Social Science: An Approach to the Study of the Social Sciences Through a Neglected Field of Biography* (1927; reprint, Port Washington, N.Y.: Kennikat, 1965). The classic midcentury studies of what I am calling the "sociological turn," all tracing a convergence or consensus in social theory around the turn of the century, are Talcott Parsons, *The Structure of Social Action: A Study in Social Theory with Special Reference to a Group of Recent European Writers* (New York: McGraw-Hill, 1937); Morton White, *Social Thought in America: The Revolt Against Formalism* (1947; reprint, New York: Oxford University Press, 1976); and H. Stuart Hughes, *Consciousness and Society: The Reorientation of European Social Thought, 1890–1930* (1958; reprint, New York: Vintage, 1977). Beginning in the 1960s, the breakdown of the Parsonian consensus generated a series of revisionist studies that emphasized the ideological roots of modern sociology, including Dusky Lee Smith, "Sociology and the Rise of Corporate Capitalism," *Science and Society* 29, no. 4 (Fall 1965): 401–18; Robert A. Nisbet, *The Sociological Tradition* (New York: Basic, 1966); Alvin W. Gouldner, *The Coming Crisis of Western Sociology* (New York: Basic, 1970); Herman Schwendinger and Julia R. Schwendinger, *The Sociologists of the Chair: A Radical Analysis of the Formative Years of North American Sociology* (New York: Basic, 1975); and Irving M. Zeitlin, *Ideology and the Development of Sociological Theory* (Englewood Cliffs, N.J.: Prentice Hall, 1994). Particularly illuminating on the ideological affinity between modern sociology and modern economics are Göran Therborn, *Science, Class, and Society: On the Formation of Sociology and Historical Materialism* (London: NLB, 1976); and Simon Clarke, *Marx, Marginalism, and Modern Sociology: From Adam Smith to Max Weber* (London: Macmillan, 1982). The definitive synthesis in recent years is Dorothy Ross, *The Origins of American Social Science* (New York: Cambridge University Press, 1991); but see also Bruce Mazlish, *A New Science: The Breakdown of Connections and the Birth of Sociology* (New York:

Oxford University Press, 1989); Peter T. Manicas, *A History and Philosophy of the Social Sciences* (Oxford: Basil Blackwell, 1987); Thomas L. Haskell, *The Emergence of Professional Social Science: The American Social Science Association and the Nineteenth-Century Crisis of Authority* (Chicago: University of Illinois Press, 1977); Lewis A. Coser, *Masters of Sociological Thought: Ideas in Historical and Social Context* (New York: Harcourt Brace Jovanovich, 1971); and Arthur J. Vidich and Stanford M. Lyman, *American Sociology: Worldly Rejections of Religion and Their Directions* (New Haven, Conn.: Yale University Press, 1985). For a provocative critique of different approaches to the history of sociology, see Donald N. Levine, *Visions of the Sociological Tradition* (Chicago: University of Chicago Press, 1995). For useful new essays on the history of social theory more broadly, see Alex Callinicos, *Social Theory: A Historical Introduction* (New York: New York University Press, 1999); and Howard Brick, "Society," in *Encyclopedia of the United States in the Twentieth Century*, ed. Stanley I. Kutler et al., vol. 2 (New York: Charles Scribner's Sons, 1996), 917–39. For an important recent effort to reconstruct the Parsonian consensus, see Jeffrey C. Alexander, *Theoretical Logic in Sociology*, 4 vols. (Berkeley: University of California Press, 1982–1983).

6. On Chicago as market metropolis, see William Cronon, *Nature's Metropolis: Chicago and the Great West* (New York: W. W. Norton, 1991).

7. Small, *General Sociology*, 487.

8. On racial nationalism in the Gilded Age and the Progressive Era, see John Higham, *Strangers in the Land: Patterns of American Nativism, 1860–1925* (1955; reprint, New York: Atheneum, 1963), esp. 131–57. On the concept of culture in modern American social science, see George W. Stocking Jr., *Race, Culture, and Evolution: Essays in the History of Anthropology* (New York: Free Press, 1968), 195–233; and Hamilton Cravens, *The Triumph of Evolution: American Scientists and the Heredity-Environment Controversy, 1900–1941* (Philadelphia: University of Pennsylvania Press, 1978), 89–153.

9. My formulation of this problem is influenced by Walter Benn Michaels's argument that the cultural pluralism of the 1920s represented a reconstruction of racial essentialism on the basis of culture rather than biology. Michaels, however, contends that it was the principle of pluralism that rendered "the modern concept of culture . . . a form of racism" by "*deriving* one's beliefs and practices *from* one's cultural identity instead of *equating* one's beliefs and practices *with* one's cultural identity." Michaels, *Our America: Nativism, Modernism, and Pluralism* (Durham, N.C.: Duke University Press, 1995). My argument, in contrast, is that the pragmatist identification of selfhood with social practice, which Michaels along with the founders of modern sociology deems the counteressentialist position, entailed a kind of cultural essentialism in its own right. Precisely because it rejected contractual models of society as rooted in an outdated understanding of universal human nature, the pragmatist position ended up conceiving of individual identity as something not freely chosen but rather conferred upon the individual without his or her conscious consent.

10. On Small's life and work, see George Christakes, *Albion W. Small* (Boston: Twayne, 1978).

11. Small, "Significance of Sociology," 113.

12. Small, *General Sociology*, 478; Albion W. Small, *Adam Smith and Modern Sociology: A Study in the Methodology of the Social Sciences* (Chicago: University of Chicago Press, 1907), 137.

13. Small, *Smith and Modern Sociology*. On "social economy" and Progressive politics in

Europe and the United States, see Daniel T. Rodgers, *Atlantic Crossings: Social Politics in a Progressive Age* (Cambridge, Mass.: Belknap Press of Harvard University Press, 1998), 76–111. On the meaning of "social economy" in the discourse of the contemporary labor movement, see Lawrence B. Glickman, *A Living Wage: American Workers and the Making of Consumer Society* (Ithaca, N.Y.: Cornell University Press, 1997), 57–91.

14. On the role of the social gospel in the rise of American sociology, see Cecil E. Greek, *The Religious Roots of American Sociology* (New York: Garland, 1992).

15. Albion W. Small and George E. Vincent, *An Introduction to the Study of Society* (New York: American Book Co., 1894), 40, 79.

16. Small, *Smith and Modern Sociology*, 65.

17. Small, *Smith and Modern Sociology*, 103–4.

18. See Herbert Hovenkamp, "The Political Economy of Substantive Due Process," *Stanford Law Review* 40 (1988): 379–447, esp. 402–39.

19. See Mary O. Furner, "The Republican Tradition and the New Liberalism: Social Investigation, State Building, and Social Learning in the Gilded Age," in *The State and Social Investigation in Britain and the United States*, ed. Michael J. Lacey and Mary O. Furner (New York: Cambridge University Press and Woodrow Wilson Center Press, 1993), 171–241, esp. 177–78.

20. See Mark Blaug, "Was There a Marginal Revolution?" *History of Political Economy* 4, no. 2 (Fall 1972): 269–80; Ronald L. Meek, "Marginalism and Marxism," *History of Political Economy* 4, no. 2 (Fall 1972): 499–511; Phyllis Deane, *The Evolution of Economic Ideas* (New York: Cambridge University Press, 1978), 93–114; Maurice Dobb, *Theories of Value and Distribution Since Adam Smith: Ideology and Economic Theory* (New York: Cambridge University Press, 1973), 166–210; Klaus Hennings and Warren J. Samuels, eds., *Neoclassical Economic Theory, 1870 to 1930* (Boston: Kluwer Academic, 1990); Mark Blaug, *Economic Theory in Retrospect*, 3d ed. (1962; reprint, New York: Cambridge University Press, 1978), 309–42; Ross, *Origins of American Social Science*, 172–95.

21. See Furner, "Republican Tradition and the New Liberalism," 179; Clarke, *Marx, Marginalism, and Sociology*, 162–65; Hovenkamp, "Substantive Due Process," 408–9.

22. For a sharp critique of such subjectivism as a basis for neoclassical theory, see Maurice Dobb, *Political Economy and Capitalism: Some Essays in Economic Tradition* (1945; reprint, Westport, Conn.: Greenwood, 1972).

23. Small, *Origins of Sociology*, 172 (emphasis in original).

24. Callinicos, *Social Theory*, 159–60; Therborn, *Science, Class, and Society*, 294; Parsons, *Structure of Social Action*, 129–77. On Simmel's psychology of capitalism in relation to the development of American social science, see Jeffrey Sklansky, "Socializing the Psyche: The Fall of Political Economy and the Rise of Social Psychology in the United States, 1830–1930," Ph.D. diss., Columbia University, 1996, 367–70. See also David Frisby, *Georg Simmel* (New York: Tavistock, 1984); Donald N. Levine, "Introduction," in Georg Simmel, *On Individuality and Social Forms: Selected Writings*, ed. Levine (Chicago: University of Chicago Press, 1971); Tom Bottomore and David Frisby, "Introduction to Translation," in Georg Simmel, *The Philosophy of Money*, trans. Bottomore and Frisby (London: Routledge & Kegan Paul, 1978).

25. See Furner, "Republican Tradition and the New Liberalism," 179.

26. See A. W. Coats, "The Educational Revolution and the Professionalization of Ameri-

can Economics," in *Breaking the Academic Mould: Economists and American Higher Learning in the Nineteenth Century*, ed. William J. Barber (Middletown, Conn.: Wesleyan University Press, 1988), 340–75, esp. 349–50.

27. See Therborn, *Science, Class, and Society*, 178–81, 241–44; Clarke, *Marx, Marginalism, and Sociology*, 122–27, 137; Small, *Origins of Sociology*, 235–73, 327.

28. Coats, "Professionalization of American Economics," 352. On the origins of the AEA more broadly, see Mary O. Furner, *Advocacy and Objectivity: A Crisis in the Professionalization of American Social Science, 1865–1905* (Lexington: University Press of Kentucky, 1975).

29. Francis Lieber, *Fragments of Political Science on Nationalism and Inter-Nationalism* (New York: Charles Scribner, 1868), 8. On Lieber, see Herbert W. Schneider, *A History of American Philosophy* (New York: Columbia University Press, 1963), 149–54; Joseph Dorfman, *The Economic Mind in American Civilization, 1606–1865*, vol. 2 (New York: Viking, 1946), 865–80; Ross, *Origins of American Social Science*, 37–42. On Burgess, see Ralph Gordon Hoxie, "John W. Burgess, American Scholar; Book I: The Founding of the Faculty of Political Science," Ph.D. diss., Columbia University, 1950; William H. Berge, "The Impulse for Expansion: John W. Burgess, Alfred Thayer Mahan, Theodore Roosevelt, Josiah Strong and the Development of a Rationale," Ph.D. diss., Vanderbilt University, 1969; Wilfred M. McClay, "Introduction," in John W. Burgess, *The Foundations of Political Science* (1933; reprint, New Brunswick, N.J.: Transaction, 1994). On the ideological affinities between the work of Lieber and that of Burgess, see Bernard Edward Brown, *American Conservatives: The Political Thought of Francis Lieber and John W. Burgess* (New York: Columbia University Press, 1951). The organicist model of society in modern American social science also drew upon the Anglo-American common law tradition; see Chapter 7 below.

30. On the social science of Jane Addams, see Mary Jo Deegan, *Jane Addams and the Men of the Chicago School* (New Brunswick, N.J.: Transaction, 1988); Dorothy Ross, "Gendered Social Knowledge: Domestic Discourse, Jane Addams, and the Possibilities of Social Science," in *Gender and American Social Science*, ed. Helene Silverberg (Princeton, N.J.: Princeton University Press, 1998), 235–64; Christopher Lasch, "Introduction," in *The Social Thought of Jane Addams*, ed. Lasch (New York: Bobbs-Merrill, 1965). For examples of Addams's innovative social psychology, see Addams, "The Larger Aspects of the Women's Movement," *Annals of the American Academy of Political and Social Science* 56 (Nov. 1914): 1–8, reprinted in *Thought of Addams*, 151–62; Addams, *Democracy and Social Ethics*, ed. Anne Firor Scott (1902; reprint, Cambridge, Mass.: Harvard University Press, 1964); Addams, "The Settlement as a Factor in the Labor Movement," in Residents of Hull House, *Hull-House Maps and Papers* (New York: Thomas Y. Crowell, 1895), 183–204; Addams, *Newer Ideals of Peace* (New York: Macmillan, 1907); Addams, *Peace and Bread in Time of War* (New York: King's Crown Press, 1945).

31. For Washington's discussion of "imitativeness," see Booker T. Washington, "The Economic Development of the Negro Race in Slavery" and "The Economic Development of the Negro Race Since Its Emancipation," in Washington and W. E. Burghardt Du Bois, *The Negro in the South: His Economic Progress in Relation to His Moral and Religious Development* (New York: Citadel, 1970), 9–75. On Park's debt to Washington, see Deegan, *Jane Addams*, 23; David Levering Lewis, *When Harlem Was in Vogue* (1979; reprint, New York: Penguin, 1997), 45–46. See also Robert E. Park, "Racial Assimilation in Secondary Groups; With Particular Reference to the Negro," *Publication of the American Sociological Society* 8 (1913): 66–83,

reprinted in Park, *Race and Culture* (Glencoe, Ill.: Free Press, 1950). Dorothy Ross notes that the founding document of the Chicago School was a 1912 research protocol written by Park's colleague, William I. Thomas, and titled, "Race Psychology: Standpoint and Questionnaire, with Particular Reference to the Immigrant and the Negro." Ross, *Origins of American Social Science*, 357–67. See also two seminal Chicago School studies of the "psychology of assimilation": W. I. Thomas and Florian Znaniecki, *The Polish Peasant in Europe and America* (1918; reprint, New York: Alfred A. Knopf, 1927); William I. Thomas, with Robert E. Park and Herbert A. Miller, *Old World Traits Transplanted* (1921; reprint, Montclair, N.J.: Patterson Smith, 1971). For a distillation of the Chicago School approach, see Robert E. Park and Ernest W. Burgess, *Introduction to the Science of Sociology* (Chicago: University of Chicago Press, 1921).

32. See W. E. B. Du Bois, *The Souls of Black Folk* (1903; reprint, New York: New American Library, 1969). For further examples of Du Bois's work during his early career as a sociologist, see Du Bois, *The Philadelphia Negro: A Social Study* (1899; reprint, New York: Benjamin Blom, 1967); *W. E. B. Du Bois on Sociology and the Black Community*, ed. Dan S. Green and Edwin D. Driver (Chicago: University of Chicago Press, 1978); *W. E. B. Du Bois Speaks: Speeches and Addresses, 1890–1919*, ed. Philip S. Foner (New York: Pathfinder, 1970). On Du Bois's studies with James and with Wagner and Schmoller and on his early engagement with German cultural nationalism generally, see Arnold Rampersad, *The Art and Imagination of W. E. B. Du Bois* (Cambridge, Mass.: Harvard University Press, 1976), 25, 43, 74–89; and Shamoon Zamir, *Dark Voices: W. E. B. Du Bois and American Thought, 1888–1903* (Chicago: University of Chicago Press, 1995), 77–79. For a related discussion of racial essentialism in Du Bois's writings, see Kwame Anthony Appiah, *In My Father's House: Africa in the Philosophy of Culture* (New York: Oxford University Press, 1992), 34–45.

33. Coats, "Professionalization of Economics," 352, 357–58, 362.

34. Small, *Smith and Modern Sociology*, 2–6, 171; quoted passage at 6.

35. Franklin H. Giddings, "The Quality of Civilization," *American Journal of Sociology* 17, no. 5 (Mar. 1912): 581–89; quoted passages at 585–86. On Giddings, see John L. Gillin, "Franklin Henry Giddings," in Odum, *American Masters*, 191–228; Robert C. Bannister, *Sociology and Scientism: The American Quest for Objectivity, 1880–1940* (Chapel Hill: University of North Carolina Press, 1987), 67–75; Frank A. Ross, "Franklin Henry Giddings," *Dictionary of American Biography*, ed. Harris E. Starr, vol. 21, supp. 1 (New York: Charles Scribner's Sons, 1944), 339–40.

36. For important historical critiques of consumer culture in the tradition of the Frankfurt School and the New Left, see Christopher Lasch, *The Culture of Narcissism* (New York: W. W. Norton, 1979); Richard Wightman Fox and T. J. Jackson Lears, *The Culture of Consumption: Critical Essays in American History, 1880–1980* (New York: Pantheon, 1983); Warren I. Susman, *Culture as History: The Transformation of American Society in the Twentieth Century* (New York: Pantheon, 1984); and William Leach, *Land of Desire: Merchants, Power, and the Rise of a New American Culture* (New York: Pantheon, 1993). For recent reappraisals more sympathetic to the democratic promise of mass consumption, see Glickman, *Living Wage*; James Livingston, "Modern Subjectivity and Consumer Culture," in *Getting and Spending: European and American Consumer Societies in the Twentieth Century*, ed. Susan Strasser, Charles McGovern, and Matthias Judt (New York: Cambridge University Press, 1998); Barry Shank, "Subject, Commodity, Marketplace: The American Artists Group and

the Mass Production of Distinction," *Radical History Review* 76 (Winter 2000): 25–52; Ann Douglas, *Terrible Honesty: Mongrel Manhattan in the 1920s* (New York: Farrar, Straus, and Giroux, 1995); Michael Denning, *The Cultural Front: The Laboring of American Culture in the Twentieth Century* (New York: Verso, 1996). See also, on the debate over consumerism in Patten and Veblen's era, Daniel Horowitz, *The Morality of Spending: Attitudes Toward the Consumer Society in America, 1875–1940* (Baltimore: Johns Hopkins University Press, 1985). For a broad overview of consumerism in the twentieth century, see Gary Cross, *An All-Consuming Century: Why Commercialism Won in Modern America* (New York: Columbia University Press, 2000).

37. Rexford G. Tugwell, "The Life and Work of Simon Nelson Patten," *Journal of Political Economy* 31, no. 2 (Apr. 1923): 153–208, esp. 156–66, 182; Daniel M. Fox, *The Discovery of Abundance: Simon N. Patten and the Transformation of Social Theory* (Ithaca, N.Y.: Cornell University Press, 1967), 13–14. On Patten's theory of consumer culture, see also Leach, *Land of Desire*, 233–42.

38. Joseph Dorfman, *Thorstein Veblen and His America* (New York: Viking, 1934), 3–16; Coser, *Masters of Sociological Thought*, 275–77; Max Lerner, "Editor's Introduction," in *The Portable Veblen*, ed. Lerner (New York: Viking, 1948), 2–3; John Kenneth Galbraith, "Introduction," in Thorstein Veblen, *The Theory of the Leisure Class* (1899; reprint, Boston: Houghton Mifflin, 1973), vii–xiii, xxi. On Veblen's life, see also Elizabeth Watkins Jorgensen and Henry Irvin Jorgensen, *Thorstein Veblen: Victorian Firebrand* (Armonk, N.Y.: M. E. Sharpe, 1999). On Veblen's social thought, see also John P. Diggins, *The Bard of Savagery: Thorstein Veblen and Modern Social Theory* (New York: Seabury, 1978); and Rick Tilman, *The Intellectual Legacy of Thorstein Veblen: Unresolved Issues* (Westport, Conn.: Greenwood, 1996).

39. Henry Rogers Seager, "Introduction," in Simon N. Patten, *Essays in Economic Theory*, ed. Rexford Guy Tugwell (New York: Alfred A. Knopf, 1924), xii–xiii; Tugwell, "Life and Work of Patten," 174, 179; Fox, *Discovery of Abundance*, 21–22, 25, 13.

40. Harvey A. Levenstein, *Revolution at the Table: The Transformation of the American Diet* (New York: Oxford University Press, 1988), 30–42. See also, Alfred D. Chandler Jr., *The Visible Hand: The Managerial Revolution in American Business* (Cambridge, Mass.: Harvard University Press, 1977), 293–302, 334–50.

41. Simon Nelson Patten, *The Premises of Political Economy; Being A Re-Examination of Certain Fundamental Principles of Economic Science* (1885; reprint, New York: Augustus M. Kelley, 1968); Patten, *The Theory of Dynamic Economics* (Philadelphia: Publications of the University of Pennsylvania, 1892); Patten, *The Theory of Social Forces* (Philadelphia: American Academy of Political and Social Sciences, 1896).

42. Patten, *Premises of Political Economy*, 10–18.

43. Patten, *The Consumption of Wealth* (Philadelphia: Publications of the University of Pennsylvania, 1889), 47–50.

44. Patten, *Dynamic Economics*, 41–44; quoted passage at 44 (emphasis in original).

45. Patten, *Social Forces*, 93.

46. Patten, "The Scope of Political Economy," *Yale Review* 2 (Nov. 1893): 264–87, reprinted in Patten, *Economic Theory*, 183 (emphasis in original).

47. William Watts Folwell, *Minnesota: The North Star State* (Boston: Houghton Mifflin, 1908), 270–76; John D. Hicks, *The Populist Revolt: A History of the Farmers' Alliance and the*

People's Party (Minneapolis: University of Minnesota Press, 1931), 60; Cronon, *Nature's Metropolis*, 376–77.

48. Martin Ridge, *Ignatius Donnelly: The Portrait of a Politician* (Chicago: University of Chicago Press, 1962), 245–46; Meridel Le Sueur, *North Star Country* (New York: Duell, Sloan & Pearce, 1945), 204–7; Hicks, *Populist Revolt*, 103–4.

49. Veblen, "Why Is Economics Not an Evolutionary Science?" *Quarterly Journal of Economics* 12 (July 1898), reprinted in Veblen, *The Place of Science in Modern Civilisation, and Other Essays* (New York: B. W. Huebsch, 1919), 56–81, esp. 73; Veblen, "The Preconceptions of Economic Science," part 2, *Quarterly Journal of Economics* 13 (July 1899), reprinted in Veblen, *Place of Science*, 114–47, esp. 123–56.

50. Veblen, "Some Neglected Points in the Theory of Socialism," *Annals of the American Academy of Political and Social Science* 2 (1892), reprinted in Veblen, *Place of Science*, 387–408; quoted passage at 399.

51. Veblen, *Leisure Class*, 81, 39.

52. Veblen, "The Limits of Marginal Utility," *Journal of Political Economy* 17, no. 9 (Nov. 1909), reprinted in Veblen, *Place of Science*, 231–51; quoted passage at 249.

53. Veblen, *The Theory of Business Enterprise* (1904; reprint, New York: Augustus M. Kelley, 1965), 136, 148.

54. Veblen, "On the Nature of Capital," part 2, *Quarterly Journal of Economics*, 23 (Nov. 1908), 352–86, esp. 353–57.

55. Patten, "The Formulation of Normal Laws, With Especial Reference to the Theory of Utility," *Annals of the American Academy of Political and Social Science* 17 (Jan.–June 1896): 426–49; quoted passage at 429.

56. Patten, *Consumption of Wealth*, 51.

57. Patten, *Theory of Social Forces*, 88, 80.

58. Patten, *Dynamic Economics*, 77.

59. Patten, "The Conflict Theory of Distribution," *Yale Review* 17 (Aug. 1908), reprinted in Patten, *Economic Theory*, 220, 238.

60. Veblen, "The Socialist Economics of Karl Marx and His Followers," parts I and II, *Quarterly Journal of Economics* 20 (Aug. 1906), reprinted in Veblen, *Place of Science*, 409–30, 431–56, esp. 418, 441.

61. Veblen, *Leisure Class*, 119.

62. Veblen, *Business Enterprise*, 148, 186, 237.

63. Veblen, *Leisure Class*, 137.

64. Veblen, "Theory of Socialism."

65. Veblen, "On the Nature of Capital," part 1, *Quarterly Journal of Economics* 22 (Aug. 1908), 324–51; quoted passages at 325, 326.

66. Ibid., 332, 337–38, 344–45.

67. See Veblen, *The Instinct of Workmanship, And the State of the Industrial Arts* (1914; reprint, New York: Augustus M. Kelley, 1964).

68. Patten, *Social Forces*, 142–43.

69. Patten, *Political Economy*, 11, 214–16. On the transnational discourse of "degeneration," see Daniel Pick, *Faces of Degeneration: A European Disorder, c. 1848–c. 1918* (Cambridge: Cambridge University Press, 1989). On the relationship between consumerism and nativism in the contemporary American labor movement, see Glickman, *Living Wage*, 78–91.

70. Patten, "Normal Laws," 443–44.

71. Patten, *The Theory of Prosperity* (New York: Macmillan, 1902), 3.

72. Patten, *The New Basis of Civilization* (New York: Macmillan, 1907), 103–4, 125, 191, 208, 211, 219; Patten, *Product and Climax* (New York: B. W. Huebsch, 1909).

73. Patten, "Normal Laws," 448–49.

74. Patten, "The Reconstruction of Economic Theory," *Annals of the American Academy of Political and Social Science,* sup. (Nov. 1912), reprinted in Patten, *Economic Theory,* 292, 323.

75. Veblen, *Absentee Ownership, And Business Enterprise in Recent Times: The Case of America* (1923; reprint, New York: Augustus M. Kelley, 1964), 9–10.

76. See esp. Veblen, "The Mutation Theory and the Blond Race," *Journal of Race Development* 3, no. 4 (Apr. 1913), reprinted in Veblen, *Place of Science,* 457–76; Veblen, "The Blond Race and the Aryan Culture," *University of Missouri Bulletin,* Science Series, vol. 2, no. 3, reprinted in Veblen, *Place of Science,* 477–96. See also, for related ideas, Veblen, "The Intellectual Pre-Eminence of Jews in Modern Europe," *Political Science Quarterly* 34 (Mar. 1919), reprinted in Veblen, *Essays in Our Changing Order,* ed. Leon Ardzrooni (New York: Viking, 1954), 219–31.

77. Veblen, *Business Enterprise,* 310–40; Veblen, *Instinct of Workmanship,* 138, 306.

78. See Jacques Donzelot, *L'Invention du Social: Essai sur le Déclin des Passions Politiques* (Paris: Librairie Arthème Fayard, 1984), 18–104; Donzelot, "The Promotion of the Social," *Economy and Society* 17, no. 3 (Aug. 1988): 395–427; Donzelot, "The Mobilization of Society," in *The Foucault Effect: Studies in Governmentality,* ed. Graham Burchell, Colin Gordon, and Peter Miller (Chicago: University of Chicago Press, 1991), 169–79.

79. On the theory of degeneration in France, see Robert A. Nye, *Crime, Madness, and Politics in Modern France: The Medical Concept of National Decline* (Princeton, N.J.: Princeton University Press, 1984); Ian Dowbiggin, "Degeneration and Hereditarianism in French Mental Medicine, 1840–90: Psychiatric Theory as Ideological Adaptation," in *The Anatomy of Madness: Essays in the History of Psychiatry,* vol. 1, ed. W. F. Bynum et al. (New York: Tavistock, 1985), 207–17; Pick, *Faces of Degeneration,* 51–106. On French crowd psychology, see Susanna Barrows, *Distorting Mirrors: Visions of the Crowd in Late Nineteenth-Century France* (New Haven, Conn.: Yale University Press, 1981). See also, on the general intellectual climate, Ruth Harris, *Murders and Madness: Medicine, Law, and Society in the Fin de Siècle* (New York: Oxford University Press, 1989).

80. Émile Durkheim, *The Division of Labor in Society,* trans. George Simpson (Glencoe, Ill.: Free Press, 1947; translation of *De la Division du Travail Social,* originally published 1893).

81. See Callinicos, *Social Theory,* 123–34; Clarke, *Marx, Marginalism, and Sociology,* 137–38; Therborn, *Science, Class, and Society,* 252–60; Donzelot, *L'Invention du Social,* 73–86; Donzelot, "Promotion of the Social," 396.

82. On the similarities and differences between Durkheim and Tarde, see Terry N. Clark, "Introduction," in Gabriel Tarde, *On Communication and Social Influence: Selected Papers,* ed. Clark (Chicago: University of Chicago Press, 1969), 7–18; Rosalind H. Williams, *Dream Worlds: Mass Consumption in Late Nineteenth-Century France* (Berkeley: University of California Press, 1982), 325–52. On Tarde's influence in the United States, see Clark, "Introduction," 65–66; Ruth Leys, "Mead's Voices: Imitation as Foundation, or, The Struggle Against Mimesis," *Critical Inquiry* 19 (Winter 1993): 277–307, esp. 278–79.

83. Tarde, "Sociology," from "La Sociologie," *Études de Psychologie Sociale* (Paris: Giard &

Brière, 1898), reprinted in Tarde, *On Communication*, 73–105; quoted passage at 94. See also Tarde, "Belief and Desire," from *Essais et Mélanges Sociologiques* (Paris: Maloine, 1895), reprinted in Tarde, *On Communication*, 195–206.

84. I borrow the point about Tarde's disavowal of the Cartesian dualism, as well as the term "solidarist," from Williams, *Dream Worlds*, 349.

85. Tarde, *The Laws of Imitation*, trans. Elsie Clews Parson (New York: Henry Holt, 1903), xxiv.

86. Ibid., 376.

87. Ibid., xxiii.

88. Ibid., 366–70.

89. Tarde, "The Public and the Crowd," *L'Opinion et La Foule* (1901; reprint, Paris: Alcan, 1922), reprinted in Tarde, *On Communication*, 277–94; quoted passages at 279, 277, 280, 284–85.

90. Ibid., 333.

91. Edward Alsworth Ross, *Seventy Years of It: An Autobiography* (New York: D. Appleton-Century, 1936), 331–33; Higham, *Strangers in the Land*, 109. See also Sean H. McMahon, *Social Control and Public Intellect: The Legacy of Edward A. Ross* (New Brunswick, N.J.: Transaction, 1999); and R. Jackson Wilson, "Edward Alsworth Ross: The Natural Man and the Community of Constraint," in Wilson, *In Quest of Community: Social Philosophy in the United States, 1860–1920* (New York: John Wiley and Sons, 1968), 87–113.

92. Ross, *Seventy Years*, 6.

93. Ibid., 11 (emphasis in original); Wilson, "Edward Alsworth Ross," 95.

94. Ross, *Seventy Years*, 19, 7, 11, 12, 286, 307–12.

95. Ibid., 126.

96. Ross, *Social Control: A Survey of the Foundations of Order* (New York: Macmillan, 1901), 3, 105.

97. Ross, *Social Psychology: An Outline and Source Book* (New York: Macmillan, 1908), vii.

98. Clark, "Introduction," 65–66.

99. Ross, *Seventy Years*, 42–43; Wilson, "Edward Alsworth Ross," 101.

100. Gillis J. Harp, "Lester F. Ward: Positivist Whig," in Harp, *Positivist Republic: Auguste Comte and the Reconstruction of American Liberalism, 1865–1920* (University Park: Pennsylvania State University Press, 1995), 109–53, quoted passage at 109; Lester F. Ward, *Dynamic Sociology, or Applied Social Science: As Based Upon Statical Sociology and the Less Complex Sciences*, 2 vols. (New York: D. Appleton, 1883).

101. Lester F. Ward, *The Psychic Factors of Civilization* (1893; reprint, New York: Johnson Reprint Co., 1970).

102. Clifford H. Scott, *Lester Frank Ward* (Boston: Twayne, 1976), 21–37.

103. Henry Steele Commager, "Introduction," in *Lester Ward and the Welfare State*, ed. Commager (Indianapolis, Ind.: Bobbs-Merrill, 1967), xxviii.

104. In a 1907 letter to Ross, President Roosevelt wrote admiringly of *Social Control*. "Justice [Holmes] spoke of it to me as one of the strongest and most striking presentations of the subject he had ever seen. I got it at once and was deeply interested in it. Since then I have read whatever you have written," Roosevelt wrote, adding that he was almost always in hearty agreement with the author. Roosevelt to Ross, 19 Sept. 1907, published in Ross, *Sin and Society: An Analysis of Latter-Day Iniquity* (Boston: Houghton Mifflin, 1907), ix. See also Walter Lippmann, *Public Opinion* (1922; reprint, New York: Macmillan, 1961).

105. Commager, "Introduction," xxii; Harp, "Lester F. Ward," 112–18; Scott, *Lester Ward*, 19–21.

106. Scott, *Lester Ward*, 85.

107. Ibid., 84; David Montgomery, *Beyond Equality: Labor and the Radical Republicans, 1862–1872* (1967; reprint, Urbana: University of Illinois Press, 1981), 415.

108. On Ward's relation to socialism, see Aleksander Gella, "Introduction," in *The Ward-Gumplowicz Correspondence: 1897–1909*, trans. Gella (New York: Essay, 1971), xxv; Scott, *Lester Ward*, 96–97. It was on behalf of this clerks' class that he wrote, while working in the Treasury Department's new Bureau of Statistics in 1869, one of his earliest political articles: an unpublished essay entitled "Washington City," decrying the exploitation of bureaucrats. Scott, *Lester Ward*, 23.

109. Ward, "Mental vs. Physical Liberty," *The Iconoclast*, 2, no. 18 (Aug. 1871), reprinted in Ward, *Glimpses of the Cosmos*, vol. 1 (New York: G. P. Putnam's Sons, 1913), 236–37.

110. Harp, "Lester Ward," 118–19; Scott, *Lester Ward*, 23–28.

111. Harp, "Lester Ward," 127–29. Ward also took from Comte a crucial insight: what the citizens of a democracy required in order to make effective use of their government was not simply scientific knowledge, but knowledge of a new science, offering a whole new way of conceiving the state itself. As he explained in a paper on "politico-social functions," which he read before the Anthropological Society of Washington in March 1881, the old political science of Adam Smith and John Stuart Mill had no place for the modern state, which exercised a new kind of power. Political economy could scarcely make sense of a state that provided for transportation, communication, and education, that regulated the railroad, managed the mail, and sent its citizens to school. Yet such a state was already a reality in Germany and France, and it was rapidly arising in England and the United States. Properly understood, the strong modern state represented not political power in the traditional sense, but "social" power—the power not of the people but of society itself. To put that power to work on their behalf, Ward argued, people would have to learn to see themselves as well as their state in a new light. Ward, "Politico-Social Functions," *Pennsylvania Monthly* 12, no. 137 (May 1881): 321–36, reprinted in Ward, *Glimpses of Cosmos*, 335–53.

112. Ward, *Dynamic Sociology*, 2:538; Small, *Origins of Sociology*, 341.

113. Ward became one of the most influential American exponents of this theory of "social progress," along with the anthropologist Lewis Henry Morgan and the geologist and ethnologist John Wesley Powell, who was a close associate of Ward's. On "social evolutionism" in the United States, see Stocking, *Race, Culture, and Evolution*, 116–28, 240–41. Powell, Morgan's leading disciple, was the director of the U.S. Geographical and Geological Survey of the Rocky Mountain Region in 1875, when Ward served as a botanist on one of Powell's famous expeditions. In 1881, Powell became director of the national U.S. Geographical and Geological Survey, where Ward went to work that same year and became a leader in the new field of paleobotany. Charles Van Doren and Robert McHenry, eds., *Webster's Guide to American History* (Springfield, Mass.: G. & C. Merriam, 1971), 1180–81; Scott, *Lester Ward*, 26, 29.

114. Ward, *Dynamic Sociology*, 1:519–20, 497, 516–17.

115. Ibid., 1:517.

116. The reason for the widening gulf between the production and acquisition of wealth lay in what Ward described in *The Iconoclast* as the wrongheaded "reverence" of labor for the illegitimate "authority" of capital. In *Dynamic Sociology*, he explained that the reign of greed had led the working poor to admire the idle rich, just as Veblen more elaborately argued.

"The poor mechanic is taught to look up, as to superior beings, to the wealthy merchant and banker, who have grown rich by the mere handling of the objects which he has produced," he wrote. Ward, *Dynamic Sociology*, 1:578.

117. Ibid., 1:579.

118. Ibid., 2:535.

119. Ibid., 1:594–95.

120. Ibid., 2:251–52.

121. See the discussion of John Stuart Mill's "developmental democracy" in C. B. Macpherson, *The Life and Times of Liberal Democracy* (New York: Oxford University Press, 1977), 44–49.

122. "Provided with the requisite knowledge, [they] will not be deceived." Ward, *Dynamic Sociology*, 1:579.

123. Ibid., 1:50, 52.

124. From this he concluded that the "practical work which sociology demands is . . . *the organization of feeling.*" Ward, *Dynamic Sociology*, 1:12, 68.

125. Ward, *Psychic Factors of Civilization*, 94, 55.

126. "It consists in a power acquired by the mind, of looking into a more or less complicated set of circumstances and perceiving that movements which are not in obedience to the primary psychic force are those that promise results." Ward, *Psychic Factors*, 145.

127. Ibid., 134–45.

128. Ibid., 114–15.

129. Ibid., 130, 289.

130. Those assembled included "Major J. W. Powell, Director of the United States Geological Survey and of the Bureau of American Ethnology; the Hon. David Jayne Hill, American Secretary of State; the Hon. William T. Harris, United States Commissioner of Education; the Hon. Caroll D. Wright, United States Commissioner of Labor and Superintendent of the Tenth Census; Dr. Frank Baker, Superintendent of the National Zoölogical Park; Mr. W. F. Willoughby, now Treasurer of Porto Rico; Mr. Edward T. Peters of the Department of Agriculture; Messrs. David Hutcheson and Roland P. Falkner of the Library of Congress; Mr. Henry F. Blount, manufacturer and banker; and Miss Sarah E. Simons, Head of the English Department of the Washington High Schools." Ward, *Pure Sociology: A Treatise on the Origin and Spontaneous Development of Society* (New York: Macmillan, 1903), vii.

131. Ward, *Pure Sociology*; Ward, *Applied Sociology: A Treatise on the Conscious Improvement of Society By Society* (Boston: Ginn and Co., 1906).

132. Ward, *Dynamic Sociology*, 1:68.

133. Ward, *Pure Sociology*, 282.

134. Ibid., 161.

135. Ibid., 105–10; Ward, *Applied Sociology*, 28.

136. Ward, *Applied Sociology*, 330.

137. Ibid., 294.

138. Ward, *Pure Sociology*, 238, 33–34.

139. Ward, *Applied Sociology*, 33.

140. The leading example of this line of analysis of Ross's America in more recent times is Robert H. Wiebe, *The Search for Order, 1877–1920* (New York: Hill & Wang, 1967).

141. Dorothy Ross notes that John Stuart Mill used the term "social control" in *On Liberty*

(1859) to mean basically the same thing that Edward Ross did in his later work. But it was the American sociologist's development of the idea that made it a fundamental feature of American social science. See Ross, *Origins of American Social Science*, 229–40.

142. Ross, *Social Control*, 3, 57.

143. Of his undergraduate years at Coe College in Cedar Rapids, Iowa, Ross wrote: "Our text in political economy was beneath all contempt, but Henry George's *Progress and Poverty* was bootlegged among us and swept me off my feet." Ross, *Seventy Years*, 15. Ross drew heavily upon his reading of George in writing a college oration called "The Coming Slavery," warning against the power of industrial organization. Wilson, "Edward Alsworth Ross," 92–93.

144. Ross, *Social Control*, 45, 46, 47.

145. Ross, *Seventy Years*, 63–64; Van Doren and McHenry, *Webster's Guide*, 1243–44.

146. Ross, *Seventy Years*, 69–71. For the other side of the story, see Jane Lathrop Stanford, *Address on the Right of Free Speech*, delivered to the Board of Trustees of the Leland Stanford Junior University, 25 Apr. 1903, 8–11.

147. Ross, "The Standard of Deferred Payments," *Annals of the American Academy of Political and Social Science*, vol. 3 (Nov. 1892): 293–305.

148. Ross, *Foundations of Sociology* (New York: Macmillan, 1905), 26–27.

149. Ross, *Social Control*, 396, 12, 17–18.

150. Ibid., 53, 54, 87.

151. Ibid., 441. "It is investigation of the kind I have attempted in this book that will enable society to go about the business of control in a scientific way." Ibid., 436.

152. Ibid., 197.

153. "The immediate cause of the location of power is prestige. The class that has the most prestige will have the most power." Ibid., 78.

154. Ibid., 104–5.

155. Ross, *Social Psychology*, 57; Ross, *Foundations of Sociology*, 102.

156. Ross, *Social Psychology*, 12.

157. Ross, *Sin and Society*, 3.

158. Ross, *Foundations of Sociology*, 145.

159. Ross, *Sin and Society*, 53, 51–52.

160. Echoing Tarde virtually word for word, Ross wrote: "Ours is not . . . as [Gustave] Le Bon insists, 'the era of crowds.' It is, in fact, the era of publics." Ross, *Foundations of Sociology*, 134. See also Ross, *Social Psychology*, 64.

161. Ross, *Sin and Society*, 41–42.

Chapter Seven

1. Charles Horton Cooley, *Human Nature and the Social Order* (1902; reprint, New Brunswick, N.J.: Transaction, 1983), 184. As Marshall Cohen notes, "Though the term 'social self' had a wide circulation in the philosophical circles of the 1890s, Cooley was the first sociologist to incorporate it into a coherent social theory." Cohen, *Charles Horton Cooley and the Social Self in American Thought* (New York: Garland, 1982), 124. See also Edward C. Jandy, *Charles Horton Cooley: His Life and His Social Theory* (New York: Dryden, 1942); Caroline Winterer, "A Happy Medium: The Sociology of Charles Horton Cooley," *Journal of the His-*

tory of the Behavioral Sciences 30 (Jan. 1994): 19–27; Lewis A. Coser, *Masters of Sociological Thought: Ideas in Historical and Social Context* (New York: Harcourt Brace Jovanovich, 1971), 305–20; Robert Cooley Angell, "Introduction," in Charles Horton Cooley, *Sociological Theory and Social Research: Being Selected Papers of Charles Horton Cooley* (New York: Henry Holt, 1930). On the history of ideas about selfhood generally, see Charles Taylor, *Sources of the Self: The Making of the Modern Identity* (Cambridge, Mass.: Harvard University Press, 1989); Wilfred M. McClay, *The Masterless: Self and Society in America* (Chapel Hill: University of North Carolina Press, 1994); Daniel Walker Howe, *Making the American Self: Jonathan Edwards to Abraham Lincoln* (Cambridge, Mass.: Harvard University Press, 1997); Philip Cushman, *Constructing the Self, Constructing America: A Cultural History of Psychotherapy* (Reading, Mass.: Addison-Wesley, 1995); Warren I. Susman, "'Personality' and the Making of Twentieth-Century Culture," in Susman, *Culture as History: The Transformation of American Society in the Twentieth Century* (New York: Pantheon, 1984); Christopher Lasch, *The Culture of Narcissism: American Life in an Age of Diminishing Expectations* (New York: W. W. Norton, 1979).

2. James Livingston, *Pragmatism and the Political Economy of Cultural Revolution, 1850–1940* (Chapel Hill: University of North Carolina Press, 1994). See also, James Mark Baldwin, *The Individual and Society; or, Psychology and Sociology* (Boston: Richard G. Badger, 1911).

3. Stephen Field, "The Centenary of the Supreme Court of the United States," *American Law Review* 24 (May–June 1890): 351–68; quoted passage at 364. On the rise of the modern business corporation in the economy and the law, see Gerald Berk, *Alternative Tracks: The Constitution of American Industrial Order, 1865–1917* (Baltimore, Md.: Johns Hopkins University Press, 1994); Martin J. Sklar, *The Corporate Reconstruction of American Capitalism, 1890–1916: The Market, the Law, and Politics* (New York: Cambridge University Press, 1988); Alfred D. Chandler Jr., *The Visible Hand: The Managerial Revolution in American Business* (Cambridge, Mass.: Belknap Press of Harvard University Press, 1977); James Willard Hurst, *The Legitimacy of the Business Corporation in the Law of the United States, 1780–1970* (Charlottesville: University Press of Virginia, 1970); Arthur S. Miller, *The Modern Corporate State: Private Governments and the American Constitution* (Westport, Conn.: Greenwood, 1976).

4. Hurst, *Legitimacy of the Business Corporation*, 14–18.

5. Berk, *Alternative Tracks*, 3, 12–13, 35, 180; Walter Licht, *Industrializing America: The Nineteenth Century* (Baltimore, Md.: Johns Hopkins University Press, 1995), 86.

6. Licht, *Industrializing America*, 133; David M. Gordon, Richard Edwards, and Michael Reich, *Segmented Work, Divided Workers: The Historical Transformation of Labor in the U.S.* (New York: Cambridge University Press, 1982), 108.

7. Gordon, Edwards, and Reich, *Segmented Workers*, 95–116; Licht, *Industrializing America*, 130–33, 159–62, 181–82. See also James Livingston, "The Social Analysis of Economic History and Theory: Conjectures on the Late Nineteenth-Century American Development," *American Historical Review* 92, no. 1 (Feb. 1987): 69–95.

8. On Thomas M. Cooley, the essential works are Alan Jones's Ph.D. dissertation in 1960 from the University of Michigan, later reprinted as *The Constitutional Conservatism of Thomas McIntyre Cooley: A Study in the History of Ideas* (New York: Garland, 1987); and Jones's several subsequent articles based upon the dissertation: "Thomas M. Cooley and the Interstate Commerce Commission: Continuity and Change in the Doctrine of Equal Rights,"

Political Science Quarterly 81, no. 4 (Dec. 1966): 602–27; "Thomas M. Cooley and 'Laissez-Faire Constitutionalism': A Reconsideration," *Journal of American History* 53 (1966–1967): 751–71; "Thomas M. Cooley and the Michigan Supreme Court: 1865–1885," *American Journal of Legal History* 10, no. 2 (Apr. 1966): 97–121. See also Phillip S. Paludan, "Law and the Failure of Reconstruction: The Case of Thomas Cooley," *Journal of the History of Ideas* 33, no. 4 (Oct.–Dec. 1972): 597–614; Phillip S. Paludan, *A Covenant with Death: The Constitution, Law, and Equality in the Civil War Era* (Chicago: University of Illinois Press, 1975), 249–73; G. Edward White, *The American Judicial Tradition: Profiles of Leading American Judges* (New York: Oxford University Press, 1976), 296–97; Stephen Siegel, "Historism in Late Nineteenth-Century Constitutional Thought," *Wisconsin Law Review* (1990): 1485–1515; Mortimer Elwyn Cooley, *The Cooley Genealogy* (Rutland, Vt.: Tuttle, 1941), 673–81.

9. Jones, "'Laissez-Faire Constitutionalism'"; Charles W. McCurdy, "Justice Field and the Jurisprudence of Government-Business Relations: Some Parameters of Laissez-Faire Constitutionalism, 1863–1897," *Journal of American History* 61, no. 4 (Mar. 1975): 970–1005; Morton J. Horwitz, *The Transformation of American Law, 1870–1960: The Crisis of Legal Orthodoxy* (Oxford: Oxford University Press, 1992), 65–107; Howard Gillman, *The Constitution Besieged: The Rise and Demise of Lochner Era Police Powers Jurisprudence* (Durham, N.C.: Duke University Press, 1993); Herbert Hovenkamp, "The Political Economy of Substantive Due Process," *Stanford Law Review* 40 (1988): 379–447. For important qualifications to the revisionist view, see Paul Kens, *Justice Stephen Field: Shaping Liberty from the Gold Rush to the Gilded Age* (Lawrence: University Press of Kansas, 1997). For the older view of "laissez-faire constitutionalism" as a reactionary effort by jurists in league with business interests to stave off popular attempts to reign in corporate capital, see Benjamin R. Twiss, *Lawyers and the Constitution: How Laissez Faire Came to the Supreme Court* (1942; reprint, New York: Russell & Russell, 1962); Clyde S. Jacobs, *Law Writers and the Courts: The Influence of Thomas M. Cooley, Christopher G. Tiedeman, and John F. Dillon upon American Constitutional Law* (Berkeley: University of California Press, 1954); Howard Jay Graham, *Everyman's Constitution: Historical Essays on the Fourteenth Amendment, the "Conspiracy Theory," and American Constitutionalism* (Madison: State Historical Society of Wisconsin, 1968); Robert Green McCloskey, *American Conservatism in the Age of Enterprise: A Study of William Graham Sumner, Stephen J. Field and Andrew Carnegie* (Cambridge, Mass.: Harvard University Press, 1951).

10. C. B. Macpherson, *The Political Theory of Possessive Individualism: Hobbes to Locke* (New York: Oxford University Press, 1962); Charles Horton Cooley, *Social Organization: A Study of the Larger Mind* (New York: Charles Scribner's Sons, 1913), 71.

11. Along these lines, see Alan Jones, "Law and Economics v. A Democratic Society: The Case of Thomas M. Cooley, Charles H. Cooley, and Henry C. Adams," *American Journal of Legal History* 36 (1992): 119–38.

12. Cf. Oliver Wendell Holmes Jr., *The Common Law* (Boston: Little, Brown, 1881). On the congruence between Holmes's legal theory and the philosophical and social-scientific revolt that produced the social self, see Morton White, *Social Thought in America: The Revolt Against Formalism* (1947; reprint, New York: Oxford University Press, 1976), 59–75; Thomas C. Grey, "Holmes and Legal Pragmatism," 41 *Stanford Law Review* (Apr. 1989): 787–870; Catharine Pierce Wells, "Old-Fashioned Postmodernism and the Legal Theories of Oliver Wendell Holmes Jr.," *Brooklyn Law Review* 63, no. 1 (Spring 1997): 59–85; G. Edward White, *Justice Oliver Wendell Holmes: Law and the Inner Self* (New York: Oxford University Press,

1993), esp. 148–95; R. Jeffrey Lustig, *Corporate Liberalism: The Origins of Modern American Political Theory, 1890–1920* (Berkeley: University of California Press, 1982), 116–20, 176–83.

13. Thomas M. Cooley, *A Treatise on the Constitutional Limitations Which Rest Upon the Legislative Power of the States of the American Union*, 1st ed. (1868; reprint, New York: Da Capo, 1972); Paludan, "Law and the Failure of Reconstruction," 598; Jacobs, *Law Writers*, 29; Jones, "'Laissez-Faire Constitutionalism,'" 758.

14. Twiss, *Lawyers and the Constitution*, 18–41; quoted passage at 18. Twiss's work was based upon his doctoral thesis in politics at Princeton University, where he received his Ph.D. in 1938. Ibid., xi–xii. See also Jacobs, *Law Writers*.

15. Jones, "'Laissez-Faire Constitutionalism'"; and his other works cited in note 8 above.

16. Berk, *Alternative Tracks*, 100–104. See also Edwin A. Gere Jr., "Dillon's Rule and the Cooley Doctrine: Reflections of the Political Culture," *Journal of Urban History* 8, no. 3 (May 1982): 271–98; Paul D. Carrington, "Law as 'The Common Thoughts of Men': The Law-Teaching and Judging of Thomas McIntyre Cooley," *Stanford Law Review* 49 (Feb. 1997): 495–546; David J. Barron, "The Promise of Cooley's City: Traces of Local Constitutionalism," *University of Pennsylvania Law Review* 147, no. 3 (Jan. 1999): 487–612. Meanwhile, more conservative legal scholars and jurists have recently laid claim to Cooley's earlier reputation as a supporter of laissez-faire. See, for example, Richard A. Epstein, *Takings: Private Property and the Power of Eminent Domain* (Cambridge, Mass.: Harvard University Press, 1985), 283–84; Richard A. Epstein, *Principles for a Free Society: Reconciling Individual Liberty with the Common Good* (Reading, Mass.: Perseus, 1998), 129–30. For a critique of U.S. Supreme Court Justice Antonin Scalia's use of Cooley in defense of a conservative interpretation of Fourth Amendment law, see David A. Sklansky, "The Fourth Amendment and Common Law," *Columbia Law Review* 100, no. 7 (Nov. 2000): 1739–1814, at 1752.

17. Jones, "'Laissez-Faire Constitutionalism,'" 754–56; G. E. White, *American Judicial Tradition*, 116–18; Gillman, *Constitution Besieged*, 55; Harry N. Scheiber, "The Road to *Munn*: Eminent Domain and the Concept of Public Purpose in the State Courts," *Perspectives in American History*, vol. 5 (Cambridge, Mass.: Charles Warren Center for Studies in American History, 1971), 329–402; William A. Fischel, *Regulatory Takings: Law, Economics, and Politics* (Cambridge, Mass.: Harvard University Press, 1995), 64–140.

18. *The People v. Salem*, 20 Mich. 452, 478, 487. See also Cooley's 1869 decision in *The East Saginaw Manufacturing Co. v. the City of East Saginaw*, 19 Mich. 259.

19. The Fifth Amendment proscribed such action on the part of the federal government; the Fourteenth Amendment extended the scope of the "due process" clause to prohibit such action on the part of the states. Though most state constitutions already contained "due process" or similar clauses, the Fourteenth Amendment made "due process" violations by the states subject to federal judicial review.

20. T. M. Cooley, *Constitutional Limitations* (1st ed.), 357.

21. Thomas M. Cooley, *A Treatise on the Law of Taxation, Including the Law of Local Assessments* (Chicago: Callaghan and Co., 1876), 89–90. On rising taxes and public finance in the postbellum era, see C. K. Yearley, *The Money Machines: The Breakdown and Reform of Governmental and Party Finance in the North, 1860–1920* (Albany: State University of New York Press, 1970), 3–35.

22. See John V. Orth, "Taking from A and Giving to B: Substantive Due Process and The Case of the Shifting Paradigm," *Constitutional Commentary* 14, no. 2 (Summer 1997): 337–45.

23. William B. Scott, *In Pursuit of Happiness: American Conceptions of Property from the Seventeenth to the Twentieth Century* (Bloomington: Indiana University Press, 1977), 138–46; Graham, *Everyman's Constitution*, 14–18; Miller, *Corporate State*, 19.

24. Sklar, *Corporate Reconstruction*, 49–50; Horwitz, *Transformation of American Law*, 65–107; Hovenkamp, "Substantive Due Process"; *County of San Mateo v. Southern Pacific R. Co.*, 13 F. 722 (1882); *County of Santa Clara v. Southern Pac. R. Co.*, 18 F. 385 (1883); *Santa Clara County v. Southern Pacific Railroad Co.*, 118 U.S. 396 (1886).

25. *The Trustees of Dartmouth College v. Woodward*, 4 Wheat. 518 (1819); Thomas Cooley, *A Treatise On the Constitutional Limitations Which Rest Upon the Legislative Power of the States of the American Union*, 2d ed. (Boston: Little, Brown, 1871), 296–97.

26. Thomas M. Cooley, "State Regulation of Corporate Profits," *North American Review* 137, no. 322 (Sept. 1883): 205–17; quoted passage at 207.

27. Thomas M. Cooley, "Labor and Capital Before the Law," *North American Review* 139, no. 337 (Dec. 1884): 503–16; quoted passages at 515, 513, 515, 514, 507–8, 514, 511.

28. See William Novak, *The People's Welfare: Law and Regulation in Nineteenth-Century America* (Chapel Hill: University of North Carolina Press, 1996), 13–15; Christopher L. Tomlins, *Law, Labor, and Ideology in the Early American Republic* (New York: Cambridge University Press, 1993), 38–97; Horwitz, *Transformation of American Law*, 27–28; Gillman, *Constitution Besieged*.

29. See Ernst Freund, *The Police Power: Public Policy and Constitutional Rights* (Chicago: Callaghan & Co., 1904).

30. T. M. Cooley, *Constitutional Limitations* (1st ed.), 572, 597, 575–76. Cooley's discussion of the police power encompassed laws concerning the sale of liquor, quarantines, health inspections, observation of the Sabbath, traffic, licensing, and the preservation of public morals.

31. T. M. Cooley, *Treatise on Taxation*, 2.

32. Horwitz, *Transformation of American Law*, 27–28.

33. *Munn v. Illinois*, 94 U.S. 130 (1876).

34. T. M. Cooley, "Labor and Capital," 504.

35. The tract, *De Portibus Maris*, published in 1787 but written more than a century earlier, had already been widely influential in nineteenth-century American jurisprudence. See Scheiber, "Road to *Munn*," 334–55. In his discussion of *Munn*'s use of Hale, however, Cooley significantly noted that "the common sense of the general public, enlightened by the broad and varied experience of the present century, must, in many cases, be far more worthy of being followed than any *dictum* coming to us from the centuries that preceded it." T. M. Cooley, "Labor and Capital," 504.

36. On the long-standing tension between the common law tradition and liberal political theory, see James R. Stoner, *Common Law and Liberal Theory: Coke, Hobbes, and the Origins of American Constitutionalism* (Lawrence: University Press of Kansas, 1992); J. G. A. Pocock, *The Ancient Constitution and the Feudal Law: A Study of English Historical Thought in the Seventeenth Century* (New York: Cambridge University Press, 1957); Carol Rose, *Property and Persuasion: Essays on the History, Theory, and Rhetoric of Ownership* (Boulder, Colo.: Westview, 1994), 71–101; Gregory S. Alexander, *Commodity and Propriety: Competing Visions of Property in American Legal Thought, 1776–1970* (Chicago: University of Chicago Press, 1997), 44–47. On the significance of the common law tradition for the jurisprudence of the

police power and the regulatory state, see Novak, *People's Welfare*, 35–39; Peter Karsten, *Heart versus Head: Judge-Made Law in Nineteenth-Century America* (Chapel Hill: University of North Carolina Press, 1997).

37. Thomas M. Cooley, "Suggestions for the Study of the Law," in Sir William Blackstone, *Commentaries on the Laws of England*, ed. Thomas M. Cooley, 3d ed., rev. (Chicago: Callaghan and Co., 1884), x. See also Cooley's approving use of Lieber's work. Ibid., xi. On Cooley's turn toward Burkean conservatism, see Jones, *Constitutional Conservatism*, 234–45; Siegel, "Historism."

38. *People v. Hurlbut*, 24 Mich. 44, at 107; quoted in Carrington, "Common Thoughts," 537.

39. Thomas M. Cooley, "The Uncertainty of the Law," *American Law Review* 22 (May/June 1888): 347–70; quoted passage at 368.

40. On Hale's evolutionary rather than reactionary interpretation of the common law, see Pocock, *Ancient Constitution*, 170–81.

41. T. M. Cooley, "Labor and Capital," 504, 505, 503.

42. Thomas M. Cooley, "The Influence of Habits of Thought Upon Our Institutions," 2d Annual Address Delivered Before the South Carolina Bar Assn., 2 Dec. 1886.

43. Jones, *Constitutional Conservatism*, 292–321. Jones notes that the ICC under Cooley "helped pioneer the new course that independent regulatory commissions would pursue in the future," representing "an approach to the problem of the industrial age which combined older traditions of a self-governing individualism with new patterns of governmental control." Ibid., 343. On Progressive regulation of corporations, see James Weinstein, *The Corporate Ideal in the Liberal State* (Boston: Beacon, 1968).

44. Charles H. Cooley, "The Theory of Transportation," *Publications of the American Economic Association* 9, no. 3 (May 1894), in C. H. Cooley, *Sociological Theory*, 41; Charles H. Cooley, "The Development of Sociology at Michigan" (1928), in C. H. Cooley, *Sociological Theory*, 5; Cohen, *Charles Horton Cooley*, 70; Jandy, *Charles Horton Cooley*, 29–30; Coser, *Masters of Sociological Thought*, 15.

45. C. H. Cooley, "Theory of Transportation," 17; C. H. Cooley, "Development of Sociology," 5; Cohen, *Charles Horton Cooley*, 70–71. Lester Ward also encouraged Cooley's sociological work. Jandy, *Charles Horton Cooley*, 30.

46. C. H. Cooley, "Theory of Transportation," 104, 108–9, 112–13, 114.

47. Ibid., 104, 66.

48. Ibid., 86–98. Further, in the "general theory of rates" with which he culminated his analysis, Cooley proposed that freight rates should be determined no longer by the cost to the shipper, as measured by the weight or bulk of the freight, but rather by the utility to the customer, as measured by the freight's market value. Ibid., 94. In this way, he implicitly adopted the utility theory of value heralded by the marginalist revolution in economics, which definitively repudiated the labor theory of value at the core of classical political economy and made the consumer rather than the producer the determinant of value. See Chapter 6 above.

49. Ibid., 60, 40, 58, 59, 61. See also, C. H. Cooley, "Development of Sociology," 7–8.

50. C. H. Cooley, *Social Organization*, 71.

51. Charles H. Cooley, "Personal Competition," in C. H. Cooley, *Sociological Theory*, 178, 187.

52. Ibid., 222, 226, 188.

53. Jandy, *Charles Horton Cooley*, 13–15, 38–39; Angell, "Introduction," vii–x; Coser, *Masters of Sociological Thought*, 314.

54. C. H. Cooley, *Human Nature*, 95, 120, 121. In a presumably autobiographical aside, he noted: "Social experience is a matter of imaginative, not of material, contacts; and there are so many aids to the imagination that little can be judged as to one's experience by the merely external course of his life. An imaginative student of a few people and of books often has many times the range of comprehension that the most varied career can give to a duller mind. . . . The idea that seeing life means going from place to place and doing a great variety of obvious things is an illusion natural to dull minds." Ibid., 139–40.

55. Ibid., 119.

56. Ibid., 66–68. However, the self-styled "social behaviorist" George H. Mead deemed Cooley's conception of selfhood insufficiently social because it inhered in subjective "imagination" rather than objective "behavior." George Herbert Mead, *Mind, Self, and Society, From the Standpoint of a Social Behaviorist* (Chicago: University of Chicago Press, 1934), 224. Cf. John B. Watson's critique of functionalist psychology. Watson, *Behavior: An Introduction to Comparative Psychology* (New York: Henry Holt, 1914), 8–9.

57. C. H. Cooley, *Social Organization*, 3, 5.

58. Ibid., 69.

59. Ibid., 81.

60. Ibid., 244, 271–72.

61. Ibid., 85, 118.

62. Charles H. Cooley, "Political Economy and Social Process," *Journal of Political Economy* 25, no. 4 (Apr. 1918): 366–74, reprinted in C. H. Cooley, *Sociological Theory*, 251–59; originally delivered as a paper before a small group of students and teachers in 1910. See also Charles H. Cooley, *Social Process* (1918; reprint, Carbondale: Southern Illinois University Press, 1966), 295–308.

63. C. H. Cooley, *Social Process*, 144–45, 57. Cf. Edward Bellamy, *Looking Backward* (1888; reprint, New York: New American Library, 1989). On Bellamy, see John L. Thomas, *Alternative America: Henry George, Edward Bellamy, Henry Demarest Lloyd, and the Adversary Tradition* (Cambridge, Mass.: Harvard University Press, 1983).

64. C. H. Cooley, *Social Organization*, 302.

65. Ibid., 304.

66. Ibid., 307, 277.

67. C. H. Cooley, *Social Process*, 326, 86–87, 328.

Conclusion

1. Ralph Waldo Emerson, "The American Scholar," in Emerson, *Selected Essays*, ed. Larzer Ziff (New York: Penguin, 1982), 83–105; quoted passages at 101, 100.

2. Ibid., 96, 87.

3. G. Stanley Hall, *Life and Confessions of a Psychologist* (New York: D. Appleton, 1923), 162–63; Burton J. Bledstein, *The Culture of Professionalism: The Middle Class and the Development of Higher Education in America* (1976; reprint, New York: W. W. Norton, 1978), 259–68.

4. Karl Mannheim, *Ideology and Utopia: An Introduction to the Sociology of Knowledge*, trans. Louis Wirth and Edward Shils (New York: Harcourt, Brace & World, 1936), 192–263; Fredric Jameson, *The Political Unconscious: Narrative as a Socially Symbolic Act* (Ithaca, N.Y.: Cornell University Press, 1981), 281–99; Sacvan Bercovitch, *The Rites of Assent: Transformations in the Symbolic Construction of America* (New York: Routledge, 1993), 1–28.

5. C. B. Macpherson, *The Political Theory of Possessive Individualism: Hobbes to Locke* (New York: Oxford University Press, 1962), 51–61.

6. The general law that revolutionary change arises from the internal contradictions of a given social system or mode of production, rather than being born of external forces, lies at the core of the 50-year-old debate among Marxist scholars over the origin of the transition from feudalism to capitalism. See Rodney Hilton, ed., *The Transition from Feudalism to Capitalism* (London: NLB, 1976). For a more recent recapitulation of that controversy, including non-Marxists as well, see T. H. Aston and C. H. E. Philpin, eds., *The Brenner Debate: Agrarian Class Structure and Economic Development in Pre-Industrial Europe* (New York: Cambridge University Press, 1985).

7. For the older view of Western European and American social science as the polar opposite of Marxism, see, for example, Robert A. Nisbet, *The Sociological Tradition* (New York: Basic, 1966); and Alvin W. Gouldner, *The Coming Crisis of Western Sociology* (New York: Basic, 1970). For an important corrective, tracing the lines of intersection and convergence as well as divergence between historical materialism and Western sociology, see Göran Therborn, *Science, Class and Society: On the Formation of Sociology and Historical Materialism* (London: NLB, 1976), esp. 119–24. For a related critique of the dialogue between Marxist and non-Marxist social theory in the twentieth century, see Perry Anderson, *Considerations on Western Marxism* (London: NLB, 1976) and, by the same author, *In the Tracks of Historical Materialism* (Chicago: University of Chicago Press, 1984). See also the contrasting views of the open border between Marxism and Pragmatism in modern American social thought in Brian Lloyd, *Left Out: Pragmatism, Exceptionalism, and the Poverty of American Marxism* (Baltimore, Md.: Johns Hopkins University Press, 1997); and James Livingston, "Marxism, Pragmatism, and the American Political Tradition," *Intellectual History Newsletter* 20 (1998): 61–67.

8. Karl Marx, *Capital: A Critique of Political Economy*, vol. 1, trans. Ben Fowkes (New York: Penguin, 1990), 705–6.

9. "Ideas which later turned out to have been only distorted representations of a past or potential social order were ideological, while those which were adequately realized in the succeeding social order were relative utopias." Mannheim, *Ideology and Utopia*, 204.

10. Adolf A. Berle and Gardiner C. Means, *The Modern Business Corporation and Private Property*, rev. ed. (New York: Harcourt, Brace & World, 1968; original edition published 1932), 312–13.

11. Howard Brick, "Optimism of the Mind: Imagining Postindustrial Society in the 1960s and 1970s," *American Quarterly* 44, no. 3 (Sept. 1992): 348–80; quoted passage at 360.

12. John Kenneth Galbraith, *The Affluent Society*, 4th ed. (Boston: Houghton Mifflin, 1984; original edition published 1958); Galbraith, *The New Industrial State* (1967; reprint, New York: New American Library, 1968); quoted passages in *Industrial State*, 68, 150.

13. For a celebration of "new management theory," highlighting its debt to the Deweyan ideal of "participatory democracy" on the New Left, see Mary Britton King, "Make Love, Not Work: New Management Theory and the Social Self," *Radical History Review* 76 (Winter 2000): 15–24. For a critical discussion of notions of "pension socialism" or "investor democracy," see Adam Harmes, "Mass Investment Culture," *New Left Review* 9 (May/June 2001): 103–24. Along similar lines, see Ernest Mandel, *Marxist Economic Theory*, trans. Brian Pearce (London: Merlin, 1962), 233–36.

14. For recent historical works ostensibly vindicating such evolutionary arguments, see Martin J. Sklar, *The United States as a Developing Country: Studies in U.S. History in the Progressive Era and the 1920s* (New York: Cambridge University Press, 1992); James Livingston, *Pragmatism and the Political Economy of Cultural Revolution, 1850–1940* (Chapel Hill: University of North Carolina Press, 1994).

15. On the "increasing one-sidedness of the class struggle" in these decades, see Mike Davis, *Prisoners of the American Dream: Politics and Economy in the History of the US Working Class* (New York: Verso, 1986), quoted passage at vii; and, from a perspective more sympathetic to the notion of a technocratic shift in the basis of social power, Harold Perkin, *The Third Revolution: Professional Elites in the Modern World* (New York: Routledge, 1996), 28–48.

16. See Mike Parker and Jane Slaughter, *Working Smart: A Union Guide to Participation Programs and Reengineering* (Detroit, Mich.: Labor Education and Research Project, 1994).

17. See American Federation of Labor–Congress of Industrial Organizations (AFL-CIO), *Common Sense Economics: The Basic Rap* (Washington, D.C.: AFL-CIO, 2000); Doug Henwood, *Wall Street: How It Works and for Whom* (New York: Verso, 1997); John Bellamy Foster and Robert W. McChesney, "Working-Class Households and the Burden of Debt," *Monthly Review* 52, no. 1 (May 2000): 1–11; Harmes, "Mass Investment Culture," 122–24.

18. See Doug Henwood, "Talking About Work," in *Rising From the Ashes? Labor in the Age of "Global" Capitalism*, ed. Ellen Meiksins Wood, Peter Meiksins, and Michael Yates (New York: Monthly Review Press, 1998), 17–27. "[T]here's no evidence that some technological revolution means that a given amount of GDP growth today generates less employment growth than in the past; if anything, the gap between GDP and job growth is narrower now than in earlier decades." Ibid., 24–25. See also Heather Boushey, Chauna Brocht, Bethney Gundersen, and Jared Bernstein, *Hardships in America: The Real Story of Working Families* (Washington, D.C.: Economic Policy Institute, 2001).

19. See Kim Moody, *Workers in a Lean World: Unions in the International Economy* (New York: Verso, 1997).